The Blue Pages

Resources for Teachers

from

INVITATIONS

Regie Routman

Shaker Heights, OH City Schools
language arts resource teacher

with

Susan Hepler

Alexandria, VA
children's literature specialist

Vera Milz

Bloomfield Hills, MI Public Schools
elementary school teacher

and

Dana Noble

Shaker Heights, OH City Schools
English teacher

HEINEMANN
Portsmouth, NH

Heinemann
A division of Reed Elsevier Inc.
361 Hanover Street
Portsmouth, NH 03801-3912
Offices and agents throughout the world

Library of Congress Cataloging-in-Publication Data
Routman, Regie.
   [Invitations. Blue Pages]
   The blue pages : resources for teachers : from Invitations / by
Regie Routman with Susan Hepler . . . [et al.].
      p.   cm.
   Includes bibliographical references and index.
   ISBN 0-435-08835-1
   1. Language experience approach in education—Bibliography.
   2. Language arts—Bibliography.   3. Teaching—Bibliography.
   4. Teachers—Bibliography.   I. Title.
Z5818.L3R68 1994
[LB1576]
016.372.6—dc20   94-31701
                                    CIP

Editor: Toby Gordon
Production: Renée LeVerrier and Melissa L. Inglis
Cover design: Jenny Greenleaf

Printed in the United States of America on acid free paper
99 98 97 96 EB 3 4 5 6 7 8 9

Contents

Acknowledgments

In verifying and providing information as well as in updating and reviewing resources, the following people were very helpful: Julie Beers, George Cannon, Marlene Cohn, Linda Cooper, Terry Cooper, Mary Costello, Elaine Farge, Barbara Gallagher, Don Gallo, Andrea Goode, Carol Levine, Loretta Martin, Nancy O'Connor, Sara Phillips, Alison Preece, Peg Rimedio, Joan Servis, Jan Shields, Barbara Speer, and Ali Sullo. Special thanks to children's librarian John Philbrook at the San Francisco Public Library for his help and comraderie in locating outstanding multicultural literature.

For all the support I received from Heinemann, I am most appreciative. A special thank you to Mike Gibbons for getting me whatever information I needed so quickly and efficiently. Thanks also to Carolyn Coman, Ray Coutu, Melissa Patten, Leigh Peake, and Sheila Peters for diligently tracking down resources and providing relevant publishing information. A special thank you to Peggy Hansen for her meticulous proofreading and copyediting efforts. A heartfelt thank you to Melissa Inglis, Production Editor, who assumed the complicated task of putting the many separate pieces together with good humor, steadfast dedication, and careful attention to detail. Thanks also to Production Manager Renée LeVerrier for skillfully coordinating and expediting production efforts and to Jenny Greenleaf for her lively cover design. To Toby Gordon, Publishing Director and wonderful facilitator of the entire process, a generous thank you.

Once again, as with the 1991 "blue pages," I am especially grateful to Susan Hepler, Vera Milz, and Dana Noble for their friendship, dedication, and first-rate contributions to *The Blue Pages: Resources for Teachers from Invitations*. Collaborating with each of these talented educators has been a pleasure and an enriching personal and professional experience. This updated, expanded, and revised edition could never have been completed without their considerable input and expertise.

Finally, I am especially appreciative of the continuing support, patience, and love from my husband Frank.

July 1994

Introduction

I am a fanatic about being well informed professionally. Partly it's because teachers are often not held in the same high regard as other professionals. Partly it's because I'm largely self-educated in the teaching of reading and writing and continue to be so. Mostly it's because I believe we teachers must be knowledgeable in order to get our message across and be taken seriously by other teachers, administrators, parents, policy makers, and other educational stakeholders. And, of greatest importance, we teachers must take responsibility for being well informed so that we provide the kinds of excellent learning experiences and environments that allow all our students to thrive.

When I wrote *Invitations: Changing as Teachers and Learners K–12* (Heinemann, 1991), I shared my and other teachers' experiences in moving toward whole language and more authentic teaching, learning, and evaluating. I dealt in depth with such issues as responding to literature, teaching for strategies, writing and spelling, integration, evaluation, learning disabled students, classroom management and organization, and establishing support networks. The response to the book from educators across the United States and Canada has been overwhelming. I am often told that the "blue pages" at the end of the book are a particularly helpful resource for supporting our teaching and professional growth.

The hope for these updated, expanded, and revised "blue pages" is that you have easy access to some of the best and most relevant current professional books, resources, and children's literature. To that end, *The Blue Pages: Resources for Teachers from Invitations* is offered as a stand-alone volume for educators who already own *Invitations*. A 1994 edition of *Invitations* that includes the new "blue pages" is also available. In this new edition, the original white pages are mostly unchanged except for the updated resources in the body of the text and at the end of chapters.

The Blue Pages is organized with integrated teaching in mind. For your easy referral, separate, annotated listings are included for evaluation, spelling, mathematics, social studies, science, author/illustrator, and parents. Many resources are provided for choosing and using quality literature in the classroom. The extensive recommended literature and supplemental literature lists for K–12 support a balanced literature/reading program. The expanded appendices include practical material for classroom use. Professional books, journals, newsletters, and articles are useful for independent reflection and for collaborative talk in your building or district. Use the table of contents to locate what you are interested in.

Because our field is changing so quickly, it is difficult to know and keep up with all the latest and most useful resources that are now available. I hope you enjoy reading through these pages, locating the resources that are just right for you, and incorporating them into your teaching and learning.

Resources for Teachers

The following annotated resources—professional books, journal articles, themed journals, journals, newsletters, and literacy extension resources—have been carefully selected to support teachers in continued professional growth in teaching and learning. A (•) before a title indicates a resource that has been found to be particularly useful, thought provoking, and outstanding in quality.

Almost all of the new professional books and resources that are included in this edition have publication dates of 1991 and beyond, and more than 60 percent of these are new to this edition. The professional books and resources from the "blue pages" of *Invitations: Changing as Teachers and Learners K–12* (1991) that are excellent, current, and worth teachers' time have been kept. Many older, less useful resources have been deleted, especially when there is an updated book by an author. For other recommended resources, up to and including 1988, see *Resources for Teachers* (Routman, 1988).

Professional Books

Annotations with Vera Milz

The following is an annotated bibliography of books other teachers, Vera Milz, and I have found helpful in furthering our knowledge of language learning, literacy, and teaching. Vera Milz, a highly talented elementary teacher and reviewer of professional books, has annotated many of the titles, and her initials *(V.M.)* appear after the annotations she has written. All titles, unless otherwise noted, are available in paperback.

Note, also, because there is enormous interest in spelling and evaluation and so many of us struggle with these issues, professional books and resources related to spelling and evaluation are listed separately for your easy reference in "Literacy Extension Resources" on pages 74b–86b.

Being Professional

Teachers ask me how I find the time to read professionally. I make it a priority, as the reading is absolutely necessary to my continued growth and development as a teacher-learner. Without exception, every teacher I know and admire who has made great professional strides in moving ahead in thinking and practice reads professionally and talks about those books with other colleagues. I, and they, deliberately set aside time to read professionally, and we consider it a necessity. For Vera Milz, professional reading breaks the isolation of teaching. By hearing the voices of others through their texts, Vera's beliefs are often confirmed. She says, "It gives me the strength to do things that are right for children." Reading widely also makes it possible for us to question assumptions, acknowledge weaknesses, try new approaches, and move toward new goals. Just as we ask our students to take increasing responsibility for their learning, we must also take responsibility for our own. So how do we find the time?

For myself, when I am working in classrooms, I try to do as much as I can when I am right there with the students. For example, during reading time, if I am meeting with a small group who needs an activity to work on independently, I try to put it together on the spot (for example, scribing an original story using the children's language) with just minimal time required later on for reproducing and assembling. In elementary writing workshop classrooms, I read and respond to the children's writing during individual or group conferences with the student(s). I do not take the papers home. In my planning in school, after school, and at home, I make an effort not to do much "busy work" but rather to get materials and plans ready that engage students and teachers to work as independently as possible. I think you will find that as your classroom becomes more student centered, and as you are negotiating curriculum and classroom decisions with your students, you will be able to make time to read and grow professionally—in spite of ever-increasing demands across the curriculum.

My recommendation is that you read through the titles and annotations, see what interests you, and choose one or more titles to get started on. You may want to choose a topic or book you're interested in or curious about, one you feel is a weak area for you, or one that is an area you're moving toward. With the busy work and family schedules that we have, it often motivates us to make time for reading if one or more colleagues is reading the same book. I always get more out of a book when I can discuss it with a colleague. One of the most wonderful things that our district did towards the close of a recent school year was to buy a copy of a professional book (from a committee-recommended list of about a dozen titles) for every K–12 teacher and administrator who chose one. Teachers had the summer to read the book. Then, a part of a professional day was set aside for teachers to get together around a table and talk about the book they had read. Those that took advantage of the opportunity found it a terrific experience for collegial exchange and professional growth.

Finally, perhaps most important are the political issues. Beyond the personal benefits to me and my students of reading professionally are the political considerations. If we teachers are to have a voice that is heard, respected and taken seriously by other educators, parents, administrators, and policy makers, we *must* be knowledgeable about current research, theory, and practice in language learning. We must be able to think for ourselves, be intelligent decision makers, and take a stand on important issues. Only when we teachers become more articulate through reading, writing, and speaking on a wide range of educational issues will we be trusted to make decisions for children and freed from the external pressures that continue to drive curriculum and evaluation.

Allen, JoBeth, and Jana M. Mason (eds.). 1989. *Risk Makers, Risk Takers, Risk Breakers: Reducing the Risks for Young Literacy Learners.* Portsmouth, NH: Heinemann.

This is a thought-provoking book with chapters by classroom teachers and university researchers who discuss how schools and parents can provide the most effective support for children labeled at-risk. Stereotypes about social class and educational expectations are examined in light of new evidence of early literacy acquisition by these children. The book is divided into four sections, moving from detailed accounts of successful individual children to descriptions of teachers and their positive learning environments to strategies for parental support, and, finally, to suggestions for literacy policies and practices designed to reduce risks for all children. The book is important reading for anyone developing programs that will increase the potential of every young child to be successful in becoming literate. (V.M.)

Allen, JoBeth, Barbara Michalove, and Betty Shockley. 1993. *Engaging Children: Community and Chaos in the Lives of Young Literacy Learners.* Portsmouth, NH: Heinemann.

This book is the story of what two classroom-based and one university-based researcher learned about six children chosen because they were the ones that they were concerned about the most in a school with many at-risk children. The teachers wanted to study the effects of whole language instruction on children who were experiencing extreme hardship in the educational setting. Each of the children's stories is compelling and unique with many successes, but no magical "learned happily ever after" ending for any of them. In the words of the authors, "Maybe one teacher can't make all the difference. But teachers can make a difference, a lasting difference, for the children we worry about the most." The book is important reading for anyone dealing with children who are at risk of failing to become literate. (V.M.)

Armour, Maureen W. 1994. *Poetry, the Magic Language: Children Learn to Read and*

Write It. Englewood, CO: Teachers Ideas Press.

Designed to take the mystery out of enjoying and writing poetry, this book is a joy to read. Using anecdotes, many examples of poetry by children, and a conversational tone, the author invites you to use poetry in a variety of fresh and interesting ways. Various poetic forms are explored, and directions for integrating poetry into the content areas are included. Poetry is also integrated into themes, such as food, pets, oceans, trees, and families, with suggestions for poems to use with the children, and examples of student poems inspired by them are given. The entire book is a delightful resource. (V.M.)

• Atwell, Nancie (ed.). 1990. *Coming to Know: Writing to Learn in the Intermediate Grades*. Portsmouth, NH: Heinemann.

Practicing teachers in grades 3–6 in Maine enthusiastically describe fresh approaches to writing in the content areas. Social studies, science, math, and art are integrated with reading and writing through the use of learning logs based on personal experiences and observations. Teachers looking for alternatives to traditional book reports and research reports will find well-documented alterative methods. The seventy pages of appendices, which include "Genres for Report Writing," "Prompts for Learning Log Entries," "Bury Yourself in Books: Children's Literature for Content-Area Study," and "Resources for Writing and Reading to Learn," are wonderfully helpful.

Atwell, Nancie. 1991. *Side by Side: Essays on Teaching to Learn*. Portsmouth, NH: Heinemann.

If you have ever had the privilege of reading an article by Nancie Atwell, or hearing her speak, this book will be a welcome reminder of her insights. It speaks of her loving involvement with her adolescent students, as well as her young daughter. She explores the conditions that allow children to become readers and writers, and proposes new revisions of the workshop model described in her book In the Middle. *Other topics include the teaching of poetry, including special education students in the reading and writing workshop, the implications of reader response theory in literature-based classrooms, and the importance of reflection through teacher research. As always, a visit with Nancie Atwell is a stimulating experience. (V.M.)*

Atwell, Nancie (ed.). 1989–1990. *Workshop 1, 2, 3, by and for Teachers*. Portsmouth, NH: Heinemann. (See Newkirk, Thomas for *Workshop 4, 5* and Barbieri, Maureen, for *Workshop 6*.)

1, Writing and Literature.
2, Beyond the Basal.
3, The Politics of Process.

This annual series of books each features about ten articles by knowledgeable, practicing teachers representing grades K–8, a discussion between an expert teacher and a professional leader, an article by a children's author, and an interview with another children's author to be shared with your students. Each issue is themed in order to give a focus that might be explored by educators and students. For example, in the first volume, Donald and Carol Carrick share their insights into writing and illustrating children's books. Cora Five shares her fifth grader's poetry, while Tom Newkirk interviews a fifth-grade teacher, Jack Wilde. Each article gives insight into the use of wonderful literature in the classroom writing program. In the second volume, Jack Prelutsky is interviewed, as well as first-grade teacher Carol Avery. Cynthia Rylant describes how easily writing comes to her, and what this might mean for the teaching of writing in school. In the third annual, Mem Fox gives her perspectives on the exercises that children must perform, instead of real writing and reading in the classroom. Patrick Shannon shows how so-called reading reformers are making their voices heard, and how educators need to use their own literacy skill to make their views known. Toby Curry and Debra Goodman are interviewed about their efforts to obtain community support for a whole language magnet school. The above are but a sampling of the thought-provoking articles by the many authors in this collection.

Each volume deserves your careful attention. (V.M.)

Avery, Carol. 1993. *. . . And with a Light Touch: Learning About Reading, Writing, and Teaching with First Graders.* Portsmouth, NH: Heinemann.

Primary-grade teachers will love this book! The author takes you inside her first-grade classroom, and shows the day-to-day interactions of teaching and learning between herself and her students at schools in Lancaster County, Pennsylvania. In the book, she shares how she organizes the classroom environment, helps children to begin writing, lists possible minilesson topics for writing, gives suggestions for reading aloud to children, structures a reading workshop, and documents student growth. Children's literature, how it is used and enjoyed, is cited throughout the book. As each of the topics is explored, case studies are used to demonstrate how the children are learning in this rich environment. (V.M.)

Barbieri, Maureen, and Linda Rief (eds.). 1994. *Workshop 6: The Writer as Teacher.* Portsmouth, NH: Heinemann. (See Atwell, Nancie, for *Workshop 1, 2, 3,* and Newkirk, Thomas, for *Workshop 4, 5.*)

The importance of personal and professional writing is considered in this sixth volume of the series. As the editors say, "Writing helps us understand why we do what we do. Writing brings us closer to our students. And writing connects us to one another." Mary Mercer Krogness begins the book with her eloquent poem, "Voice." Mike Steinberg illustrates how writing nourishes his teaching and his life. Teacher-author Susan Benedict and author Betty Green are interviewed and share their insights on how writing contributes to the richness of their lives. The editors hope that the book will inspire teachers to take their writing beyond the classroom— I believe it meets their goal! (V.M.)

Barth, Roland S. 1990. *Improving Schools from Within: Teachers, Parents, and Principals Can Make the Difference.* San Francisco: Jossey-Bass Publishers.

For all those who have become fasci-nated with school change and staff development, as I have, this is an inspiring book. Barth sees collegiality as central to a healthy school where everyone is a teacher and a learner. He defines collegiality as teachers and principals talking to each other about practice, observing each other in their work, sharing their knowledge with each other, and teaching each other what they know. "The quality of adult relationships within a school has more to do with the quality and character of the school and with the accomplishments of students than any other factor" (p. 163). Barth's faith in teachers seems to make it possible for us to break the isolation of teaching and develop more collegiality.

• Baskwill, Jane. 1989. *Parents and Teachers: Partners in Learning.* Richmond Hill, Ontario: Scholastic Canada.

The author, who is a whole language teacher, parent, and principal, honestly shares how she went about improving parent-teacher communication. Using the "family model" built on trust, understanding, and open communication, Baskwill describes the projects and procedures she initiated in her move toward a reciprocal communication model. Specifics are given in the text and the appendix for how she used a survey, booklets for parents, notes to parents, dialogue journals, newsletters, book bags, parent bags, "lunch box launchers," special kits, and more. An extremely valuable resource for any teacher wishing to significantly improve parent-teacher communication. Be sure your school library and administrator have a copy of this book.

Bayer, Ann Shea. 1990. *Collaborative-Apprenticeship Learning: Learning and Thinking Across the Curriculum, K–12.* Mountain View, CA: Mayfield. Co-distributed by Richard C. Owen, Katonah, NY.

This terrific text (156 pp.) discusses, demonstrates, and applies a collaborative teacher-learner model that is relevant for teachers at the kindergarten through university level. Teachers ready to shift more responsibility for learning to students and to use language and writing as a tool for learning—especially in the content areas—will find much support here. Specifics for management, eliciting prior knowledge (especially through focused free writing), focused reading, writing to learn, and peer interaction are invaluable for revising approaches to planning and implementing curriculum.

Bissex, Glenda L., and Richard H. Bullock (eds.). 1987. *Seeing for Ourselves: Case-Study Research by Teachers of Writing.* Portsmouth, NH: Heinemann.

Bissex defines a teacher-researcher as "an observer, a questioner, a learner, and a more complete teacher" (pp. 4–5), while Bullock discusses the power of teacher research to change the way teachers regard their students, themselves, and their profession (p. 27). Case-study research is described as a powerful tool to discover what is happening to the children we teach, as well as a way of looking at both ourselves and our profession. Classroom teachers from first grade to university level then present their findings from their studies of poetry usage, writing process, writing conferences, journal usage, and so on. An especially interesting chapter brings the various authors together for a roundtable discussion on their research. (V.M.)

Bloome, David (ed.). 1989. *Classrooms and Literacy.* Norwood, NJ: Ablex.

Twenty researchers examine literacy activity and learning in natural settings—classrooms in elementary schools. The researchers explore the relationships between classrooms and literacy through four related issues: the classroom community, intellectual consequences, access to literacy, and distribution of power. Educators and teacher-researchers interested in how the functions and functioning of classrooms affect students' literacy will be interested in these long-term, descriptive studies.

Two quotes:

"Children from low-income and working class communities tend to have a literacy curriculum different from that of their middle and upper class counterparts" (Bloome, p. 19); "In order to move into a higher group, students must not

simply work harder and learn more; they must also learn qualitatively different reading skills, participation styles, and teacher orientations" (Borko and Eisenhart, p. 124).

• Boomer, Garth, Nancy Lester, Cynthia Onore, and Jon Cook (eds.). 1992. *Negotiating the Curriculum: Educating for the 21st Century.* London: The Falmer Press.

Teachers and learners are advised to ask four questions about a topic of study and together negotiate the answers.

1. What do we know already?

2. What do we want, and need, to find out?

3. How will we go about finding out?

4. How will we know, and show, that we've found out when we've finished? (p. 21)

This book is must reading for all educators struggling to move to a more student-centered, meaningful curriculum. It is also the most helpful book I have read for creating an integrated, inquiry-based curriculum that both engages students' interests and meets district requirements. Very provocative reading for coming to grips with sharing power in the classroom (as compared to limited decision making by students), real choice for students (as opposed to required choosing from options), intention (as compared to external motivation), collaborative talk and learning (as compared to planned cooperative learning) and integrated learning contexts. Terrific for discussion and rethinking your teaching.

Bredekamp, Sue (ed.). 1987. *Developmentally Appropriate Practice in Early Childhood Programs Serving Children from Birth Through Age 8.* Expanded ed. Washington, DC: National Association for the Education of Young Children.

This position statement (91 pp.) has become a highly acknowledged document for looking at appropriate and inappropriate practices for infants, toddlers, preschoolers, and primary-grade students. It is an outstanding reference for all teachers, administrators, parents, and policymakers who want to ensure the development of favorable early childhood practices in language and literacy learning. Be sure your school library has a copy of this publication.

Bredekamp, Sue, and Teresa Rosegrant (eds.). 1992. *Reaching Potentials: Appropriate Curriculum and Assessment for Young Children. Volume 1.* Washington, DC: National Association for the Education of Young Children.

Guidelines are presented to determine what is included in early childhood curriculum and assessment decisions. One chapter addresses the relationship of child development and curriculum while giving many examples of age-appropriate and individually appropriate curriculum decisions. Another section is concerned with antibiased, multicultural curriculum in general. Finally, educators describe their own growth as teachers as they implemented more appropriate classroom practices in their primary classrooms. This book takes learning beyond just "hands-on" activities, and its suggestions are bound to stimulate discussion among educators looking to improve programs for young children. (V.M.)

- Brooks, Jacqueline, and Martin Brooks. 1993. *In Search of Understanding: The Case for Constructivist Classrooms.* Alexandria, VA: Association for Supervision and Curriculum Development.

  The authors elaborate on the guiding principles of constructivism:
  "(1) posing problems of emerging relevance to learners
  (2) structuring learning around 'big ideas' or primary concepts
  (3) seeking and valuing students' points of view
  (4) adapting curriculum to address students' suppositions
  (5) assessing student learning in the context of teaching" (viii).
  If you agree with these principles and the accompanying constructivist view that children formulate their own understandings of the world, then we teachers must provide meaningful learning environments that foster inquiry and speculation. The authors of this outstanding text (144 pp.) elaborate on each of the guiding principles and provide excellent informa-
  tion and examples for becoming constructivist teachers. Don't miss reading this fascinating book!
  A few quotes to think about:
  "In order to understand, students must search for meaning. In order to search for meaning, students must have the opportunity to form and ask questions" (p. 54).
  "Posing narrow questions for which one seeks a singular answer denies teachers the opportunity to peer into students' minds" (p. 86).

- Brown, Rexford. 1991. *Schools of Thought: How the Politics of Literacy Shape Thinking in the Classroom.* San Francisco: Jossey-Bass Publishers.

  For educators and policymakers interested in creating schools that promote a "literacy of thoughtfulness," this is one of the best books I have ever read. Brown visited a representative sampling of North American schools and classrooms "where thinking and problem-solving activities were supposed to be a major part of the curriculum." In seeking to determine how and if educational policy impacted a "literacy of thoughtfulness," Brown and his team interviewed, observed, and talked extensively with elementary through secondary teachers and administrators. The results, while disturbing, were not surprising. With the exception of an Ontario school district and small pockets of whole language classrooms, there were few classrooms where a literacy of thoughtfulness was observed, that is, a literacy "that goes beyond basic skills and includes enhanced abilities to think critically and creatively; to reason carefully; to inquire systematically into any important matter; to analyze, synthesize, and evaluate information and arguments; and to communicate effectively to a variety of audiences in a variety of forms" (xiii). Despite the fact that educators believe that you have to aim at students' higher mental processes and profess to do so, most instruction relied on the textbook and aimed at the lower mental processes. The book ends with a copy of "Resource Guidelines for Program Review from the Ontario Ministry of Education." Use these excellent guidelines, which are listed on a continuum, to self-evaluate where you and your school are in having a child-centered, subject-integrated, problem-solving, instruction/evaluation program that leads to learner independence.

Some quotes to think about (from pp. 232–233):

"If you want young people to think, you ask them hard questions and let them wrestle with the answers. If you want them to analyze something or interpret it or evaluate it, you ask them to do so and show them how to do it with increasing skill. . . . If you want them to think the way scientists or historians or mathematicians do, you show them how scientists and historians and mathematicians think, and you provide opportunities for them to practice and compare those ways of thinking."

"Schools and districts that are farthest along in developing more thoughtfulness among students have also created more thoughtful environments and conditions for the adults in the system."

Browne, Ann. 1993. *Helping Children to Write.* London: Paul Chapman Publishing.

For teachers who struggle with how to implement and sustain a developmental approach to writing, this practical guide (158 pp.) incorporates the best of current research and practice and presents it in a readable, well-organized manner. "There are three important elements of designing a writing curriculum for children: firstly, that they are given tasks that involve real reasons to communicate meaning through writing; secondly, that they are initially given time to work on a piece of writing and time to return to it later either alone or with the teacher's help; and, thirdly, that they have opportunities to write in different styles and with different degrees of concentration depending on the task" (p. 21). Browne analyzes children's writing samples with in-depth comments on content, handwriting, and spelling, and she suggests future teaching directions for the child's continued progress. She answers common questions about writing in practice, addresses the teaching of writing to bilingual pupils, discusses explaining de-

velopmental writing to parents, and much more. If you are planning a writing curriculum for young children (preschool through primary), you will want to track down this book.

Caine, Renate Nummela, and Geoffrey Caine. 1991. *Making Connections: Teaching and the Human Brain.* Alexandria, VA: Association for Supervision and Curriculum Development.

How the brain functions, and how the brain (and learning) are affected by health, stress, and teaching approaches is the subject of this fascinating book. Over and over, the authors demonstrate how rote practice on isolated skills is inappropriate for acquiring knowledge. Instead, they show how a deeper understanding of the complexity of the brain supports holistic education. For example, content to be taught when spelled out in state curriculum frameworks can be fragmented and meaningless to individual students. Instead, subject matter to be studied should be organized around themes developed in the classroom setting to allow students to relate new and unfamiliar information to their background of experience. The book complements the work of Frank Smith, and also provides theoretical support for integrated, meaning-centered education. (V.M.)

Calkins, Lucy McCormick. 1994. *The Art of Teaching Writing.* New Edition. Portsmouth, NH: Heinemann.

In this new edition of her original breakthrough book, Calkins writes about helping students find and develop the significance in their lives through writing. "In this new edition I describe writing episodes that do not begin with a topic and a draft but instead with noticing, a question. When writing begins with something that has not yet found its significance, it is more apt to become a process of growing meaning" (p. 8). In rethinking her ideas, Calkins shares with us how to create a writing workshop in the elementary classroom that delights in what children can do and encourages them to find meaning in the moments and stories of their lives.

Among some of the topics she discusses in depth are rehearsal for writing, development of conventions in writing, conferencing, revising, publication ("the beginning, not the culmination of the writing process"), writing poetry, writing memoir, reading/writing connections through author and genre study, and writing nonfiction. She also addresses issues in assessment, theme studies, curriculum, and home-school connections. Each chapter ends with an excellent recommended bibliography of children's literature and professional literature.

• Calkins, Lucy McCormick, with Shelley Harwayne. 1991. *Living Between the Lines*. Portsmouth, NH: Heinemann.

This is an unusual, personal, and thoughtful book on the teaching of writing. There is no index to look up minilessons, conferencing, or specific procedures to follow. Instead, the reader is completely immersed in the recent work, thoughts, images, and writings of the teachers and students of the Teachers College Writing Project in New York City and is asked to rethink the teaching of writing.

In this sensitively and beautifully written text, the reader gets a feel for what the promise of writing can hold when writing workshop moves from writing folders and published pieces to notebooks and projects. We are asked to reexamine the writing workshop in broader, more flexible ways so we provide—among other elements—"silent spaces," "commitment," "genre study," "longer, slower conferences," ourselves as joyfully literate role models, real-life connections and purposes for writing, and lots of opportunities to help children develop their most promising "seed ideas." "In a sense, everything in this book addresses how we can help youngsters write with an intensity and life force" (p. 271). The changes Calkins has made in her own thinking and teaching since she wrote The Art of Teaching Writing (Heinemann, 1986) are humbling and inspiring for us all.

• Cambourne, Brian. 1988. *The Whole Story: Natural Learning and the Acquisition of*
Literacy in the Classroom. Richmond Hill, Ontario: Scholastic-TAB.

In whole language circles, Brian Cambourne is to Australia what Don Holdaway is to New Zealand and Ken Goodman is to the United States. For teachers ready to take the time to understand the theory behind whole language, this text (201 pp.) offers detailed insight into the language learning process. The in-depth discussion of Cambourne's eight conditions of learning is thought provoking and applicable to the classroom. While mostly a theoretical text, the reader is taken into a grade 5 Australian classroom and given a picture of theory into practice. There is a useful section on evaluating literacy development. There is no index.

Cazden, Courtney. 1992. *Whole Language Plus: Essays on Literacy in the United States and New Zealand*. New York: Teachers College Press.

This collection of essays on language learning is challenging, thought-provoking reading. Cazden takes the view that as children become literate, "they need deliberate help in attending to parts as well as wholes" (ix). She believes that children do not learn to read in school just as easily as they learn to speak at home (a tenet of whole language) because schools cannot duplicate the conditions of oral language immersion that exist in the home. Along with Marie Clay, she suggests the "instructional detour"—a momentary diversion, when needed, on the main road of meaningful language use (pp. 14–15). The last section of this text deals with education in New Zealand, and I found the essay "Richmond Road: A Multilingual/Multicultural Primary School in Auckland" especially fascinating. It is the remarkable story of an unusually successful, inner-city, multicultural school and how the vision of its educational leader, Jim Laughton, powerfully influenced the entire school community—even after his death. It is worth getting a hold of this book just to read this uplifting essay, originally published in Language and Education: An International Journal in 1989. We see what is possible when "kids always come first," *and teachers respect and value families' cultures and each other while also taking responsibility for their own learning.*

Chase, Penelle, and Jane Doan. 1994. *Full Circle: A New Look at Multiage Education.* Portsmouth, NH: Heinemann.

Increasingly, schools are restructuring with multiage groupings in order to have more developmentally appropriate programs and to reap the benefits of children of various ages learning from each other. Two teachers who have collaborated in teaching a primary-grades, multiage classroom since 1988 describe how they structure their day, support children as learners, use ongoing assessment strategies, use thematic units to integrate the curriculum, incorporate a workshop approach to learning, and involve parents in their program. What comes through in this 197-page text is the caring, secure community the children and teachers develop together and the responsibility the children assume for their behavior and learning. Additional perspectives are offered on multiage groupings in chapters written by a parent, a principal, and other teachers. The book ends with an extensive review by Diane McClellan of the literature on multiage grouping and useful appendices for classroom use. Valuable for educators interested in multiage classrooms, holistic teaching, and co-teaching.

Christenbury, Leila. 1994. *Making the Journey: Being and Becoming a Teacher of English Language Arts.* Portsmouth, NH: Boynton/Cook.

As an experienced, reflective teacher of English, Leila Christenbury has written this thorough, theoretical and practical text (247 pp.) to help prepare middle and high school teachers for the realities and demands of the profession. Christenbury discusses various teaching models and recommends "exploration and discussion" instead of "teaching by telling." She explores and discusses a myriad of ongoing issues such as fear of not knowing enough, classroom management, literature young people should read, characteristics of a reader-response classroom, guidelines for dealing

with average, gifted, and alienated students, teaching Shakespeare, teaching language and grammar, questioning techniques, and much more. Christenbury raises philosophical questions, gives suggestions, and encourages the reader to reflect on the ideas presented in the text by engaging in personal journal writing and further exploration with cited resources. Lots of practical ideas for teaching literature, including an annotated bibliography of recommended young adult novels and selected, multicultural literature.

Clay, Marie. 1991. *Becoming Literate: The Construction of Inner Control.* Portsmouth, NH: Heinemann.

To become a reader and writer is a complex process! This book looks at the acquisition of literacy from the preschool years to the early years of school when a child reaches the stage that allows them to read independently from new texts. Clay argues that successful readers develop an inner control, and a self-extending system, that allows them to work with print even though they have been taught by very different programs. Children who do not develop strategies to organize and control their reading processes will fail to become literate. She pleads that teachers recognize that "some children need extra resources and many more supportive interactions with teachers." One example would be the Reading Recovery program developed in New Zealand. The book is very detailed in tracing how children learn to write and read, and it will be very useful to primary teachers attempting to understand the process in an effort to support the children in their classroom. (V.M.)

Clay, Marie. 1993. *Reading Recovery: A Guidebook for Teachers in Training.* Portsmouth, NH: Heinemann.

This is the guidebook that is used by all Reading Recovery teachers in training and in practice and that replaces Early Detection of Reading Difficulties *(Clay, 1985.) The intensive program that this text outlines in great detail is for the small percentage of first graders in any classroom that are hardest to teach. Marie*

Clay cautions that 80 to 90 percent of all children will learn to read without the meticulous and rigorous procedures of Reading Recovery. While I had read this difficult and comprehensive text before becoming a Reading Recovery teacher, it was most useful to me after I had received the teacher training. See also the companion volume, An Observation Survey of Early Literacy Achievement *(Clay, 1993), which presents ways of observing young children's literacy development, (annotation p. 75b). (If you are unfamiliar with Reading Recovery, see pages 479–485 in* Invitations *for information.)*

Cochrane, Orin (ed.). 1992. *Questions and Answers About Whole Language.* Katonah, NY: Richard C. Owen.

Twenty-one questions about whole language are answered by educators from England, Canada, Australia, and the United States. The book is substantial in content, yet informal enough for a relaxing read. It covers such topics as defining whole language, the role of literature study, evaluation in a whole language classroom, and where whole language is going in the future. The answers will be helpful to parents, teachers, administrators, and anyone inquiring about whole language methodology. (V.M.)

Cochrane, Orin, and Ethel Buchanan (eds.). 1993. *Teachers' Stories: Starting the Year with Whole Language.* Winnipeg, Manitoba: Whole Language Consultants.

This quick, enjoyable read includes stories by sixteen teachers from kindergarten through university. They each explain how they begin the school year in their classrooms. Their routines, structure, struggles, parent communications, and honest sharing give teachers support and ideas for a successful beginning.

Collerson, John (ed.). 1988. *Writing for Life.* Portsmouth, NH: Heinemann.

I found this Primary English Teaching Association publication a very welcome addition to books on the teaching of writing. This practical, readable, 120-page book goes beyond the process-conference approach and gives specific suggestions for teaching writing across the curriculum. There are lots of ideas for teaching children to write in different genres: reports, scripts, descriptions, and factual accounts, as well as narratives. The point is well made that we need to demonstrate expository as well as narrative forms of writing to have a balanced writing program. Applicable for secondary school too.

• Cordeiro, Pat. 1992. *Whole Learning: Whole Language and Content in the Upper Elementary Grades.* Katonah, NY: Richard C. Owen.

This book shows what worked for the author in her self-contained classroom as she began to utilize whole language techniques through her use of process writing methods. As a learner, she describes how she changed, why she was proceeding the way she did, and how her upper elementary students learned. A flexible schedule allowed her students to focus on thematic work centered around the content areas of social studies, science, and math. Suggestions for literature books to support the various topics abound in every chapter. A very important section is her thoughts on reflection and assessment. It includes ways of documenting student growth through portfolios and self-evaluations, as well as her own narrative accounts of the student's progress. This is an important book for teachers who are seeing whole language students enter the upper levels of elementary school. (V.M.)

Crafton, Linda K. 1994. *Challenges of Holistic Teaching: Answering the Tough Questions.* Norwood, MA: Christopher-Gordon.

This is a practical book that can be used in many ways. It could be read from cover to cover, but probably will be used to find information as a concern becomes pressing and needs a response. A wide variety of topics are covered from ability grouping to writing workshop. A unique feature of the book is the Related Questions section, which allows readers to network their way through the book. Suggestions for further reading and any children's books cited are listed at the end of each question. I especially enjoyed the sections on Skills and Strategies, Parents, and Literature Discussions. (V.M.)

Crafton, Linda K. 1991. *Whole Language: Getting Started . . . Moving Forward.* Katonah, NY: Richard C. Owen.

This is a comprehensive handbook dealing with the realities of starting and continuing a whole language classroom. It is grounded in theory, yet is full of practical ideas. Beginning with the differences between traditional, product-oriented, teacher-controlled education and holistic, student-centered, process-driven, language-based teaching, the author notes that the two philosophies are total opposites. She then lists six guiding principles and how they are applied in the whole language classroom. Crafton worked with six classroom teachers from various grade levels, including a high school teacher, and their stories are told throughout the book. One especially valuable chapter contains twenty-five strategies that can easily be integrated into the classroom setting. Another tells how each teacher begins the school year with her students. This is a supportive as well as challenging book for evolving whole language teachers. (V.M.)

Crawford, Leslie W. 1993. *Language and Literacy Learning in Multicultural Classrooms.* Boston: Allyn and Bacon. (hardbound)

The student population in the United States is rapidly changing as children who were considered representative of minority groups are now becoming the majority. This book is a comprehensive resource for teachers who are concerned that students from varied ethnic, cultural, and language backgrounds become literate in a pluralistic society. Strategies for learning that benefit all children are identified, as well as suggestions for assessment and evaluation. A "Teacher's Resource Kit" contains a fine selection of children's books for multicultural teaching themes and topics. (V.M.)

Cullinan, Bernice (ed.). 1992. *Invitation to Read: More Children's Literature in the Reading Program.* Newark, DE: International Reading Association.

Information to build or strengthen your use of children's literature in the reading program is presented in this thoughtful book. From Tomie dePaola's opening words to Bill Martin, Jr.'s afterword, it is loaded with vital information for teachers. The first section deals with genre studies, including books for emergent readers, poetry appreciation, realistic fiction, and informational books. In the next section, suggestions for enriching the arts and humanities, conducting author studies, extending multicultural understandings, and introducing award-winning books are given. The last portion considers reader response, at-risk readers, censorship, resources to find children's books, and suggestions for organizing a literature/reading program. Throughout the book, practical and innovative teaching ideas are featured. All in all, this is a very helpful book for busy classroom teachers. (V.M.)

Cullinan, Bernice, and Lee Galda. 1994. *Literature and the Child.* 3rd ed. Fort Worth, TX: Harcourt Brace. (hardbound)

This is an updated and more concise edition of one of my favorite reference books. I often refer to it when I am developing a thematic unit, studying an author or illustrator's work, or considering a genre study. As with Charlotte Huck's Children's Literature in the Elementary School, *a landmark anthology of children's books, books are described, criteria are given as to what to look for in a children's book, and many suggestions are given for their use in the classroom. Yet this book has several unique features, which make it especially useful in the classroom, such as a chapter on the readers of children's books— the children themselves, and how they respond to reading, read to learn, and read to enjoy. Another strong chapter is one that focuses on multicultural books as a distinct genre. Brief profiles of authors/illustrators are placed throughout the book, as well as a list of their birthdays in one of the appendices. Though the book is expensive for an individual teacher to purchase, it is well worth requesting as an addition to the school library. (V.M.)*

• Dahl, Karin L. (ed.). 1992. *Teacher as Writer: Entering the Professional Conversation.*

Urbana, IL: National Council of Teachers of English.

The voices of teachers are needed for sharing their insights and knowledge about educational issues, but many do not know where to start. This book begins with the personal accounts of teachers who are writing for the profession, and encourages others to take the plunge. Advice for tackling all aspects of the writing process, how to find support within writers' groups, as well as how to develop articles and get them published, is offered by teacher educators from all levels of education. This book is a treasure chest of practical support and encouragement for anyone planning to write for publication. (V.M.)

Davidson, Jane L. (ed.). 1988. *Counterpoint and Beyond: A Response to "Becoming a Nation of Readers."* Urbana, IL: National Council of Teachers of English.

This publication was written to explore concerns that the NCTE Commission on Reading found in the highly publicized BNR (Becoming a Nation of Readers), which was released in 1985. They believed that while BNR presented some sound theoretical positions and offered practical suggestions, it had several serious faults that needed to be addressed in a new publication. Commission members felt BNR was biased, did not present a full picture, and was inconsistent in the theory of reading presented and in the suggestions made for beginning reading instruction. BNR blithely dismissed whole language theory and research with the statement, "In the hands of very skillful teachers, the results can be excellent. But the average result is indifferent when compared to approaches typical in American classrooms, at least as gauged by performance on first and second grade standardized reading achievement tests" (p. 45, BNR). Several chapters describe how minority concerns were largely ignored in BNR. The place of literature in the reading program was barely mentioned beyond suggesting that parents should read to their children. Another problem was the relationship between phonics and comprehension. In one statement, BNR stressed that children construct meaning from their first experiences with reading, while the report stressed that children be taught basic letter-sound relationships first, or they would be unable to comprehend. Both the original report and Counterpoint should be read together and the dialogue continued! (V.M.)

DeFabio, Roseanne Y. 1994. *Outcomes in Process: Setting Standards for Language Use.* Portsmouth, NH: Boynton/Cook.

Acknowledging that national standards and outcomes are present realities and that "someone" will be setting the standards, the author, who is a language arts consultant at the State Education Department in New York, contributes to the national conversation by explicitly defining and recommending standards for the language arts. She also reports the results of a pilot study of a group of teachers who used specific standards, outcomes, and criteria in their high school classrooms to assess students' language learning. This is a thoughtful, useful text for educators and stakeholders interested in standards and outcome-based assessment as well as in improving instructional practices.

I appreciated the clarification of common terms as these terms have taken on different meanings depending on one's educational context and past experiences. Outcomes are defined as the "knowledge, skills, and understandings that individuals can and do habitually demonstrate as a result of instruction and experience." Outcomes without standards are insufficient. "While the outcome describes what an individual knows, can do, or is like, the standard indicates how well or to what degree the individual knows, can do, or is like the behavior indicated in the outcome." Furthermore, DeFabio asserts, in order to make the standard clear, some specific criteria or performance indicators of observable behaviors are necessary. I found chapter 4, "Standards, Benchmarks, and the Continuum," particularly definitive and relevant to my own school district's debate on curriculum/assessment standards and outcomes. The Appendix, "Revised Draft of Outcomes with Eight Levels of Performance," will be helpful to groups writ-

ing their own outcomes. This text is applicable across the grades even though most examples come from secondary level.

DeFord, Diane E., Carol A. Lyons, and Gay Su Pinnell (eds.). 1991. *Bridges to Literacy: Learning from Reading Recovery.* Portsmouth, NH: Heinemann.

For teachers, parents, administrators, and school districts who want to know how Reading Recovery training and teaching operate and are implemented, reading this text will give much information and insight. Marie Clay's unique early-intervention program for the lowest-achieving readers in a first-grade class is detailed. The New Zealand and Ohio research bases are summarized. In the chapter, "Reading Recovery Surprises," Marie Clay notes the long-term, surprising outcomes/successes for "slow-learning" children and thus makes a convincing case for implementing Reading Recovery. In Part 2 of the book, Diane DeFord, Kathy Short, Barbara Peterson, and Kathleen Holland describe rich literary experiences and contexts in school and in the home that promote strategic reading and success for "at-risk" children. Many of the principles, examples, and strategies they cite and use are applicable to all students learning to read and write. In fact, since many teachers (myself included, until I became a Reading Recovery teacher) have never had good instruction in understanding and teaching the beginning reading process, this 240-page text can serve as an invaluable resource. Early primary teachers will find that the explanations of leveling of books for Reading Recovery and the bibliography of leveled books provided by Barbara Peterson in chapter 6 are very useful. In Part 3, Gay Su Pinnell, Daniel Woolsey, Carol Lyons, and Charlotte Huck address Reading Recovery teachers as learners and describe the powerful impact of Reading Recovery training and teaching on teacher thinking, attitudes, and classroom practice. The final section, "Constructing Literacy Lessons" (pp. 222–231), provides an essential framework of six components that some experienced Reading Recovery teachers in Ohio adapted to their classrooms:

reading aloud, shared reading, rereading stories, writing—including shared writing, dictation, independent writing, ongoing assessment, and honoring children's reading and writing.

Dyson, Anne Haas, and Celia Genishi (eds.). 1994. *The Need for Story: Cultural Diversity in Classroom and Community.* Urbana, IL: National Council of Teachers of English.

In this book, the basic need for story to organize and bring meaning to our life experiences is vividly illustrated. Nineteen contributors look at many aspects of storying—from its nature to its power in the classroom. I was especially interested in how Vivian Gussin Paley used an ongoing story she wrote to influence the way three African-American kindergartners viewed their racial identity. Courtney Cazden looked at the critical role of teachers in responding to the stories children tell at sharing time. Other essays looked at the performance of African-American student writers, the influence of gender in what children write, and teachers as authors of children's literature. The questions raised within these pages will increase the potential that the power of story has in your classroom. A very thought-provoking volume! (V.M.)

Edelsky, Carole, Bess Altwerger, and Barbara Flores. 1991. *Whole Language: What's the Difference?* Portsmouth, NH: Heinemann.

This book has been written with the intention of helping educators become more knowledgeable about the theoretical bases of whole language. For the teacher who already has some understanding of whole language, the detailed theoretical framework that is presented—as well as the scenes from whole language classrooms—makes whole language theory very explicit.

Elbow, Peter. 1990. *What Is English?* New York: Modern Language Association of America.

This book is a very personal and challenging picture of the English profession from early elementary to college. Reflecting on the 1987 English Coalition Conference, Elbow identifies the major issues confronting our profession: what does "English" mean?, theory and practice in the teaching of reading and writing, should there be a "canon" of books that all students should read?, and assessment. Interspersed between Elbow's reflections are pieces by participants who attended the conference. This is a thought-provoking book for teachers of any grade or age level. (V.M.)

- Ernst, Karen. 1994. *Picturing Learning: Artists and Writers in the Classroom*. Portsmouth, NH: Heinemann.

  The author was an eighth-grade language arts and social studies teacher for many years when a budget crisis eliminated her job; but since she was certified as an art teacher she was assigned to teach art to K–4 elementary school students. Having used the principles of the reading/writing workshop for many years, she decided to apply them in her art program. She says, "Just as writing led my students into the process of discovery, learning, and making meaning, I wanted creating pictures to do the same." This book is the exciting journey she and her students undertook together. It is also the story of an unusual collaboration between Ernst and the classroom teachers she worked with. She often visited their classrooms and wrote notes to the children that reflected on her visits. Their teachers in turn often stayed as the children began their art classes. In the classroom, as children began to write they were already often planning how they would express their written thoughts in art projects they could do when they could go to the art room. Choice of projects, writing, or pictures to create meaning became a central issue, just as choice of topics is important in a reading/writing workshop. Ernst illustrates the book with her own line drawings and notes, which adds another level of understanding to her work. This is an important book in considering the integration of art into the curriculum, and should be read both by classroom and art specialist teachers alike. (V.M.)

Fearn, Gloria Wilber. 1993. *Building the Good School: Participating Parents at Charquin*. Hayward, CA: Ohlone Press.

This book is a tribute to the empowerment of students, parents, and teachers in creating a holistic environment that is growing and changing to meet the needs of the learners within its walls. The Charquin Program is an alternative school within the Markham Public School that dates back about twenty years. It began with the active participation of parents in developing a philosophical base utilizing the open-classroom model, and has evolved into one also using whole language practices. Both theoretical and practical, this book shows how a school community can work together to support educational programs that will allow children to meet the demands of the future. It will be enjoyed by educators who might be interested in creating a school within a school, and shared with parents who support their vision. (V.M.)

Feathers, Karen. 1993. *Infotext: Reading and Learning*. Markham, Ontario: Pippin Publishing, and Portsmouth, NH: Heinemann.

By infotexts, the author means the oral and written texts that we read (such as books, journals, newspapers, speeches) to gather information on specific topics. In Feathers's words, this book is about "strategies that will help students read infotexts of all descriptions with greater understanding and better retention of information." I especially appreciated this book for its student-centered approach and all the current, excellent, and usable information on content reading.

Fisher, Bobbi. 1991. *Joyful Learning: A Whole Language Kindergarten*. Portsmouth, NH: Heinemann.

This book describes what an observant, knowledgeable kindergarten teacher does in her classroom in a typical day and why she does it. It is a remarkably clear and pragmatic explanation of a classroom based on Don Holdaway's Natural Learning Model. Each chapter highlights a specific aspect of the classroom. The chapters on assessment, dramatic play, and questions teachers ask are especially strong. Although the book is focused on the kindergarten level, teachers from pre-kindergarten through grade 2 will find many ideas, routines, themes, and record-keeping suggestions that will directly apply to their whole language classrooms.

Five, Cora Lee. 1991. *Special Voices.* Portsmouth, NH: Heinemann.

The stories of eight children with special needs are told as they lived in a regular classroom instead of an isolated setting. Their teacher describes how she helped the children develop into readers and writers while learning from them. She began by building an accepting, supportive environment that allowed children to have time to create, ownership of their ideas, and response from herself and fellow students. As this design worked for general education students, she began to question if it would nurture special children and enable them to do their best. Each year for six years, she had one or two students who were labeled ESL, were disruptive, or labeled "learning disabled." All proved they could work and learn in a language-rich environment with their peers. Their stories will provide many answers to problems facing learners in our own classrooms. Their successes can become those of our special learners. The possibilities are endless. (V.M.)

Fletcher, Ralph. 1991. *Walking Trees: Teaching Teachers in the New York City Schools.* Portsmouth, NH: Heinemann.

This is a sensitively written, honest account of the author's struggles and successes during one school year when he worked as a staff developer for the Teachers College Writing Project. In a book that reads like a novel, Fletcher poignantly describes his daily experiences in teaching the writing process to administrators, teachers, and children in the New York City schools. Compelling reading.

• Fletcher, Ralph. 1993. *What a Writer Needs.* Portsmouth, NH: Heinemann.

This is one of my favorite books on the teaching of writing. It is short, personal, well written, original, and terrifically useful. Fletcher, a talented writer and teacher, shares anecdotes and details of the craft of writing, and, in so doing, helps us become better writers and better teachers of

writing. Some of the writing topics he discusses and develops in individual chapters include: character, setting, specificity, voice, tension, beginnings, endings, unforgettable language, playfulness with time, and significant subjects. The Appendix gives many examples of books, poems, and stories that develop each of those topics well. Elementary and middle school teachers will appreciate the wealth of strategies and supporting examples of Fletcher's and students' writing. A wonderful resource for getting students and ourselves to write well.

Some favorite quotes:

"The writing becomes beautiful when it becomes specific" (p. 47).

"Voice in writing has to do with a unique personality-on-paper" (p. 77).

"We need to teach students how to write small, not just in terms of detail . . . but also in terms of moments, time" (p. 132).

• Forester, Anne D., and Margaret Reinhard. 1989. *The Learner's Way.* Winnipeg, Manitoba: Peguis.

This outstanding text (315 pp.), based on the belief that children learn from models and by being immersed in doing, combines a strong theory base with very specific practice. For the primary teacher, especially in K–2, who wants to visualize the whole language classroom and make it a reality, there is no book that is more helpful. Teachers will find the details and scheduling of actual classroom teaching presented in a clear, relaxed, applicable manner.

Activities and strategies such as story time, book time, reading groups, unison reading, individualized reading, writing workshop, author's circle, and news time are fully explained. News time is viewed as "our most comprehensive way of modeling all of the writing skills" (p. 90). During news time, children share their news of the day orally as the teacher writes and demonstrates the reading-writing connection through spelling, phonics, handwriting, punctuation, capitalization, and rereading.

Forester, Anne D., and Margaret Reinhard. 1991. *On the Move: Teaching the Learn-*

ers' Way in Grades 4–7. Winnipeg, Manitoba: Peguis.

Theory and practice are blended into a comprehensive handbook that supports teachers who are attempting to bring holistic teaching methods into the intermediate grades. It continues the work the authors began in their text designed for primary-grade teachers. They encourage teachers to learn by doing and observing their students, and give many suggestions to start with. Topics include: Establishing a Climate for Learning, Classroom Management, Aspects of Reading and Writing Workshops, Moving Across the Curriculum to Teach Social Studies, Science, the Arts, Combination and Nongraded Classrooms, and Assessment. All of their suggestions are grounded on their research in the classrooms of three outstanding classroom teachers, which makes the book even more useful to busy teachers wanting to make substantive changes in their classrooms. (V.M.)

Foster, Harold M. 1994. *Crossing Over: Whole Language for Secondary English Teachers.* Fort Worth, TX: Harcourt Brace.

English teachers in middle and high school settings who are beginning to receive whole language–oriented students will appreciate this resource. The opening chapters define and describe the growing whole language movement in the secondary schools. The next part of the book is used to illustrate aspects of whole language teaching in the classroom setting. Topics such as conducting a reading workshop, leading a reader-response book discussion, and assessing writing are included. Last, becoming a whole language teacher, planning for the classroom, and remaining a whole language teacher are considered. This book would be very helpful as a guide for a discussion group of teachers interested in learning more about, or beginning to implement, whole language methodology. (V.M.)

• Fox, Mem. 1993. *Radical Reflections: Passionate Opinions on Teaching, Learning, and Living.* San Diego: Harcourt Brace.

Written in a humorous, engaging style, this collection of a well-known author's articles and presentations makes thought-provoking, inspiring reading for what it means to be a teacher of reading and writing. Two favorite quotes:

"If you don't open up and share who you are with your students, they will not learn to trust you as a teacher and as a fellow human being; this will limit their engagement in class" (p. 163).

"The best 'teacher' you will ever have is careful reflection on your own experience as a teacher of whole language in your own classroom" (p. 165).

Freeman, Yvonne S., and David E. Freeman. 1992. *Whole Language for Second Language Learners.* Portsmouth, NH: Heinemann.

The authors do not believe that whole language instruction is a panacea that will cure all problems facing bilingual students, but they are convinced that the application of seven principles found in whole language will give each of their ESL students a better chance for school success. They are the following: lessons should proceed from whole to part, lessons should begin with what the student knows, lessons should be meaningful to the students, lessons should encourage students to share their ideas, lessons should develop both oral and written language together, learning should take place in the first language before English is acquired, and teachers should believe that their students will learn. These principles are each developed in a supporting chapter with an explanation of underlying theory, as well as possible practices. This is essential reading for any teacher with ESL students in his or her classroom. (V.M.)

Galda, Lee, Bernice E. Cullinan, and Dorothy S. Strickland. 1993. *Language, Literacy and the Child.* Fort Worth, TX: Harcourt Brace. (hardbound)

Beginning teachers, as well as those wanting to learn the latest information on language learning and literacy development, will enjoy this resource. It brings theory and practice together in a careful and thoughtful manner. The opening chap-

ters look at oral language, listening, reading, and writing from the beginnings to proficiency. Later chapters apply these concepts through descriptions of teachers and students in their classrooms, along with suggestions for planning and implementation. Scattered throughout the text are helpful teaching ideas, which are conveniently listed on the front endpapers of the book. (V.M.)

Glover, Mary Kenner. 1993. *Two Years: A Teacher's Memoir*. Portsmouth, NH: Heinemann.

This little book gives a glimpse of life in a private, alternative school in a first, and then second, grade taught by the author. The value of having one teacher for two consecutive years is beautifully illustrated as Glover describes her classroom experiences in such a setting. Many anecdotes and examples of children's work bring the classroom to life, and will provide inspiration to build a child-centered curriculum. This is a rich environment filled with a love for learning and a stimulating academic atmosphere. (V.M.)

Goswami, Dixie, and Peter R. Stillman (eds.). 1987. *Reclaiming the Classroom: Teacher Research as an Agency for Change*. Portsmouth, NH: Boynton/Cook.

This exciting collection of essays addresses the "how's" as well as the "why's" of classroom research. The importance of teacher-researchers can be summed up in James Britton's statement, "What the teacher does not achieve in the classroom cannot be achieved by anybody else." Though the book is not a step-by-step procedure manual, a teacher can gain valuable information on how to carry out classroom research. Essays such as "A Quiet Form of Research," "Research as Odyssey," "Class-Based Writing Research: Teachers Learning from Students," and "Planning Classroom Research" were quite useful to me. The final section of the book documents the practices and insights of seven teacher-researchers learning in their classrooms. (V.M.)

• Graves, Donald H. *A Fresh Look at Writing*. 1994. Portsmouth, NH: Heinemann.

What I love about Don Graves's newest book is his stance, "I'll show you how to do this so you can do it too." We hear and see Graves's thinking, verbalizing, and writing before he asks us to undertake what he calls "ACTIONS." "An ACTION is something you do that will help you become an active teacher of writing." We are also privy to the changes in thinking and practice Graves has undergone since Writing: Teachers and Children at Work was published by Heinemann in 1983. Bothered by some of the orthodoxy that resulted from that landmark book, he gives us the conditions for creating good writing and relooks at conferencing, sharing, revising, and writing fiction in detail. One of the early quotes I was glad to see was, "We've learned that teachers need to teach more, right from the outset." By this Graves refers to teaching children how to read their own writing, how to share their writing, how to listen and respond to others' writing, and how to teach spelling and other conventions writers use.

One of the most important ACTIONS for optimal learning that Graves models for us is how to get to know our students well and learn from them. Throughout the text, he models that by letting us get to know him well—not just as a writer but as a person who is always learning and changing. Graves's book is a gift to us and our students.

Some quotes to ponder:

"If students are not engaged in writing at least four days out of five, and for a period of thirty-five to forty minutes, beginning in Grade One, they will have little opportunity to learn to think through the medium of writing."

"You, the teacher, are the most important condition for creating learning in the classroom. Your students will observe how you treat writing in your own life, how you learn, and what is important to you through the questions you ask of the world around you."

"The purpose of the writing conference is to help children teach you about what they know that you may more effectively help them with their writing."

"Our data show that when a writer makes a good choice of subject the voice booms through. When the voice is strong, writing improves as well as all the skills that go to improve writing. Indeed, voice is the engine that sustains writers through the hard work of composing, the drafts and redrafts."

Graves, Donald H. 1989–1992. *The Reading/Writing Teacher's Companion.* Portsmouth, NH: Heinemann.

> *Investigate Nonfiction*
> *Experiment with Fiction*
> *Discover Your Own Literacy*
> *Build a Literate Classroom*
> *Explore Poetry*

> This series of books brings together Graves's thoughts and insights since his groundbreaking book Writing: Teachers and Children at Work *(1983). Whereas his earlier book focused more on the process of writing, these books explore the richness of reading and writing together in a literate classroom. Examples of teachers and children sharing both fiction and nonfiction books they enjoy and writing in various forms are given. Teachers are encouraged to examine their own reading and writing, what they do as listeners and speakers, to rethink their own learning and their use of time in the classroom, and to read aloud as well as help children write poetry. Throughout the series, actions/reflections are suggested to encourage teachers to reach out to new possibilities in their language arts teaching. (V.M.)*

Graves, Michael, and Bonnie Graves. 1994. *Scaffolding Reading Experiences: Designs for Student Success.* Norwood, MA: Christopher-Gordon.

> *A scaffolded reading experience is an instructional procedure that assists students to learn by allowing them to meet a goal or carry out a task that could be beyond their unassisted efforts. Just as a mother sharing a book with a young child might page through to familiarize the child with the general content before reading, a teacher provides essentials that will make the reading experience worthwhile and more meaningful. This book contains prereading, reading, and postreading activities, as well as comprehensive ones that incorporate all three types, for a particular group of students reading certain texts. Various chapters discuss the reasoning behind such experiences, how to incorporate them into the classroom, and how they fit into a total reading program. Two helpful appendices suggest ways to choose appropriate text material, as well as where to locate information on books. Author, title, appropriate grade level, and subject are indexed for children's books, as well as author and subject for professional books. This book has a wealth of strategies that can be accessed to meet the needs of various students from first to eighth grade. (V.M.)*

Hall, Nigel. 1987. *The Emergence of Literacy.* Portsmouth, NH: Heinemann.

> *For the educator who wants to examine the worldwide research behind emergent literacy but who doesn't have time to read all the primary sources, this 101-page volume provides a solid foundation. This remains an important book for increasing your knowledge about language learning and for implementing meaningful literacy instructional practices.*

• Hansen, Jane. 1987. *When Writers Read.* Portsmouth, NH: Heinemann.

> *This comprehensive text brings writing and reading instruction together based on insights found in writing process classrooms. It begins with Hansen's own questioning as she learned new methods of reading instruction while observing in Ellen Blackburn Karelitz's first-grade classroom. However, much of the book is based on her research at Mast Way, a public school in New Hampshire. Guidelines are given for structuring the classroom, evaluation, the teacher's role, the place of phonics, and basal readers based on real happenings in the classrooms where Hansen was working. Chapters are devoted to the ways that librarians, administrators, Chapter 1 teachers, and even college professors can support the classroom teacher. Teachers who are looking for alternatives to basal programs will find this book an invaluable resource. (V.M.)*

• Harp, Bill (ed.). 1993. *Bringing Children to Literacy: Classrooms at Work*. Norwood, MA: Christopher-Gordon.

The reader is taken into exemplary grades 1–6 literacy classrooms to see whole language principles and practices in action: theme cycles, literature study, shared reading, portfolios, journaling, to name a few. In great depth, classroom teachers describe their organization, planning, management, teaching and evaluation strategies, and reading-writing programs. Second-grade teachers Deborah Manning and Jean Fennacy broaden our understanding and use of shared reading in a primary classroom. First-grade teacher Mary Giard explains her role and the students' in her excellent guided-reading program. Mary Kitagawa demonstrates how she sets up her excellent writing program and responds to her fifth- and sixth-grade writers. Donna Byrum and Virginia Lazenby Pierce describe how they organize for theme cycles as a way to involve their fifth graders in investigation of meaningful, self-chosen topics. Kittye Copeland shares how she organizes her multiage (ages 5–12) classroom for reading and writing. Each chapter provides a wealth of information and workable ideas for teachers. Don't miss reading this valuable resource!

Harris, Violet J. (ed.). 1992. *Teaching Multicultural Literature in Grades K–8*. Norwood, MA: Christopher-Gordon. (hardbound)

This is a collection of essays by writers reflecting both their expertise and their cultures. An especially helpful chapter by Rudine Sims Bishop presents guidelines for teachers who are trying to select authentic multicultural literature. In other chapters, African-American, Asian Pacific, Native American, Puerto Rican, Mexican-American, and Caribbean children's literature is discussed with great insight. Each author presents the development of children's literature within his or her culture while helping the reader to become aware of stereotypes and negative images that might inadvertently be promoted. Annotated lists of highly recommended books are given at the end of each chapter. The final chapter has an excellent listing of small presses, related organizations, journals, and bookstores for finding multicultural books. The entire volume is a fabulous resource for the selection of, discussion of, and debate on appropriate multicultural literature for children. (V.M.)

• Harste, Jerome C., and Kathy G. Short, with Carolyn Burke and contributing teacher-researchers. 1988. *Creating Classrooms for Authors: The Reading-Writing Connection*. Portsmouth, NH: Heinemann.

This is an in-depth text (416 pp.) for the experienced reading-writing teacher who already applies the theoretical knowledge of language learning in the classroom along with effective management techniques. The authors view "The Authoring Cycle" as a model for all learning in a curriculum that focuses on life experiences. The reader is given much direction to get and keep the cycle going. Teachers will find the second section of the book, where many specific classroom activities are described, especially valuable. "Author's Chair," "Classroom Newspaper," "Family Stories," "Learning Logs," "Literature Circles," "Reader's Theatre," "Save the Last Word for Me," "Sketch to Stretch," and "Written Conversation" are among some of the curricular activities delineated.

• Harwayne, Shelley. 1992. *Lasting Impressions: Weaving Literature into the Writing Workshop*. Portsmouth, NH: Heinemann.

This book is bound to become a well-used and well-worn classic in an elementary teacher's professional library. It is filled with practical ideas based on the author's experiences with Antoinette Ciano's fifth graders in P.S. 148 in Queens, New York. However, as a co-director of the Teachers College Writing Project, Shelley Harwayne also explores the relationship between reading and writing at many grade levels, thus giving the book a universal appeal. She explores the writing workshop structures over a school year, and includes thoughts on minilessons, conferences, author visits, book talks, and assessment. Literature is brought into every aspect of the classroom setting. As she completed the book, Harwayne moved into a new position as the director of an alternative public school that will have literature as the heart of the curriculum. She outlines her hopes and dreams for the new school, and ends this valuable resource with the words, "To be continued." I look forward to her future comments. (V.M.)

Heald-Taylor, Gail. 1989. *The Administrator's Guide to Whole Language.* Katonah, NY: Richard C. Owen.

This is a handy text (189 pp.) to give to the administrator who wants to know more about whole language and how to facilitate its implementation. Especially useful is the extensive section on the research supporting whole language teaching, the comparison between whole language and skills-based approaches, the activities and strategies principals should expect to see in whole language classrooms, the suggestions for informing and educating parents about whole language, and the section on assessment. Excellent for teachers as well.

• Heard, Georgia. 1989. *For the Good of the Earth and Sun: Teaching Poetry.* Portsmouth, NH: Heinemann.

A practicing poet and teacher with a love of language and respect for students takes us "inside" the process of poetry writing by describing her own thinking-writing-reading processes. In so doing, she makes reading and writing poetry seem natural, desirable, and possible for us all. The book is practical, inspiring, and lovely to read. For the classroom teacher, there are suggestions and strategies for reading poetry, getting started writing poetry, creating visual images with words, choosing original words, revising, conferencing, and creating line-breaks and white spaces as well as examples of various minilessons. Although Heard sees a place for rhymed poetry, as well as haiku and cinquain, which she calls "the hamburger and hot dog of American poetry classrooms" (p. 96), she goes beyond formula writing to encouraging exploration with various forms and ideas in a poetry-rich environment. Lots of examples of what actually transpires in her poetry workshops with children are included along with many poems by chil-

dren. There are also useful bibliographies of poetry books for children and reference books for teaching poetry. Reading this extraordinary and powerful book will change the way you approach the teaching of poetry.

Hearne, Betsy, and Roger Sutton (eds.). 1993. *Evaluating Children's Books: A Critical Look: Aesthetic, Social, and Political Aspects of Analyzing and Using Children's Books.* Urbana-Champaign, IL: University of Illinois Graduate School of Library and Information Science.

Taken from a conference devoted to evaluating books for children and young adults, the speakers/writers of this text take us inside the book review process. Reading this text sensitized me to the criteria and issues surrounding the selection of nonfiction books, picture books, and especially books about minority groups. With literature being the mainstay of the reading program in many schools and classrooms, teachers—as well as librarians—are making decisions about literature to purchase. This is an important text for developing a "culturally conscious literature" collection. The chapter "Evaluating Children's Books for Whole-Language Learning" by Violet Harris is particularly helpful to teachers.

A favorite quote: "Books can make a difference in dispelling prejudice and building community: not with role models and recipes, not with noble messages about the human family, but with enthralling stories that make us imagine the lives of others. A good story lets you know people as individuals in all their particularity and conflict; and once you see someone as a person—flawed, complex, striving—you've reached beyond stereotype" (p. 134).

• Heath, Shirley Brice, and Leslie Mangiola. 1991. *Children of Promise: Literate Activity in Linguistically and Culturally Diverse Classrooms.* Washington, D.C.: National Education Association.

This sixty-four-page publication urges us to address the literacy education needs of culturally and linguistically diverse students by seeing them as "children of promise" rather than "at risk." Citing several literacy programs that have dramatically influenced the literacy skills and attitudes of low-achieving, language-minority students by involving them in cross-grade tutoring, lots of opportunities for talk, and other specific approaches to language-based learning that are powerful for all students, this is a must-read book for all educators. Detailed suggestions for developing literate behaviors—for example, successful small-group conversations in the classroom—are included. Practical for all K–12 teachers.

- Hickman, Janet, and Bernice E. Cullinan (eds.). 1989. *Children's Literature in the Classroom: Weaving Charlotte's Web.* Norwood, MA: Christopher-Gordon.

    Designed as a tribute to Charlotte Huck's teaching and her philosophy about literature for children, this book reflects the influence this remarkable teacher has had on her students. Following the opening tribute describing Huck's career and her vision of literature as the heart of the school curriculum, the book is divided into three sections: understanding the uses of literature in the classroom; celebrating books and authors in the picture book, fantasy, historical fiction, and poetry genres; and developing literature-based programs. The various chapters are contributed by her former students and several children's authors. The Epilogue, "No Wider Than the Heart Is Wide," is a piece by Huck herself. The entire volume is a rich and unique legacy for all of us to savor and treasure. (V.M.)

- Hickman, Janet, Bernice Cullinan, and Susan Hepler (eds.). 1994. *Children's Literature in the Classroom: Extending Charlotte's Web.* Norwood, MA: Christopher-Gordon.

    This book is a companion book to Children's Literature in the Classroom and continues with the fine scholarship and tone of the first volume. It covers completely new topics, such as poetry in the classroom, responses to literature, learning from the illustrations in picture books, literature across the curriculum, using literature in Reading Recovery programs, as

well as adapting Reading Recovery principles for adults. The prologue is by Charlotte Huck, who cites many uses and abuses of children's literature. These fine authors leave the reader with much food for thought. (V.M.)

Hiebert, Elfrieda H., and Barbara M. Taylor (eds.). 1994. *Getting Reading Right from the Start: Effective Early Literacy Interventions.* Boston: Allyn and Bacon.

The purpose of this book is to show that early literacy intervention programs with the focus on authentic reading and writing tasks can prevent many first-grade children from failure to learn to read. Seven different successful programs, designed to accelerate the literacy learning of children who enter school behind their peers in emergent reading skills, are discussed in the various chapters of the book. The programs take various forms, such as tutoring efforts, small-group efforts, and classroom/school restructuring, but all stress the need for activities like reading stories aloud, using big books, extending text through drama or art, and writing experiences in print-rich environments. (V.M.)

- Hill, Susan, and Joelie Hancock. 1993. *Reading and Writing Communities: Co-operative Literacy Learning in the Classroom.* Victoria, Australia: Eleanor Curtain

    While we know that classroom climate is especially important for developing readers and writers, most of us struggle with how to attain a classroom where students assume responsibility for their own behavior and for the successful functioning of the class. Australian educators Hill and Hancock clearly show us—through words, charts, and photographs—how to organize our classrooms and build a cohesive community. Specific strategies for getting students to successfully read and write in different genres are demonstrated. An easy-to-read, theoretically sound "how-to" book for the elementary grades.

Hill, Susan, and Tim Hill. 1990. *The Collaborative Classroom.* Portsmouth, NH: Heinemann.

Based on the cooperative learning work of David and Roger Johnson, the authors *present lots of detailed examples of activities for successful cooperative group work. Very useful for the teacher who wants children to work together but who needs specific classroom management information to set up the collaborative classroom.*

Holland, Kathleen E., Rachael A. Hungerford, and Shirley B. Ernst (eds.). 1993. *Journeying: Children Responding to Literature.* Portsmouth, NH: Heinemann.

Major and current research based on Louise Rosenblatt's transactional theory of reader response is reported in this book about children's responses to literature. Studies are cited from early and upper elementary, middle school/junior high, and across grade levels. Practicing teachers will be able to find many ideas on how to use literature more effectively in their classroom. The whole book is a stimulating blend of theory and practice that will be useful to those reading it, and is especially helpful in noting how the children's responses develop as they grow older. (V.M.)

• Hubbard, Ruth Shagoury, and Brenda Miller Power. 1993. *The Art of Classroom Inquiry: A Handbook for Teacher-Researchers.* Portsmouth, NH: Heinemann.

This is a wonderfully supportive book for any teacher contemplating teacher research. I loved the quote: "Research is a high-hat word that scares a lot of people. It needn't. It's rather simple. Essentially research is nothing but a state of mind . . . a friendly, welcoming attitude toward change . . . going out to look for change instead of waiting for it to come" (xv–xvi, quoting Charles Kettering). Some of the important topics the book deals with include finding and framing the research question, designing the research study, collecting and analyzing the data, writing up the research, getting rid of writer's block, and finding funds for your research. An appendix lists the names and addresses of over forty teacher-researchers and invites you to write to them. We need more teachers writing for teachers. This book invites you to become a teacher-researcher and share your story.

• Huck, Charlotte, Janet Hickman, and Susan Hepler. 1993. *Children's Literature in the Elementary School.* 5th ed. Fort Worth, TX: Harcourt Brace.

This updated edition of an acclaimed text (866 pp.) should be readily accessible to all teachers and librarians as it is one of the most comprehensive and outstanding reference books on children's literature. Part 1 discusses the value of literature and gives guidelines for evaluation of literature. Chapter 2, "Understanding Children's Response to Literature," is valuable for understanding, observing, encouraging, and examining what goes on between a book and its reader. In Part 2, all types of literature are discussed in depth: books to begin on including wordless books, ABC books, and concept books; picture books; traditional literature including folktales, fables, myths, legends, and the Bible; modern fantasy; poetry; contemporary realistic fiction; historical fiction; biographies and informational books. Some of these are complete enough to stand as individual anthologies. Part 3 focuses on developing a literature program in the school. The specific suggestions and examples for guiding in-depth studies of books with webbing and questioning techniques are especially helpful. Numerous charts list books that share similar patterns and may be taught together. "Teaching Features" focus attention on actual classroom programs. At the end of each of the thirteen chapters are "Suggested Learning Experiences" that give ideas that can be adapted to the classroom, "Related Readings" with a brief description of each reference cited, and "References" with recommended book titles specific to each topic.

Karelitz, Ellen Blackburn. 1993. *The Author's Chair and Beyond: Language and Literacy in a Primary Classroom.* Portsmouth, NH: Heinemann.

This author takes us into her first-grade classroom over the period of one school year. She describes what she does, her students' responses, and her own questions and decision making. It is easy to picture a "typical" day, as examples of children's writing, transcripts of confer-

ences, and samples of record keeping illustrate the various points that the author makes. I especially enjoyed the chapter on note writing between the students and their teacher, as well as the information about the integration of reading and writing across the curriculum. The significance of the "author's chair," where children gather to talk about their books and those of professional children's authors, is discussed in the last chapter. Throughout the book, transcripts of the children's conversations reveal things that are important to them, and show how they bring the written word into their own perspectives. This is a valuable book for primary-grade teachers with many practical ideas based on a solid theoretical framework. (V.M.)

Kasten, Wendy C., and Barbara K. Clarke. 1993. *The Multi-Age Classroom: A Family of Learners.* Katonah, NY: Richard C. Owen.
The multiage classroom model has been used for many years in England and New Zealand, and, of course, in the one-room schoolhouses scattered across the U.S. Yet, only recently are researchers taking a second look at the benefits that such groupings of children might have. These authors have been doing research in this field for several years, and in this book have summarized the history and benefits of multiage classrooms. In all instances, they advocate multiage groupings as very positive environments for learning language. They describe several outstanding classroom communities with intermediate, K–1, K–3, or grade 5–6 students, and give advice for implementing them. The last chapter contains questions frequently asked by teachers and parents. (V.M.)

Katz, Lilian G., Demetra Evangelou, and Jeanette Allison Hartman. 1990. *The Case for Mixed-Age Grouping in Early Education.* Washington, DC: National Association for the Education of Young Children.
Multiage grouping is explored and advocated for young children. Both academic and social benefits are seen for the youngest as well as the oldest members of the classroom, and the benefits are explained in detail. Teaching strategies, such

as peer tutoring and cooperative learning, are suggested. Several programs are described, and areas of future research are suggested. (V.M.)

Kirby, Dan, and Carol Kuykendall. 1991. *Mind Matters: Teaching for Thinking.* Portsmouth, NH: Boynton/Cook.
This book is not a "how-to" manual. Instead, it is a book that challenges you as a teacher to "embark on adventures of the mind that may or may not have anything to do with your students." Its central premise is "it takes thinking teachers to develop thinking students." There are many "assisted explorations" designed to take you into the territory of thinking, as well as models to spark ideas that might be implemented in your classroom. Designed almost as a conversation between friends, this book is stimulating but informal. It's the kind of book that would be enjoyable on a summer break when you have time to dream and stretch, or it could be the focus of a discussion group between colleagues. Whatever way you choose to use it, both you and your students will benefit by considering the challenges it presents. (V.M.)

Kobrin, Beverly. 1988. *Eyeopeners! How to Choose and Use Children's Books about Real People, Places, and Things.* New York: Penguin.
Kobrin views fiction and nonfiction as "literary coequals" and states that children need TLC—the total literature connection. Asserting that children have natural curiosity and are fascinated by facts, she discusses over 500 engrossing nonfiction books and groups them by categories such as biographies, dinosaurs, grandparents, and holidays, to name a few. Each book annotation includes a brief summary, recommended age ranges, and teaching tips. This valuable resource book for teachers, parents, and librarians also includes criteria for evaluating nonfiction as well as an extensive "Quick-Link Index" to aid the teacher looking for specific topics or themes.

• Krogness, Mary Mercer. 1995. *Just Teach Me, Mrs. K! Talking, Reading and Writing with Resistant Adolescent Learners. Portsmouth, NH: Heinemann.*

"Resistant learners deserve a good intellectual and creative workout even if they claim not to want it." So believes Mary Krogness, an extraordinary teacher of low and underachieving seventh and eighth graders who are anxious, angry, and fearful about school learning. Taking us inside her classroom, she shares her story of how she attempts to hook these students on talking, reading, and writing through nurturing their imaginations, respecting them as individuals, and getting them to take responsibility for their behavior and their learning. Believing that a language arts class must deal with everything that touches the lives of students, Krogness helps her students feel free to talk and use language to learn through interviews, improvisational drama, theater games, word play, language exercises, reading aloud, conversations, listening, field trips, questioning, literature discussions, reading and writing poetry, plays, personal histories, fairy tales, and more.

While much has been written about the teaching challenges of nonmainstream students with language learning problems, little has been written about successfully engaging these students. In this elegantly written account, Krogness writes about "the class that made me question my worth as a teacher and as a person" and how with great effort and compassion she reaches many of these recalcitrant, yet mostly able, adolescents. The voices and increasing self-esteem of the students shine through in their conversations and in their writing.

Lane, Barry. 1993. *After THE END: Teaching and Learning Creative Revision.* Portsmouth, NH: Heinemann.

In answer to the question, "I can get them to write, but how do I get them to revise?" Lane addresses many concerns of teachers of writing. He carefully takes us through lots of activities, approaches, and questions we can use in the classroom to encourage and help students to write well. Some of the topics for writing and revision he discusses and demonstrates include writing leads, writing with descriptive detail, creating characters and building scenes using dialogue, "exploding a moment," conferencing, editing, freewriting, and writing with voice. Very helpful to teachers of grades three through college and beyond.

Langer, Judith A. (ed.). 1992. *Literature Instruction: A Focus on Student Response.* Urbana, IL: National Council of Teachers of English.

This book brings together a series of essays advocating student-response literature instruction from elementary years to college. In a piece especially helpful to elementary teachers, Jayne DeLawter presents the idea that teachers must become exploration leaders in order to lead students into and beyond the author's text. She deplores the use of patterned and sequenced instruction guides for literature, and instead focuses on a classroom where children discuss and reflect as they work through their understandings of a particular piece of literature. Other essays provide a picture of what a response-based classroom might look like, as well as call for changes in literature instruction and new ways of evaluation of day-to-day learning. This book will be especially useful to upper elementary through high school teachers. (V.M.)

Lott, Joyce. 1994. *A Teacher's Stories: Reflections on High School Writers.* Portsmouth, NH: Boynton/Cook.

Joyce Lott, a senior high English teacher, began keeping a daily journal as a way to reflect on her teaching and on students who were not progressing with traditional methods. While on a sabbatical, she examined and analyzed her journal entries and the stories they told about individual students and herself. In this engaging, retrospective telling of stories, she comes to realize that "knowing who my students were as people not only affected my interaction with them, it also affected their writing and whether it progressed or not." Lott is able to acknowledge cross-cultural dilemmas and the importance of knowing, valuing, and accepting a student's culture *in order to understand and appreciate his or her writing style. She questions her approaches to peer editing, grading, and responding to students' writing. She also acknowledges her many successes and realizes, "My task had been not so much to teach them as to encourage learning" (p. 94). In Part V, she shares why and how she uses portfolios and how it has shifted the focus away from grades and towards improving the writing. Secondary teachers will find the information on portfolios excellent for getting students to have more ownership and involvement in their writing. This 202-page book is interesting reading for all reflective teachers.*

Lyons, Carol A., Gay Su Pinnell, and Diane E. DeFord. 1993. *Partners in Learning: Teachers and Children in Reading Recovery.* New York: Teachers College Press.

For the many educators interested in Reading Recovery (the early-intervention program developed in New Zealand by Marie Clay to prevent reading failure), this significant text discusses the research base, implementation, principles, teacher training, lesson elements, teaching strategies, and change process. Excellent for clear insights into Reading Recovery, teacher and institutional change, the reading process, and literacy education.

• Manning, Maryann, Gary Manning, and Roberta Long. 1994. *Theme Immersion: Inquiry-Based Curriculum in Elementary and Middle Schools.* Portsmouth, NH: Heinemann.

The authors define theme immersion (TI) as an "in-depth study of a topic, issue, or question" that is of importance and interest to many members of the learning community. The topic, materials, activities, direction, and outcomes are determined by a negotiated partnership between students and teachers through a process that fosters student exploration, choice, risk taking, social interaction, knowledge construction, and autonomy. Manning, Manning, and Long differentiate between a theme immersion and theme unit, viewing the latter as mostly a teacher-designated, skills-oriented topic study where all areas of the
curriculum are often forced into a unit. In their TI focus, the authors realistically consider district and state requirements, what areas of the curriculum can be taught through a TI, and how to plan, manage, implement, and evaluate a TI. Chapter 4 is devoted to demonstrating and developing research skills such as raising questions, note taking, and interviewing. Chapter 5 presents many multimedia suggestions from ancient arts to modern technology for demonstrating and sharing knowledge. A list of over a hundred ways students can express their knowledge through writing is also included. Chapter 7 details two theme immersions—environment in a fourth-grade class and oceanography in an eighth-grade classroom. Interviews with theme-immersion teachers follow in the next chapter. The final chapter consists totally of TI photographs. The book ends with an extensive listing of resources to support the TI process, including annotations of recommended professional texts and journal articles, titles and authors of literature for selected theme immersions, and names and addresses of magazines and selected organizations for student research and information. What I especially appreciated and admired about this 206-page resource is its emphasis on meaningful principles, guidelines, and strategies. The authors continually demonstrate how we can effectively apply the theme-immersion, inquiry process to our own classrooms. A first-rate resource!

• Marzano, Robert J. 1992. *A Different Kind of Classroom: Teaching with Dimensions of Learning.* Alexandria, VA: Association for Supervision and Curriculum Development.

This is a captivating, enlightening book for expanding your thinking and your current instructional paradigm about how children learn. "Dimensions of Learning" is Marzano's highly respected, research-based, K–12 model of classroom instruction. "The Dimensions framework is structured on the premise that the process of learning involves the interaction of five types, or dimensions, of thinking: (1) posi-

tive attitudes and perceptions about learning, (2) thinking involved in acquiring and integrating knowledge, (3) thinking involved in extending and refining knowledge, (4) thinking involved in using knowledge meaningfully, and (5) productive habits of mind" (vii). Marzano defines and discusses each of these dimensions and makes them come to life through classroom stories that explore teachers' and students' thinking and decision making. The final chapter, "Putting It All Together," presents specific, helpful guidelines to help teachers use the "Dimensions" to organize instruction. An excellent resource for curriculum development in all areas and for learning-centered schooling.

McClure, Amy A., with Peggy Harrison and Sheryl Reed. 1990. *Sunrises and Songs*. Portsmouth, NH: Heinemann.

The reader is taken through a school year in a fifth- and sixth-grade whole language classroom where students are immersed in poetry daily. The teachers, avid readers and writers of poetry, inspire their students to read and respond to poetry; to write, critique, revise, and publish poetry; and to write daily in their poetry journals. For teachers ready to connect poetry meaningfully to children's lives, this text is a valuable resource.

Meek, Margaret. 1992. *On Being Literate*. Portsmouth, NH: Heinemann.

This book is a companion book to Learning to Read (1982) and is designed to help parents understand reading and writing and their importance in today's society. It is also valuable for teachers of any grade level to read. Traditional views of literacy are being challenged by universal schooling, the advent of television, and computer technology. Meek helps the reader to understand that literacy has never been static, and that the definition changes as society makes new demands to meet current conditions. It is up to us to help children deal with these new challenges. (V.M.)

• Mills, Heidi, and Jean Anne Clyde (eds.). 1990. *Portraits of Whole Language Classrooms: Learning for All Ages*. Portsmouth, NH: Heinemann.

Whole language teachers in varied settings—home day care, preschool, elementary, middle school, high school, university education lab—describe their experiences with students in their classrooms. The book assumes the reader already has a good understanding of whole language theory and classroom management. The final chapter, by John McInerney and Jerome Harste, nicely clarifies some beliefs about whole language. For description of chapters dealing with holistic teaching in remedial settings, see "Resources" at the end of chapter 14.

• Ministry of Education (Wellington, NZ). 1993. *Dancing with the Pen: The Learner as a Writer*. Katonah, NY: Richard C. Owen.

This is a handbook designed to help teachers understand how children learn to write as well as provide ways to help them facilitate the learning process. Many samples of children's writing illustrate the various stages of development. The ways that children write—from personal experiences to poetry—are considered in one chapter. Classroom environments, scheduling tips, and resources are suggested, as well as ways to monitor individual writing development. The format of this book will be familiar to readers of the outstanding book on reading published by the Ministry, Reading in Junior Classes. All in all, this is a very complete guide that would be very useful to a beginning elementary teacher. (V.M.)

Mooney, Margaret E. 1990. *Reading to, with, and by Children*. Katonah, NY: Richard C. Owen.

Teachers, especially K–2, who want a full description and understanding of approaches to reading (reading aloud, shared reading, language experience, guided reading, and independent reading) and how these approaches can be used in the classroom will treasure this guide (92 pp.). Sample lessons for emergent, early, and fluent readers model strategies and questions teachers can use to get children to enjoy literature as well as predicting, sampling, confirming, and self-correcting on text.

Morrow, Lesley Mandel. 1993. *Literacy Development in the Early Years.* 2nd ed. Boston: Allyn and Bacon.

For educators interested in current research and theory in early literacy development and how to apply that knowledge to the preschool through grade 1 classroom, this academic text (411 pp.) discusses the development of early literacy in depth and includes strategies for promoting oral language development and reading and writing development. Chapter 5, "Developing Positive Attitudes Toward Reading Through the Use of Children's Literature," deals with promoting voluntary reading and organizing well-planned library corners/literacy centers. Also, particularly useful to classroom teachers are chapter 7, "Developing Reading Through Learning About Print," and chapter 9, "Organizing and Managing the Learning Environment for Literacy Development at School." Pages 183–188 are very specific for how to guide a child's story retelling.

Murray, Donald M. 1989. *Expecting the Unexpected: Teaching Myself—and Others—to Read and Write.* Portsmouth, NH: Boynton/Cook.

This is a diverse collection of twenty-four pieces full of introspection and sharing. Divided into four sections—Listening to the Page, Learning by Sharing, Exploring Form, Sitting to Write—it reveals Murray's thinking about his own process of writing and teaching writing to others. Along with essays and speeches, he even includes handouts used with his students—one of which was a piece written to describe revision by revealing it, "Revision as Visible Craft." He shares how he wrote and later revised a very personal piece, which he submitted to the Boston Globe for his "Over Sixty" column. In another piece, he answers questions from high school students. In paging through the book, I'm sure that you will feel the joy of learning through the writing of this distinguished teacher/writer. (V.M.)

• Murray, Donald M. 1990. *Shoptalk: Learning to Write with Writers.* Portsmouth, NH: Boynton/Cook.

As a teenager, Murray was fascinated by writers talking about their writing, and he began a collection of quotations that eventually filled twenty-four thick notebooks. This book is a selection of his favorites organized into sixteen categories, such as "Why Write," "The Beginning Line," "Waiting for Writing," and "The Writing Habit." However, it is not just a book of quotations, for each section begins with a personal essay on Murray's own experiences with the topic. Both we and our students can join the company of writers as we browse through this book. Murray described it well: "I am comforted by what they say to me as we leave the writing desk together. My collection of quotes allows me to learn from fellow writers, to laugh and mourn with them, to know that others have experienced what I have often thought was eccentric or inappropriate." I'm glad that he took the time to share his quotes and insights with us! (V.M.)

• Nagy, William E. 1988. *Teaching Vocabulary to Improve Reading Comprehension.* Urbana, IL: National Council of Teachers of English and Newark, DE: International Reading Association.

This concise book (42 pp.) is the best I have read for combining research and practice in the teaching of vocabulary on a conceptual level. While the author states that "the single most important thing a teacher can do to promote vocabulary growth is to increase students' volume of reading" (p. 38), he also makes it clear that there is an important place for intensive instruction. Three necessary properties of vocabulary instruction are defined: integration ("tying in new words with familiar concepts and experiences"), repetition (having many encounters with a word), and meaningful use. Many useful activities for classroom application are included.

Neuman, Susan B., and Kathleen A. Roskos. 1993. *Language and Literacy Learning in the Early Years: An Integrated Approach.* Fort Worth, TX: Harcourt Brace.

Neuman and Roskos examine oral and written language processes in young chil-

dren's development and suggest appropriate practices for creating effective learning environments. This text takes a balanced approach in its comprehensive analysis of how children acquire language and literacy. Topics addressed include setting up the physical environment for learning, child-centered activity planning, integrated learning activities, and assessment, to name a few. Packed with usable information and activities for pre-K and K educators, parents, and childcare providers.

• Newkirk, Thomas. 1989. *More Than Stories: The Range of Children's Writing.* Portsmouth, NH: Heinemann.

Every once in a while I find a book that makes me think, "Ah, that says what I am thinking, but I haven't been able to put it into words yet." This book is one of that kind for me. Newkirk clearly explains the semiotic position on language development in the opening section, and then he carefully describes the diversity of writing done by young children as they develop the ability to write expository prose. An especially meaningful chapter is an interview of Kathy Matthews, a second-grade teacher, who focuses on the many uses for writing found in her classroom. The book blends theory and practice in a way that stretched me as a teacher and gave me a lot to think about. (V.M.)

Newkirk, Thomas (ed.). 1992–1994. *Workshop 4, 5 by and for Teachers.* Portsmouth, NH: Heinemann. *(See Atwell, Nancie for Workshop 1, 2, 3 and Barbieri, Maureen, for Workshop 6.)*

4, The Teacher as Researcher
5, The Writing Process Revisited
The need for and purpose of teacher research in the language arts is explored in the fourth volume. It challenges teachers to consider what they should include and omit in their writings, and encourages teachers to reflect on what they do. The teacher interview is with Regie Routman, and this issue's author interviews are Jean Craighead George and Barbara Cooney. Cross-age tutoring, writing across the curriculum, and assessment are just a few of the topics addressed by the teacher-

researchers. As with the other workshop volumes, teacher writers are encouraged to submit their professional writing for publication. In the fifth volume, Donald Graves is interviewed, as well as two African-American educators, Dawn Harris-Martine and Isoke Nia. Portfolios, fiction writing, integration of writing and the arts, and the importance of storytelling are considered in light of the writing process movement. (V.M.)

• Newkirk, Thomas, with Patricia McLure. 1992. *Listening In: Children Talk About Books (and Other Things).* Portsmouth, NH: Heinemann.

In this little book, Newkirk visits McLure's first/second-grade classroom where he focuses on her 9:30 A.M. book discussions of thirty to forty-five minutes each. In these daily sessions, the children's understandings of their reading developed as they connected literature with their own everyday lives. The rich "talk" of this classroom challenges the teacher-dominated comprehension questioning with one right answer that occurs in many classrooms. You have to read this book, and its fascinating transcripts, to begin to realize the depth of understanding that these children reach. (V.M.)

• Newman, Judith. 1991. *Interwoven Conversations: Learning and Teaching Through Critical Reflection.* Portsmouth, NH: Heinemann.

This is a remarkable text for rethinking how we teach reading and writing in our classrooms! Judith Newman takes us inside her university classroom during a two-week institute and shows us her thinking, process, and practice in teaching and setting up conditions for learning. The reader becomes an "insider" in seeing how Newman helps establish a community of learners, how she organizes and manages her classroom, how she responds to teachers by conferencing with them about their own writing as well as how she handles revising and editing, literature discussions, reading/writing relationships, and evaluation. We not only hear the honesty of Newman's voice; we also hear the voices of the K–12 teachers as they interact and reflect with Newman, each other, and themselves through conversations and written reflections. More than any other book I have read recently, this book caused me to reflect on my practice and read and think "with pencil in hand." (I wrote all over the margins.) This is a provocative text for extending your thinking and learning about whole language and language processes and for becoming aware of your own questions and contradictions in your teaching.

- Norton, Donna E. 1991. *Through the Eyes of a Child: An Introduction to Children's Literature.* 3rd ed. New York: Macmillan. (hardbound)

  This comprehensive text (779 pages) about all aspects of children's literature is a first-rate resource that you will want to have access to. The organization of the book is unique. The content includes such topics as history of children's literature; selecting and evaluating children's literature; artists and their illustrations; picture books; traditional literature including folktales, fables, myths, and legends; modern fantasy, poetry, contemporary realistic fiction; historical fiction; multicultural literature; and nonfiction biographies and informational books. Following each chapter on the characteristics, history, and discussion of books for each genre is a chapter on involving children in that genre. These chapters present many activities and strategies for webbing, extending, and appreciating the literature and give teachers lots of terrific, practical ideas for use in the classroom.

  Also unique to this text are the controversial issues raised in each chapter, the personal portraits and statements by well-known authors and illustrators about themselves and their books, and the illustrated flashbacks that highlight significant people, books, and events in the history of children's literature. Each chapter also ends with a summary, suggested activities, references, and an annotated bibliography of children's literature with approximate reading level by grade and interest level by age. Useful appendices to the text in-

clude book-selection aids, publishers and their addresses, and a bibliography of book awards.

Ohanian, Susan. 1994. *Who's in Charge? A Teacher Speaks Her Mind.* Portsmouth, NH: Boynton/Cook.

In this book is an inspiring collection of materials written by a practicing teacher that include letters written to editors, articles published in magazines, and poetry. You may not always agree with Ohanian, but her concerns for children and the profession are very real and her voice shatters a mood of complacency. In past years, I have read some of the articles, and spoken with the author, and I have come to see her as a "conscience" for teachers. It is quite an experience to see her work brought together, and to look at what she has written over the last twenty years. As she has touched the lives of her students, she has touched mine as she writes about topics as diverse as Japanese educational methodology, bringing real reading into the reading program, the basalization of literature, problems with a literary canon, and much more. This is a book for educators of all kinds who want to improve schools and our profession. It will validate concerns you have, stretch your thinking, and cause both some laughter and some tears. (V.M.)

Pappas, Christine C., Barbara Z. Kiefer, and Linda S. Levstik. 1990. *An Integrated Language Perspective in the Elementary School: Theory into Action.* White Plains, NY: Longman.

Educators wanting to plan and implement thematic units will find much support in this scholarly, comprehensive text (384 pp.). The authors present the theoretical and practical aspects of an integrated language perspective that includes integration of the language arts as well as integration across the curriculum. Marginal notations throughout the text cite references, note useful resources, and highlight and explain concepts. Chapter 4, "Prototypes for Integrated Language Classrooms," includes eight prototypes (thematic units). Each prototype includes a WEB, a weekly schedule, a typical day in an actual classroom, a summary, and a bibliography of children's literature and resources. The one thing I found missing in the prototypes were the major concepts and understandings. Teachers will find the thematic units excellent models but will need to be sure to put the "big understandings" into their own integrated language units. I found the chapters "More Ideas to Integrate Curricular Areas," "More on How-to: Ideas for Implementation in Integrated Language Classrooms," and "An Integrated Language Perspective Effecting Change" to be particularly useful for the classroom teacher.

Patterson, Leslie, Carol Minnick Santa, Kathy G. Short, and Karen Smith (eds.). 1993. *Teachers Are Researchers: Reflection and Action.* Newark, DE: International Reading Association.

If you believe that "teachers are professionals who should take an active role in educational change" (p. 173), this supportive text for elementary through college teachers makes teacher inquiry possible in the realm of day-to-day teaching. Teachers describe their inquiry processes, beginning with finding and framing their questions and continuing with their various methods of observation and data collection to their reflections and changes in practice as a result of their teacher research.

Peregoy, Suzanne F., and Owen F. Boyle. 1993. *Reading, Writing, & Learning in ESL: A Resource Book for K–8 Teachers.* White Plains, NY: Longman.

In this concise text, you will find a practical resource to help teachers provide literacy instruction for second-language learners. Several chapters are devoted to background information on how second-language acquisition occurs. Process writing, literature-based reading instruction, and reading across the curriculum are discussed with an emphasis on adapting instruction to the child with limited English. In so doing, the classroom environment can be a richer place for all students. (V.M.)

Perrone, Vito. 1991. *A Letter to Teachers: Reflections on Schooling and the Art of Teaching.* San Francisco: Jossey-Bass Publishers.

Perrone, director of programs in teacher education at the Harvard Graduate School of Education, eloquently urges us to carefully reflect on our teaching and to construct for ourselves "a more powerful voice." He challenges us to discuss and rethink such critical issues as deciding what to teach, engaging students, valuing differences, making school more accessible to parents, evaluating and grading, and empowering teachers. The chapter "Refining the Craft of Teaching" offers specific questions and helpful suggestions to us for continuing our own professional growth. "Only when teachers themselves assume the dominant position in regard to issues of teaching and learning in their classrooms, and begin to speak more broadly and authoritatively on matters of education, will we see significant improvement" (xiii). Each time I reread parts of this inspiring book (160 pp.), I rethink some of my assumptions about teaching and learning.

Peterson, Ralph. 1992. *Life in a Crowded Place: Making a Learning Community.* Portsmouth, NH: Heinemann.

Peterson quickly makes the point that "life in classrooms is an intense social experience." Many teachers cope by restricting everything they can think of, yet he notes there are some teachers who trust students, expect them to take the initiative, and value what they think. These teachers' expectations are nurtured and used to support learning in the best way possible. In this book, the author identifies ways that teachers can work with students to make a learning community that supports language acquisition. Vignettes of teachers and students working together are used throughout the book to illustrate the various points. I especially enjoyed the chapter on "Authority: Empowering Students." If students are to become lifelong learners, they must assume the authority to think for themselves, and to be responsible for their actions. (V.M.)

• Peterson, Ralph, and Maryann Eeds. 1990. *Grand Conversations: Literature Groups in Action.* Richmond Hill, Ontario: Scholastic-TAB.

For teachers who are already comfortable with a literature approach to reading, this eighty-page text dealing with literature study of "books that have layers of story action and meaning" (p. 26) gives inspiration, organization, specific techniques, and lots of examples for constructing meaning through dialogue and interpretation. Developing children's awareness of, and response to, literary elements—story structure, plot, characters, place, tensions, point of view, mood, time, symbols and metaphors, theme—is fully discussed and demonstrated with examples from excellent literature. Examples of teacher-developed forms for organization and evaluation are also cited. A terrific, high-level resource.

Pierce, Kathryn Mitchell, and Carol J. Gilles (eds.). 1993. *Cycles of Meaning: Exploring the Potential of Talk in Learning Communities.* Portsmouth, NH: Heinemann.

Twenty teachers and teacher educators share their perspectives on "talk" in the classroom setting. This is a thoughtful text considering various aspects of talk in the learning community, talk as a strategy to explore writing or content-area reading, the role of the teacher in literature discussion groups, and evaluation of talk in the literature discussion group. Lots of classroom examples are found in the individual essays, making this a very helpful book for teachers who have established collaborative literature studies in their classrooms. (V.M.)

• Probst, Robert. 1988. *Response and Analysis: Teaching Literature in Junior and Senior High School.* Portsmouth, NH: Boynton/Cook.

This book brings literature into students' lives. Probst believes literature should be a vital, personal experience and not presented as the object of tests and exercises. Drawing heavily on Louise Rosenblatt's work of almost fifty years ago, this text tries to show that literature should be personally significant, that readers be respected as they respond in different ways, and that readers acknowledge the role of literature in their world. The book is or-

ganized into three parts: a rationale of response-based teaching, literature choices, and the overall program. Many suggestions for the classroom are given, and there is an excellent listing of literary works that will stimulate students to think. Two sensitive themes, sexuality and violence, are discussed in detail, while representative books are listed under various themes. Other useful chapters include suggestions for response-based evaluation, as well as one in which film and television are considered as visual literature. Lots of practical and theoretical information for a teacher wanting a response-based literature program. (V.M.)

Raines, Shirley C., and Robert J. Canady. 1990. *The Whole Language Kindergarten.* New York: Teachers College Press.

Early childhood teachers will appreciate this handbook for creating a learning environment to support literacy development. Play, group time, library corners, thematic teaching, science areas, and art guidelines are just some of the many topics considered in a whole language framework. Many anecdotes of actual happenings from various kindergartens support the suggestions and strategies suggested by the authors. (V.M.)

Rathbone, Charles, Anne Bingham, Peggy Dorta, Molly McClaskey, and Justine O'Keefe. 1993. *Multiage Portraits: Teaching and Learning in Mixed-Age Classrooms.* Peterborough, NH: Crystal Springs Books.

The opening section of this book contains University of Vermont researcher Charles Rathbone's observations in Anne Bingham's multiage classroom. In the second part of the book, the four coauthors' voices are heard as they each write a chapter about their multiage classrooms. The last portion of the book contains Rathbone's reflections and questions about multiage classrooms. The book will be useful to teachers who are considering this type of organization, as well as teachers who are looking for support for what they do. The book will stretch and inspire you. (V.M.)

Rhodes, Lynn K., and Curt Dudley-Marling. 1988. *Readers and Writers with a Differ-*

ence: *A Holistic Approach to Teaching Learning Disabled and Remedial Students*. Portsmouth, NH: Heinemann.

For the teacher ready to look at teaching learning disabled and remedial students holistically, this well-documented, comprehensive text (329 pp.) provides a wealth of information on all aspects of language learning. The authors discuss many instructional approaches for assessing, teaching, and extending meaningful reading and writing. The chapter "Developing Fluency in Reading and Writing" provides specific, detailed instructional strategies such as assisted reading, repeated reading, Readers Theatre, choral reading, sustained silent reading, freewriting, journal writing, and written conversation. Most of the strategies and activities recommended are appropriate for all learners. An extensive list of predictable trade books for young children is included.

- Rief, Linda. 1992. *Seeking Diversity: Language Arts with Adolescents*. Portsmouth, NH: Heinemann.

This highly respected, acclaimed text by an exemplary, eighth-grade language arts teacher has already influenced many teachers' practices across the grades. With a passionate, caring voice, Linda Rief takes us into her classroom and the literate lives of the adolescents she teaches to share how she organizes the literacy environment, immerses her students in reading and writing in all genres, encourages students to express themselves through writing and the visual arts, and gets students to take responsibility for their learning. A few of the many areas she gives teaching strategies for are conducting an interview, getting to know your students better, having students take more responsibility for reading, and reading and writing about grandparents and the elderly. The sections on evaluation, which include grading, portfolios, and "close-up snapshots" from student portfolios (in Appendix A), are outstanding and provide a wealth of information for getting students to be the primary evaluators of their writing. References at the end of each chapter, and extensive appendices at the end of the text, include all kinds of useful information and practical support for literature, reading, writing, book-making, communicating with parents, and evaluation. Wonderful student writing samples abound throughout the text.

Everything Rief does connects to a well-grounded theory of language learning, reading and writing as reciprocal processes, wonderful literature, and the real lives of her students. By sharing what she has learned from other experts and from her students, what strategies and activities she uses, and what is working and not working in her classroom, she invites us to look at our own classrooms and build rich learning environments. Rief writes, "At the end of every year I ask students, 'If you had to pick the one thing I did that helped you the most as learners, what would it be?' They inevitably say, 'You write with us, and you read with us'" (p. 10). Rief helps us and challenges us to do better with our own students. Don't miss reading this powerful book!

Robb, Laura. 1994. *Whole Language, Whole Learners: Creating a Literature-Centered Classroom*. New York: William Morrow. (hardbound)

Based on thirty years of classroom teaching, this book is a treasure trove of practical ideas for bringing literature into the classroom. Some of the topics considered are getting support, getting started, reading and writing experiences, inquiry and content-area journaling, authentic assessment, and planning theme cycles. A unique feature of this book is the fifteen essays by children's authors and illustrators—Steven Kellogg, Jerry Pinkney, Lois Lowry, Karla Kuskin, and others—that are placed throughout the book. The appendix contains a series of forms to stimulate the development of your own parent letters, newspapers, and evaluation forms. (V.M.)

- Romano, Tom. 1987. *Clearing the Way: Working with Teenage Writers*. Portsmouth, NH: Heinemann.

"Our responsibility as writing teachers is to help students learn personal processes for creating writing that enable them *to create their best writing" (p. 52). Drawing on his own experiences as a high school English teacher, Tom Romano eloquently describes how in a safe writing workshop, he enables students to use language to discover thought and to find their individual voices and styles. Romano demonstrates his craft with samples of his own and students' writing—drafts, revisions, and finished pieces in which meaning comes before correctness and form—examples of purposeful writing prompts, and meaningful ways of evaluating and grading with the goal that "above anything else, we want them to write again" (p. 128).*

I began this book because I had been invited to speak with interested secondary teachers in our district. I had intended to skim the book, to get a feel for it. The power of Romano's voice grabbed me and never let up until I had ingested every word. I was surprised to find many references to Don Graves and Lucy Calkins and to see high school practice in an effective writing workshop very similar to what we are striving for at the elementary level. I savored fresh insights, new visions, clear writing by a teacher-learner, and validation that the writing process is inherently the same from kindergarten through grade twelve. This is a remarkable book that should be read by every serious teacher of writing.

Routman, Regie. 1988. *Transitions: From Literature to Literacy.* Portsmouth, NH: Heinemann.

A personal, honest account of a public school teacher's transition from basal texts and worksheets toward a literature program in reading and a process approach in writing. Some of the topics that are fully discussed include the use of predictable books, how to teach reading and writing with children's books, the place of phonics in the reading-writing program, journal writing, parental involvement, and evaluation. While the book's emphasis is on the primary grades, the theory, ideas, and extensive annotated resources are applicable across the grades. Educators beginning to move toward whole language have found this book both practical and inspiring.

Rudman, Masha Kabakow (ed.). 1993. *Children's Literature: Resource for the Classroom.* 2nd ed. Norwood, MA: Christopher-Gordon.

This book is an updated paperback version of the first edition. Many of the original chapters have been reprinted in this edition along with three new ones. Experts in the field share their insights about censorship, multicultural literature, technology, poetry in the classroom, and global education. Two chapters feature interviews with noted children's authors Virginia Hamilton, Eve Bunting, Ashley Bryan, and others. This is a reference book that should be in every library. It is helpful for teachers to consider current issues in the field, as well as for sharing information with your students. (V.M.)

- Semler, Ricardo. 1993. *Maverick: The Success Story Behind the World's Most Unusual Workplace.* New York: Warner Books.

Although this is not a book about education, I found it such fascinating, stimulating reading, with so much that could apply to teaching, that I have included it. The author is the head of Semco, one of the most successful companies in Brazil, a company that manufactures and distributes industrial parts for heavy machinery. In fact, the company is so successful and well thought of that one-quarter of all graduating college students in Brazil apply to work there. Semler describes his unorthodox, common-sense philosophy and methods for running a company where employees set their own hours and salaries, design their own working environments, examine all financial statements, and decide with their coworkers how to run their particular section of the company. In Semco, the power does not reside at the top; decisions are made by consensus, and flexibility, respect, and freedom are part of the fabric of the company. Some basic premises of the company that schools would do well to think about and adopt are the following: change is normal and necessary; the need for many rules and the need for innovation are incompatible; all memos are restricted to a single page with the most important information at the top; put quality of life first, and quality of product and productivity of workers follow. The book includes the company's evaluation questionnaire, given to employees twice each year to evaluate their supervisors. I recommend all supervisors in education give this excellent questionnaire to teachers and use the responses as a self-evaluation tool.

A few quotes to think about:

"We simply do not believe our employees have an interest in coming in late, leaving early, and doing as little as possible for as much money as their union can wheedle out of us. After all, these same people raise children, join the PTA, elect mayors, governors, senators, and presidents. They are adults. . . . We treat them like adults. We trust them. . . . We get out of their way and let them do their jobs" (p. 59).

"Democracy has yet to penetrate the workplace" (p. 170).

"Most businesses today are still organized much the same way they were in 1633, with stultifying top-down management, close and dutiful supervision, and little room for creativity. . . . Technology is transformed overnight; mentality takes generations to alter" (pp. 283–284).

Shannon, Patrick. 1989. *Broken Promises: Reading Instruction in Twentieth-Century America.* Granby, MA: Bergin & Garvey.

A must for every classroom teacher and administrator to read! The message is that commercially packaged basal reading materials control reading instruction and are doing a "good job of teaching students to decode words and to reproduce the meaning of texts." However, this goal is preventing children from becoming fully literate—"able to understand the connections among their lives and those of others, and to act on their new knowledge to construct a better, a more just, world" (viii). Shannon describes the technologizing and marketing of reading in a detailed history of the basal reader and shows how these systems have actually de-skilled teachers by their detailed instructions on how to manage the worksheets, reading selections, and students. He cites research, some of it

his own, as to why so many teachers rely on basal materials and follow their directions, yet want to be professionals able to make critical judgments to meet student needs. Finally, he devotes the last chapter of the book to the "possibilities of constructive change," such as collective seminars in which teachers analyze their dependence on basals or conduct research in their own classrooms. Although he believes that it will not be easy, Shannon thinks that it is possible for teachers and students to resist the management of their literacy and lives and to "gain their rightful place in reading programs." (V.M.)

• Shannon, Patrick. 1990. *The Struggle to Continue: Progressive Reading Instruction in the United States.* Portsmouth, NH: Heinemann.

This book was written to describe the underlying practices and promises of the child-centered and critical literacy programs—mentioned as positive alternatives to the controlling technological management of literacy decried in Broken Promises. *Shannon also gives a historical perspective to the whole language movement by noting it as a recent development of a hundred-year-old movement to provide literacy programs based on the child within a social context. This is a challenging book but worthwhile reading for any teacher who has lived with the domination of reading instruction by the basal reader industry and is attempting to struggle with alternatives. As he helps teachers make connections with the rich progressive past, Shannon encourages teachers to continue to work for better and more compassionate literacy programs for their students and future generations. (V.M.)*

• Shannon, Patrick, and Kenneth Goodman (eds.). 1994. *Basal Readers: A Second Look.* Katonah, NY: Richard C. Owen.

This book is a follow-up to the groundbreaking Report Card on Basal Readers *(1988). After its publication, basal reader companies attempted to change their materials, often claiming that they had met the recommendations at the end of the Report Card. However, when a group of* educators was assembled to analyze the latest basal editions, various problems still were inherent in the materials. Each author examines one aspect of basal reader production, such as workbook exercises, multiculturalism, poetry inclusion, and others. Four classroom teachers also respond with their concerns. A particularly provocative chapter is written by Mem Fox in which she pleads for the use of real writing, real books, and real relationships in our classrooms. This book should be read by anyone involved in determining what books children will be given in the classroom. (V.M.)

• Short, Kathy Gnagey, and Kathryn Mitchell Pierce (eds.). 1990. *Talking About Books: Creating Literate Communities.* Portsmouth, NH: Heinemann.

Fourteen teachers and teacher educators share their experiences with literature study. This is a very thoughtful text for the teacher who already has a collaborative atmosphere in a whole language classroom. Literature circles, which include small-group discussions in which students read and react to the same book or small-group discussions on text sets in which students read different but thematically related texts, are discussed fully. Lots of specific examples are given, not only for individual books but also for integrated literature study across the curriculum. The introductory chapter by Charlotte Huck sets the tone for the power of literature.

Sloan, Glenna Davis. 1991. *The Child as Critic: Teaching Literature in Elementary and Middle Schools.* 3rd ed. New York: Teachers College Press.

This book supports the belief that the use of literature is the best way to support genuine literacy development. It combines theory and practice to show how to implement reading/writing programs that support the study of literary works or literary criticism. The first section of the book argues that literature must be central in the reading program. Research evidence for the positive effects of literature programs in reading is clearly presented in chapter 2. The next portion gives teachers a theo-

retical framework on which to base the teaching of literature. It examines the work of Northrop Frye to show that even young children can understand the universal patterns present in literature. The final part gives specific examples of techniques and strategies that may be appropriately undertaken in elementary and middle schools. An excellent bibliography will help teachers locate appropriate books for their classroom. (V.M.)

• Smith, Frank. 1990. *To Think.* New York: Teachers College Press.

The process of thinking is examined from all angles in this comprehensive book. As with his previous books, Smith celebrates the power of humans to learn! He expresses concern about complaints that students are unable to think, and, therefore, must be carefully taught, and believes that attempts to teach "thinking skills" can actually hamper the development of thinking. Two especially interesting chapters, "Thinking Creatively" and "Thinking Critically," demystify these aspects of thinking and show how they are not so difficult and distinctive after all. Finally, he looks at educational implications for both teachers and students. He suggests, "Students—and teachers—must learn to doubt. . . . Certainty stunts thought, in ourselves and others. . . . Thought flourishes as questions are asked, not as answers are found" (p. 129). Smith also stresses the importance of functional, relevant reading and writing when he states, "Reading and writing are two activities that promote thought—provided that what is read is worth thinking about and that writing is used for extending the imagination of the writer" (p. 128). Last, he warns that "thinking cannot be broken down into parts, specified in objectives, and taught in isolated exercises and drills. All of this interferes with thought" (p. 128). This is a relevant, challenging book with implications affecting the entire school curriculum. (V.M.)

Smith, Frank. 1994. *Understanding Reading: A Psycholinguistic Analysis of Reading and Learning to Read.* 5th ed. Hillsdale,

NJ: Lawrence Erlbaum Associates, Publishers.

In this new edition of his classic text on how reading is learned (not how it is taught), Smith provides a theoretical analysis of all aspects of reading—linguistic, psychological, social, and physiological—based on current research and Smith's own brand of brilliant thinking. "Reading is seen as a creative and constructive activity having four distinctive and fundamental characteristics—it is purposeful, selective, anticipatory, and based on comprehension, all matters where the reader must clearly exercise control" (p. 3). Smith also deals with recent developments, issues, and alternative points of view in reading—especially the ideological clash between whole language and direct instruction. As well, he gives ways to support learners' reading until they are able to take over the process. Noting that reading defies "simplistic analysis," he believes it is up to sensitive teachers, who he views as "the essential element in literacy instruction," to have a solid understanding of learning to read and an understanding of their students. Then teachers can make the necessary decisions about reading in the classroom.

Spear, Karen, and others. 1994. *Peer Response Groups in Action: Writing Together in Secondary Schools.* Portsmouth, NH: Boynton/Cook.

English teachers describe their struggles, efforts, and strategies to establish successful peer-response groups in the writing process classroom. The power of collaboration, the constraints of time and scheduling, the need for modeling, the ways to teach students how to communicate in writing-response groups, and the benefits of peer review are just some of the issues they tackle. The first-person accounts from mostly middle and secondary school teachers provide engaging reading and workable ideas for the writing-response process. Applicable for the intermediate grades through postsecondary.

Stires, Susan (ed.). 1991. *With Promise: Redefining Reading and Writing Needs for Special Students.* Portsmouth, NH: Heinemann.

This is a book about teaching reading and writing to any elementary students considered to be "at risk" of failure. All of us have encountered children who learn in unique ways, and how to help them to learn in the best possible way is always a major question. This book asks those hard questions, and it shares the insights of educators who are attempting to meet the needs of these children. Issues of testing, labeling, effective environments, and programs are considered. In an especially moving piece, Donald Graves pleads that children with learning problems not be disenfranchised from literacy, that they can and should be encouraged to write. (V.M.)

• Strickland, Dorothy S., and Lesley Mandel Morrow (eds.). 1989. *Emerging Literacy: Young Children Learn to Read and Write.* Newark, DE: International Reading Association.

This book is highly recommended for preschool–grade 2 teachers for developing a meaningful literacy program. Kindergarten teachers, especially, will find this book particularly helpful for tying theory and practice together and for incorporating appropriate classroom practices. In addition to gaining a current and broad understanding of issues and principles of early literacy, teachers are presented with a wealth of practical ideas and activities. The importance and application of oral-language experiences, story book reading, and all kinds of writing for promoting children's language and literacy growth are clearly delineated.

Strickland, Kathleen, and James Strickland. 1993. *Uncovering the Curriculum: Whole Language in Secondary and Postsecondary Classrooms.* Portsmouth, NH: Heinemann.

For high school and college teachers who want to understand and implement whole language principles and practice to make their teaching more relevant to students' lives, this is a fine text. Practicing secondary and postsecondary teachers share stories and strategies that lend support and specifics to the reading/writing workshop, application of reader-response theory, classroom management, questioning in literature discussion, conferencing in writing, writing to learn, grading, and evaluation. The final chapter, "Whole Language—A Political Issue" is important reading for dealing with resistance to whole language and the change process. Also applicable to the elementary and middle grades.

Sumner, Deborah (ed.). 1993. *Multiage Classrooms: The Ungrading of America's Schools: The Multiage Resource Book.* Peterborough, NH: Society for Developmental Education.

This resource book contains a collection of articles reprinted from educational journals and research reports on multiage grouping and supportive practices. An extensive bibliography and descriptions of multiage models provide a wealth of material for teachers or administrators wanting to explore this program for their school. Finally, an assortment of forms and charts currently in use by schools with multiage classrooms are reprinted for adaptation to your educational settings. This compilation provides a good starting point in organizing your own program. (V.M.)

• Taylor, Denny. 1993. *From the Child's Point of View.* Portsmouth, NH: Heinemann.

In this provocative collection of her papers, Taylor uses rich ethnographic portraits of learners to show that simplistic testing methodology does not tap the complex ways that children become literate. All of the children with whom she has worked have thick special education folders focusing on the errors that these children have made—not on how they use language in nontesting situations. She shows how we must observe children and learn from their strengths—not from what is missing—before beginning to define practice and assessment of curriculum. The final section addresses an "Advocacy Model of Instructional Assessment," in which support teams focus on what students can

do, along with problem solving from the student's point of view. I found myself considering my students with new eyes after reading this book. I encourage you to make this book required reading. (V.M.)

Taylor, Denny. 1991. *Learning Denied.* Portsmouth, NH: Heinemann.

This little book is the story of a family's bitter clash with the public school, and special education bureaucracy, that their son attended. It shows the wrongness of assessments that reduce learning to scores on tests administered and interpreted by "experts" who rarely work with the child and only focus on what the child is unable to do. As doubts about Patrick's abilities increased in the school setting, the testing became a self-fulfilling prophecy—he met the low expectations and stopped performing in school. Yet at home, and in sessions with Taylor, he read and wrote increasingly difficult material. He was finally abandoned to a home-schooling program, and the school district washed its hands of this child. Taylor questions whether the school district will ever acknowledge his literacy, and make room for him. This book raises more questions than it answers. I wonder how many other "Patricks" are in our schools. (V.M.)

• Taylor, Denny, and Catherine Dorsey-Gaines. 1988. *Growing Up Literate: Learning from Inner-City Families.* Portsmouth, NH: Heinemann.

This poignant, moving ethnographic study of urban black families living well below the poverty line focuses on families who have first-grade children successfully learning to read and write. Through their carefully documented observations, the authors dispel the common myths and stereotypes of poor, black families. We see overwhelming confirmation that the families effectively use reading and writing daily for their survival, to communicate with others, to fulfill educational requirements, and for pleasure. The authors state, "it is evident that the families with whom we are working are more than the fillers in of forms—they are active members in a print community in which literacy is used for a *wide variety of social, technical, and aesthetic purposes, for a wide variety of audiences, and in a wide variety of situations"* (p. 200). *Educators, researchers, and policymakers are urged to take a close look at these families—and other functioning families—to begin to close the wide gaps between home and school literacy.*

- Thomas, Joan Krater, Jane Zeni, and Nancy Devlin Cason. 1994. *Mirror Images: Action Research in Multicultural Writing Classrooms.* Portsmouth, NH: Heinemann.

    "What can we as teachers do to improve the writing of African-American students in our classrooms?" This was the action research question that a group of white, female, middle school (grades 7–10) teachers working in integrated classrooms sought to answer. Looking closely at their own role in lower black achievement, this personal, inspiring account tells the story of how they question their assumptions, come to value and build on the strengths of black males, and transform their attitudes and daily classroom teaching so all students benefit. "We realized that if we were committed to teaching all students, we must change how we view our 'mirror reflections'—the kids who most differ from us in race, class, and gender." "Individualizing and personalizing" is what they call their approach of stressing relationships, valuing of culture, and developing self-awareness. It is affirming a child first for who he is, not what he does. And it is being willing to make adjustments for students' needs and interests in the reading/writing process classroom. This is a powerful book for taking a critical look at our own instructional contexts and for finding ways to maximize the potential of alienated, struggling students. This moving account is also testimony to the fact that major change is possible if we are willing to look critically at our own behaviors and get to know and value our students and their cultures. Lots of excellent teaching strategies and sample lessons are woven into this extensive text and the appendices. Don't miss reading this remarkable story of teacher/student change and

growth! Also encouraging for starting your own action research. Applicable and practical for all grades.

Tierney, Robert J., Mark A. Carter, and Laura E. Desai. 1991. *Portfolio Assessment in the Reading-Writing Classroom.* Norwood, MA: Christopher-Gordon.

Based on research and practice, K–12, of the use of reading and writing portfolios in several school districts, this scholarly and practical text provides teachers with a flexible framework for implementing and using portfolios in the classroom. The text fully discusses and gives specific examples for topics such as the following: getting started with portfolios, selecting pieces for the portfolio, involving parents in the portfolio assessment process, understanding the teacher's role in the portfolio process, fostering students' self-evaluation of selected items in the portfolio, sustaining portfolios over time, and using portfolios to evaluate students. Lots of specific examples and ideas.

- Tobin, Lad. 1993. *Writing Relationships: What REALLY Happens in the Composition Class.* Portsmouth, NH: Boynton/Cook.

    "Why haven't we been more honest about how hard it is to teach writing?" (p. 144). I guess that's why I appreciated this book so much. In a first-person, confessional tone that is refreshing, engaging, and unconventional, Tobin takes us inside his process-oriented, college composition classes and private thoughts to share honestly the frustrating and rewarding daily interactions and decision-making processes with his students. In telling us "stories about actual situations from my classes that evoked powerful responses from me and my students" (p. 16), he invites us to identify our own unconscious behaviors, biases, problems, and successes. Tobin moves beyond the simplistic assumptions of process classrooms and examines provocative issues about grading, collaboration, competition, power, and peer review with new lenses, suggesting, for example, that "our grades reflect our own attitudes and tastes as much as they reflect something about

the essay in front of us" (p. 68) and that "competition and cooperation are not mutually exclusive or even necessarily conflictual" (p. 90).

Tobin's premise, that supportive interpersonal relationships in the classroom are necessary for improving student writing, is an important one for all classrooms: "writing students succeed when teachers establish productive relationships with— and between—their students" (p. 6). He challenges us as writing teachers to examine the central role we and other students play in students' composing processes when we give students guidelines, suggest changes, and read their essays. All of us who struggle with establishing and sustaining successful process writing classrooms will find much support and ideas for reading student essays, responding to student writing, leading a discussion of an essay, running a writing workshop, grading, setting up peer and coauthoring groups, conferencing, and publishing. Most importantly, though, by acknowledging and understanding what is really going on in our writing classrooms, we can take the first, necessary step to improve and change how we help students learn to write. Written for secondary and postsecondary teachers; also recommended for elementary and middle school.

Tompkins, Gail E. 1994. *Teaching Writing: Balancing Process and Product.* 2nd ed. New York: Macmillan.

Many practical strategies for teaching writing are found in this comprehensive text on the writing process. However, it is not just a recipe book! The author worked closely with classroom teachers and has included many vignettes to show how the ideas are implemented in classrooms. Many student samples are used to show possible outcomes of the various lessons and projects suggested in the book. (V.M.)

Vacca, Jo Anne L., Richard T. Vacca, and Mary K. Gove. 1991. *Reading and Learning to Read.* 2nd ed. New York: HarperCollins. (hardbound)

For educators who want to understand and implement a current view of reading, *this scholarly and practical text connects beliefs with practice in an informative, readable fashion. The hallmarks of a literate environment for early readers are described along with workable recommendations for creating such an environment in the classroom. Approaches, guidelines, and strategies to teach and promote beginning reading, connect writing and reading, reading comprehension, vocabulary knowledge, oral and silent reading, literature use across the curriculum, and authentic assessment are described. Activities in Appendix A and B are very helpful for determining and assessing your own theoretical beliefs about reading and reading instruction. Vacca, Vacca, and Gove have taken the best of reading research and practice and organized it into a 616-page text with lots of useful strategies for guiding the reading process.*

Vacca, Richard T., and Timothy V. Rasinski. 1992. *Case Studies in Whole Language.* Orlando, FL: Harcourt Brace.

The authors take us inside the classrooms of preschool through grade five teachers who are moving towards whole language and describe their beliefs and practices along with some principles underlying whole language. Each chapter focuses on one teacher and grade, including a multigrade primary classroom, and includes a typical day, organization and management, strategies, and teaching issues. For teachers in various stages of transition to whole language, this is an excellent book for understanding whole language and refining your own beliefs and practices.

Walmsley, Sean. 1994. *Children Exploring Their World: Theme Teaching in Elementary School.* Portsmouth, NH: Heinemann.

The author devotes the first third of this book to a consideration of the theory and practice of teaching through themes. Walmsley looks at different kinds of themes—content area, conceptual, calendar-based, form, and biographical—and then turns the book over to practicing classroom teachers of grades K–6. These teachers share their experiences of developing and teaching specific themes on top-

ics including insects, the human body, a fish hatchery, historical architecture, and Egyptian mummies. Some of the individual stories show how involved children can get in a certain topic if they're given choices about the direction they want their project to take. This book offers professional resources as well as resources for each specific theme.

Watson, Dorothy, Carolyn Burke, and Jerome Harste. 1989. *Whole Language: Inquiring Voices*. Richmond Hill, Ontario: Scholastic-TAB.

   This seventy-one-page volume, a companion book to Ken Goodman's What's Whole in Whole Language?, *sees teaching as inquiry as the necessary direction for whole language teachers. Teachers are guided to reflect on their own learning in order to foster a community of inquiring learners. Conditions of inquiry—vulnerability, community, generation of knowledge, democracy, and reflexivity—are discussed and demonstrated. This is a very readable and sophisticated book for the teacher who already has a whole language foundation.*

• Weaver, Constance. 1994. *Reading Process and Practice: From Socio-Psycholinguistics to Whole Language*. 2nd ed. Portsmouth, NH: Heinemann.

   For all educators who want the latest tie-in between theory and practice on all aspects of language learning, this comprehensive (731 pp.) and readable text offers a wealth of information in an integrated, useful manner. In addition to detailed discussions of the reading process (including phonics, miscue analysis, research studies supporting whole language practices, Reading Recovery) and extensive, current resources and activities, this new edition also includes two informative chapters on whole language that address whole language principles, common misconceptions, and whole language teaching as a continuing process of development. The chapter "Reading, Literature, and the Dramatic Language Arts" by Ruth Beall Heinig is full of suggestions for combining the dramatic language arts with whole language.

"Whole Language Learning and Teaching for Second Language Learners" by Yvonne Freeman and David Freeman addresses approaches to teaching and supporting second-language students. An amazing resource!

Weaver, Constance. 1994. *Success at Last! Helping Students with Attention Deficit (Hyperactivity) Disorders Achieve Their Potential*. Portsmouth, NH: Heinemann.

   Written to help students with Attention Deficit (Hyperactivity) Disorders, this timely book includes articles by and discussions among young adults with AD(H)D as well as articles by parents and teachers. Based on current research and her conversations with students with AD(H)D, Weaver recommends a "system-theory perspective combined with whole language, learning, and teaching." Always valuing and respecting the learner, she and other contributing authors offer many specific suggestions for ways that parents, teachers, and psychologists can work more effectively with AD(H)D students. Fascinating, informative reading that is applicable for all special-needs students.

Weaver, Constance. 1990. *Understanding Whole Language: From Principles to Practice*. Portsmouth, NH: Heinemann.

   Weaver provides an extensive research and theoretical background to support a whole language approach to teaching and learning and discusses how whole language principles can be applied to the classroom. For educators who already have a rudimentary understanding of whole language, this thorough, scholarly text (336 pp.) provides as in-depth an understanding of whole language as can be found. Weaver devotes fifty-eight pages to phonics—comprising as complete an overview of the research as exists (including research from whole language classrooms), the implications of the research, and suggestions for teaching. An extensive section on assessment (79 pp.) includes current information regarding standardized testing, reading assessment, and a variety of meaningful assessment procedures.

Weaver, Constance, and Linda Henke. 1992. *Supporting Whole Language: Stories of Teachers and Institutional Change.* Portsmouth, NH: Heinemann.

This provocative text deals with success stories and struggles faced by whole language educators and schools. The first part of the book deals with teacher change, and the second part deals with institutional change. What I found especially worrisome were case studies of places where whole language had once thrived but had now disappeared. "The staff began thinking on the activity level. They continued to do message board, written conversation, book making, graphs, and so on, but the activities were ends in themselves rather than strategies for communication, reflection, and learning" (p. 180). The caution is there for us all. Change in practice without a change in beliefs brings no lasting change. Our practice must be theory-driven. For success, support, and suggestions in the change process, teachers and administrators will want to read and discuss this book.

• Wells, Gordon, and others. 1994. *Changing Schools from Within: Creating Communities of Inquiry.* Toronto: OISE Press and Portsmouth, NH: Heinemann.

For every teacher who seeks to be a teacher-researcher but feels uncomfortable with the title and the process, this book is for you. Wells and a group of teachers in Canada report on their own "action research" in their classrooms. Action research means being deliberately reflective about one's teaching and then using that new knowledge to take specific action to improve one's teaching "so that one's students, in turn, are enabled to become intentional learners" (pp. 30–31). Outstanding for teachers ready to question, observe, analyze, and change their practice and for school-based inquiry and discussion.

Wilde, Jack. 1993. *A Door Opens: Writing in Fifth Grade.* Portsmouth, NH: Heinemann.

I found this to be a very supportive book (138 pp.) for intermediate and mid-dle school teachers, especially those beginning to establish writing process classrooms. Wilde, a fifth-grade teacher, is very explicit on how he teaches poetry, fiction, report writing, persuasive writing, and writing across the curriculum. I appreciated the depth of information on how to write fiction stories—a difficult genre for many students—how to take students from prose to poetry, and how to write a research report. Fast-paced and enjoyable to read, Wilde's teacher stories, assignments, and classroom experiences provide much information and encouragement.

Wood, Karen D., with Anita Moss (eds.). 1992. *Exploring Literature in the Classroom: Contents and Methods.* Norwood, MA: Christopher-Gordon.

Bringing literature and reading education together is the goal of this timely text. It is filled with many suggestions and activities suggested by experts in their respective fields. Lapp, Flood, and Farnan present ways to use trade books and basal readers to complement each other in a well-rounded reading program. Other chapters consider technological support, multicultural literature, use of drama, and ways to turn kids on to reading. Last, children's author Natalie Babbitt traces her own journey as a reader. This is a comprehensive book for elementary teachers who are moving from a basal-equipped classroom to one that includes children's literature. (V.M.)

Zemelman, Steven, and Harvey Daniels. 1988. *A Community of Writers: Teaching Writing in the Junior and Senior High School.* Portsmouth, NH: Heinemann.

The authors, co-directors of the Illinois Writing Project, have written a thoughtful and practical text (288 pp.) for teachers of grades 6–12. Drawing on the research of the integrated language arts movement of the 1970s and 1980s, the authors present a complete theoretical and practical framework for the implementation of a process writing classroom. While they honestly acknowledge the obstacles of implementing process writing at the junior and senior high levels, they also stress its necessity "because this is the part of school we most desperately need to reform" (p. 11). Teachers from the upper elementary grades onward will find a wealth of usable ideas for developing classroom management techniques, sensitizing students to working in groups, structuring and designing many types of writing activities, and evaluating student writing beyond copyediting. Three approaches to writing are advocated and explained in depth: student-initiated writing (journals, writing workshop), teacher-assigned writing, and writing to learn. A strong rationale and specific suggestions are given for prewriting, drafting, revising, and conferencing. Teachers will find this book very supportive, realistic, and filled with meaningful writing activities.

Zemelman, Steven, Harvey Daniels, and Arthur Hyde. 1993. *Best Practice: New Standards for Teaching and Learning in America's Schools*. Portsmouth, NH: Heinemann.

This is a tightly organized volume that looks at the best practices in the subject areas of reading, writing, mathematics, science, and social studies. Each of the standards is followed by a description of an exemplary program, and then a summary of how schools should change in this area. Methods for encouraging the implementation of these new approaches, as well as a ten-year program for districtwide staff development, are described. Finally, the Washington Irving School in Chicago is cited as an example of how teachers can be encouraged to work together to enact new curriculum in city school settings. This book should be helpful to administrators and teachers who are looking for an overview of the best educational practices, and places where they are being implemented. (V.M.)

Journal Articles

For other annotated journal articles related specifically to spelling, whole language, journal writing, evaluation, and learning disabilities, see "Resources" at the end of respective chapters in *Invitations*.

Alverman, Donna. October 1991. "The Discussion Web: A Graphic Aid for Learning Across the Curriculum." *The Reading Teacher*, pp. 92–99.

The author defines and describes "the Discussion Web," a procedure that encourages students to work together to make more meaningful and frequent comments in group discussions. An encouraging strategy for getting students to focus critically on the "why" and not just the "what" of an issue.

• Atwell, Nancie. Spring 1989. "The Thoughtful Practitioner." *Teachers Networking: The Whole Language Newsletter*, Vol. 9, no. 3, pp. 1, 10–12.

Atwell encourages us to become teacher-researchers, that is, "thoughtful practitioners" who constantly examine and evaluate our own teaching and learning. Terrific for thoughtful discussion.

Babbitt, Natalie. November–December 1990. "Protecting Children's Literature." *The Horn Book Magazine*, pp. 696–703.

Children's author Natalie Babbitt eloquently reminds us that good fiction is meant to be enjoyed on a human, personal level. She warns against the lessons and discussions designed "to teach" that often accompany the use of literature in the reading program: "Because if we weigh the stories down with the baggage of unrelated lessons, they will sink and disappear" (p. 703).

Braddock, Jomills Henry II, and James M. McPartland. April 1990. "Alternatives to Tracking." *Educational Leadership*, pp. 76–80.

Citing the harmful effects of tracking, the authors offer specific modifications and alternatives. Among them are postponing and limiting tracking, experimenting with different placement criteria, and providing support for teachers in untracked classes.

Brent, Rebecca, and Patricia Anderson. October 1993. "Developing Children's Classroom Listening Strategies." *The Reading Teacher*, pp. 122–126.

Recognizing that effective listening skills do not develop automatically, the authors

model how to get students to be good lis-
teners. I have found the suggested activities and strategies especially valuable for
improving students' listening abilities during sharing time at the end of writing
workshop.

Bruce, Joyce, and Beverly Showers. February
1980. "Improving Inservice Training: The
Messages of Research." *Educational Leadership*, pp. 379–385.

*Many successful staff-development pro-
grams still base their models on the Joyce
and Showers paradigm, which evolved
from a review of over two hundred research studies. This classic article by two
well-respected researchers gives the components of successful staff-development programs—presentation of theory, demonstration of skill, practice, feedback, and
coaching. Educators wanting to design effective staff-development programs will
find this a very useful article.*

Church, Susan. February 1994. "Is Whole
Language Really Warm and Fuzzy?" *The
Reading Teacher*, pp. 362–370.

*Concerns about teachers "doing" whole
language without examining their own beliefs prompted Church to explore the com-
plexities of understanding whole language
theory and practice. One of the questions
she raises is, "Why do so many teachers
seem to believe that whole language means
they should not play an active role as
teacher?" (p. 363). Church convincingly
argues that we need ongoing, school-based
inquiry that focuses on the "why" of language learning. An excellent article for
discussion and reflection.*

Cooper, Harris. November 1989. "Synthesis
of Research on Homework." *Educational
Leadership*, pp. 85–91.

*Cooper reviews and summarizes almost
120 research studies on the effects of homework. He concludes that homework has a
neglible effect on achievement at the elementary level, a moderate effect at the
junior high level, and a positive effect at
the high school level as long as the material is not too complex or unfamiliar. Cooper includes a useful recommended homework policy for districts, schools, and*

teachers. Share these policy guidelines
with parents and administrators.

• Copenhaver, Joby. Spring 1993. "Instances of
Inquiry." *Primary Voices*, pp. 6–12.

*Copenhaver describes how she collabo-
rated with Carolyn Burke and fifth-grade
teacher Rise Paynter to help students generate inquiry questions that would sustain
their individual research for several weeks.
Students then chose a way to share their
new knowledge with the class. Self-evaluation was a major part of the inquiry process. I and many of our teachers have used
the wonderful self-evaluation idea, "Three
Plusses and a Wish," with students and
parents as a positive way to hear their
voices. Excellent for supporting child-in-
itiated inquiry in the classroom and for
promoting self-evaluation.*

Cordeiro, Pat. Winter 1992–1993. "Becoming
a Learner Who Teaches." *Teachers Networking: The Whole Language Newsletter*, pp. 1, 3–4.

*Cordeiro describes how she has moved
from integrated curriculum, where the
teacher brings separate elements of the
curriculum together in a meaningful way,
to "generative curriculum," where teacher
and students collaboratively shape the
curriculum through talk and exploration
in the classroom community. "Teachers
must be learners first, and teachers second" (p. 4). Great for self-reflection and
looking at where you are with curriculum
integration.*

Cudd, Evelyn T., and Leslie Roberts. February
1989. "Using Writing to Enhance Content
Area Learning in the Primary Grades."
The Reading Teacher, pp. 392–404.

*This excellent article is full of specific
demonstrations, ideas, and examples for
writing in the content areas in grades 1–3.
Very useful to teachers who want to move
beyond narrative writing.*

Daiute, Colette. October 1989. "Research Cur-
rents: Play and Learning to Write." *Language Arts*, pp. 656–664.

*The importance of collaborative writing
and the benefits of playful talk for children's writing development are emphasized. The research indicates that collabo-*

rative composing (especially on the computer) is "productive and enriching" and that a "little noise and laughter" contribute to writing.

Donaldson, Gordon A., Jr. October 1993. "Working Smarter Together." *Educational Leadership*, pp. 12–16.

Our K–12 Language Arts Committee found this article very helpful for working together collaboratively through the curriculum-change process. By "working smarter," Donaldson refers to being able to direct our new efforts wisely and monitor what we do so that we benefit children and do not exhaust ourselves in the process. "The cycle of progress requires that a school staff redefine itself as a community responsible for setting and reaching its own goals and capable of managing its own resources" (p. 15). Donaldson helps us achieve this worthy goal.

Dowhower, Sarah L. March 1989. "Repeated Reading: Research into Practice." *The Reading Teacher*, pp. 502–507.

The benefits and procedures of repeated reading ("multiple readings of connected text") are discussed and demonstrated. Specific, practical, and useful for all teachers.

Duffy, Gerald G. February 1992. "Let's Free Teachers to Be Inspired." *Phi Delta Kappan*, pp. 442–447.

The author provides a much-needed, balanced perspective to the debate on which approach to instruction is best. "No matter what is being taught, there seem to be two prevalent approaches to instruction. One is direct; the other, holistic" (p. 442). Rather than carrying one approach to extremes, Duffy recommends that teachers use professional judgment and combine the best of prevailing theory and practice. "Effective teaching is associated with being empowered to combine tenets of various positions in order to arrive at instructional decisions that make sense in a particular instructional situation" (p. 444). Excellent for reflection and discussion.

Farris, Pamela J. Summer 1989. "Story Time and Story Journals: Linking Literature and Writing." *The New Advocate*, pp. 179–185.

The author details specific ways to link literature with writing through story journals, literary journals, and dialogue journals. Useful for the primary-grade teacher.

Fielding, Linda, and Cathy Roller. May 1992. "Making Difficult Books Accessible and Easy Books Acceptable." *The Reading Teacher*, pp. 678–685.

Fielding and Roller recognize the importance of classroom time each day for independent reading and the accompanying reality that some children do not engage with print during this time. The authors offer workable suggestions for getting struggling readers reading the print during independent reading time. Excellent ideas for across the grades.

Five, Cora Lee. Spring 1988. "From Workbook to Workshop: Increasing Children's Involvement in the Reading Process." *The New Advocate*, pp. 103–113.

A fifth-grade teacher describes how she moved to a reading program that complemented her writing program in which students had "time, ownership, and response." Very useful and specific for teachers who want to use literature in a reading workshop approach.

• Fractor, Jann Sorrell, Marjorie Ciruti Woodruff, Miriam G. Martinez, and William H. Teale. March 1993. "Let's Not Miss Opportunities to Promote Voluntary Reading: Classroom Libraries in the Elementary School." *The Reading Teacher*, pp. 476–484.

A quality classroom library positively impacts the amount of voluntary reading students do and increases literacy activities. Yet, the authors found that while most elementary classrooms have library centers, only a very small percentage of these are excellent. Criteria and suggestions for setting up excellent libraries are detailed. Photos and features of some exemplary classroom libraries are included. Read this article, and self-evaluate your own classroom library.

• Fullan, Michael G., and Matthew B. Miles. June 1992. "Getting Reform Right: What Works and What Doesn't." *Phi Delta Kappan*, pp. 745–752.

The authors explain why reforms fail and what must happen in order for reform efforts to succeed. They note that "the implementation dip"—things going wrong before they go right—and anxiety and uncertainty are "intrinsic to all successful change." Use this article in your district, as we did, to help gain support and understanding for the difficult process of change.

Gamoran, Adam. October 1992. "Is Ability Grouping Equitable?" *Educational Leadership*, pp. 11–17.

Negative achievement effects of grouping and tracking are documented with the recommendation that there be less tracking and grouping and an improved use of ability grouping.

Garan, Elaine M. March 1994. "Who's in Control? Is There Enough 'Empowerment' to Go Around?" *Language Arts*, pp. 192–199.

Garan realistically discusses management and control issues in a whole language classroom. Based on her ethnographic study as a participant-observer in a whole language classroom, she urges the sharing of control with students while acknowledging how difficult this is for most of us. Very useful for looking at our own teaching and for effectively structuring the whole language classroom.

• Glasser, William. February 1990. "The Quality School." *Phi Delta Kappan*, pp. 425–435.

A provocative, thought-provoking article on how to manage our teaching so that the majority of students do high-quality schoolwork. Excellent for discussion, K–12.

• Goodlad, John I., and Jeannie Oakes. February 1988. "We Must Offer Equal Access to Knowledge." *Educational Leadership*, pp. 16–22.

"Study after study reveals the dominance of telling, lecturing, questioning the class, and monitoring seatwork. The inquiring, questioning, probing, hypothesizing kind of intellectual endeavor often associated with learning is not usually found in classrooms" (p. 17). Furthermore, poor and minority children, overrepresented in the lowest groups, and with little chance of access to the highest groups, receive the most inferior schooling. Educators are urged to examine tracking practices and consider different ideas: implementing small cooperative learning groups, providing concept-based (rather than fragmented skills) curriculums, and altering the way we perceive individual differences.

Goodman, Kenneth S. Winter 1988. "Look What They've Done to Judy Blume!: The 'Basalization' of Children's Literature." *The New Advocate*, pp. 29–41.

Goodman reiterates that authentic text, the way the author wrote it, is the easiest to read and to learn to read. He decries common tampering with stories by well-known authors to fit basal schemes. Teachers and administrators desirous of using real literature instead of basal texts will find this a supportive article.

• Hammond, Catherine. February 1993. "The Internal Screen: A Powerful Tool for Writing." *Language Arts*, pp. 116–122.

This is the most useful article I have read on getting students to write well. Hammond demonstrates how she gets students to write with specific, powerful images by using their "screens" (the place where we see things in our heads) to capture and visualize exact moments in their lives.

Henke, Linda. Winter 1988. "Beyond Basal Reading: A District's Commitment to Change." *The New Advocate*, pp. 42–51.

For school districts ready to look at alternative reading program options, this article describes how a district that decides against a new basal adoption implements a program that accommodates use of the old basal while adding lots of trade books, daily independent reading, and daily writing workshop time, as well as staff development and parent communication.

• Hepler, Susan. Summer 1988. "A Guide for the Teacher Guides: Doing It Yourself." *The New Advocate*, pp. 186–195.

This gem of an article gives specific guidelines to teachers who want to work together to develop meaningful guides for specific books. Meaningful questions, responses to literature, and appropriate ac-

tivities are discussed and demonstrated. The article is not only useful for making your own guides for books but it is also valuable for looking at commercial guides critically.

Herman, Patricia A., and Janice Dole. September 1988. "Theory and Practice in Vocabulary Learning and Instruction." *The Elementary School Journal*, pp. 43–54.

The authors discuss three approaches to vocabulary instruction—definitional, contextual, and conceptual—while also acknowledging that most words are learned incidentally; "an average reader learns the meaning of 800–1,200 words per year through free reading alone" (p. 44). A combination of the three approaches is recommended, and specifics are provided. The definitional approach, by itself, is seen to be mostly ineffective. With the contextual approach, the importance of teacher demonstration is illustrated through an example of a teacher verbalizing thought processes to figure out the meaning of a word in natural context. A series of activities that demonstrates a conceptual approach to learning a word is clearly delineated. Current research about vocabulary and its effect on reading comprehension is also discussed. An excellent article for gaining perspective on vocabulary acquisition.

Hudelson, Sarah, Julia Fournier, Cecilia Espinosa, and Renee Bachman. March 1994. "Chasing Windmills: Confronting the Obstacles to Literature-Based Programs in Spanish." *Language Arts*, pp. 164–171.

While Spanish-speaking children and bilingual programs are increasing in the United States, the quantity, quality, and cultural authenticity of literature available in Spanish is still very limited. The authors discuss the challenges of getting quality Spanish-language literature into the literature classroom. Excellent criteria, references, and literature cited to aid selection.

• Juliebo, Moira, and Joyce Edwards. January 1989. "Encouraging Meaning Making in Young Writers." *Young Children*, pp. 22–27.

The authors demonstrate what happens when writing tasks are artificially created by the teacher. They concur with already existing studies that support the need for topic choice, real purpose, and a varied audience for obtaining children's best written work. Although the writing samples discussed are from primary children, the characteristics that are found to encourage—or restrict—written composition apply to all the grades. An important article for understanding the need for authentic writing experiences.

Lambert, Linda. May 1988. "Staff Development Redesigned." *Phi Delta Kappan*, pp. 665–668.

Lambert urges expanding the teacher's role in staff development from "passive receiver" to leadership and inquiry. Teachers ready to take an active, decision-making role in restructuring staff development in their school will find lots of support and valuable information in this thought-provoking article. Great for discussion.

Larrick, Nancy. Spring 1991. "Give us Books! But Also . . . Give Us Wings!" *The New Advocate*, pp. 77–83.

Nancy Larrick makes an impassioned plea to keep the joy of reading quality literature alive in the classroom. She notes that many teachers are using real books with students, but many are also using accompanying teachers' guides that ruin the joy and beauty of the books. She cites the problems with many of these guides. Good for discussion and for self-checking your own use of literature in the classroom.

Lee, Nancy G., and Judith C. Neal. December 1992/January 1993. "Reading Rescue: Intervention for a Student 'At Promise.'" *Journal of Reading*, pp. 276–282.

The authors describe how an adaptation of Marie Clay's intensive, 1:1 approach is used successfully with a very poor reader in middle school. The specific components and strategies used are clearly delineated. Guidelines for classroom teachers who work with struggling ("at promise") readers are given. Helpful and applicable across the grades.

Lipson, Marjorie Y., Sheila W. Valencia, Karen K. Wixon, and Charles W. Peters. April

1993. "Integration and Thematic Teaching: Integration to Improve Teaching and Learning." *Language Arts*, pp. 252–263.

Everyone I know struggles with meaningful integration of the curriculum. The authors provide a realistic overview of where we are in the profession and provide a rationale—as well as suggestions—for teaching with integrated, thematic units. Helpful for being able to develop thematic units that deal with important, big ideas that are authentically connected to meaningful content.

• Maeroff, Gene I. "Assessing Alternative Assessment." December 1991. *Phi Delta Kappan*, pp. 272–281.

"For all its attractiveness, alternative assessment is fraught with complications and difficulties." Maeroff notes, for example, "if students themselves are to take responsibility for their own work, the criteria must be spelled out in ways that are understandable to children." Looking at existing alternative assessments in various states and schools, Maeroff discusses the benefits and the problems. Great for gaining perspective and ideas on alternative assessments.

Manning, Maryann, Gary Manning, and Constance Kamii. November 1988. "Early Phonics Instruction: Its Effect on Literacy Development." *Young Children*, pp. 4–8.

The authors describe what happened to one six-year-old (who entered school reading predictable books) when she received a heavy dose of phonics instruction in kindergarten. "With the exception of digraphs and consonant blends, the instruction caused confusion and reduced her confidence in her own ability to figure things out." The authors are not against phonics instruction, but they do question an imposed, time-consuming phonics program that may not fit the child's stage of development. Rather, they urge an emphasis on meaning with lots of time for reading and writing so children can work out their own system of rules.

Means, Barbara, and Michael S. Knapp. December 1991. "Cognitive Approaches to Teaching Advanced Skills to Educationally Disadvantaged Students." *Phi Delta Kappan*, pp. 282–289.

A summary of the research supporting the teaching of "advanced" skills to "at-risk" learners is presented along with strategies for doing so. Offers helpful suggestions for reshaping the curriculum so all students receive "higher-order" content and thinking.

• Newmann, Fred M., and Gary G. Wehlage. April 1993. "Five Standards of Authentic Instruction." *Educational Leadership*, pp. 8–12.

Five standards for engaging students in high-quality work that uses students' minds well are presented with specific criteria. The standards are described with a five-point scale for rating lessons and include higher-order thinking, depth of knowledge, connectedness to the world, substantive conversation, and social support for student achievement. Discuss and use this excellent framework in your school, as we did, to self-evaluate current practices and to move toward more "authentic," higher-level instruction and achievement. Applicable to all grade levels and subject areas.

• O'Brien, Kathy L. Winter 1991. "A Look at One Successful Literature Program." *The New Advocate*, pp. 113–123.

Many teachers now incorporate literature into their reading programs, but, in some cases, not without basalization of the literature. The author describes and recommends specific, successful practices which maintain the integrity of the text and the reader and which promote high level dialogue and analysis. Read and discuss this excellent article, and apply the practices to your own literature program.

• Ohanian, Susan. Fall 1988. "My Word! A Plea for More Disorderliness." *Teachers Networking: The Whole Language Newsletter.*

Ohanian argues that rather than trusting kids to become readers and celebrating children's literature, many teachers and publishers ruin the literature for kids by trying to extract as many skills as possible. Must reading for teachers tempted to have kids do lots of activities to go along with books!

• Ohlhausen, Marilyn M., and Mary Jepsen. Winter 1992. "Lessons from Goldilocks: 'Somebody's Been Choosing My Books But I Can Make My Own Choices Now!'" *The New Advocate*, pp. 31–46.

Ohlhausen and Jepsen recommend a process for teaching children how to select books that are characterized as "too easy," "just right," and "too hard." Through teacher modeling and guided practice, children learn to independently judge book difficulty for themselves and to choose books to read from all three categories. I, and many of our teachers, use the "Goldilocks Strategy" in the independent reading program. See Appendix D, p. 189b.

Pace, Glenellen. January 1991. "When Teachers Use Literature for Literacy Instruction: Ways That Constrain, Ways That Free." *Language Arts*, pp. 12–25.

Many teachers now use literature to support literacy development. "But frequently what teachers have children do with literature is at odds with a whole language paradigm." Pace identifies key premises from whole language theory, gives supporting examples from elementary classrooms, and asks specific questions about classroom practice as a way for us to evaluate our teaching. Excellent for reflection and discussion and for making our theory and practice congruent with holistic, learner-centered views. Applicable for K–8.

Rasinski, Timothy V. May 1989. "Fluency for Everyone: Incorporating Fluency Instruction in the Classroom." *The Reading Teacher*, pp. 690–693.

This highly practical, research-based article gives the classroom teacher specific strategies for promoting and supporting reading fluency of students. Repetition, modeling, direct feedback, tape recording, choral reading, and use of easy materials are fully discussed. I have found this article to be especially useful for helping "at-risk" students become more proficient readers.

Reardon, S. Jeanne. Winter 1988. "The Development of Critical Readers: A Look into the Classroom." *The New Advocate*, pp. 52–61.

An intermediate-grade classroom teacher describes the necessary elements for development of critical readers. Her specific demonstrations of how she reads to her class every day and how she conducts a small-group literature discussion are extremely helpful to the teacher who wants insight into promoting high-level thinking by connecting authors' purposes to literature. Applicable for all the grades.

Reimer, Becky L., and Leslie Warshow. April 1989. "Questions We Ask of Ourselves and Our Students." *The Reading Teacher*, pp. 596–606.

Teachers who have made meaningful and major changes in their teaching tell their personal stories. Supportive, informative, and inspiring to all teachers in the change process.

Rosenblatt, Louise M. October 1991. "Literature—S.O.S.!" *Language Arts*, pp. 444–448.

Louise Rosenblatt asks us "to be clear theoretically about efferent and aesthetic reading" and to take care not to use literature to teach "skills." Important for understanding Rosenblatt's important ideas on how readers transact with texts and for looking carefully at how we use literature in the classroom.

Scharer, Patricia L., and Deana B. Detwiler. March 1992. "Changing as Teachers: Perils and Possibilities of Literature-Based Language Arts Instruction." *Language Arts*, pp. 186–192.

A sixth-grade teacher describes her transition to literature-based teaching and shares her struggles and successes. Recommendations for supporting teacher change are included. Very helpful to teachers and schools in transition.

Sears, Sue, Cathy Carpenter, and Nancy Burstein. May 1994. "Meaningful Reading Instruction for Learners with Special Needs." *The Reading Teacher*, pp. 632–638.

This fine article details how to balance the need for explicit instruction with whole language principles for special-needs learners. The authors describe a reading program that consists of assisted reading (reading grade-level texts aloud with help), informal assessment (taking running records and responding to comprehension questions), and contextualized strategy instruction (minilessons based on identified needs). Very helpful to anyone who works with struggling readers.

- Shannon, Patrick. October 1989. "The Struggle for Control of Literacy Lessons." *Language Arts*, pp. 625–634.

  The author argues that, in a democratic educational and social setting, the control of literacy lessons should be properly shared by teachers and students. Even when materials are substantially improved over traditional basal texts, publishers still maintain control by predetermining the possible choices. Shannon raises weighty questions about control of literacy lessons and suggests that as long as a commercial program is used, it is the publisher's choices that control the lessons.

Shepard, Lorrie A., and Mary Lee Smith. May 1990. "Synthesis of Research on Grade Retention." *Educational Leadership*, pp. 84–88.

  The authors note that "the large body of research on grade retention is almost uniformly negative." Given that 5 to 7 percent of children in public schools in the United States are retained annually at a cost of almost $10 billion a year, this is an article to be taken seriously. Retention leads to increased risk of dropping out of school, poor self-esteem, and lower achievement in later grades. The authors recommend "promotion plus remediation" and suggest alternative ways to provide specific and additional instructional help.

Silva, Cecilia, and Esther L. Delgado-Larocco. October 1993. "Facilitating Learning Through Interconnections: A Concept Approach to Core Literature Units." *Language Arts*, pp. 469–474.

  For teachers and districts who implement literature and literature-based programs, the authors present a model for developing meaningful literature units with conceptually related books. Helpful for focusing on meaning and enjoyment and avoiding trivialising of the literature.

Slavin, Robert E. September 1988. "Synthesis of Research on Grouping in Elementary and Secondary Schools." *Educational Leadership*, pp. 67–77.

  Slavin, perhaps best known for his comprehensive research analysis on ability grouping ("Ability Grouping and Student Achievement in Elementary Schools: A Best Evidence Synthesis." Review of Educational Research, Vol. 57, no. 3 [1987], pp. 213–336), summarizes the research on achievement effects of ability grouping at the elementary and secondary levels. This scholarly article is important reading for all educators. It calls into question many common grouping practices for regular, gifted, and special education students.

- Smith, Frank. February 1992. "Learning to Read: The Never-Ending Debate." *Phi Delta Kappan*, pp. 432–441.

  Conflicting views of how children learn to read and how reading should be taught are examined with thoughtful rhetoric and uncommon good sense. Frank Smith elaborates on how children learn to read and on current theories of teaching reading, specifically, the phonics or "skills" approach and the whole language or "naturalistic" approach. "Methods can never ensure that children learn to read. Children must learn from people: from the teachers (formal and informal) who initiate them into the readers' club and from the authors whose writing they read" (p. 440). Read this powerful essay and continue the debate in your own school. You may also want to read the response to Smith, "The Debate Continues" by Kenneth J. Smith, Valerie F. Reyna, and Charles J. Brainerd (Phi Delta Kappan, January 1993, pp. 407–410).

Smith, Frank. January 1989. "Overselling Literacy." *Phi Delta Kappan*, pp. 353–359.

  "Individuals become literate not from the formal instruction they receive, but from what they read and write about and who they read and write with" (p. 355). Smith cautions against the promotion of literacy as a cure-all for society's ills and reminds us that literacy is most valuable and productive when it is meaningful and carried out in association with literate people who read and write for pleasure.

Rather than relying on instructional programs and evaluation, school environments need to foster collaborative relationships that free the imagination and empower both teachers and students. A great article for group discussion.

Taylor, Denny. November 1989. "Toward a Unified Theory of Literacy Learning and Instructional Practices." *Phi Delta Kappan*, pp. 184–193.

The author argues that "reductionist" and "hierarchical" research views of children's early literacy development do not take into consideration the complex individual and personal ways children have been observed to learn and use language, and, therefore, these views are too narrow to be taken seriously. Taylor urges educators to establish theoretical frameworks that broaden and enhance children's opportunities for dynamic reading and writing experiences. "Our task is to insure that the voices of children become embodied in the ways in which we teach" (p. 193). An important article for thinking about our own understandings and beliefs about literacy.

Throne, Jeanette. September 1988. "Becoming a Kindergarten of Readers?" *Young Children*, pp. 10–16.

A well-respected kindergarten teacher in our school district argues that good kindergarten teachers have always taught reading—not through formal, decontextualized materials—but through all kinds of authentic language experiences. Throne discusses how she fosters reading through shared book experiences, repeated readings, creative dramatics, related writing and art activities, and group discussions about stories. An excellent article for early childhood educators who want a developmentally appropriate curriculum.

Topping, Keith. March 1989. "Peer Tutoring and Paired Reading: Combining Two Powerful Techniques." *The Reading Teacher*, pp. 488–494.

The author, an educational psychologist who developed a parent-child paired-reading procedure that is widely practiced in the United Kingdom, discusses the bene-fits, organizational procedures, and evaluation research of paired-reading programs in classrooms, in which a more able child assists a less able one in reading. "All the major research reviews on the effectiveness of peer tutoring in reading have shown that the tutors accelerate in reading skill at least as much as, if not more than, the tutees" (p. 489). This very specific article gives complete information to the K–12 teacher who is interested in setting up a paired-reading program.

• Turner, Richard L. December 1989. "The 'Great' Debate–Can Both Carbo and Chall Be Right?" *Phi Delta Kappan*, pp. 276–283.

An educational researcher responds to two extreme positions on the teaching of phonics in beginning reading: "Debunking the Great Phonics Myth" by Marie Carbo (Phi Delta Kappan, November 1988) and "Learning to Read: The Great Debate 20 Years Later—A Response to 'Debunking the Great Phonics Myth'" by Jeanne Chall (Phi Delta Kappan, March 1989). In reviewing the research literature on the place of phonics in beginning reading instruction, Turner reviews the "best evidence" studies—those "that were free from bias, that directly addressed the research question of interest, and that inspired confidence in the results" (p. 276). He concludes, "If systematic phonics influences reading vocabulary and comprehension at all, it does so very, very slightly" (p. 283). Read all three articles for perspectives on phonics in beginning reading.

Urzúa, Carole. Fall 1994. "Faith in Learners Through Literature Studies." *Voices from the Middle*, pp. 19–30.

The rationale and procedures for a literature study—where students meet with their peers to read and discuss an agreed-upon book in "book club" sessions—are described in detail. Excellent for organizing your own literature study.

Walmsley, Sean A., and Ellen L. Adams. April 1993. "Realities of 'Whole Language.'" *Language Arts*, pp. 272–280.

Interviews with a group of teachers confirmed that whole language instruction is very difficult to put into practice, manage, and assess. The authors state, "We had the feeling that most of the teachers were still grappling with a concept that they did not fully understand." This controversial article is important for looking at whole language realistically, for making sure that teachers receive sufficient support for the rigorous demands of whole language teaching, and for addressing the politics of whole language.

Wason-Ellam, Linda. March 1988. "Using Literary Patterns: Who's in Control of the Authorship?" *Language Arts,* pp. 291–301.

The author warns against overuse of literary patterns from predictable texts and suggests that beginning writers need to focus on communicating ideas. While innovating on patterned text can be meaningful (especially in oral-language activities), often it is overworked and restrictive. "At times, this is carried to such an extreme that the task often resembles workbook activities" (p. 292). Teachers who are spending a lot of time having children extend specific patterns should read this article for perspectives and for suggestions of how predictable books can serve as models to promote authentic writing.

Wheelock, Anne. October 1992. "The Case for Untracking." *Educational Leadership,* pp. 6–21.

For schools thinking about "untracking" and giving all students equal access to valued knowledge, this article provides incentive and support. Wheelock identifies characteristics of schools that have successfully eliminated tracking by ability and improved instruction and learning.

Whitmore, Kathryn F., and Caryl G. Crowell. Winter 1994. "What Makes a Question Good Is . . ." *The New Advocate,* pp. 45–57.

The authors describe how literature study in a third-grade community evolved from children's probing questions about a world event. The power of children's questioning as a literature study discussion strategy is demonstrated through the students' conversations and high-level questions.

Wiggington, Eliot. February 1989. "Foxfire Grows Up." *Harvard Educational Review,* pp. 24–49.

The developer of the "Foxfire approach," a democratic, experiential, and hands-on approach and philosophy of education describes Foxfire's core educational practices and how he and others work with teachers to achieve them. The approach believes that all-age students "benefit from examining the culture, traditions, and history of their communities, urban or rural, and then documenting and publishing what they found" (p. 24). The Foxfire approach has much in common with whole language in that education is student centered and connected to the real world. Texts are used as resources as the need arises; group work and collaboration are highly valued; the teacher is a facilitator and guide; self-evaluation is intrinsic to the learning process. A provocative article for educators interested in learning about the Foxfire approach.

Yaffe, Stephen H. March 1989. "Drama as a Teaching Tool." *Educational Leadership,* pp. 29–32.

The benefits of drama as a response to literature for gifted as well as at-risk students K–12 are discussed and demonstrated.

• Zarrillo, James. Fall 1991. "Theory Become Practice: Aesthetic Teaching with Literature." *The New Advocate,* pp. 221–233.

Many elementary teachers are unaware of Rosenblatt's seminal work, The Reader, The Text, The Poem: The Transactional Theory of the Literary Work (Carbondale, IL: Southern Illinois University Press, 1978) and her enormous, worldwide impact. Zarrillo translates Louise Rosenblatt's transactional theory of reading to the elementary grades and demonstrates his interpretation of aesthetic teaching. "Aesthetic teaching relies on literature and supports the personal reading choices and unique responses of students" (p. 231). Be sure to read and discuss this terrific article. Excellent for understanding Rosenblatt's "efferent" and "aesthetic" approaches to reading and for creating a literature program that is theoretically sound, intensely personal, response centered, and respectful of children's needs and choices.

Zucker, Carol. May 1993. "Using Whole Language with Students Who Have Language and Learning Disabilities." *The Reading Teacher,* pp. 660–670.

Based on a whole language philosophy, a learning disabilities resource teacher specifically describes her classroom reading-writing activities and the benefits to the children. Helpful and applicable to all learners with special needs.

Themed Journals

These themed journals are wonderful springboards for thinking about practices, processes, and changes in literacy learning and teaching K–12. Many of the articles in these journals have been discussed in our weekly language arts support groups. It is recommended that your school library have a copy of each journal for your reference.

Baumann, James F. (guest ed.). May 1990. *The Reading Teacher: Whole Literacy.* Newark, DE: International Reading Association.

This issue explores possibilities and challenges in implementing whole language. The introductory article, "'Possibilities, Daddy, I Think It Says Possibilities': A Father's Journal of the Emergence of Literacy" by Lester L. Laminack is both scholarly and delightful for taking a look at a preschooler's attempts to interact with print in his world. Preschool, kindergarten, and grade one teachers will find "Dramatic Play: A Context for Meaningful Engagements" by James F. Christie valuable for noting the importance of providing opportunities for literacy-related dramatic play and for specific suggestions on theme centers and teacher involvement. "Language, Literature, and At-Risk Children" by Nancy L. Roser, James V. Hoffman, and Cynthia Farest describes how a literature program was successfully organized and implemented in a large, impoverished county school system. "Whole Language in the Middle School" by Anna M. McWhirter, which describes a reading

workshop approach, will be instructive for middle and high school teachers seeking alternatives to traditional language arts teaching. "Assessment and Accountability in a Whole Literacy Curriculum" by Kathryn H. Au, Judith A. Scheu, Alice J. Kawakami, and Patricia A. Herman will be very useful to teachers, administrators, and school districts looking for accountability in incorporating holistic measures for monitoring and documenting learning. Other fine articles discuss the use of computers, parent involvement, reading-spelling links, and how a grade one teacher incorporated whole language in her classroom.

Brandt, Ronald (executive ed.). April 1989. *Educational Leadership: Redirecting Assessment.* Alexandria, VA: Association for Supervision and Curriculum Development.

If you are interested in improving evaluation and assessment, don't miss this outstanding issue. Lorie Shepard's opening article, "Why We Need Better Assessments" addresses the limitations of standardized testing and points the way to more authentic assessment. "High-Stakes Testing in Kindergarten" by Samuel J. Meisels discusses the harmful effects and misuse of readiness testing for labeling, placing, and retaining children. "There are presently no readiness or achievement tests sufficiently accurate to serve the high-stakes functions they are being asked to perform" (p. 20). "On Misuse of Testing: A Conversation with George Madaus" by Ron Brandt addresses the concerns of the director of the Center for the Study of Testing, Evaluation, and Educational Policy and is a terrific article for group discussion. Among other things, Madaus notes that high test scores do not correlate with high skills levels; measurement-driven instruction makes teaching easier but "deprofessionalizes" it; ranking school districts by test results uses tests in a way that was never intended. In "Testing and Thoughtfulness," Rexford Brown notes that thinking skills cannot be broken down and tested. He calls for more thoughtful tests such as those that students create themselves. Dennie Palmer Wolf's article, "Portfolio As-

sessment: Sampling Student Work," is outstanding for understanding the concepts behind portfolio assessment. In a very significant article, "Teaching to the (Authentic) Test," Grant Wiggins calls for a redesign of assessment procedures at the high school level that reflects authentic literacy behaviors. "Theory and Practice in Statewide Reading Assessment: Closing the Gap" by Sheila Valencia, David Pearson, Charles Peters, and Karen Wixon describes the statewide reading comprehension tests in Illinois and Michigan that are based on current reading theory. "How Do We Evaluate Student Writing? One District's ANSWER" by Melva Lewis and Arnold Lindaman gives specifics on how a district measures students' growth as writers in grades 1–12 using fall and spring writing samples, student and parent evaluative responses of those samples, and holistic assessment of the samples.

- Flores, Barbara (guest ed.). January 1994. *Primary Voices K–6. Challenge for Change: Theme Cycles.* Urbana, IL: National Council of Teachers of English.

   This is a great issue for understanding integration and gaining a meaningful framework for classroom inquiry focused on critical questions, problem solving, and constructing knowledge. In the opening article, Barbara Flores and Bess Altwerger rethink learning and teaching and explain what they mean by "theme cycle." In a theme cycle, "Teachers and students select and negotiate topics of study, and based upon the collective knowledge of the class, they delineate questions and issues of interest, seek out resources, and plan learning experiences." The new knowledge is presented and shared, leading to other questions and further study that continues the learning cycle. In the articles that follow, elementary school bilingual teachers, a principal, a seventh-grade humanities teacher, and a sixth-grade bilingual teacher describe in detail how theme study has evolved and transformed instruction and learning in their classrooms and schools. Don't miss this enlightening issue for rethinking your own curriculum. Lots of usable ideas for the classroom.

Froese, Victor (guest ed.). April 1989. *The Reading Teacher: Empowering Both Teachers and Students.* Newark, DE: International Reading Association.

   Each of the articles in this thought-provoking journal is noteworthy for thinking about how literacy is taught and learned in schools and for incorporating recent research into practice. I was particularly impressed by "Building Communities of Readers and Writers" by Trevor Cairney and Susan Langbien, who stress the importance of the social and collaborative nature of learning in all learning environments. "Empowered Students; Empowered Teachers" by William T. Fagan is a very important article for understanding the crucial role teachers play in determining whether or not reading and writing are meaningfully connected to children's lives. "Questions We Ask of Ourselves and Our Students" by Becky L. Reimer and Leslie Warshow describes the struggles and breakthroughs of specific classroom teachers in trying to teach reading and writing with "real life connections." "The Teacher's Role in Students' Success" by Mariam Jean Dreher and Harry Singer calls upon teachers to move from activity managers who follow teacher manuals to professional decision makers who determine goals, materials, and methods.

- Gadsden, Vivian L. (guest ed.). Autumn 1992. *Theory into Practice: Literacy and the African-American Learner.* Columbus, OH: The Ohio State University, College of Education. (1945 N. High St., 43210)

   The collective voices of the authors and researchers in this provocative issue discuss the social and cultural contexts, approaches, and experiences that appear to support and/or hinder literacy learning and access to literacy for African-Americans. I will highlight just a few contributors, but the entire issue is high level, excellent, and worth reading and discussing.

   Violet Harris discusses the historical perspective of literacy and notes that educators working with African-Americans need to know and learn from the lessons of the past and use materials and methods that affirm African-Americans and their *culture. In her article, "Acquisition of Literate Discourse: Bowing Before the Master?" Lisa Delpit challenges some conventional views of teaching African-Americans. She believes it is not enough for students to speak and write freely in their own language and voice; they must also be taught to speak and write eloquently with correct grammar, form, and style in the dominant discourse in order to have access to the culture of power. She shares the stories of two successful African-American men who grew up "in an era of overt racism" and who had no aspirations beyond their immediate neighborhoods. These men made major achievements in life because of teachers who had unflappable visions of what they could become and who gave them access to the subtle and mechanical features of middle-class discourse. Their teachers set high standards for them, expected them to meet them, and gave them the necessary, explicit help needed to succeed in mainstream America. Delpit's work is critical reading for all teachers. "In Reading Between the Lines and Beyond the Pages: A Culturally Relevant Approach to Literacy Teaching," Gloria Ladson-Billings describes how two exemplary teachers, who appreciate and celebrate their students "both as individuals and as members of a specific culture" facilitate learning for the African-American students in their classrooms. The descriptions of how these teachers and classrooms operate provide important information for teaching African-American students. So do the articles by Emilie V. Siddle Walker and Michele Jean Sims. The final article, by Patricia A. Edwards, "Involving Parents in Building Reading Instruction for African-American Children," describes a successful book-reading program for low-income, African-American parents that assists and supports them in sharing books with their children. The strategies presented are powerful and workable for other similar communities.*

Good, Thomas L. (ed.). November 1989. *The Elementary School Journal: Special Issue on Whole Language.* Chicago: University of Chicago Press.

This is a superb issue for examining the theory, history, and applications of the whole language movement as well as for getting perspectives and implications for teaching and learning. Yetta Goodman begins the issue with a scholarly article that gives a history of the whole language movement. Kenneth Goodman discusses characteristics of whole language and the strong research base for whole language, as well as research possibilities. Other articles define and describe whole language, Reading Recovery, and current and potential views of teacher education. Two commentaries on whole language respond to the articles in this issue and give varying perspectives. The concluding article by Jerry Harste addresses the future of the whole language movement and is important reading for all those concerned with schooling in a democratic society.

Hardt, Ulrich H. (ed.). Fall 1988. *Oregon English. Theme: Whole Language.* Portland: Oregon Council of Teachers of English. (Available for purchase through National Council of Teachers of English, Urbana, IL.)

Favorite articles include "Reflections on Whole Language: Past, Present and Potential" by Dorothy Watson, "Evaluation in the Holistic Reading/Language Arts Curriculum" by Richard Ammon, "Whole Language Teaching: Support from Instructional and Research Models" by Jane B. Braunger. Other articles deal with curricular change, integrating fairy tales into language arts, teaching skills, organizing a student publishing company, integrating letter writing across the curriculum, using children's literature (including picture books) with junior high students, incorporating the arts to reach turned-off high school students, thinking beyond biased textbooks in teaching U.S. history. This entire journal is outstanding for deepening understanding of whole language theory and practice.

Jongsma, Eugene, and Roger Farr (guest eds.). April 1993. *Journal of Reading: Literacy Assessment.* Newark, DE: International Reading Association.

For districts that are ready to question their assessment practices, this provocative issue examines the changes taking place in reading assessment and raises important questions about portfolio assessment systems, creative performance tasks, and national standards. Informed (informal) assessment by teachers, preparation for state-mandated tests, the present practice of portfolios from elementary through postsecondary contexts, and attempts to incorporate more authentic assessments are examined from both problematic and promising perspectives. Because of the national interest in portfolios, I was particularly struck by "Student Portfolios: Opportunities for a Revolution in Assessment" by Robert C. Calfee and Pam Perfumo. In that article and others, the editors and authors caution that without knowledgeable educators and adequate support, the changes taking place in assessment may fizzle and disappear. A terrific issue for discussion and for helping establish workable and meaningful assessment practices.

Shannon, Patrick, and Kenneth S. Goodman (guest eds.). Autumn 1989. *Theory into Practice: Perspectives on Basal Readers.* Columbus, OH: The Ohio State University.

This journal presents varying viewpoints about basal reading materials and raises philosophical questions about literacy learning and teaching. The volume goes way beyond basal texts and raises critical questions about assessment, textbook adoption, reading programs, students' perceptions about reading, reading comprehension, and more. Important reading for all teachers, administrators, and policymakers who are interested in the effects of reading programs on literacy instruction and development and in bringing about constructive change.

Wood, George (coordinator). Fall 1990. *Democracy and Education: Alternatives to Standardized Testing.* Athens, OH: Institute for Democracy in Education at Ohio University.

Don't miss this powerful, thought-provoking issue! This outstanding journal includes articles that discuss how stand-

ardized testing demeans and disempowers educators and students by devaluing classroom teachers' judgment and by overrelying on test makers, and it offers alternatives for authentic evaluation. The lead article, "Toward Authentic Assessment," by the editorial board of Democracy and Education, is a clear statement about standardized testing that contains what's wrong with standardized testing (including a statement from Fair Test, the National Center for Fair and Open Testing) as well as options open to teachers to deal with testing. The second essay is a position statement on standardized testing from the National Association for the Education of Young Children. Educators in early childhood programs will find much support here for restricting test use. The remainder of this issue includes inspiring articles by elementary and secondary teachers and students—and a parent—who offer personal and practical insights into the necessity of valuing and involving students in an authentic evaluation process.

Journals

Democracy & Education
4 issues per year/subscription $20
The Institute for Democracy and Education
College of Education
313G McCracken Hall
Athens, OH 45701–2979

A quality journal written by and for teachers that focuses on issues related to democratic practice. For example, recent themed issues have addressed tracking and ability grouping, democratic management, alternatives to standardized testing, classroom and community building, and project-centered learning. The Institute sponsors a conference in Athens, Ohio, every June.

Educational Leadership
8 issues per year/subscription $32
Association for Supervision and Curriculum Development
1250 North Pitt Street
Alexandria, VA 22314–1453

A journal for elementary, middle school, and secondary teachers and administra-

tors interested in being on the cutting edge of current educational theory and practice. For anyone interested in being well informed about good ideas regarding today's educational practices. ASCD offers many excellent professional development opportunities through an annual conference, continuing workshops, and many publications and resources for administrators and teachers.

Elementary School Journal
5 issues per year/subscription $29.50 (individual); $56 (institutions); $22.25 (NAESP); $19.50 (students)
University of Chicago Press
Journals Division
5720 South Woodlawn
PO Box 37005
Chicago, IL 60637

Geared toward a more scholarly audience, this journal contains studies, research reviews, and analyses of ideas for elementary teachers, administrators, teacher educators, and researchers.

• **English Journal**
8 issues per year/subscription $40 (individual); $50 (institutions) (includes membership in NCTE)
National Council of Teachers of English
1111 W. Kenyon Road
Urbana, IL 61801–1906

By teachers for teachers in middle, junior, or senior high school, English Journal contains quality, thought-provoking articles about theory, practice, and new ideas in learning, reading, and writing in the classroom.

The Horn Book Magazine
6 issues per year/subscription $35 (individual); $42 (institutions)
11 Beacon Street, Suite 1000
Boston, MA 02108

For anyone interested in quality writing about books for children and young adults, The Horn Book Magazine provides the most complete, responsible, and thoughtful coverage. Contains reviews of children's and young adult titles; articles from and about authors and their work; articles on books from parallel cultures, using literature in the classroom, and many more topics of interest.

Journal of Reading
8 issues per year/subscription $38 (individual); $41 (institutions)
International Reading Association
800 Barksdale Road
PO Box 8139
Newark, DE 19714–8139

The audience is adolescent and adult-level teachers. Contains insights into theory, research findings, reviews of professional and adolescent books, and reviews of institutional materials.

• **Language Arts**
8 issues per year/subscription $40 (individual); $50 (institutions)
National Council of Teachers of English
1111 W. Kenyon Road
Urbana, IL 61801–1096

Theory and practice in language learning are combined with exceptional literary style in monthly themed journals. This official journal of NCTE (for the elementary grades) notes its new publications, forthcoming conferences, and reviews of children's and professional books.

Note that NCTE sponsors an annual conference in late November and a spring conference that focus on current professional issues. State and local affiliates also sponsor meetings of interest to English/language arts teachers at all levels. NCTE also publishes numerous professional publications for teachers.

Learning
8 issues per year/subscription $18
Learning Magazine
Education Center, Inc.
1607 Battleground Avenue
PO Box 9753
Greensboro, NC 27429

PO Box 2580
Boulder, CO 80322 (subscriptions)

This lively journal contains creative suggestions from teachers for teachers, practical applications for the classroom, activities, tips, and a reader exchange. For those interested in teaching K–8. Teachers new to the field should be aware that articles cover a broad spectrum from traditional to whole language approaches.

- **The New Advocate**
4 issues per year/subscription $27
The New Advocate
480 Washington Street
Norwood, MA 02062

Noted authors, illustrators, and educators share their perspectives on children's literature and related issues in this outstanding literary journal. Book and media reviews are included.

Phi Delta Kappan
10 issues per year/subscription $35
Eighth & Union
PO Box 789
Bloomington, IN 47402

Concerned with issues relating to leadership, research, trends, and policy, Phi Delta Kappan (named for the educational fraternity) is a must for those truly interested in what's happening in our schools today. Contains an annual Gallup poll of this country's attitude toward public schools.

- **Primary Voices K–6**
4 issues per year/subscription $15
National Council of Teachers of English
1111 W. Kenyon Road
Urbana, IL 61801–1096

This relatively new journal for teachers (first issue, April 1993) aims to explore current thinking in literacy education and to promote open discussion. Each themed issue is completely written and edited by outstanding educators of a "literacy community" who propose their topic of interest to NCTE. Some topics of past issues include: "Asking Questions/Making Meaning: Inquiry Based Instruction" (Fall 1992), "Making Meaning Through Writing: Writing to Learn" (August 1993), and "Challenge for Change: Theme Cycles" (January 1994). This is a terrific journal—extremely high level and practical with lots of clearly presented teaching strategies. Educators are encouraged to submit a proposal for a themed issue. Submission guidelines and back issues are available.

- **The Reading Teacher**
8 issues per year/subscription U.S. $38
International Reading Association (IRA)
800 Barksdale Road

PO Box 8139
Newark, DE 19714–8139

This practical journal for preschool and elementary teachers focuses on teaching approaches and techniques and also includes reviews of children's books, tests, and other teacher resources. Subscription includes "Reading Today," a bimonthly newspaper on news of the profession.

Note that IRA sponsors an annual conference, a World Congress, as well as state and local conferences; publishes professional publications and brochures for teachers and parents; and identifies and distributes "Children's Choices"—a yearly list of books children vote as their favorites.

Teaching K–8
8 issues per year/subscription $19.77
40 Richards Avenue
Norwalk, CT 06854 (correspondence)

PO Box 54805
Boulder, CO 80323 (subscriptions)

This publication, subtitled "The professional magazine for teachers," carries columns on reading, math, science, technology, professional growth, assessment, school and classroom libraries, parenting—all written by well-known educators. It carries ten reader exchange networks, such as Art Pals, Whole Language Network, Substitute Teachers Network, and Paraprofessionals Exchange. Each issue includes reports on innovative schools and teachers throughout the country, which the editors have personally visited. It also features a monthly personal interview with well-known authors and illustrators of children's books. Editorial content includes emphasis on multiage, whole language, integrated curriculum, and professional growth.

Voices from the Middle
4 issues per year/subscription $15
National Council of Teachers of English
1111 W. Kenyon Road
Urbana, IL 61801–1096

This excellent, new journal (first issue, Fall 1994) written by a team of experienced educators is both reflective and practical and is geared to upper elementary and middle school teachers of language *arts. Each issue focuses on a curricular topic or concept. In the first themed issue, "Students Responding to Literature," the teacher-authors invite you into their classrooms, and readers see the organization, planning, student work samples, and theory-into-practice teaching. Teachers will appreciate the rich descriptions of middle school classrom practices in this journal. Educators are encouraged to write for guidelines and submit a proposal for an issue in literacy education.*

Young Children

6 issues per year/subscription $25
National Association for the Education of Young Children
1509 16th Street, NW
Washington, DC 20036–1426

Early childhood educators will find this journal to be thought provoking, informative, and supportive in the area of professional growth. Major issues and ideas in the field are discussed. Contains such items as a calendar of conferences, book reviews, Washington public policy updates, and a section of reader commentary.

Newsletters/Other Periodicals

Book Links

bimonthly magazine/subscription $20
Booklist Publications
The American Library Association
50 E. Huron St.
Chicago, IL 60611

Aptly described by its subtitle, Connecting Books, Libraries, and Classrooms, this bimonthly magazine is for teachers, librarians, parents, and anyone else who works with books and children. Each issue explores the connections between literature and the learning experience for children preschool to grade eight, and contains articles, recommended reading lists, and interviews that provide strategies for using books effectively in teaching.

The Five Owls

5 bimonthly issues per year/subscription $20
The Five Owls, Inc.
Hamline University Crossroads Center
Mailing Code MS–C1924

1536 Hewitt Avenue
St. Paul, MN 55104

This publication is intended for teachers, librarians, and parents interested in staying involved and current with the best of children's literature. Includes in-depth book reviews, practical ideas for using books with children, specialized bibliographies, and thoughtful articles, essays, and interviews.

The Kobrin Letter. Concerning Children's Books About Real People, Places and Things.

7 issues per year/subscription $12
The Kobrin Letter
732 Greer Road
Palo Alto, CA 94303

This is the only publication that deals exclusively with the review and recommendation of children's nonfiction. Two or three themes or topics are dealt with in each issue, and information from six to eight books per topic is included. For example, one issue dealt with "Trees" and "About AIDS" and included information from approximately six books for each topic.

Portfolio, The Newsletter of Arts PROPEL

[five back issues published from 1987–1989 (Vol. I, nos. 1–5)/$2 (nos. 1, 2, and 4); $2.25 (no. 3); $2.50 (no. 5)]
Harvard University
Graduate School of Education
Harvard Project Zero
323 Longfellow Hall, Appian Way
Cambridge, MA 02138

This outstanding, occasional newsletter of the Arts PROPEL project (the five-year collaborative effort that involved artists and researchers from Harvard Project Zero and Educational Testing Service, as well as students, teachers, and administrators from the Pittsburgh Public Schools) shares experiences from the project and offers insightful articles on creative approaches to learning and assessment and evaluation in middle and senior high school classrooms. Lots of terrific information on portfolio assessment.

Rethinking Schools

Rethinking Schools Limited
4 issues per year/subscription $12.50

1001 East Keefe Avenue
Milwaukee, WI 53212

Rethinking Schools *is a nonprofit, activist, independent newspaper published by Milwaukee-area teachers. This provocative, thoughtful publication focuses on local and national reform in urban elementary and secondary schools. Articles and issues connect classroom practice with broad policy issues and are written by educators from all over the country. Recent issues dealt with such topics as teaching for social justice, school choice in education, charter schools, the role of teachers' unions, multicultural videos and audiotapes, and funding education. This is an important publication for dealing with equity and social-justice issues in a forthright, constructive manner. Back issues and bibliographies are available.*

• **Teachers Networking: The Whole Language Newsletter**
4 issues per year/subscription $15 (U.S.); $18 (Canada)
For group membership at one address, each subscription over ten ordered is half price.
Richard C. Owen Publishers, Inc.
PO Box 585
Katonah, NY 10536

Features thought-provoking articles by leading whole language educators as well as reviews of professional and children's literature, issues of concern and interest to parents and educators, and a whole language calendar of upcoming conferences. A particularly well-done newsletter.

• **The WEB: Wonderfully Exciting Books**
3 issues per year/subscription $10
The Web, Ohio State University College of Education
200 Ramseyer Hall, 29 West Woodruff
Columbus, OH 43210–1177

Comprehensive book reviews, which include excellent teaching ideas, are presented by teachers and librarians. The center spread in each issue—a teaching web focusing on activities centered on a book, group of books, genre, or theme—is especially helpful for integrating literature across the curriculum. For more examples

of well-done "webs," back issues of The WEB *are available for purchase.*

The Whole Idea
4 issues per year/subscription $12 (U.S.); $15 (Canada)
The Wright Group
19201 120th Ave NE
Bothell, WA 98011–9512

Practical articles, activities, and ideas for teachers interested in whole language. Includes ideas from practicing teachers as well as well-known educators. Very useful for the elementary classroom teacher.

Whole Language Special Interest Group of IRA Newsletter
2 issues per year with membership/$5 (U.S.)
WLSIG Newsletter
Margaret Y. Phinney
740 Cherokee Avenue
St. Paul, MN 55107

This thoughtfully literate newsletter has lead articles by well-known whole language educators as well as reprints of newsworthy articles about whole language. Also includes news of the teaching profession as related to whole language, reviews of recent whole language materials, and a calendar of future events.

The Whole Language Umbrella Newsletter
4 issues per year/subscription included with membership in the Whole Language Umbrella, a confederation of Whole Language support groups and individuals ($25 U.S. member; $30 Canadian member per year). Group memberships ($25 U.S. or $30 Canadian plus $1 either per member) include 5 subscriptions, additional subscriptions $3 U.S. or $3.25 Canadian.

The Whole Language Umbrella
Membership Office
PO Box 2029
Bloomington, IN 47402–2029

The newsletter describes the activities and business of the Whole Language Umbrella, primarily helping whole language teachers and support groups to network with each other. Includes articles and news about whole language issues and teaching, information about other newsletters and support groups in the United

States and Canada, support group publications, and upcoming conferences, including the annual Whole Language Umbrella conference.

Literacy Extension Resources

Annotations with Vera Milz

The following resources are ones I, Vera Milz, and other teachers have found especially useful for supporting our teaching and professional growth. Resources in this section can be used to support the integration of the language arts across the curriculum. You will also find much information and many ideas for selecting, using, and responding to quality literature. For your easy reference, this edition of "Literacy Extension Resources" lists separate categories for assessment and evaluation, spelling, math, social studies, science, and author/illustrator. There is also a separate listing for parent resources to promote parent communication and education. Check with your school and public librarians, other teachers, local bookstores, and journals for additional, new, and updated resources for teaching. All resources listed are available in paperback unless otherwise noted.

American Library Association Publishing Services. 50 East Huron Street, Chicago, IL 60611.

Publishes professional books for teachers and librarians and Booklinks *(see annotation, p. 58b). Some recent resources include* Against Borders: Promoting Books for a Multicultural World *by Hazel Rochman (1993),* Handbook for Storytellers *by Caroline Feller Bauer (1993),* The Newbery and Caldecott Award: A Guide to the Medal and Honor Books *(1993, continually updated),* Mock Newbery and Caldecott Election Kit *by Kathleen Staerkel, Linda Callaghan, Nancy Hackett, and Susan Reisner;* Genre Favorites for Young Adults *by Sally Estes (ed.), and* Venture into Cultures: A Resource Book of Multicultural Material and Programs, *edited by Carla Hayden (1992). Because neither Heinemann nor I was able to obtain review copies from ALA, I was unable to read and review these titles.*

Bare Books. 1987. Racine, WI: Treetop Publishing.

Publishes reasonably priced blank books (about $1 each) and sturdy line guides for writing in the blank books. Each Bare Book contains twenty-eight blank white pages and a hard cover that measures 6 3/8 by 8 1/8 inches. Minimum order ten books. Adds a nice touch for special projects.

Baskwill, Jane, and Steve Baskwill. 1991. *Language Arts Sourcebook: Grades 5 & 6.* Richmond Hill, Ontario: Scholastic Canada. (hardbound)

Four themes and accompanying four week plans for "In the Days of the Knights," "Imagine That," "Take Flight," and "The Sea" make up the major part of this resource. I found the section on routines, which includes minidemonstration routines and activity routines, especially helpful and applicable across the elementary grades. See also Language Arts Sourcebook: Grades 3–4 *(1988) and* Language Arts Sourcebook: Grades 1–2 *(1986). Three-ring binder format. Expensive.*

• Bauer, Marion Dane. 1992. *What's Your Story? A Young Person's Guide to Writing Fiction.* New York: Clarion.

Written for upper elementary and middle school students, this terrific book lets young writers "inside" the fiction writing process. Well-known author Marion Bauer gives a wealth of specific, workable suggestions for getting and developing ideas for stories, for creating realistic characters, and for writing a satisfying story from beginning to end. I plan to lend this book to students who show promise and interest in fiction writing. Bauer's book will also enable me to do a better job teaching fiction writing, a difficult genre for many students.

Beaty, Janice J. 1994. *Picture Book Storytelling: Literature Activities for Young Children.* Fort Worth, TX: Harcourt Brace.

This is a delightful book filled with ways to bring young children and picture books together. Nearly 200 picture books are described, along with ways to extend the enjoyment with songs, projects, and games. Many suggestions are given to enhance the presentation of the books through storytelling, and the books are categorized into themes such as dinosaurs, food, space, families, and beauty. A feature I especially enjoyed was the "Authors of Interest" statements scattered throughout the book. Interesting facts about authors and illustrators were given that I could take back to my classroom to share with my students. (V.M.)

- Benedict, Susan, and Lenore Carlisle (eds.). 1992. *Beyond Words: Picture Books for Older Readers and Writers.* Portsmouth, NH: Heinemann.

    As an adult reader, I have always loved picture books. It always seemed a shame to hear a librarian label them "baby" books, and encourage children to move on to chapter books. This book is an especially welcome addition to my professional library as it eloquently argues that picture books belong to all ages. Within its pages, teachers of various grade levels show how they use picture books in their reading/writing programs. Several authors and illustrators provide a glimpse into their creative worlds, while two teenage writers detail how they use picture books to enhance their own writing processes. This is an especially helpful resource for teachers of older students, but there are plenty of ideas for every grade level. (V.M.)

Bishop, Rudine Sims (ed.). 1994. *Kaleidoscope: A Multicultural Booklist for Grades K–8.* Urbana, IL: National Council of Teachers of English.

    Over 400 books published between 1990 and 1992 explore the lives of people of color, primarily African-Americans, Asian-Americans, Hispanic Americans/Latinos, and Native Americans. Books are grouped and annotated by genre or theme rather than by cultural group and include nonfiction, fiction, picture books, poetry, biography, folktales, myths, and legends. Indexes and multicultural resources are particularly helpful for developing teaching units and locating specific books.

- Blatt, Gloria T. (ed.). 1993. *Once upon a Folktale: Capturing the Folklore Process with Children.* New York: Teachers College Press.

    Outstanding contributors—such as Bette Bosma, Patricia Cianciolo, Eric Kimmel, and Margaret Read MacDonald—share how they use folklore to engage and educate children. Folklore, the oldest form of literature, relishes the oral tradition and is the telling of old fairy tales, myths, rhymes, jingles, family stories, urban stories. Believing that, through folklore, we understand literature, and that "folklore fits the intellectual and emotional development of children" (p. 5), the authors give a convincing rationale and a myriad of possibilities for using folklore in the classroom, the home, and the community. Bibliographies of folklore materials are included. Terrific ideas and plans for the classroom.

Bohning, Gerry, Ann Phillips, and Sandra Bryant. 1993. *Literature on the Move: Making and Using Pop-Up and Lift-Flap Books.* Englewood, CO: Teacher Ideas Press.

    This resource book offers guidelines for making eight basic pop-up and lift-flap action books, along with numerous variations for you to try with your students. The last part of the book offers many creative ideas that teachers can use to develop thematic units. They are organized by topic and include children's books, as well as springboards for reading/writing projects. Some of the topics are biographies, animals, holidays, sports, and transportation. The directions are so simple and well-written that I have been able to put the book out in my second-grade classroom as an idea book for children to use as they "publish" their stories. (V.M.)

Bosma, Bette. 1992. *Fairy Tales, Fables, Legends, and Myths: Using Folk Literature in Your Classroom.* 2nd ed. New York: Teachers College Press.

    For the elementary and intermediate levels, this useful resource can be used to heighten children's awareness of and appreciation for folk literature. Four types of folktales—fairy tales, animal tales, legends, and myths—are explained and elaborated upon. Suggested activities include involving students in reading, writing, storytelling, dramatizing, improvising, and illustrating folktales. This second edition includes new information on multicultural folktales and an extensive bibliography of recommended folk literature with annotations for 180 books. Lots of ideas and lesson plans for developing units on folk literature are included.

Brinkerhoff, Stevie Auld. 1993. *Linking: Developing Strategic Readers and Writers in the Primary Classroom.* Grand Rapids, MI: Michigan Reading Association (P.O. Box 7509, 49510).

In an easy-to-read, personal tone, Brinkerhoff and colleagues have put together a useful, eighty-page spiral-bound booklet to help teachers "make the transition from teaching skills to teaching with a strategy focus." Building on the work of Marie Clay and other practitioners, Brinkerhoff discusses and demonstrates early reading strategies in a manner that is helpful and specific to early primary grade teachers.

Bromley, Karen. 1993. *Journaling: Engagements in Reading, Writing, and Thinking.* New York: Scholastic Professional Books.

An elementary teacher has compiled pre-K through high school teachers' experiences using many different types of journals to suggest ways to build a journal-writing program. Some of the journals that are described are the buddy journal, learning log, double-entry journal, home-school journal, writer's journal, and daily group journal. Especially useful to teachers who are new to journal writing and to those looking for fresh ideas. Many examples from student journals are provided.

Bryant, Patricia, and Luceille Werner (compilers). 1992. *Reading and Writing . . . Can Be a Child's Talk Written Down.* Updated ed. Peotone, IL: Early Prevention of School Failure.

Written to assist kindergarten and first-grade teachers to connect reading and writing through language experience and whole language approaches, this sourcebook is full of activities, thematic ideas, and projects for teachers who want to move away from programs and worksheets. Lots of photographs and visuals make the book a functional resource.

Canavan, Diane D., and LaVonne H. Sanborn. 1992. *Using Children's Books in Reading/Language Arts Programs: A How-To-Do-It Manual for School and Public Libraries.* New York: Neal-Schuman Publishers.

The authors have selected quality trade books to use in the K–8 reading program. Sections include many titles and annotations of books for developing beginning reading, vocabulary through word play, text comprehension, language concepts, and literary awareness. This 216-page resource is particularly helpful for teachers moving towards a literature approach. Lots of ideas for using children's books.

Chatton, Barbara. 1993. *Using Poetry Across the Curriculum: A Whole Language Approach.* Phoenix, AZ: Oryx Press.

This amazing reference shows teachers how to integrate poetry across the curriculum. Two thematic units, "Eats" and "Conversation," are given for use in the classroom. Each is filled with suggested poems, books, activities, and projects. Although the purpose of the book is to cross curricular lines, for convenience, most of the chapters have been arranged by content areas, such as science, mathematics, social studies, language arts, health, and music. Each chapter is further divided by subject with many poems listed, along with bibliographic information to help you locate the appropriate poem. The index in the back of the book is invaluable in locating a particular poem, or the work of a certain poet. (V.M.)

The Children's Book Council, Inc. 568 Broadway, New York, NY 10012.

Publishes a newsletter with information about children's books, book publishers, and inexpensive publishers' materials. Sells pamphlets, posters, and bookmarks that support reading and writing; sponsors an annual Children's Book Week and distributes accompanying materials. Distributes annually: "Children's Choices" (a yearly selection of newly published books that children prefer), "Outstanding Science Tradebooks for Children" (first published in spring issue of Science and Children), *and "Notable Children's Trade Books in the Field of Social Studies" (first published in spring issue of* Social Education).

Cole, Joanna (compiler). 1989. *Anna Banana: 101 Jump-Rope Rhymes,* illustrated by Alan Tiegreen. New York: Morrow Junior Books. (Beech Tree Paperback)

Traditional jump-rope rhymes are great for shared reading and chanting in the classroom and on the playground. Students can also be encouraged to write their own jump-rope rhymes. Sources for finding additional jump-rope rhymes are included.

Cullinan, Bernice E. (ed.). 1993. *Children's Voices: Talk in the Classroom; Fact and Fiction: Literature Across the Curriculum;* and *Pen in Hand: Children Become Writers.* Newark, DE: International Reading Association.

Noting that children's literature is now widely used in classrooms, these three slim volumes with contributions by notable educators give suggestions and examples for meaningfully connecting literature with reading-writing-speaking processes. Some of the many activities that are discussed are literature circles, storytelling, creative drama (in Children's Voices), *literature in the science and math program, nonfiction in the social studies program, diversity education (in* Fact and Fiction), *literature and children's writing, reading assessment through written response, and writing nonfiction (in* Pen in Hand). *An excellent, practical resource for teachers.*

Cutting, Brian. 1990. *Getting Started in Whole Language.* Bothell, WA: The Wright Group.

This is an excellent, all-purpose, highly practical resource (120 pp.) to see, feel, and read about how a whole language classroom looks and functions. Although this resource is based on the commercially produced "Sunshine Books," the verbal and visual examples for shared reading experiences, writing connections, language experiences, paired reading, independent reading, scheduling, and evaluation are very useful to any K–1 teacher interested in whole language.

Cutting, Brian, with Helen Dupree. 1988. *Language Is Fun: Teacher's Book.* Level 2. Bothell, WA: The Wright Group.

This practical collection of ideas for K–2 whole language classrooms extends to drama, art, and literature. Particularly useful are the colorful photographs and samples of children's work from New Zealand classrooms. While many of the literature extension ideas stem from specific books in a reading series, ideas on the resource's theme "I Can . . ." are applicable across the curriculum.

Danielson, Kathy Everts, and Jan LaBonty. 1994. *Integrating Reading and Writing Through Children's Literature.* Boston: Allyn and Bacon.

This 251-page resource focuses on ways to use literature in the integration of reading and writing. In addition to extensive children's literature bibliographies, the authors offer excellent background information on current views of reading and writing as well as many ideas and sample activities for using literature to enhance reading comprehension, responding to literature through writing, involving students with poetry, and dealing with skills and assessment. While some ideas for using the literature are overstructured and directive, teachers can choose the ones that suit their contexts. Especially helpful to teachers who are beginning to use literature as the mainstay of the reading/writing program and for teachers seeking additional ideas.

Davies, Anne, Colleen Politano, and Caren Cameron. 1993. *Making Themes Work: Building Connections.* Winnipeg, Manitoba: Peguis.

For teachers who want to promote learning through meaningful "themes" that capitalize on children's interests, this seventy-six page book is full of practical ideas for beginning, planning, exploring, and evaluating the thematic topic under discussion.

Day, Frances Ann (compiler). 1994. *Multicultural Voices in Contemporary Literature.* Portsmouth, NH: Heinemann.

Information about thirty-nine inspiring multicultural authors and illustrators, their noted works, and optional activities to go along with designated books are included in this comprehensive teacher reference. This is a great resource for planning author or illustrator units and for balancing the literature program with diversity. Also, teachers who struggle with ways to meaningfully extend the literature will find excellent models in the suggested optional activities.

Doiron, Ray. May 1994. "Using Nonfiction in a Read-Aloud Program: Letting the Facts Speak for Themselves." *The Reading Teacher*, pp. 616–624.

Because fiction predominates in the selections teachers make for read-aloud and discussion books in the classroom, this is an important article for balancing our literacy programs. In addition to presenting a convincing case for reading more nonfiction, Doiron provides a starter, annotated bibliography of nonfiction read-alouds.

Eisele, Beverly. 1991. *Managing the Whole Language Classroom: A Complete Teaching Resource Guide for K–6 Teachers*. Cypress, CA: Creative Teaching Press.

If you are a teacher who is just beginning to move to a whole language philosophy, you will enjoy this "how-to" book. It contains basic information on creating a classroom environment, suggestions for professional development, ideas for scheduling the school day, ways to plan instruction, ways to organize classroom materials and supplies, how to evaluate, and ways to inform parents and colleagues. There are lots of guides and forms that can be adapted for classroom use. Very well illustrated and teacher friendly! (V.M.)

Fairfax, Barbara, and Adela Garcia. 1992. *Read! Write! Publish! Making Books in the Classroom Grades 1–5*. Cypress, CA: Creative Teaching Press.

Materials, techniques, and directions are given for making all kinds of books. Teachers looking for creative ways for children to publish will find many clearly written and illustrated ideas that are easy to put into practice.

Fox, Carol, and Margery Sauer. 1989. *Celebrate Literature*. Logan, IA: The Perfection Form Company.

These spiral-bound, comprehensive resource books for each grade level from kindergarten through grade six promote the use of a literature curriculum. Each literature unit is presented by genre—poetry, picture books, traditional literature, fiction, nonfiction, biography—and includes goals and objectives, background information, author study, featured books and resources, lots of student activities, and evaluation activities. Lots of good ideas for the classroom teacher.

Freeman, Evelyn B., and Diane Goetz Person (eds.). 1992. *Using Nonfiction Trade Books in the Elementary Classroom: From Ants to Zeppelins*. Urbana, IL: National Council of Teachers of English.

Informational books are highlighted in this fine collection of articles in which the genre itself is explained, its place in the elementary curriculum is considered, and strategies to use it in the classroom are given. Several award-winning authors, such as Russell Freedman and Patricia Lauber, reflect on their experiences in writing nonfiction. In other chapters, practitioners share how these books are used in their classrooms. The index of titles and authors is helpful in locating a particular book on a topic your class is studying. A listing of Nonfiction Book Awards is useful in finding the highest quality books of this genre. (V.M.)

• Gilles Carol, Mary Bixby, Paul Crowley, et al. (eds.). 1988. *Whole Language Strategies for Secondary Students*. Katonah, NY: Richard C. Owen.

This 208-page resource is very useful to the middle school and secondary teacher wishing to understand and apply whole language teaching strategies in the classroom. The first section of the book lays the theoretical foundation for whole language. The second section consists of specific strategy lessons from whole language classrooms that tie theory and practice together. Each full-page strategy lesson contains the rationale for the lesson, specific procedures, and extensions and variations on the lesson. Strategy lessons encompass literature, the content areas, reading and writing, computers, and other areas.

Goforth, Frances S., and Carolyn V. Spillman. 1994. *Using Folk Literature in the Classroom: Encouraging Children to Read and Write.* Phoenix, AZ: Oryx Press.

This book was written for teachers to encourage children to make connections with literature and respond to it. The first two chapters provide a background for the study of folk literature, and the theoretical base for the literary transaction process. The remaining chapters present summaries of fifty-four stories and verses from twenty countries around the world. The stories are organized by thematic units, such as magical animals, overcoming odds, special gifts, and many more, along with instructional strategies and activities. As I looked over this book, some of the tales were familiar, but many were new to me. This is definitely a book that will stretch your knowledge of folk literature, and expand your use of it in the classroom. (V.M.)

Green, Joseph. 1993. *The Word Wall: Teaching Vocabulary Through Immersion.* Markham, Ontario: Pippin Publishing, and Portsmouth, NH: Heinemann.

A sixth-grade classroom teacher tells how a Word Wall, initially posted for room decoration, became the focus of his curriculum and a terrific way to expand students' vocabulary. Green describes how he uses Word Walls as a daily tool for teaching phonics, grammar, spelling, new vocabulary and as a thesaurus and spellcheck. Some teachers will find the approach too structured, but most will be able to meaningfully adapt ideas to their own contexts. Applicable to elementary and secondary classrooms.

Green, Pamela. 1992. *A Matter of Fact: Using Factual Texts in the Classroom.* Winnipeg, Manitoba: Peguis (distributors).

This theory-into-practice book is for the primary-grades teacher who wants students to read and write competently in a range of factual genres such as reports, descriptions, explanations, and procedural texts. Lots of classroom-created charts and children's work samples included. Applicable to the intermediate grades.

Hall, Susan. 1990, 1994. *Using Picture Storybooks to Teach Literary Devices: Recommended Books for Children and Young Adults.* Volumes 1 and 2. Phoenix, AZ: Oryx Press.

The primary purpose for a picture book must always remain in the pleasure of its reading, but, in addition, older students can begin to utilize these books to enhance their own writing skill. These two books are very useful in locating literary elements used by various authors, such as flashback, inference, irony, simile, metaphor, and others. Each reference contains actual quotes from the cited picture book, and is cross-referenced to other devices that the author uses. In volume 2, the author also shows how students can learn to appreciate the color, power, and nuances of picture book art while learning about literary devices. (V.M.)

• Hamilton, Martha, and Mitch Weiss. 1990. *Children Tell Stories: A Teaching Guide.* Katonah, NY: Richard C. Owen.

The authors, professional storytellers, demonstrate how to teach children to tell stories—especially simple folktales—and to make storytelling an essential part of the curriculum. The benefits of storytelling by children, including improvement in self-esteem, expressive language skills, group dynamics, and new learnings, are convincing. Many exercises and strategies for teaching children all aspects of storytelling are clearly delineated. Handouts for students and parents, as well as extensive bibliographies, are included. The book is so well organized and specific, you will feel storytelling is possible and desirable for your classroom. An outstanding resource for all grade levels.

Hart-Hewins, Linda, and Jan Wells. 1992. *Read It in the Classroom: Organizing an Interactive Language Arts Program, Grades 4–9.* Portsmouth, NH: Heinemann.

This little handbook is designed to help teachers incorporate literature into their reading programs. Guidance for theme development, related books, ways of organizing the classroom, and record-keeping forms are given. A series of bibliog-

raphies list books that can be used to focus on a particular topic. The suggestions can be easily adapted to younger or older students. (V.M.)

Heller, Ruth. 1991. *Up, Up and Away: A Book About Adverbs.* New York: Grosset & Dunlap. (Sandcastle)

This gorgeous picture book uses playful, rhymed text to introduce students to adverbs. A wonderful resource for sensitizing students in the intermediate grades and beyond to the interesting use of adverbs. See other equally engaging, language concept/vocabulary books by Ruth Heller: A Cache of Jewels and Other Collective Nouns *and* Many Luscious Lollipops: A Book About Adjectives.

Hill, Susan. 1993. *Jump for Joy: More Raps & Rhymes.* Winnipeg, Manitoba: Peguis.

Hill has selected raps, chants, and rhymes for reading aloud, having fun, and building group cohesion in the classroom. Builds on her earlier Raps & Rhymes *(Peguis, 1990).*

Hill, Susan. 1992. *Readers Theatre: Performing the Text.* Winnipeg, Manitoba: Peguis (distributors).

Hill gives lots of examples on how to bring poems, picture books, and stories to life through Readers Theatre (see Invitations, *p. 98). Useful for getting more oral language, drama, and performance of texts into the primary classroom.*

Hurst, Carol Otis. 1990. *Once Upon a Time . . .: An Encyclopedia for Successfully Using Literature with Young Children.* Allen, TX: DLM. (hardbound)

This comprehensive, spiral-bound resource (370 pp., 8½ by 11 inches) by a highly knowledgeable children's librarian is written and compiled to assist teachers who don't have time to research authors, illustrators, and themes. The book is well organized into four sections: "Authors and Illustrators," "Individual Picture Books," "Themes," and "Special Pages." Each prominent author and illustrator listing (there are about forty-five) includes a mailing address (when available), biography, books published, awards received, relevant topics to "notice and talk about," and activity

ideas for selected books. The "Special Pages" section includes annotated listings of patterned books, wordless books, Big Books, whole language and children's literature resource books, poetry resources, children's records and tapes, children's magazines, books about color, math, social studies, science, the seasons, and more. A wealth of valuable and useful information. Expensive.

Irvine, Joan. 1992. *How to Make Super Pop-Ups.* New York: Morrow Junior Books.

For teachers who are interested in making different types of pop-up books, this resource gives easy-to-follow instructions with clear illustrations. The book includes needed materials, directions for cutting, folding, and measuring and many examples of pop-up projects. See also, How to Make Pop-Ups *(1987).*

Jenkins, Esher C., and Mary C. Austin. 1987. *Literature for Children About Asians and Asian Americans: Analysis and Annotated Bibliography, with Additional Readings for Adults.* New York: Greenwood Press.

Although this text has not been updated, it is still the most comprehensive resource for books by and about Asians (as of 1994), and therefore, it is included. In addition to recommended literature, the book includes criteria for selecting books for a cross-cultural curriculum.

Jensen, Julie M., and Nancy L. Roser (eds.). 1993. *Adventuring With Books: A Booklist for Pre-K–Grade 6.* 10th ed. Urbana, IL: National Council of Teachers of English.

Nearly 1800 annotations of books published between 1988 and 1992 are included in this latest edition. The book is designed to help anyone introducing books to children to choose those of literary and artistic merit, and it is a sampling of the over 20,000 books actually published during that period. The introduction is especially interesting as the editors note their observations of current trends in the publishing field. The annotations are grouped under headings, such as Celebrations, Sciences and Mathematics, Historical Fiction, Poetry, and more. In addition, the book has a listing of selected literary awards, publishers' addresses, and descriptions of popular booklists. (V.M.)

Johnson, Paul. 1992. *A Book of One's Own: Developing Literacy Through Making Books*. Portsmouth, NH: Heinemann.

For a very complete look at every stage of the book-creating process, you will want to check this book. It has everything from simple folded-paper books to hardcover, bound books. There are lots of examples and step-by-step instructions for you to make books with your students. Every classroom publishing center needs one. (V.M.)

Johnson, Paul. 1993. *Literacy Through the Book Arts*. Portsmouth, NH: Heinemann.

With paper, pens, and a pair of scissors, you can learn over fifty ways to make a book. Johnson believes that children can combine writing and visual communication through the book arts, and this book is filled with examples of wonderful student creations. Two basic books are explained in detail, along with many variations: the Concertina from China, and Origami from Japan. No matter what grade you teach, there are plenty of ideas to get your students started on creating unique books to share their writings. (V.M.)

Kaufman, Ronne L. (executive ed.). 1990. *Innovations: Teaching with Literature in the Classroom*. New York: Scholastic.

Lesson plan guides have been developed to go along with quality books such as The Hundred Dresses *by Eleanor Estes,* Nettie's Trip South *by Ann Turner, and* Lon Po Po *by Ed Young. Each guide (there are about fifty available) includes a story overview, information about the genre and the author/illustrator, and many suggested activities for reading and reacting to the book. While there are too many activities suggested, teachers can choose the ones that will work best for them.*

Kenney, Anne, Lori Morgan, Jane Owen, Chris Sherman, and Russell Walsh (team leaders). 1992. *Teens' Favorite Books: Young Adults' Choices 1987–1992*. Newark, DE: International Reading Association.

For anyone looking to choose a high-interest book for a teenager, this useful re-source includes descriptions of over 100 books for young adult readers that are grouped by subject. For recommended books for children aged 4–13, see Kids' Favorite Books: Children's Choices 1989–1991, *also published by the International Reading Association.*

• King, Laurie, and Dennis Stovall. 1992. *Classroom Publishing: A Practical Guide to Enhancing Student Literacy*. Hillsboro, OR: Blue Heron. (Also available from the International Reading Association.)

This magnificent guide to publishing for grades K–12 is one you will not want to miss. It is packed with practical information and limitless possibilities for publishing. The first section of this 224-page guide, "Tales from the Classroom," contains rich examples and successful publishing stories from teachers in diverse K–12 classrooms. The second section, "Publishing: Who, What, When, Where, Why & How," contains a history of modern publishing, a description of how it's done, career options, how to get funding for student projects, and legal and social issues of publishing. The last section of the book, "Resources," provides detailed lists and addresses of contests, publishing programs, markets for young writers, and an extensive bibliography of sources of further information. Even if you are an experienced writing/publishing teacher, you will find inspiration, new ideas, and much to apply in your own classroom from this fascinating, useful resource.

Kruse, Ginny Moore, and Kathleen T. Horning. 1991. *Multicultural Literature for Children and Young Adults*. 3rd ed. University of Wisconsin-Madison: Cooperative Children's Book Center.

Summaries and publishing information of carefully selected literature by and about African-Americans, American Indians, Asian-Americans, and Hispanic Americans make up this notable bibliography. Books are grouped in sixteen broad categories, such as "History, People and Places," "Seasons and Celebrations," "Issues in Today's World," "Biographies," and "Fiction for Teenagers." Appendices include authors and illustrators of color, a listing of the titles categorized by ethnic or cultural groups, annotations of recommended resources, and a public policy statement.

Larrick, Nancy. 1991. *Let's Do a Poem! Introducing Poetry to Children.* New York: Delacorte Press.

This is a handbook with many ideas for bringing poetry and children together. Complete poems are found in each chapter, along with suggestions for movement, music, drama, and pantomime. I especially like the author's suggestions for interactive reading between two or more children. A list of poetry books, by the poets whose works are cited in the book, is found in the back, along with indexes by author, title, subject, and first lines of the poem. This is a valuable resource for teachers who want their students to come to love the sound and feel of poetry. You'll never just "read" a poem again after reading this book. (V.M.)

• Ledoux, Denis. 1993. *Turning Memories into Memoirs: A Handbook for Writing Lifestories.* Lisbon Falls, ME: Soleil Press, and Portsmouth, NH: Heinemann.

Noting the importance of story for entertainment, reassurance, and making meaning, Ledoux encourages us to connect with our own lifestories and write them down. The step-by-step strategies and exercises that are demonstrated make it possible for us and our students to write successful lifestories from our family histories. An intriguing book!

Levine, Michael. 1993. *The Address Book: How to Reach Anyone Who Is Anyone.* 6th ed. New York: Putnam.

This book is continually updated to provide current mailing addresses of thousands of interesting and famous people and organizations. Teachers and students find this a motivating letter-writing resource for the writing classroom. See also Levine's The Environmental Address Book *and* The Kid's Address Book.

Lipson, Eden Ross. 1991. *The New York Times Parent's Guide to Children's Books.* New York: Random House.

This guide of "best books" published in

the United States has been written "to help you look for the next book to give to your favorite child." Many book titles, accompanied by brief descriptions, are listed alphabetically by title in each of the following categories: wordless books, picture books, story books, early reading books, middle reading books, and young adult books. Thirty-four indexes allow looking up books in multiple ways. Preschool through middle school (through grade nine) teachers will find this a useful reference to share with parents.

Lynch-Brown, Carol, and Carl M. Tomlinson. 1993. *Essentials of Children's Literature.* Needham Heights, MA: Allyn and Bacon.

This is a wonderful resource text (350 pp.) for learning about and using children's trade books in the classroom and for planning literature units. Lots of background information and recommendations are provided for notable poetry books, picture books, traditional literature, science fiction, realistic fiction, nonfiction, multicultural literature, and authors in various genres. Appendices include an extensive listing of award-winning books, popular children's magazines, and professional resources. A wealth of information for K–8 teachers using a literature approach is provided in this practical, readable text.

McClure, Amy A., and Janice V. Cristo (eds.). 1994. *Inviting Children's Responses to Literature: Guides to 57 Notable Books.* Urbana, IL: National Council of Teachers of English.

Teachers who move to a literature approach and feel they are not doing enough with a book will feel comforted by the solid, yet minimalist, activities included in this resource. Each brief book guide includes suggested grade levels, a plot summary, teaching suggestions, and related books. The "Introduction" and the guides provide rationale and ideas for deepening readers' responses to text through conversation, reading, writing, and listening.

Macon, James M., Diane Bewell, and Mary-Ellen Vogt. 1991. *Responses to Literature Grades K–8.* Newark, DE: International Reading Association.

For teachers who have moved, or are moving, to using a literature approach and trade books as the foundation of the language arts program, this twenty-nine page booklet provides specific support on how to respond meaningfully to literature. The authors discuss theories of response to literature, engagement activities, and management issues. Teachers will appreciate and use the sample writing activities that are included.

Miller-Lachmann, Lynn. 1992. *Our Family, Our Friends, Our World: An Annotated Guide to Significant Multicultural Books for Children and Teenagers.* New Providence, NJ: R.R. Bowker. (hardbound)

This extensive reference text (710 pages) provides a critical bibliography and reference guide for multicultural fiction and nonfiction for children and young adults. Acknowledging that "many of the best multicultural works have shortcomings and blind spots" the authors point out the biases and inaccuracies in these texts so that "with the help of sensitive adults, young people will learn to read critically and to look behind stereotypes to the richness, diversity, and universal elements within each culture" (xi). A wealth of information that is helpful to any educator involved in selecting multicultural books for purchase or use.

Moir, Hughes, Melissa Cain, and Leslie Prosak-Beres (eds.). 1992. *Collected Perspectives: Choosing and Using Books for the Classroom.* 2nd ed. Norwood, MA: Christopher-Gordon.

Over 1000 children's books written between 1984 and 1990 are reviewed in depth in this book. Curriculum suggestions, related books on similar topics, and resources are given for each book. The books are organized according to audience and genre, and an extensive subject index will be very useful for thematic study planning. This is a book written by educators who work daily with children, and their suggestions are very useful to busy teachers. Though the book is expensive for a teacher to purchase singly, it is well worth requesting as an addition to

the school library, or asking colleagues to go together to purchase a copy for shared use. (V.M.)

Monson, Dianne (project chair). 1994. *Teachers' Favorite Books for Kids: Teachers' Choices 1989–1993.* Newark, DE: International Reading Association.

This annotated list of more than 150 books of high literary quality for K–8 classrooms is a great guide for selecting and using outstanding books. "These are books that might not be discovered or fully appreciated by children without introduction by a knowledgeable adult." A fine source for families too. (IRA also publishes Children's Choices *and* Young Adults' Choices.*)*

Morgan, Norah, and Juliana Saxton. 1991. *Teaching, Questioning and Learning.* London and New York: Routledge.

This unique text offers elementary through postsecondary teachers models, techniques, activities and lots of detailed examples to promote relevant, appropriate, and substantial questioning in the classroom. The authors believe "effective teaching depends primarily upon the teacher's skill in being able to ask questions which generate different kinds of learning." They classify questions into three categories: questions that elicit information, questions that shape understanding, and questions that press for reflection, and then they demonstrate limitless possibilities within these categories. This practical text is particularly useful and specific for getting the language of good questioning into the classroom and for promoting effective classroom discourse.

Moss, Joy F. 1994. *Using Literature in the Middle Grades: A Thematic Approach.* Norwood, MA: Christopher-Gordon.

For use in reading-writing classrooms in grades 4–8, the author has developed integrated literature units (focus units) that are organized around a topic, genre, theme, or narrative element. Each focus unit includes a variety of related texts, reading experiences, dialogue groups, and responses. Complete, detailed plans and suggested activities are included. Some of the focus units and chapters are: "Friendship Stories," "Modern Fairy Tales and Traditional Literature," "Internal Conflict in Realistic Fiction," "Family Stories," and "War and Peace: Historical Fiction and Non-fiction." Each chapter/focus unit ends with a literature bibliography. A terrific resource!

Moss, Joy F. 1990. *Focus on Literature: A Context for Literacy Learning.* Katonah, NY: Richard C. Owen.

This practical text connects theory and practice and offers in-depth literature units around the following focuses: transformation tales, Baba Yaga tales, devil tales, cat tales, magic object tales, bird tales, wish tales, horse tales, Cinderella tales. Each unit includes plans for daily sessions, meaningful literature extensions, and bibliographies or tales.

NOVA Books. 1990. New York: Simon & Schuster.

Produced in association with the award-winning public television series "NOVA," these outstanding informational paperback science books on a variety of topics are a visual delight. All books include an index, and all are fascinating reading for intermediate grades upward.

- O'Toole, Mary. Illustrated by Ruth Moodie and Nel Pianta. 1993. *Relevant Reading Resources: Strategies for the Teaching of Reading.* Kew, Victoria, Australia: Yarra Publications; distributed in the U.S. by A.U.S.S.I.E. (Australian United States Services in Education, 1636 Third Avenue, #292, New York, NY 10128).

This remarkable resource offers a multitude of meaningful activities for creating a literary environment, reading to and with children, organizing a language program, developing positive reading attitudes, developing effective reading and learning strategies, and focusing on how texts work. Each page, which is packed with clearly written text supported by black-and-white illustrations, gives practical information and many suggested teaching activities. Teachers will love all the wonderful ideas in this unique resource! Spiral bound.

- Peck, David. 1989. *Novels of Initiation: A Guidebook for Teaching Literature to Adolescents.* New York: Teachers College Press.

This excellent guidebook for secondary teachers contains analyses of twelve American novels commonly read in secondary English classes. Each of these novels is connected by the theme of initiation, that is, the main characters move on a "perilous passage" from childhood to adulthood. Each chapter discusses a different novel and includes an analysis of the novel that encompasses story and setting, characters, themes, style, and language; teaching suggestions for discussion and writing; and other related literary works that can be used with the particular novel. The useful appendices list other American novels of initiation as well as other thematic unit possibilities with suggested novels to fit each theme.

Raffi. 1989. *The Raffi Everything Grows Songbook.* New York: Crown.

For early-childhood teachers who want to connect reading and singing, this spiral-bound book contains the printed music and words of fifteen songs to go along with Raffi's album Everything Grows. *See also* Raffi Songs to Read *for other materials on the singing-reading connection.*

Raines, Shirley C., and Robert J. Canady. 1989–1994. *Story S-T-R-E-T-C-H-E-R-S: Activities to Expand Children's Favorite Books.* Mt. Rainier, MD: Gryphon House.

Story S-T-R-E-T-C-H-E-R-S: Original Volume

More Story S-T-R-E-T-C-H-E-R-S

Story S-T-R-E-T-C-H-E-R-S for the Primary Grades

450 More Story S-T-R-E-T-C-H-E-R-S for the Primary Grades

These four volumes contain exciting lists of children's books that could be used to build a literature program in early-childhood through primary-grade classrooms. The first two books were especially written for preschool use, but many primary-grade teachers used them, and requested that the format be extended beyond first grade. The books are organized into themes such as friends, plants, science, seasons, environment, and multicultural concerns. Each cited book is summarized, and several pages of creative ideas to expand its enjoyment are listed from which teachers can pick and choose. These books are a helpful resource for lower-grade teachers who want to integrate learning across the curriculum. (V.M.)

Rasinski, Timothy V., and Cindy S. Gillespie. 1992. *Sensitive Issues: An Annotated Guide to Children's Literature K–6.* Phoenix, AZ: Oryx Press.

This is a fine reference book for teachers to find high-quality literature dealing with serious problems that children often must confront on a daily basis both in and out of school. Often I have found that when children read about someone dealing with a similar problem to their own, it can help them to begin to work through it themselves. Books and possible activities are listed for topics such as substance abuse, death, divorce, cultural differences, relocation, and nontraditional home environments. (V.M.)

Rhodes, Lynn K. (ed.). *LINK PAKS.* 1986–1994. Lakewood, CO: LINK, the Language Company.

A LINK (Language Instruction Natural to Kids) PAK includes meaningful activities to go along with a quality title for pre-K through grade seven as well as a copy of the designated book. Some suggested activities include reading and comparing other versions and other related books, and writing as a response to reading. LINK also publishes guidelines for creating your own book units.

Roettger, Doris. 1986–1992. *BOOK PROS.* Johnson, IA: Heartland Area Education Agency.

Teaching guides for notable picture story books and novels are available for kindergarten through upper elementary grades. Each guide is teacher developed and describes activities to do before reading, during reading, and after reading. These guides are helpful in the transition process to a literature program. Many activities are suggested, so you will need to be selective to keep the focus on enjoying and appreciating the literature.

Roettger, Doris. 1988–1993. *Reading Beyond the Basal Plus.* Logan, IA: Perfection Learning.

Teacher resource guides for novels for upper elementary and middle school levels. Teacher- and student-tried suggestions to involve students in using their own experiences to better understand the concepts and ideas in the story, keeping a journal, exploring the use of language, critical thinking, drama and oral language activities, exploring an author's writing styles, authentic writing activities, and exploring across-the-curriculum activities. Author information and an annotated bibliography are also included.

Sharkey, Paulette Bochnig, and Jim Roginski (eds.). 1992. *Newbery and Caldecott Medal and Honor Books in Other Media.* New York: Neal-Schuman Publishers. (hardbound)

"For librarians, teachers, and parents, this is the place to find the answer to the question, 'What filmstrips, posters, videos, etc., have been made from this Newbery/Caldecott book, or about its author or illustrator?'" (ix). Appendices in this 143-page volume include "Newbery Medal and Honor Books, 1922–1992," "Caldecott Medal and Honor Books 1938–1992," "Bibliography of Resources," "Directory of Media Producers and Distributors," and a "List of Titles by Media Formats."

Slapin, Beverly, and Doris Seale (eds.). 1992. *Through Indian Eyes: The Native Experience in Books for Children.* 3rd ed. Philadelphia, and Gabriole Island, British Columbia: New Society Publishers.

This 312-page resource on Native Americans includes texts written by Native Americans about the Native American experience. This is an excellent book for sensitizing non–Native Americans to Native American issues and points of view and for selecting materials that represent Native Americans accurately. At the heart of the book are "Book Reviews" that point out what is accurate and inaccurate to the Native culture. While my sensitivity to how

Indians are represented in literature has been greatly heightened through this text, note that parts of some book reviews seem overly emotional.

Slaughter, Judith Pollard. 1993. *Beyond Storybooks: Young Children and the Shared Book Experience.* Newark, DE: International Reading Association.

Giving credit to Don Holdaway's original work in shared-book experiences in New Zealand, detailed in his book The Foundations of Literacy *(Sydney: Ashton Scholastic, 1979), Slaughter suggests many ways to make and introduce Big Books and to use shared-book experiences across the curriculum. An excellent resource for teachers new to shared-book experience as well as those looking for additional teaching ideas.*

Smith, Jennifer. February 1988. "Periodicals That Publish Children's Original Work." *Language Arts,* pp. 202–208.

This informative journal article features twenty-two children's magazines that publish children's original writings and art work. Magazines cited are easily accessible and intended for children preschool through grade six. Information for each magazine listed includes the title, address, subscription price, frequency of publication, intended audience, and type of material accepted from children.

Stoll, Donald R. (ed.). 1994. *Magazines for Kids and Teens: A Resource for Parents, Teachers, Librarians, and Kids!* Glassboro, NJ: Educational Press Association of America, and Newark, DE: International Reading Association.

This publication alphabetically includes entries for 249 magazines for preschool through secondary age/grade levels. Each entry includes the goals and philosophy of the magazine, its subject matter, intended audience, whether or not readers' work is published, circulation, and complete publishing/ordering information. An introduction by Bernice Cullinan gives a rationale and suggestions for using magazines in the classroom and at home. Indexes include an age/grade level index, a subject index that lists magazines by topics, and maga-

zines that publish readers' work. Be sure to take advantage of all the sources that welcome and publish student writing. You and your students may first want to write to order sample copies of these appealing magazines. A great resource!

Sweet, Anne P. 1993. *State of the Art: Transforming Ideas for Teaching and Learning to Read.* Washington, DC: United States Department of Education. (Available in packages of 25 from Superintendent of Documents, P.O. Box 371954, Pittsburgh, PA 15250)

This eighteen-page booklet on effective reading instruction is organized into ten interrelated ideas "for transforming the teaching and learning of reading." Ideal to give to teachers, parents, administrators, and policymakers to promote understanding of reading as a strategic and meaning-constructing process.

Thomas, Rebecca. 1993. *Primaryplots 2: A Book Talk Guide for Use with Readers Ages 4–8.* New Providence, NJ: R.R. Bowker. (hardbound)

Thomas focuses in depth on 150 exemplary picture books published between 1988 and 1992. The book is organized into eight broad chapters focusing on such topics as self-image, folktales, illustrations, and everyday experiences. Teachers and librarians will appreciate the plot summaries, information for booktalking, suggested activities for natural extension of the books, and related book titles. See also Primaryplots *(1989). Check with R.R. Bowker for other useful, annotated book guides and bibliographic resources across the curriculum, K–12.*

Trelease, Jim (ed.). 1992. *Hey! Listen to This: Stories to Read Aloud.* New York: Penguin.

A wonderful collection of stories for reading aloud has been gathered in this volume. Each of the selections could probably be easily found in original form, but what makes this book unique is the background information given in each section about the author or the selection itself. The stories are organized by topics, such as School Days, Food for Thought, or Gigantic Creatures. When excerpts are used from chapter books, I found that Trelease has a wonderful sense of what will catch a child's interest. As I read the portions that he chose, I frequently found that my students would track down the full book and begin to read it on their own. It was a great way to introduce children to a wider range of chapter books when I knew I wouldn't have enough time to read the entire book. See also Read All About It! Great Read-Aloud Stories, Poems, and Newspaper Pieces for Preteens and Teens *(Penguin, 1993). (V.M.)*

Trelease, Jim. 1990. *The New Read-Aloud Handbook.* New York: Penguin.

The author of the inspiring and popular The Read-Aloud Handbook *offers this edition for parents and teachers. The first half of the book deals with the need to read aloud to children and how and when to carry through. Trelease offers valuable suggestions to teachers and parents to promote and implement reading aloud and reading for pleasure at home and in the classroom. The second half of the book, the "Treasury of Read-Alouds," presents an extensive listing of picture books and novels that includes brief annotations, related books, and other books by the author. A small listing of poetry books and anthologies is also included. As great read-alouds are most often memorable literature, this text is also an excellent resource for choosing books for children to read with teacher guidance or independently.*

Watt, Letty S., and Terri Parker Street. 1994. *Developing Learning Skills Through Children's Literature: An Idea Book for K–5 Classrooms and Libraries.* Volume 2. Phoenix, AZ: Oryx Press.

Don't be mislead by the title of this book, as it is very useful for the planning of a literature study. It is organized by topics, often utilizing the books of an individual author or illustrator. Each unit has suggested books and activities to develop the theme. These activities are varied to meet the needs of individual students, and suggestions are written to be used independently by the upper-grade children. The strength of this book lies in the inter-esting and unusual ways that topics are pulled together. Some of them are Presenting Information with Gail Gibbons, Feelings Shared by Cynthia Rylant, The Surreal World of Chris Van Allsburg, Character Development with Bill Wallace, and It's a Mystery to Me. If you can't get a copy for your classroom, ask your librarian to purchase one for the library. It will be well used. (V.M.)

Webb, Anne C. 1993. *Your Reading: A Booklist for Junior High and Middle School.* 9th ed. Urbana, IL: National Council of Teachers of English.

Over 600 quality fiction and nonfiction books have been selected for annotation in this latest edition. Junior high/middle school teachers looking to engage their students and update and balance their literature collections will find this a handy resource. See also other quality booklists published by NCTE that are continually updated: Adventuring with Books *(pre-K through grade six),* Books for You *(senior high), and* High Interest—Easy Reading *(junior/senior high reluctant readers).*

Wells, Jan, and Linda Hart-Hewins. 1994. *Phonics, Too! How to Teach Skills in a Balanced Language Program.* Markham, Ontario: Pembroke Publishers, and Bothell, WA: The Wright Group.

The authors demonstrate lots of activities and strategies for integrating the teaching of phonics and skills into the language-based K–3 classroom. While some teachers may find the approach too structured, teachers in transition especially will appreciate the wealth of specific information.

Whisler, Nancy, and Judy Williams. 1990. *Literature and Cooperative Learning: Pathway to Literacy.* Sacramento, CA: Literature Co-op.

K–8 teachers who want some structured, yet meaningful, activities to use with literature will find this 176-page resource very valuable. Lots of sample lessons that include strategies for cooperative learning and for moving through literature—before, during, and after reading—are included.

Wilson, Lorraine, with David Malmgren, Shirl Ramage, and Leanne Schulz. 1993. *An*

Integrated Approach to Learning. Portsmouth, NH: Heinemann.

In this book, the authors show how integrated learning works in the classroom. They outline how they plan authentic activities with real purposes relating to what the children want to learn. Classroom environment and scheduling are also discussed. The appendices contain several integrated learning units developed by the authors with their classes. These units are especially helpful as starting points for building a unit with your own students. (V.M.)

Wilson, Lorraine. *Write Me a Poem: Reading, Writing, and Performing Poetry.* 1994. Portsmouth, NH: Heinemann.

This short, practical resource for the elementary grades gives suggestions and demonstrations for getting children to write various types of poetry: free verse, rhyming poems, noisy poems, poems for two voices, and poems that express emotions.

• Zarnowski, Myra. 1990. *Learning about Biographies: A Reading-and-Writing Approach for Children.* Urbana, IL: National Council of Teachers of English.

In this book written for elementary and middle school teachers, Zarnowski demonstrates how to actively engage students with the nonfiction genre of biographies. Suggestions and examples are given for reading and discussing biographies and encouraging children to research a particular historical figure and then write their own biographical versions. Includes annotated sources for teachers to locate quality biographies, some recommended children's biographies, and samples of biographies written by students.

Assessment and Evaluation Books and Resources

For additional information and resources on assessment and evaluation, see *Invitations,* pp. 295–375.

• Anthony, Robert J., Terry D. Johnson, Norma I. Mickelson, and Alison Preece. 1991. *Evaluating Literacy: A Perspective for Change.* Portsmouth, NH: Heineman.

This remains my favorite book on evaluation. The authors begin with basic principles of language learning and continue with exemplary models of assessment and evaluation. They include a detailed framework for gathering, organizing, interpreting, and reporting information for student learning. They share samples of anecdotal comments, interviews, letters to parents, observational checklists, self-evaluation forms, children's work, reporting forms, language indicators of progress, and more. I am particularly impressed with the indepth inclusion of the child and the parents in the evaluation process. In our school district, many of us initially relied heavily on chapter 10, "Responsive Evaluation: Reporting to Parents," to initiate student-led parent-teacher conferences. For educators moving toward more holistic and student-centered evaluation, this 196-page text is invaluable.

"Assessment procedures should be contextually grounded. Tasks employed during assessment should be as similar as possible to the tasks required during instruction and the demands placed on real people in real language situations. It is unreasonable to expect learners to behave in one way during instruction and another, for which they have not been prepared, during assessment" (p. 70).

Austin, Terri. 1994. *Changing the View: Student-led Parent Conferences.* Portsmouth, NH: Heinemann.

In this engrossing, first-person account, Terri Austin, a sixth-grade teacher in Alaska, describes how she moved from controlling the assessment process to having her students take leadership and ownership. She shares how she first builds community and trust in her process classroom and, then, how she prepares her students to become active participants in assessment. I was struck by how she engaged her class in exploration of what it means to be a "good student" and how those discussions positively influenced students' future efforts. Most of the book concentrates on the student-led portfolio conference with parents and how Austin lays the groundwork for its success. Austin takes us through exactly *how she prepares students for the conferences including all the communications with parents, modeling and practice sessions with students, student self-formulation of their grades and report cards, and individual conferences with Austin. The highlight is the conference evening when families come to class, and students independently take them through their portfolios and explain their strengths, progress, and goals. I was impressed with how Austin ties home knowledge into assessment by continually inviting and including feedback and information from the parents. If you are sorting out your own evaluation procedures or beginning the process of student-led conferences, this book will give you much information and support. Conversations, reflections, and forms from the conference process are included. Austin also shares what she is still struggling with and refining. Applicable K–12.*

Barrs, Myra, Sue Ellis, Hilary Tester, and Anne Thomas, all of the Centre for Language in Primary Education, London. 1988. *The Primary Language Record: Handbook for Teachers.* Portsmouth, NH: Heinemann.

This handbook is another tool for educators who are interested in developing holistic evaluative records of a child's progress in language development. It has a detailed explanation of procedures, along with many examples of evaluations of actual children. Copies of the assessment forms are given with permission to photocopy. A unique feature of the suggested evaluation is the involvement of parents throughout the procedure. Primary teachers considering the use of observation-based, anecdotal record-keeping will find this book to be very helpful for organizing their gathered information to provide a detailed picture of a child's literacy development. (V.M.)

Batzle, Janine. 1992. *Portfolio Assessment and Evaluation: Developing and Using Portfolios in the K–6 Classroom.* Cypress, CA: Creative Teaching Press.

This spiral-bound handbook is an open-ended resource with lots of ideas to get you thinking about possible materials you might ask students to collect in a portfolio.

Many child samples are shown, and one chapter is devoted to a collection of over twenty pages of forms and checklists. Many portfolio concerns are considered in the book: Definition, Kinds, Who Is Involved in the Collection of Materials, Organization, and Use in Reporting to Parents, and more. This is an easy-to-understand, very practical reference. (V.M.)

• Bouffler, Chrystine (ed.). 1993. *Literacy Evaluation: Issues and Practicalities.* Portsmouth, NH: Heinemann.

The author examines issues in accountability and some of the recent developments in language assessment in the United States, the United Kingdom, and Australia. What authentic evaluation is, how to balance district evaluation demands and whole language teaching, how to use a portfolio approach to assess students, what the Primary Language Record is and how it has been used in the U.K., how to assess student writing, how to develop and use literacy profiles, and how to communicate with parents are all delineated with clear language, sample reports, and usable forms. This is a terrific book (116 pp.) for putting classroom-based assessment into practice.

Clay, Marie. 1993. *An Observation Survey of Early Literacy Achievement.* Portsmouth, NH: Heinemann.

Written for educators who work with young children, this ninety-three page guidebook describes the principles and procedures for systematically observing, analyzing, and summarizing the early literacy skills and book behaviors of young children. Explicit directions are given for the following observation tasks: running records (observing and analyzing a child's oral reading behaviors), letter identification, concepts about print, word tests, writing, and hearing sounds in words (dictation). These are the same tasks that make up "the Observation Survey" for Reading Recovery, used for selecting the children that need supplementary teaching. Especially useful for kindergarten and grade one teachers for making instructional decisions. See also the companion volume on p. 9b, Reading Recovery: A Guidebook for Teachers in Training *(Clay, 1993), which details procedures in the Reading Recovery program.*

Clemmons, Joan, Lois Laase, DonnaLynn Cooper, Nancy Areglado, and Mary Dill. 1993. *Portfolios in the Classroom: A Teacher's Sourcebook.* New York: Scholastic Professional Books.

This 120-page sourcebook is very helpful for getting started with portfolio assessment and for getting new ideas to adapt to your own particular school context. Educators in one elementary school share the rationale for using portfolios in the reading-writing classroom, how to get started, possible components of a portfolio, how to engage students in self-evaluation, and lots of management and teaching tips. The extensive, useful appendices offer workable criteria, charts, and checklists for parent communication and student self-evaluation. The organization, photos, and student samples throughout the book make it an easy-to-use resource.

Cohen, S. Alan. 1988. *TESTS: Marked for Life?* Richmond Hill, Ontario: Scholastic-TAB.

This fifty-eight-page book clearly explains norm-referenced and criterion-referenced tests and notes the limitations of the former. Share this book with parents and administrators.

Cooper, Winfield, and B. J. Brown. February 1992. "Using Portfolios to Empower Student Writers." *English Journal,* pp. 40–45.

A junior high and a high school teacher share their research in using portfolios in the writing-process classroom. They discuss the contents of the student-writing portfolio and how categories for inclusion were decided, share results and insights from the portfolio process, and recommend helpful teacher resources on portfolio assessment.

• Davies, Anne, and others. 1992. *Together is Better: Collaborative Assessment, Evaluation and Reporting.* Winnipeg, Manitoba: Peguis.

Written by educators in British Columbia, this terrific resource gives practical suggestions and a wealth of examples for how to meaningfully involve teachers, parents, and students in three-way conferencing and reporting. There are samples of letters to parents, evaluation/reporting forms, goal-setting plans, anecdotal narratives, feedback and reflections from the conference, and more. Blackline masters (18 pp.) of forms used for preparing for the conference and reflecting on the conference are included.

• Farr, Roger, and Bruce Tone. 1994. *Portfolio and Performance Assessment: Helping Students Evaluate Their Progress as Readers and Writers.* Fort Worth, TX: Harcourt Brace.

"Whatever purpose a teacher, school, district, or even state may set for portfolio assessment, it should not in any way override the primary purpose and potential of all language-arts portfolios: to develop the students' inclinations and abilities to evaluate their own language use!" (p. 39). Farr and Tone see the other role of portfolios as providing a back-up system for informing educational decision makers. With lots of specific examples and strong theoretical underpinnings, the authors detail how portfolios can encourage students to become self-assessors. In this superb 356-page resource, they include materials that can go into a portfolio, samples of record keeping by students and teachers, indicators to look for when examining the portfolio, activities that encourage self-assessment, guidelines to follow in using portfolios for evaluation of student growth and development, suggestions for developing your own performance assessments, and extensive appendices with reproducible forms, information, and resources for putting portfolios into practice. Teachers will appreciate the "nuts and bolts" of portfolio management, including choosing the physical portfolio holder, keeping the portfolios accessible to students, deciding on the variety of materials that go in the portfolio, managing the content of portfolios, succeeding with and finding the time for student/teacher conferences, and communicating with parents.

The authors recognize that to use port-

folios wisely for ongoing informal assessment in the language arts, we need to have a well-developed understanding of how children develop as language users and a broad understanding of assessment issues. "The bottom line in selecting and using any assessment should be whether it helps students" (p. 167). In addition to cautions about present assessment practices, we are cautioned not to grade portfolios or use portfolios only for best work but to allow students to struggle with the bulk and variety of their materials so they can begin to make sense of their language development. I have not read a more comprehensive, useful text for meaningfully applying the portfolio assessment concept to the classroom. I did wish, however, that parents were included as a more ongoing part of the portfolio process. You may find, as I did, that the sheer amount of information presented in this guidebook is overwhelming. As with any other useful resource, you will want to adapt the information and ideas to suit your own particular contexts.

Francis, David (executive director). 1994. *English—A Curriculum Profile for Australian Schools.* Carlton, Victoria, Australia: Curriculum Corporation, and Portsmouth, NH: Heinemann.

This document provides a detailed framework that is "designed to assist in the improvement of teaching and learning and to provide a common language for reporting student achievement." Specific outcomes are listed for speaking and listening, reading and viewing, and writing in increasingly complex levels. Along with each level, criteria—performance indicators—are provided as evidence to observe for, and some examples of student work used as evidence are included. Teachers and administrators across the grades will find the language used in describing desired outcomes terrifically helpful for curriculum planning and reporting to parents.

Gill, Kent (ed.). 1993. *Process and Portfolios in Writing Instruction.* Urbana, IL: National Council of Teachers of English.

Elementary, secondary, and college-level teachers will find many practical ideas in this book. In the first section, teachers describe their successes with building students' interest in and appreciation of writing. These students faced problems such as reluctance to begin writing, writer's block, and a lack of ideas. I particularly liked the chapter by high school teacher Betty McWilliams who encourages students to share their work with classmates as they develop stories from their own lives. The second part focuses on the use of writing portfolios both for instruction and evaluation. Various authors describe how students take responsibility for selecting the materials to be placed in their portfolios, and how they learn to evaluate their work. These essays are a testimony to the power of reflective teachers who help their students to write better by becoming writers themselves. (V.M.)

Glazer, Susan Mandel, and Carol Smullen Brown. 1993. *Portfolios and Beyond: Collaborative Assessment in Reading and Writing.* Norwood, MA: Christopher-Gordon.

Developing instruments that would help teachers to assess the holistic, literature-based instruction used in their classrooms was the goal of the authors of this interesting text. They provide a theoretical base to explain the step-by-step alternative procedures that have evolved in their work. I particularly liked the chapter that Lynn Searfoss was invited to contribute that places all assessment in relation to the classroom environment. He believes that the classroom must be the context in which language is to be observed and assessed, with products displayed, shared, and saved. He gives many suggestions for determining if the environment truly is a "print-rich" setting. Further chapters look at actual assessment of reading, writing, comprehension processes and products, as well as how reporting should be a collaboration between parents, student, and teacher. A chapter of questions that teachers ask is full of helpful answers. (V.M.)

Goodman, Kenneth, Lois Bridges Bird, and Yetta Goodman (eds.). 1992. *The Whole Language Catalog: Supplement on Authen-*

tic Assessment. Blacklick, OH: SRA Division of Macmillan/McGraw-Hill.

More than 100 whole language educators contributed material to this comprehensive guidebook on authentic assessment. Strategies and suggestions for new ways of evaluation are given that include use of anecdotal records, holistic checklists, portfolios, interviews, and learning logs. Indexes and cross-references allow readers to find information to meet their own particular needs. Classroom demonstrations throughout the book help make the suggested assessment techniques especially useful to teachers. (V.M.)

Goodman, Kenneth, Yetta Goodman, and Wendy Hood (eds.). 1989. *The Whole Language Evaluation Book*. Portsmouth, NH: Heinemann.

This powerful book encourages teachers to value their students and to find ways to help them—instead of showing them they have failed. Whole language practitioners across the United States and Canada contributed the various chapters describing alternatives to traditional evaluation techniques. They believe that evaluation should be a way of documenting the learning growth occurring daily—never as an assessment of decontextualized, abstract skills unrelated to the functional use of language. A variety of evaluation strategies, such as anecdotal records, learning logs, miscue analysis, journal samples, portfolios or folders, writing samples, and teacher notes, are described as they are implemented by the authors in various classroom settings from elementary to senior high school, adult education, and with bilingual and special education students. Many useful suggestions are given for record keeping. The book is an excellent resource for persons who are grounded in whole language practices and who are now interested in making student evaluation an integral part of the learning process. (V.M.)

Graves, Donald H., and Bonnie S. Sunstein (eds.). 1992. *Portfolio Portraits*. Portsmouth, NH: Heinemann.

An informative picture of how portfolios are being developed by educators from first-grade level through graduate education is found in this book. What I really like about this book is that portfolios are not packaged with a bunch of rules or mandates. Instead, the book shows the diversity and potential that keeping portfolios might have. One of the most fascinating chapters was the one where a superintendent developed his own portfolio before asking his staff to consider a portfolio project in their school district. Anyone considering the use of portfolios should read this book! (V.M.)

• Harp, Bill (ed.). 1994. *Assessment and Evaluation for Student Centered Learning*. 2nd ed. Norwood, MA: Christopher-Gordon.

The opening chapters of this book update the first edition by exploring issues about the whole language movement that have arisen in the past three years. Harp begins by looking at the principles underlying whole language instruction and its relationship to assessment and evaluation. Further chapters look at primary, intermediate, special education and multicultural classrooms, and suggest appropriate ways of assessment. This is both a practical and theoretical handbook that should be in every classroom teacher's library. (V.M.)

Herman, Joan L., Pamela R. Aschbacher, and Lynn Winters. 1992. *A Practical Guide to Alternative Assessment*. Alexandria, VA: Association for Supervision and Curriculum Development.

The authors present clear information and a strong rationale for linking quality alternative assessments with good instruction. "Good assessment reliably measures something beyond the specific tasks that students are asked to complete. The results of good assessment identify what students can do in a broad knowledge or skill domain" (p. 9). Alternative assessments examine the processes as well as the products of learning and may include performance testing, portfolio assessment, exhibits, demonstrations, and other authentic assessments. Guidelines and procedures for designing alternative assessments are given, including determining outcomes to be measured, managing the assessment admini-

stration process, deciding the actual question/problem/prompt, developing and evaluating your own criteria and rubrics, and ensuring reliable scoring and validity. I found the brief information on portfolio assessment very helpful for clarifying what must take place if portfolios are to be more than collections and are truly to be used for assessment. For rethinking, redesigning, and balancing assessment strategies in your educational context, this is a very useful guide. (134 pp.)

- Hill, Bonnie Campbell, and Cynthia Ruptic. 1994. *Practical Aspects of Authentic Assessment: Putting the Pieces Together.* Norwood, MA: Christopher-Gordon.

  If you want a very specific and practical book full of ways to assess learning in the elementary classroom, you will want to get this book. It contains over 120 reproducible forms for possible teacher use, along with commentary explaining their usage. The forms are organized according to purpose: emergent literacy, writing, reading, content areas, developmental spelling, writing conferences, reading logs, literature circles, problem solving, and many more. Several chapters address the use, collection, and organization of portfolios in a classroom setting. The entire book is a wealth of information for teachers to consider. (V.M.)

- Jett-Simpson, Mary, and Lauren Leslie (eds.). 1994. *Ecological Assessment: Under Construction.* Schofield, WI: Wisconsin State Reading Association (94809 Sternberg Avenue, 54476).

  Ecological assessments combine authentic literacy tasks with authentic texts; that is, tasks and materials are natural to what readers, writers, and speakers do in the real world. With this approach, knowledgeable teachers work side by side with students to capture the complexity of language processes primarily by observing, recording, and analyzing reading and writing processes as they occur in the classroom. How and why teachers have moved to ecological assessment is detailed in this impressive, 255-page monograph. In a straightforward, organized manner that

combines theory and practice, this guide provides an abundance of information and work samples for observing reading and writing behaviors, strategies, attitudes, and interests. Lots of specific, useful information, sample forms, and work samples involving parent communication, holistic scoring, developing rubrics, and the portfolio process are included. An excellent source for teachers, administrators, and policy makers for understanding and moving to authentic assessment practices in the classroom.

- Johnston, Peter H. 1992. *Constructive Evaluation of Literate Activity.* New York: Longman.

  This is a challenging, complex, comprehensive book on literacy and assessment that is worth the effort involved to read it. "I have based this book on the premise that there is one central reason for evaluating children's literate activity, and that is so that we might ensure optimal instruction for all children. *All other reasons are secondary to that goal" (p. 9). Johnston believes the most important evaluation is self-evaluation—for us and our students—and that teachers obtain their most useful information about students in one to one conferences and through uninterrupted observation in the classroom when students are working independently and teachers can step back. To that end, the author helps us set up contexts for constructive evaluation, look and listen better when we are observing students ("reflection in action"), describe the learner and his development through narrative reports that capitalize on the learner's strengths, match readers with texts, understand the role of choice in learning, analyze children's errors, help our students become good self-evaluators, and much more. Strategies for recording, keeping track, promoting, and analyzing literacy development are explained in great depth. Johnston demonstrates how we can evaluate a student's concepts about print, oral reading, thinking process, written language, and more through the use and analysis of running records (an audiotape for learning how to take a running record of a child's oral*

reading accompanies this text), other observational records, the portfolio process,
dialogue journals, thinking aloud, to name
just a few. Johnston also examines the in-
adequacy of standardized tests and testing
and suggests ways to reduce the amount
of testing in schools. For teachers who are
ready to rethink literacy assumptions, become more reflective about their teaching,
and view evaluation through a constructive perspective, this remarkable book (426
pp.) is important reading. Read this book
slowly. It is packed with a wealth of
thoughtful information and feasible ideas.

Some quotes to think about:

"Any evaluation procedure that interferes with or reduces optimal instruction
to any child should be regarded as highly
suspect, probably invalid, and generally
unacceptable" (p. 10).

"The more independent literate activity
that is going on in the classroom, the easier and more consistent evaluation will be.
The more students are reading and writing, and talking about the reading and
writing, the more examples are available
to be observed, and the less critical it is for
the teacher to notice every single one" (p. 8).

"Possibly the biggest obstacle to development in evaluation practices has been the
rather restricted view of what constitute
appropriate data" (p. 307).

Kamii, Constance (ed.). 1990. *Achievement Testing in Early Grades: The Games Grown-
Ups Play*. Washington, DC: National Association for the Education of Young
Children.

The contributing authors to this thoughtful text (181 pp.) give research and rationale to demonstrate the harmful effects
of achievement testing in kindergarten
through second grade. In place of standardized testing with its emphasis on fragmented skills, they recommend evaluation
(with teachers in charge) that is rooted in
classroom practice and that informs us of
students' thinking processes over time. Provocative, important reading for teachers,
administrators, parents, and policymakers.

Linek, Wayne M. February 1991. "Grading
and Evaluation Techniques for Whole

Language Teachers." *Language Arts*,
pp. 125–131.

An elementary principal gives specific
and realistic suggestions for evaluating
and grading in a whole language classroom and focuses on the issues of philoso-
phy/policy and record keeping. "The process you use will be a unique combination
of policy requirements, professional knowledge, and personal choice." Linek provides many practical possibilities for rec-
onciling accountability and grading issues
with whole language principles.

Little, Nancy, and John Allan. 1988. *Student-
Led Teacher Parent Conferences*. Toronto,
Ontario: Lugus Productions.

Written to give guidance and motivation
to teachers in grades 1–7 to implement
student-led parent-teacher conferences, this
thirty-seven-page booklet includes pre-
paratory steps, procedures, methods of
evaluation, and several sample letters and
forms. You will want to adapt the format
presented to your own conference contexts. Great for support in getting started.

Ministry of Education, Victoria, Australia.
1990. *Literacy Profiles Handbook: Assess-
ing and Reporting Literacy Development*.
(Available in the U.S. from Brewster, NY:
TASA [Fields Lane, P.O. Box 382, 10509].
A U.S. version, *The American Literacy
Profiles*, by Patrick Griffin, Patricia G.
Smith, and Lois Burrill is in the works and
will be available from Heinemann in the
spring of 1995.)

"A literacy profile is an array of information that describes and evaluates a student's reading and writing." The profile
includes attitudes and interests and strategies and accomplishments. When a K–12
language arts committee in my school district met to write a district language arts
course of study, we found the profiles to
be a helpful reference for language, content, and format.

• Murphy, Sandra, and Mary Ann Smith. *Writing Portfolios: A Bridge from Teaching to
Assessment*. 1991. Markham, Ontario: Pippin Publishing, and Portsmouth, NH: Heinemann.

The authors and twenty secondary teachers, all connected with the Bay Area Writing Project in California, collaborated on a research project experimenting with writing portfolios. In this first-rate, ninety-six-page book, they discuss the rationale for using portfolios, the decision making process teachers used in setting up portfolio programs, the pitfalls and successes teachers had, and the practices that worked best. The chapter, "What Can Students Learn from Reflecting?" (pp. 37–45), has pages of excellent questions teachers can ask in conferences and to encourage self-reflection. "The word 'portfolio,' by itself, means little. It's the individual decisions that define the portfolio assessment" (p. 83). While the portfolio context in this book is high school, as an elementary teacher I found the information very useful and applicable.

Perrone, Vito (ed.). 1991. *Expanding Student Assessment*. Alexandria, VA: Association for Supervision and Curriculum Development.

This is a fascinating book that raises questions about assessment and takes the stance that knowledgeable teachers can use observation and performance samples in the classroom context to formally and informally assess student learning. In such authentic assessment, classroom teachers and students are central to the process, and students are empowered as learners. In the first chapter, Kathe Jervis reports on how standardized testing disrupted the everyday rhythm of a grade 3–4 class in New York City and how the classroom teacher made an effort to deemphasize the tests. In chapter 2, Edward Chittenden looks at assessment first as an attitude of "keeping track" and "checking up" and suggests that classroom activities, such as story time and independent reading, are natural settings for reading assessment. In chapter 3, Ron Berger, a sixth-grade teacher, shares his assessment beliefs and practices, which center around conferences, critique, and the use of portfolios. A terrific chapter by Rieneke Zessoules and Howard Gardner deals with the importance of student reflection and shows how two high school teachers encourage

it. These two authors also explore key practices of authentic assessment for teachers and administrators. In chapter 6, twelfth-grade English teacher Patricia Lambert Stock, who integrates teaching, learning, and assessment, describes the impressive improvement of a struggling writing student. In chapter 8, Judah Schwartz raises important questions about the secrecy of mathematics tests and the fact that the media only see the scores (not the questions), and that recognizing a solution on a multiple choice test is not the same as producing a solution. I found this entire 179-page book provocative and thoughtful.

• Rhodes, Lynn K. (ed.). 1993. *Literacy Assessment: A Handbook of Instruments*. Portsmouth, NH: Heinemann.

All of the various assessment instruments discussed in Windows into Literacy, along with directions for administration, are found in this useful handbook. These forms include interviews and attitude surveys, miscue analysis, comprehension checklists, spelling analysis, emergent reading and writing evaluations, and instruments for self-evaluation. They may be photocopied by teachers for classroom use, but the editor hopes that they will be reviewed and revised to fit your particular needs. (V.M.)

• Rhodes, Lynn K., and Nancy Shanklin. 1993. *Windows into Literacy: Assessing Learners K–8*. Portsmouth, NH: Heinemann.

This text is a very inclusive look at literacy assessment. It is built on the principle that the most effective assessment takes place most often in the midst of instruction and should inform that instruction. The book values the teacher as the decision maker in determining what materials should be used to support learning after gathering information on the students' strengths and interests. Chapters in this book define assessment and the principles that should guide it. They cover a wide range of assessment methods in order to discover the following: students' perceptions of their own reading and writing strategies, reading ability, writing processes with emphasis on spelling and written products, emergent reading and writing ability. Suggestions are given as to how to use standardized, norm-referenced tests and literacy collections including portfolios, and to deal with educational change as it relates to assessment. Though the book can be overwhelming when viewed as a whole, each chapter stands alone, and teachers can read those sections that address their particular needs. It is an outstanding resource. (V.M.)

• Stenmark, Jean Kerr (ed.). 1991. *Mathematics Assessment: Myths, Model, Good Questions, and Practical Suggestions.* Reston, VA: The National Council of Teachers of Mathematics.

Geared to teachers, this seventy-one page handbook gives a convincing rationale and lots of practical assistance to implement alternative assessments that focus on student thinking. Some of the useful topics and techniques that are discussed and demonstrated are creating open-ended questions, conducting interviews and conferences, managing the classroom with observational assessment, recording observations, developing criteria for performance tasks, and keeping and evaluating a mathematics portfolio. Sample assessment forms are included. I was struck by the fact that the principles that apply to good assessment in mathematics are the same principles that apply across the curriculum. A first-rate resource for all teachers.

Traill, Leanna. 1993. *Highlight My Strengths: Assessment and Evaluation of Literacy Learning.* Crystal Lake, IL: Rigby.

This ninety-two-page sourcebook for primary teachers shares assessment procedures and record keeping for observing, recording, and interpreting reading behaviors as well as for taking running records. Some of the information and procedures are adapted from the work of Marie Clay, Richard Gentry, and others. Attractively organized with photos, charts, forms, and student work samples. Easy to use and read.

Turbill, Jan, and Brian Cambourne (eds.). 1994. *Responsive Evaluation.* Portsmouth, NH: Heinemann.

Seeking a workable model of evaluation that is congruent with language learning

theory, a group of Australian classroom teachers, school principals, directors, and university researchers collaborated in a five-year research project. The model of evaluation they adopted, Responsive Evaluation, shares the same fundamentals as a parental model of responsive evaluation in the everyday world. Some of these common fundamentals include opportunities to gather data and observe language learning in naturally occurring settings, a special relationship with and commitment to those who are being evaluated, a sense of responsibility to set up learning contexts that facilitate literacy development, a set of markers or benchmarks that can be used to recognize students' literacy growth and development. With the help of their co-researchers, teachers focused on "episodes" (literacy lessons, such as sustained silent reading or sharing circle) in their daily teaching and examined the following questions:

1. Why do I have this episode in my daily schedule?

2. What data-gathering procedures (i.e. assessment procedures) can I employ that won't break into or stop the flow of teaching and learning?

3. What markers can I use during this episode that will inform me that students are/are not learning within this episode?

4. What sense or meaning can I make from what I collect? (p. 23)

Through this daily examination, teachers and principals became more insightful and explicit about their beliefs and practices and more confident, competent, and rigorous in their evaluation procedures. Use this thoughtful, practical resource as a staff-development model and to examine and improve your own teaching/evaluation practices.

Valencia, Sheila W., Elfrieda H. Hiebert, and Peter P. Afflerbach (eds.). 1994. *Authentic Reading Assessment: Practices and Possibilities.* Newark, DE: International Reading Association.

For everyone who is struggling with the implementation of authentic assessment and portfolios (and who isn't?), this book is for you. Through case studies that are followed by thoughtful, analytical commentaries, the reader gains perspective on approaches to authentic assessment that are taking place at the classroom, district, and state levels in parts of the United States and Canada. This detailed, critical account of successes and failures is very helpful to any individual, school, or district tackling nontraditional assessment. Lends support to classroom-based assessment projects.

Wiggins, Grant. May 1992. "Creating Tests Worth Taking." *Educational Leadership,* pp. 26–33.

A national expert on testing and assessment lists questions and criteria to consider when developing authentic performance assessments. He discusses how to design tasks that involve "higher-order" thinking, scoring considerations, constraints of performance assessment, and how to report progress. He argues that quality assessment must be designed locally since good teaching and good assessing cannot be separated.

• Woodward, Helen. 1994. *Negotiated Evaluation: Involving Children and Parents in the Process.* Portsmouth, NH: Heinemann.

This gem of a book (92 pp.) lends practical help to elementary-grades teachers who want evaluation processes to actively involve the child and his or her parents as well as the teacher. I particularly appreciated all the honest information on what works and what doesn't when teachers use informal observation, such as anecdotal records and checklists. This is a must-read book for teachers who want to take responsibility for evaluation in the classroom but who need specific help with the management, organization, and procedures to make it possible. Lots of usable letters and forms included, especially for parents and student self-evaluation.

Spelling Books and Resources

For integrating spelling into the reading-writing classroom and for additional spelling resources, see *Invitations,* pp. 235–262.

Bloodgood, Janet W. November 1991. "A New Approach to Spelling Instruction in Language Arts Programs." *The Elementary School Journal,* pp. 203–211.

Within the integrated language arts classroom, Bloodgood describes how periodic spelling assessments can enable teachers to plan appropriate word study activities for students. Specific word-sorting and word-hunting activities that help students notice particular features and patterns of words are described. Underscores the need for accurate spelling assessment as part of the spelling program. Many good ideas for teaching spelling.

Bolton, Faye, and Diane Snowball. 1993. *Ideas for Spelling.* Portsmouth, NH: Heinemann.

The main emphasis of this book is on creating a balanced spelling program, and teachers will appreciate the multitude of suggested activities that go along with the various stages of children's spelling development. Viewing spelling in the context of writing, Bolton and Snowball first provide a framework for spelling development that connects spelling relationships in the English language (morphemic, phoneme-grapheme, semantics, and syntax) with strategies used by competent spellers. How to assess and evaluate children's spelling development is also included.

Bolton, Faye, and Diane Snowball. 1993. *Teaching Spelling: A Practical Resource.* Portsmouth, NH: Heinemann.

The authors believe that the only authentic reason for students to learn to spell conventionally is to assist others to read their writing. Students must not only write often, but also form hypotheses about words, try out spellings, receive feedback, and refine their hypotheses. Building on Ideas for Spelling (Heinemann, 1993), which documents the nature of learning to spell, in this 154-page resource Bolton and Snowball provide strategies and management for the elementary school classroom spelling program. Strategies that competent spellers use are demonstrated. Many examples of classroom charts, spelling resources, patterns to be taught, games for playing with words, assessment procedures, and student work samples are provided. Teachers *looking for how and what to teach in spelling will appreciate the abundance of word lists (such as homophones, common derivatives, prefixes, suffixes, abbreviations), ideas, and activities in this useful resource.*

Booth, David (ed.). 1991. *Spelling Links: Reflections on Spelling and its Place in the Curriculum.* Markham, Ontario: Pembroke Publishers, and Bothell, WA: The Wright Group.

For the teacher who is unsure of how to teach spelling and which approach to use, the solid, yet varying, perspectives presented in this 157-page text will prove useful and thought provoking. Booth passionately asks us to rethink our spelling programs, to become lifelong spelling mentors who promote word awareness and teach spelling "through writing, through poetry, through puzzles and games, through reading, through discussion and debate about words, through linguistic exploration, through second languages, through reference helps, through modeling by effective and affective teachers" (pp. 9–10). Suggesting that we must first understand how children learn to spell before we can choose words to teach, Part 1 has an essay by Rosemary Courtney dealing with the history of spelling, and Part 2 deals with developmental nature of spelling with chapters by Carol Beers and James Beers, Richard Gentry, and Edmund Henderson and Shane Templeton. Part 3, on choosing a spelling program, presents perspectives by Judith Preen, a whole language advocate, and Robert and Marlene McCracken, who offer a slightly different approach. Part 4, "What Do I Teach Monday?" has chapters by Janice Merrifield and Larry Schwartz, and offers strategies, activities, and games to develop good spellers. Part 5 offers practical help with assessment with chapters by Kristine Anderson and Ruth Scott. Next, a fascinating chapter by Sharon Siamon chronicles her daughter's growth in spelling and is a great piece for thinking about and discussing the development of spelling. Bob Barton's short essay about word consciousness concludes this fine resource.

Cunningham, Patricia M., and James W. Cunningham. October 1992. "Making Words: Enhancing the Invented Spelling-Decoding Connection." *The Reading Teacher,* pp. 106–115.

Believing that writing with invented spelling is important but that some readers and writers will not learn enough about letter-sound relationships from this practice alone, the authors developed the "Making Words" activity for first- and second-grade writing classrooms. In "Making Words," children are given a specific group of letters that they use to make words. The steps for planning and teaching a "Making Words" lesson are delineated. K–2 teachers that I know have used this activity and find it excellent for increasing phonemic awareness and spelling knowledge. I found the management of it so time consuming that I adapted the lesson for easier management.

Gentry, Richard, and Jean W. Gillet. 1993. *Teaching Kids to Spell.* Portsmouth, NH: Heinemann.

This is a great book for teachers who already have a reading-writing classroom where children are reading, writing, risk taking, inventing, and interacting with language and each other throughout the day. For teachers ready to take a workshop approach to spelling, Gentry and Gillet give us the research, theory, rationale, organization, instructional techniques, and activities for developing spellers. We are taken through the stages of invented spelling and shown how to give K–2 students a developmental spelling test, analyze the spellings to determine the child's developmental spelling level, and support the child's growing competence. For older students, we learn that expert spellers internalize phonetic, semantic, historical, and visual knowledge of words, and we are shown many ways to help children acquire all four of these necessary systems. To support that teaching, extensive appendices at the end of the book provide Latin and Greek stems, useful prefixes, familiar sound and letter patterns ("Children learn to spell pattern by pattern, not word by word" p. 89.), most frequently used words in children's writing, and words most commonly misspelled. What I especially like about this book is the balanced approach it takes with whole language and explicit teaching. "In addition to reading and writing daily in a language-rich environment, children must be taught phonetic, semantic, etymological, and visual knowledge of words both directly and indirectly in order to internalize them and use them interactively for producing correct spelling" (p. 56).

Phenix, Jo, and Doreen Scott-Dunne. 1991. *Spelling Instruction That Makes Sense.* Markham, Ontario: Pembroke Publishers, and Bothell, WA: The Wright Group.

For teachers looking for an alternative to weekly spelling lists, the authors of this practical, 103-page book strike a balance between having children write freely and teaching spelling directly. The easy-to-read text includes the logic, history, and development of spelling along with many specific strategies, techniques, and rules worth teaching. Chapter 5, "Evaluation and Record Keeping" is very helpful for the samples of written analyses of children's work that demonstrate "what the student knows" and "what can reasonably be taught." An excellent resource for understanding how to teach, evaluate, and develop spellers in the classroom.

Powell, Debbie, and David Hornsby. 1993. *Learning Phonics and Spelling in a Whole Language Classroom.* New York: Scholastic.

Teachers who are developing a whole language environment for their students often have concerns and questions about the place of phonics and spelling in the classroom. This teacher-friendly book is full of strategies and activities designed to integrate phonics and spelling into the context of literature and other authentic texts. One section I particularly liked was on recording, evaluation, and reporting. It contained many suggestions for evaluation within the context of everyday reading and writing, as well as ways to keep parents informed of changes in instructional meth-

odology. The book also has many forms that could be adapted for your particular classroom use. (V.M.)

Routman, Regie. May/June 1993. "The Uses and Abuses of Invented Spelling." *Instructor*, pp. 35–39.

Routman examines the use of invented spelling in classrooms and notes that it was never meant to be "anything goes." She discusses the need for raising our expectations and expecting students to spell high-frequency words correctly, to utilize reliable rules and patterns, and to apply spelling strategies to their daily writing. Suggestions are given for encouraging students to become good spellers.

Scott, Ruth. 1993. *Spelling: Sharing the Secrets.* Toronto: Gage Educational Publishing.

Scott gives lots of practical assistance on how to set up the language-based classroom to explore the systems of spelling. She clearly explains the spelling stages all children move through and how to analyze and assess these stages and move children forward. I found the strength of the book to be the multitude of activities and spelling strategies (phonological, visual, and morphological [meaning]) that Scott clearly presents. Teachers who are ready to integrate the teaching of spelling into the language arts will find this a very useful resource.

• Tarasoff, Mary. 1992. *A Guide to Children's Spelling Development.* Victoria, British Columbia: Active Learning Institute, and Winnipeg, Manitoba: Peguis.

For teachers who have moved to an integrated approach to spelling but need the structure, rules, and assistance the published spelling program provided, this book is for you. Tarasoff's easy-to-use, well-organized resource (177 pages) gives specific guidance and strategies for supporting children at each stage of spelling development. Extensive tables and appendices provide rules worth knowing, common letter and sound patterns and sequences, most frequently used words, commonly used prefixes and suffixes, and more. A whole chapter is devoted to spell-

ing multisyllabic words. Using annotated samples of children's writing at different stages, Tarasoff notes the knowledge and strategies the child is using to construct words and gives suggestions for helping the child develop further. A favorite resource of many teachers. See also, Mary Tarasoff's Spelling: Strategies You Can Teach (Peguis, 1990).

Templeton, Shane. November 1991. "Teaching and Learning the English Spelling System: Reconceptualizing Method and Purpose." The Elementary School Journal, pp. 185–201.

Within the language-based, process classroom, Templeton elaborates on the need for systematic, formal spelling instruction that addresses both the structure of words and vocabulary development. Noting that many students do not automatically pick up the structural and semantic patterns of words without teacher guidance, he provides specific strategies and demonstration lessons for the elementary grades. Based on the current concern of teachers and parents regarding the teaching of spelling, this is an important article for educators who recognize the need for some explicit instruction in the context of the reading-writing classroom.

• Wilde, Sandra. 1991. You Can Red This! Spelling and Punctuation for Whole Language Classrooms, k–6. Portsmouth, NH: Heinemann.

Teachers who want to understand how children develop spelling and punctuation competencies will enjoy this comprehensive handbook. It will especially appeal to teachers who sense that spelling instruction should be more than using a workbook, or memorizing a weekly list of words. Wilde very clearly shows how development takes place over time, using many examples of student writing. Many practical teaching ideas are given, and a series of sample minilessons are especially valuable. Her insights into the use and support of invented spelling by children will be especially helpful in defining the process to their parents. (V.M.)

Mathematics Books and Resources

• Apelman, Maja, and Julie King. 1993. Exploring Everyday Math: Ideas for Students, Teachers, and Parents. Portsmouth, NH: Heinemann.

Many practical ideas that can be used by anyone helping children to understand mathematical concepts are found in this book. It allows teachers and parents to tap and enhance the opportunities for math that surround a child in daily life. An appendix contains reproducible recording sheets and sample letters to parents. Each activity that I have tried with my second graders and their parents has been received with enthusiasm, and I continue to integrate many of the suggestions from this book into my math program. (V.M.)

Baker, Ann, and Johnny Baker. 1991. Counting on a Small Planet: Activities for Environmental Mathematics. Portsmouth, NH: Heinemann.

Using a thematic approach, the authors suggest activities to help children develop an awareness of environmental problems, such as trash accumulation, erosion, and water use or abuse. Each topic has a Math Fact File that helps the student to relate local problems to a global level. Upper-grade teachers will find this book useful in developing ecology units. (V.M.)

Baker, Ann, and Johnny Baker. 1991. Maths in the Mind: A Process Approach to Mental Strategies. Portsmouth, NH: Heinemann.

Strategies to encourage children to become independent thinkers in math are found in this book. It emphasizes process rather than one right answer, and is filled with examples of children's work. Many of the activities are appropriate for second graders or older students. (V.M.)

Baker, Ann, and Johnny Baker. 1990. Mathematics in Process. Portsmouth, NH: Heinemann.

Elementary teachers who are ready to apply the conditions and principles of whole language to the teaching and learning of mathematics will want to read this book.

The authors, Australian educators, advocate applying the writing process and shared-book experience to a process approach to mathematics. Lots of examples of open-ended math activities in which children have opportunities to experiment with ideas, develop their own strategies, and communicate and reflect about their experiences are presented.

Baker, Dave, Cheryl Semple, and Tony Stead. 1990. *How Big Is the Moon? Whole Maths in Action.* Portsmouth, NH: Heinemann.

As they explore real-life problems and issues, young children are encouraged to learn math concepts in this book. It describes how to establish a learning environment in which children take responsibility for their own learning and share in the planning and implementation of the curriculum. Many examples of student projects are shown throughout the book that make the different topics very understandable. A section on evaluation and record keeping has many useful ideas. (V.M.)

Braddon, Kathryn L., Nancy J. Hall, and Dale Taylor. 1993. *Math Through Children's Literature: Making the NCTM Standards Come Alive.* Englewood, CO: Teacher Ideas Press/Libraries Unlimited.

As the title suggests, this book is organized around the NCTM Standards. The first five (problem solving, communication, reasoning, connections, and estimation) are considered processes to be woven into the other eight elementary standards. Each of the content standards (number sense and numeration, measurement, etc.) has its own chapter, which contains appropriate books with suggested activities for K–6 students. A list of related books is included for each standard. This is a wonderful resource with many ideas for busy classroom teachers. (V.M.)

Burk, Donna, Allyn Snider, and Paula Symonds. 1992–1993. *Math Excursions Series.* Portsmouth, NH: Heinemann.

This innovative series of project-based mathematics units for primary teachers will seem prescriptive at first glance, but the activities invite exciting, open-ended exploration in the classroom. The books are organized by grade level (Math Excursions K, Math Excursions 1, and Math Excursions 2). Each book includes five complete units, and each unit creates a delightful story line that sets up situations in which there's a reason to use mathematics. Many of the units are based on children's literature, traditional folktales, or familiar nursery rhymes. The books are generously illustrated and well organized, and provide a wonderful introduction to the kind of open mathematical exploration called for by the NCTM Standards. The authors are all practicing classroom teachers and this is clearly revealed in their thoughtful approach to each of the books in the series.

- Burns, Marilyn. 1992. *About Teaching Mathematics: A K–8 Resource.* Sausalito, CA: Math Solutions Publications. Distributed by Heinemann.

  This book argues that math should be taught through problem solving, and clearly demonstrates why traditional math teaching based on pencil-and-paper computation has little relevance for using math in daily life. The author looks at issues in mathematics teaching, how children learn, and how to organize the classroom environment. Many classroom-tested activities are described in each section of the book, and an extensive bibliography of books and resources is in the back. This is an extremely valuable resource for the K–8 classroom teacher. (V.M.)

Burns, Marilyn. 1987–1990. *A Collection of Math Lessons.* Sausalito, CA: Math Solutions Publications. Distributed by Heinemann.

From Grades 1 Through 3, with Bonnie Tank.

From Grades 3 Through 6.

From Grades 6 Through 8, with Cathy McLaughlin.

Each of these wonderful books presents interesting ideas for teaching mathematics through problem solving. Students are encouraged to work cooperatively to find solutions, and to incorporate writing into each activity. Each chapter contains a lesson presented to real children, shows how the teacher prepared the lesson, and how the children responded. I have tried many of these lessons, and found that my students responded with enjoyment and interest. (V.M.)

Burns, Marilyn. 1992. *Math and Literature (K–3).* Sausalito, CA: Math Solutions Publications. Distributed by Heinemann.

This valuable resource gives detailed descriptions of how ten children's books were used in various classrooms. After reading the story, teachers encouraged problem-solving investigations by asking questions and giving children time to think and explore. I especially enjoyed looking at the written responses by children that are included with each lesson. In addition, twenty-one additional books are briefly described with instructional ideas included for each. (V.M.)

Charles, Linda Holden, and Micaelia Randolph Brummett. 1989. *Connections: Linking Manipulatives to Mathematics (Grades 1–6).* Sunnyvale, CA: Creative Publications.

Each grade-level resource contains twenty manipulative lessons that connect to important mathematical topics. Each lesson is structured to be used with the whole class as well as with a small group. As part of each lesson, students discuss, organize, report, display, and write about their findings. A fine resource for teachers looking to encourage more active learning experiences to help build understanding in mathematics.

Griffiths, Rachel, and Margaret Clyne. 1990. *Books You Can Count On: Linking Mathematics and Literature.* Portsmouth, NH: Heinemann.

This resource for the primary grades takes first-rate children's literature and outlines activities for developing mathematical concepts. Books are presented individually as well as thematically. Two final sections on classroom organization and evaluation are very useful.

• Kamii, Constance. 1985, 1989. *Young Children Reinvent Arithmetic: Implications of Piaget's Theory.* New York: Teachers College Press.

Grade 1, with Georgia DeClark.

2nd Grade: Young Children Continue to Reinvent Arithmetic, with Linda Leslie Joseph.

These two books can be read separately, but together they will trace children's mathematical development across first and second grade. Basing her work on Piaget's theory, Kamii demonstrates that children do not learn math, but instead reinvent it, or construct it from within—with or without direct instruction. Instead of skill and drill, children are encouraged to use arithmetic in daily living situations and in math games. These books explained many of my "gut" feelings about why my students might be having difficulty with certain concepts. For example, learning place value and double-column addition/subtraction is developmentally too difficult for young children. This book gave me alternatives and better ways to work with my students. There is much food for thought, as well as a vast assortment of games and activities, in these two volumes. I would highly recommend them to anyone working with primary-grade children, and I would suggest that teachers of older students watch for volumes at their grade level. (V.M.)

Lilburn, Pat, and Pam Rawson. 1994. *Let's Talk Math: Encouraging Children to Explore Ideas.* Portsmouth, NH: Heinemann.

This book is designed for students in grades 3–6. It contains forty group activities that encourage children to talk and write mathematically about various everyday problems related to number, space, and measurement. Each activity is carefully described and illustrated by examples of student responses and comments by teachers who have tried them. (V.M.)

National Council of Teachers of Mathematics. 1906 Association Drive. Reston, VA 22091-1593. (telephone 703-620-9840)

The National Council of Teachers of Mathematics (NCTM) has been a driving force in the reform of mathematics education with the publication of the Curricu-

lum and Evaluation Standards for School Mathematics *and* Professional Standards for Teaching Mathematics *(see annotations)*. *NCTM publishes several professional journals, including* Teaching Children Mathematics *for teachers of grades pre-K–6,* Mathematics Teaching in the Middle School *for teachers of grades 5–9, and* Mathematics Teacher *for teachers of grades 8–12. NCTM also publishes the* Journal for Research in Mathematics Education *and a wide variety of books and videotapes on all aspects of mathematics education. NCTM sponsors an annual, national conference as well as several regional conferences and many mathematics award programs.*

National Council of Teachers of Mathematics. 1989. *Curriculum and Evaluation Standards for School Mathematics.* Reston, VA: National Council of Teachers of Mathematics.

This comprehensive document (266 pp.) recognizes and addresses the need for major instructional reform in the content and emphasis in mathematics K–12. Fifty-four standards are delineated and divided into four areas: K–4, 5–8, 9–12, and evaluation. Embedded in the Standards is the belief that "First, 'knowing' mathematics is 'doing' mathematics. A person gathers, discovers, or creates knowledge in the course of some activity having a purpose" (p. 7). Also in each standard are the expected student activities associated with doing mathematics. The document bases its curriculum and evaluation of mathematical literacy on five goals for all students: learning to value mathematics, becoming confident in one's own ability, becoming a mathematical problem solver, learning to communicate mathematically, and learning to reason mathematically. All educators interested in improving the quality of school mathematics will want to become familiar with this highly impressive and workable document.

National Council of Teachers of Mathematics. 1991. *Professional Standards for Teaching Mathematics.* Reston, VA: National Council of Teachers of Mathematics.

This document has been created to provide specific direction and support to teachers for creating mathematical environments, actions, and activities that complement the goals set out in the landmark document for reform, Curriculum and Evaluation Standards for School Mathematics *(NCTM, 1989; see annotation). This text provides guidance for the development of professionalism in the teaching of mathematics and includes standards for teaching mathematics and for evaluating the teaching of mathematics, to name a few. Each professional standard for teachers is explained in depth and illustrated by vignettes depicting excellent teaching. For teachers using the NCTM Standards for how and what students should learn and be taught (1989), this companion document for professional development is a must for meeting the challenges and making the changes in mathematics teaching in the classroom.*

Ohanian, Susan. 1992. *Garbage Pizza, Patchwork Quilts, and Math Magic: Stories about Teachers Who Love to Teach and Children Who Love to Learn.* New York: W. H. Freeman. Distributed by Heinemann.

With a grant from the Exxon Corporation Foundation, the author spent a year visiting K–3 classrooms in which exciting math projects were happening. The resulting book reads like a novel, as teachers make the NCTM Standards come alive with innovative, creative teaching techniques, such as making a pie graph of types of environmental waste, which became the "garbage pizza" of the book's title. The book conveys the enthusiasm of teachers, parents, and administrators who are working together to excite children about the potential of mathematical learning. (V.M.)

Rowan, Thomas, and Barbara Bourne. 1994. *Thinking Like Mathematicians: Putting the K–4 NCTM Standards into Practice.* Portsmouth, NH: Heinemann.

This very practical resource will be appreciated by teachers who want to implement the NCTM Standards. Each chapter is filled with strategies that are explained through vignettes and anecdotes. Specific chapters discuss planning and implementing the program, evaluation, and questions that teachers might have. I especially enjoyed the case study of a student who is thinking and growing as a mathematician while using the concepts embedded in the NCTM Standards. (V.M.)

Welchman-Tischler, Rosamond. 1992. *How to Use Children's Literature to Teach Mathematics.* Reston, VA: The National Council of Teachers of Mathematics.

This seventy-nine-page resource, part of the NCTM "how to . . ." series, describes ways to use children's literature to develop mathematical concepts and connections. Specific plans and sample activities are given for many children's books. Elementary teachers, especially primary teachers, find this a helpful resource. See also The Wonderful World of Mathematics: A Critically Annotated List of Children's Books in Mathematics *by Diane Thiessen and Margaret Matthias (NCTM, 1992).*

Whitin, David J., Heidi Mills, and Timothy O'Keefe. 1990. *Living and Learning Mathematics: Stories and Strategies for Supporting Mathematical Literacy.* Portsmouth, NH: Heinemann.

This text brings the reader into a transitional first-grade classroom where children learn about mathematical principles through daily exploration and sharing of their own problem-solving strategies. Mathematics is explored through children's interests, curricular themes, classroom events, children's literature, as well as through graphing. Numbers are used for real purposes as children write original mathematical stories about such everyday concerns as losing and growing teeth and fish living and dying in the classroom. The primary-grade teacher will find this a useful resource for meaningfully connecting mathematics to the lives of children.

Whitin, David J., and Sandra Wilde. 1992. *Read Any Good Math Lately? Children's Books for Mathematical Learning, K–6.* Portsmouth, NH: Heinemann.

In this volume many interesting books are suggested that will support growing mathematical literacy. Each chapter is organized around a topic, such as multiplication, fractions, or estimation. After a general discussion of the suggested books, the reader is taken into a classroom at various levels (K–2, 3–4, 5–6) where children's responses related to specific books are described. Further explorations are suggested, and a comprehensive bibliography ends each chapter. This book is a treasure chest of ideas for bringing literature into the mathematical curriculum. (V.M.)

Social Studies Books and Resources

"If American history is being studied, a novel about colonial life will be valuable, but only as primarily an aesthetic experience, a sharing of what it would have been like to live in those days. If the story has been read with a primarily aesthetic emphasis, one can later, of course, ask students to recall incidental information about, for example, methods of transportation. But it would often be helpful to suggest that the author of the poem or novel had acquired that information through verified historical sources" (Rosenblatt, 1991, p. 447).

For easy reference, both the Social Studies and Science Books and Resources have been listed in alphabetical order by title.

Adventures with Social Studies Through Literature by Sharron L. McElmeel. 1991. Englewood, CO: Teacher Ideas Press.

In integrating language arts with social studies, McElmeel looks at other times and places through such topics as folklore, Laura Ingalls Wilder's books, Gary Paulsen's books, books related to coming to America, and American heroes. For each of these chapter topics and others, she gives background information, concepts to be highlighted, literature and authors to be discussed, and suggested response activities. Many addresses for authors and poets featured in this volume are included to promote student correspondence.

• *Children's Literature & Social Studies: Selecting and Using Notable Books in the*

Classroom, edited by Myra Zarnowski and Arlene F. Gallagher. 1993. Washington, DC: National Council for the Social Studies.

This treasure of a resource for K–8 teachers gives a wealth of practical information for using excellent trade books in the social studies program. Part 1 of the book examines the selection of books; Part 2 addresses ways to purposefully use these books. In-depth information is given for choosing and using nonfiction to read aloud, picture books, biographies, autobiographies, and historical novels. Suggested ways to use these books in discussion and writing about significant social issues are included. Excellent bibliographies, some of which are annotated, abound throughout this terrific book (80 pp.).

Cobblestone Publishing, Inc. 7 School Street, Peterborough, NH 03458.

During the school year, Cobblestone publishes monthly and bimonthly themed magazines for young people, ages 8–16: Cobblestone: The History Magazine for Young People; Calliope: World History for Young People; Faces: The Magazine About People; *and* Odyssey: Science That's Out of This World. *These quality magazines, which contain well-researched, well-written articles supported by photographs and illustrations, can be used to support an integrated curriculum. All back issues can be ordered.*

Constructing Buildings, Bridges, and Minds: Building an Integrated Curriculum Through Social Studies by Katherine A. Young. 1994. Portsmouth, NH: Heinemann.

Any teacher wanting to implement a "learning across the curriculum" project will want to read this book detailing the integration of the curriculum through a year-long classroom social studies project. Two major projects on Washington, DC, and Latin America were undertaken in the upper-elementary classroom taught by the author. The author describes the planning, the children and what they did, and what happened. She does not offer a "how-to" manual, but instead shows the often spontaneous, but carefully planned, activities that took place over the year. This is an intriguing book with many ideas to consider and think about if we are to help children to take charge of their learning and become lifelong learners. (V.M.)

"Developing Social Studies Concepts Through Picture Books" by Pamela J. Farris and Carol J. Fuhler. February 1994. *The Reading Teacher,* pp. 380–385.

Geared to middle- and upper-elementary students, this article demonstrates how picture books can be used to teach social studies. Criteria for choosing picture books and examples of how these books can be used to extend students' thinking and knowledge are included.

From Sea to Shining Sea: Ohio by Dennis Brindell Fradin. 1993. Chicago, IL: Children's Press.

This is but one title in a clearly written and illustrated series about our states that is written for the upper-elementary grades. In addition to a text of about fifty pages, each book includes a table of contents, a "Did You Know?" section of interesting and unusual facts, an information section of vital facts, a listing of important historical dates and events, a state map, a glossary, and an index. Appealing content and format.

- "Historical Literacy: A Journey of Discovery" by Cynthia Stearns Nelson. April 1994. *The Reading Teacher,* pp. 552–556.

A fifth-grade teacher does a terrific job explaining how she develops historical literacy in her classroom. She begins with three important questions: (1) What are the big understandings or concepts to be developed? (2) What cultural beliefs and values influence our perceptions of this content? (3) What resources are available for studying this content? (p. 553). Nelson's framework and "Sample Unit, the Stories of Mildred Taylor" provide an excellent model for any teacher who wants to meaningfully integrate the teaching of social studies into the curriculum.

History Workshop: Reconstructing the Past with Elementary Students by Karen L. Jorgensen. 1993. Portsmouth, NH: Heinemann.

"I realized that learning about history,

like learning to read and write, was a process in which children create or construct personal and social meaning." So writes teacher Karen Jorgensen who shares her three-year exploration in grades three through five of how she came to apply the writing workshop model to teaching history. This honest, personal narrative (167 pp.) lets us in on classroom conversations between Jorgensen and her students and also gives us many examples of activities employed in the history workshop. Recommended for teachers making the transition to teaching history so it connects with all language learning. Applicable to all the elementary grades.

Literature-Based Social Studies: Children's Books and Activities to Enrich the K–5 Curriculum by Mildred Knight Laughlin and Patricia Payne Kardaleff. 1991. Phoenix, AZ: Oryx Press.

Many themes with suggested books and activities to extend the social studies curriculum are found in this excellent reference text. Topics include Economics of Family Living, Pioneer Communities, Urban Living, World Neighbors, the American Frontier, the Civil War Era, and many more. This is a helpful book that should be in every elementary library. (V.M.)

National Council for the Social Studies. 3501 Newark Street, NW, Washington, DC 20016-3167. (telephone 202-966-7840)

The National Council for the Social Studies publishes Social Studies and the Young Learner *for elementary teachers (see annotation),* Social Education *for middle school and college teachers,* Curriculum Standards for the Social Studies *(Fall 1994), and many other publications related to teaching and learning in social studies. Also holds an annual conference, as well as regional and state conferences, to focus on issues in social studies.*

New True Books. 1990–1993. Chicago, IL: Children's Press.

There are dozens of interesting books with lots of photographs on a wide range of subjects in this social studies and science series. Books deal with such social studies topics as Congress, newspapers, Mexico,

North America, and money. Written for the primary grades.

"Notable Children's Trade Books in the Field of Social Studies." Children's Book Council, 568 Broadway, New York, NY 10012.

Published annually and jointly with the National Council for the Social Studies, this resource is a great way to keep up with the latest and best new books—including folktales and legends. (See Children's Literature and Social Studies [1993] for ways to use these titles in the classroom.) Send a self-addressed, stamped envelope for your copy.

Social Education. Washington, DC: National Council for the Social Studies.

This scholarly journal on the teaching of social studies is published seven times a year. Includes position statements, research, articles, and practical ideas for the teaching of social studies. The annual April/May issue includes "Notable Children's Trade Books in the Field of Social Studies," a specially selected annotated bibliography for children in grades K–8.

Social Studies and the Young Learner. Washington, DC: National Council for the Social Studies.

A quarterly journal for K–6 teachers to support the creative teaching of social studies. Some issues are devoted to a specific theme. Includes related children's literature, reviews of books and resources for the classroom, discussions of contemporary issues, and practical ideas and strategies for the elementary teacher. Very informative journal with lots of applicable information.

Social Studies Through Children's Literature: An Integrated Approach by Anthony D. Fredericks. 1991. Englewood, CO: Teacher Ideas Press.

Fredericks describes many projects and activities for enhancing the teaching of social studies through literature in the elementary classroom. Questions and activities are presented for about thirty titles. While there are too many questions and activities presented for each book, many of the activities can serve as good models for creating your own meaningful exten-

sions. The annotated literature and resources for social studies included in the appendices are excellent.

- *The Story of Ourselves: Teaching History Through Children's Literature* by Michael Tunnell and Richard Ammon. 1993. Portsmouth, NH: Heinemann.

  We are reminded as we read this wonderful resource for making history come alive for students that the word "history" is made up mostly of the word "story" and that historians have always been storytellers of human events and behaviors. The authors of this 204-page text convincingly give the research and rationale for using historical trade literature as the best way to help children develop historical judgment. As compared to textbooks, trade books offer richer vocabulary, greater detail, a more engaging writing style, enhanced coherence and drama as well as broader perspectives.

  This book is terrific for a close-up look at the creative process that writers of historical fiction and nonfiction use, the process of researching and writing historical literature—including a comparison of textbooks and trade books—and useful strategies and units for teaching history with trade books. The extensive, annotated bibliographies include an "Anne Frank Unit" and books specific to "Americans at War," "Human Rights," "Governing America," and "Settling New Lands." This is an invaluable resource for K–8 educators ready to meaningfully integrate the teaching of social studies into the curriculum and for becoming familiar with the best nonfiction and historical fiction writers for young people.

Understanding American History Through Children's Literature: Instructional Units and Activities for Grades K–8 by Maria A. Perez-Stable and Mary Hurlbut Cordier. 1994. Phoenix, AZ: Oryx Press.

  This volume has been organized into two sections: Part 1 for primary grades, and Part 2 for the intermediate and middle school grades. Within each section, units of instruction are planned that explore the history of the United States from

pre-Columbus to the present. In each section, many books are annotated so teachers can easily choose and select appropriate materials for their classrooms. (V.M.)

Science Books and Resources

Following are some selected resources to go along with "big understandings" and independent reading and research in an integrated science program. For understanding integration see pp. 276–294 in *Invitations*, as well as professional books and resources in these "blue pages."

The Astonishing Curriculum: Integrating Science and Humanities Through Language, edited by Stephen Tchudi. 1993. Urbana, IL: National Council of Teachers of English.

  In this collection of essays, teachers from first-grade level through graduate school share classroom practices that bridge the gap between science and the humanities. I especially enjoyed how the students of Karen Gallas use "science talks" and "science journals" to find the answers to difficult questions. Regardless of your teaching level, there are many ideas for educators to consider as they plan science experiences for children. (V.M.)

- *Benchmarks for Science Literacy: Project 2061* by the American Association for the Advancement of Science. 1993. New York: Oxford University Press.

  Carefully written by six school-district teams and extensively reviewed and rewritten, this companion book to Science for All Americans *(American Association for the Advancement of Science, 1990) provides school districts with benchmarks, "statements of what all students should be able to do" in science, mathematics, and technology. Benchmarks are provided for the end of grades two, five, eight, and twelve, and are meant to be used as a tool to guide school districts in designing and developing their own science curriculum and instructional materials for what students should know, understand, and be able to do scientifically. An essential re-*

source and exemplary model for curriculum reform.

Connections: The Living Planet, edited by Jenifer Ludbrook, Sharon Stewart, and Jocelyn Van Huyse-Ludbrook. 1993. Scarborough, Ontario: Ginn Publishing Canada.

This exciting series of twelve books for the intermediate grades is organized around three environmental issues: Life and the Planet, People and the Planet, and Planetary Change. The books explore basic concepts about ecology, requirements of human life, and ways that humans influence the ecosystem. Some titles include Water in Our World, The Remarkable RainForest, *and* The Earth Feeds Us.

Creepy Crawlies and the Scientific Method: Over 100 Hands-On Science Experiments for Children by Sally Stenhouse Kneidel. 1993. Golden, CO: Fulcrum Publishing.

This book for parents and teachers demonstrates how to use insects and crawling creatures to teach children the five steps of the scientific method: question, hypothesis, methods, result, and conclusion. Each chapter is clearly formatted with background information, lots of experiments, and clear procedures. Great for getting kids excited about science and thinking about and testing their own questions. Written for elementary teachers but suitable for secondary also.

Dear World: How Children Around the World Feel About Our Environment, edited by Lannis Temple. 1993. New York: Random House.

A collection of letters, drawings, and photos from around the world beautifully illustrates schoolchildren's concerns about environmental pollution. Students are encouraged to add their own letters and drawings.

Earth Science for Every Kid: 101 Easy Experiments That Really Work by Janice VanCleave. 1991. New York: John Wiley.

Students and teachers love this book because the experiments can be done easily at home or at school, and they really work. Experiments and activities are detailed with step-by-step instructions and illustrations. An easily understood scien-

tific explanation is given for the results of each experiment. Check the other books in this workable series.

Exploring Nature by Peter Garland. 1992. Crystal Lake, IL: Rigby

These six twenty-four-page books for the primary grades include vivid color photography and interesting text. Titles include Animals of the Rocky Shore, The Housefly, The Frog, The Ladybug, The Marvelous Mosquito, *and* The Pond.

First Discovery Books by Nancy Krulik. 1992. New York: Scholastic.

These unique, beautifully illustrated little books include brightly colored transparent overlays and laminated pages to entice the reader into making discoveries and seeing connections. Some titles in the series are Airplanes and Flying Machines, The Earth and Sky, The Egg, The Tree, *and* Weather. *Appealing for preschool through early intermediate grades.*

First Library Paperbacks by Kate Petty. 1990. New York: Franklin Watts.

This information-packed picture book series for the primary grades includes six nonfiction books: Crocodiles and Alligators, Dinosaurs, Frogs and Toads, Sharks, Snakes, *and* Spiders.

Green Giants: Rainforests of the Pacific Northwest by Tom Parkin. 1992. Buffalo, NY: Firefly Books.

This is but one book (48 pp.) in a series of Earth Care Books *that are full of accurate text and illustrations that describe the topic, what the problems are, and what we must do environmentally. Other books in the series for the intermediate grades include* For the Birds, Trash Attack!, Garbage and What We Can Do About It, Get Growing! How the Earth Feeds Us, *and* The Heat is On: Facing Our Energy Problem.

Ideas for Environmental Education in the Elementary Classroom by Kath Murdoch. 1994. Portsmouth, NH: Heinemann

This unique guidebook (204 pp.) for the primary grades focuses on activities and strategies to develop key understandings about the environment. Well-organized, workable plans include broad understandings, preparations, procedures, sam-

ples of children's work, and resource materials. Terrific for integrating environmental education across the curriculum and for problem-solving issues related to living on Earth.

Informazing!, edited by Stephen Moline. 1988–1990. Crystal Lake, IL: Rigby.

Eight, sixteen-page, little books and Big Books dealing with topics such as insects, the universe, animals, dinosaurs, and the body captivate children's imaginations with their lively, clear text and bright, realistic photographs. Geared to the primary grades.

Keeping Minibeasts by Barrie Watts. 1989. New York: Franklin Watts.

Simple text and close-up color photographs depict how to care for small creatures (such as caterpillars, frogs, ladybugs, and spiders) in this nature series for the primary grades. Ten titles in the series. Ideal for supporting independent research.

Let's-Read-And-Find-Out Science. 1992–1994. New York: HarperCollins Publishers.

This is a well-written and illustrated series of over sixty picture books for the primary grades. Some new titles include Be a Friend to Trees *by Patricia Lauber, illustrated by Holly Keller,* Where Does the Garbage Go? *by Paul Showers, illustrated by Randy Chewing,* What Makes a Shadow *by Clyde Robert Bulla, illustrated by June Otani, and* Baby Whales Drink Milk *by Barbara Juster Esbensen, illustrated by Juster Esbensen. Basic science concepts are introduced in an organized manner, and easy to follow hands-on activities are included. Topics include the* Human Body, Plants and Animals, *the* World Around Us, Dinosaurs, Outer Space, Weather and the Seasons, *and* Our Earth. *Great for the classroom library and supporting young children's natural curiosity.*

My World. 1989–1992. Austin, TX: Steck-Vaughn.

This high-interest science and social studies, nonfiction collection for grades 1–3 includes 144 titles dealing with animals, sports, nature, and nations of the world. Each sixteen-page book includes sizable

text, full-color photographs, and an index. Some titles are available in Spanish.

National Science Teachers Association. 1840 Wilson Boulevard, Arlington, VA 22201. (telephone 703-243-7100)

The National Science Teachers Association publishes Science and Children *for elementary teachers (see annotation),* Science Scope *for teachers of grades 5–9,* The Science Teacher *for teachers of grades 7–12,* The Journal of College Science Teaching *for college teachers, and many useful books and resources to support science teaching. NSTA also publishes* Quantum, *a student magazine of math and science and* "NSTA Reports!," *a science education newspaper. Also sponsors an annual, national conference as well as three regional conferences and many science award programs.*

Picture Library Paperbacks by Norman Barrett. 1989–1991. New York: Franklin Watts.

This series of about twenty nonfiction books (can be ordered individually) is packed with information, beautiful photographs, and clear, simple text for grades K–4 and is a welcome addition to the classroom library. Some titles include Polar Animals, Elephants, Bears, Airliners, Trail Bikes, *and* Helicopters.

Primary Ecology Series, edited by Bobbie Kalman. 1993. New York and Toronto: Crabtree Publishing.

Beautifully photographed with elementary school children in natural settings to support the books' subjects, these thirty-two-page picture books are full of information and invite participation in caring for our world. Some titles in the series include How Trees Help Me *and* The Air I Breathe. *Very appealing.*

Rookie Read-About Science by Allan Fowler. 1993. Chicago, IL: Children's Press.

A delightful, informative series of thirty-two-page little books on topics that interest young children. Some of the titles in this extensive series include If It Weren't for Farmers, It's a Good Thing There Are Insects, It's Best to Leave a Snake Alone, *and* It Could Still Be a Dinosaur. *Real-life photos, large, clear text, and only several sentences per page make this a welcome addition to the early primary classroom and school library.*

Science and Children. Washington, DC: National Science Teachers Association. 1840 Wilson Boulevard, Arlington, VA, 22201

This informative and practical science journal for elementary and middle school teachers and administrators is published eight times a year and is available with membership to NSTA. Provides thoughtful articles, practical and creative teaching suggestions, reviews of books and resources, colorful posters, and inserts as well as the annual "Notable Science Tradebooks for Children" in a spring issue.

Science and Language Links: Classroom Implications, edited by Johanna Scott. 1993. Portsmouth, NH: Heinemann.

Although it was written halfway across the world in Australia, this book could be a companion book to The Astonishing Curriculum: Integrating Science and Humanities Through Language *(Tchudi, 1993). This book looks at the relationships between science and talking, writing, and reading. It helps teachers to realize that language supports science learning, and science concepts can be used to develop language. Examples of student projects enhance the insights in this book. (V.M.)*

Science for All Americans: Project 2061 by the American Association for the Advancement of Science. 1990. New York: Oxford University Press.

Science for All Americans *is the highly respected philosophical treatise on what constitutes adult literacy in science. Literacy in science is defined broadly, to encompass concepts of mathematics and technology as well as the natural and social sciences. Used widely in the U.S. to help guide reform efforts, this scholarly text (272 pp.) deals with the nature of science, basic world knowledge from the scientific perspective, what scientific concepts people should understand, and the "habits of mind" that are necessary for science literacy.*

Recommendations for what scientifically literate students should know and be able

to do by the time they graduate from high school are stated. See the companion book, Benchmarks for Science Literacy, *and watch for the upcoming* Blueprints for Reform *and* Designs for Science Literacy.

Science Through Children's Literature by Carol M. Butzow and John W. Butzow. 1989. Englewood, CO: Teacher Ideas Press.

This useful resource geared to the elementary grades connects fiction books with scientific concepts by describing many activities to go along with specific books. Activities for each science topic are centered around a work of fiction. Related books and references are cited.

Science Workshop: A Whole Language Approach by Wendy Saul, et al. 1993. Portsmouth, NH: Heinemann.

Concepts and ideas developed in the reading/writing workshop are shown to be applicable in the study of science in this book. Wendy Saul provides the introductory theoretical framework in the opening chapter. Four teachers present ways of getting started, developing a questioning atmosphere, and ways of assessing the program. The final chapter gives suggestions for topic development as well as sources for materials and further information. This is a hands-on, practical approach that will be appreciated by classroom teachers eager to bring student-centered learning to the science area. (V.M.)

Sierra Club Books for Children. 1992–1994. 730 Polk Street, San Francisco, CA 94109.

The Sierra Club publishes some first-class books for children. The inspiring books include engaging text and full-color photographs to tackle environmental issues, present accurate information, and share how children and adults can make a difference. A favorite, highly acclaimed book is Come Back, Salmon *by Molly Cone, photographs by Sidnee Wheelwright (1992), the compelling story about how a group of fifth-grade students adopted a polluted stream that had once been a spawning ground for salmon and brought it back to life.*

Snapshot, edited by Mary Ling. 1994. New York: Covent Garden Books.

Titles in this series for the primary

grades, which devotes one to two pages (a snapshot in enlarged print and pictures) to each subtopic, include Wild Animals, Things on Wheels, Animal Antics, and Funny Faces.

Sunshine Science, Level 2 by Brian Cutting and Jillian Cutting. 1993. Bothell, WA: The Wright Group.

These information books with such titles as Keeping Warm! Keeping Cool!, How Flies Live, The Survival of Fish, and Our Eyes are a good addition to the classroom library. Each twenty-four-page book has sizable text, clear concepts, and color photo/illustrations. First and second graders will enjoy reading these independently or with support.

Author/Illustrator Books and Resources

• *Art for Children.* 1994. New York: Chelsea House Publishers. (hardbound)

Written with conversational text from the viewpoint of inquiring students, this fascinating series of books takes the reader into the life, thoughts, times, and art of some of the most renowned artists: Brueghel, Chagall, Leonardo da Vinci, Degas, Gauguin, Matisse, Picasso, Rousseau, and Van Gogh. Each book is about sixty pages and includes photographs related to the artists' lives along with color reproductions of their paintings. Engaging reading for grades 3–6.

Blair, Gwenda. Illustrated by Thomas B. Allen. 1981. *Laura Ingalls Wilder.* New York: Putnam. See annotation, p. 152b.

Chevalier, Tracy. 1990. *Twentieth-Century Children's Writers,* 4th ed. Chicago: St. James Press. (hardbound)

This useful teacher reference features over 800 contributors in literature. For each author, there is a lengthy, interesting narrative biographical account and a list of publications. Lots of information for in-depth author study.

• Commire, Anne (ed.). 1994: *Something About the Author.* Detroit: Gale Research. (hardbound)

Written for teachers and students, this is the most complete and extensive resource on children's authors and illustrators. Most entries are autobiographical and include the following information: personal, career, writings, and sidelights. Updated every year since 1972, there are over sixty volumes in this reference series, and each volume includes a cumulative index. If your school district does not own this outstanding series, check with your local public library.

Copeland, Jeffrey S. 1993. *Speaking of Poets: Interviews with Poets Who Write for Children and Young Adults.* Urbana, IL: National Council of Teachers of English.

Sixteen poets are interviewed by Copeland about what they hope to accomplish as they write for children. Many of them, such as Arnold Adoff and Myra Cohn Livingston, are recipients of the NCTE Award for Excellence in Poetry for Children. Bibliographies of each poet's works follow each interview. This is a valuable book for background information about the poets, as well as for assistance in locating a selection of their poetry. (V.M.)

Cummings, Pat (ed.). 1992. *Talking With Artists.* New York: Bradbury Press.

Questions asked of artists such as Leo and Diane Dillon, Lois Ehlert, Tom Feelings, Jerry Pinkney, Lane Smith, Chris Van Allsburg, and David Wiesner include where they get their ideas, whether family is included in their work, and how they make pictures. Illustrations include early work by the artists, a childhood and an adult photograph, and art work from a well-known book. Excellent resource material for author background and for discussing how artists get their ideas. Fourteen picture book illustrators are included.

Day, Frances Ann (compiler). 1994. *Multicultural Voices in Contemporary Literature.* Portsmouth, NH: Heinemann. See annotation, p. 63b.

dePaola, Tomie. 1989. *The Art Lesson.* New York: Putnam. (Sandcastle)

The popular author-illustrator tells and draws about growing up wanting to be an artist and his not-very-encouraging early school experiences. Very appealing for K–2 students and everyone who is determined to be uniquely creative.

Fox, Mem. 1992. *Dear Mem Fox, I Have Read All Your Books Even the Pathetic Ones: And Other Incidents in the Life of a Children's Book Author.* San Diego: Harvest/Harcourt Brace.

The best-selling author of Possum Magic *and* Hattie and the Fox *shares her early life experiences, and tells how she came to create her unique books. From lighthearted to serious, this book gives her insights on teaching, authoring, her brush with cancer, and life in general. An inspiring and delightful book to read! (V.M.)*

Gallo, Donald R. (ed.). 1992. *Authors' Insights: Turning Teenagers into Readers and Writers.* Portsmouth, NH: Boynton/Cook.

A group of distinguished young adult writers contributed essays on the subject of teaching literature to teenagers in this book. They cover topics such as the importance of using "readable" books in the classroom, censorship, response to books, teaching writing, and bringing authors into the classroom. Their unique experiences give teachers a lot to think about as they plan for their students. (V.M.)*

Gherman, Beverly. 1992. *E.B. White: Some Writer!* New York: Beech Tree.

Illustrated with photographs, this book gives us a chance to meet the man behind Charlotte's Web, Stuart Little, *and* The Trumpet of the Swan. *White wrote extensively for adults, but these three books he created for children have become classics. I especially enjoyed the chapters describing the creation of these wonderful books. There are many anecdotes that can be shared with your students. (V.M.)*

Holtze, Sally Holmes. 1989. *Sixth Book of Junior Authors and Illustrators.* New York: H. W. Wilson.

This teacher reference, the sixth in the series, offers complete and interesting autobiographical and biographical sketches of about 250 noted children's authors and illustrators. A new volume is published every five to six years.*

Hyman, Trina Schart. 1989. *Self-Portrait:*
Trina Schart Hyman. New York: Harper & Row. See annotation, p. 153b.

Immell, Myra (ed.). 1992. *The Young Adult Reader's Adviser: The Best in Literature and Language Arts, Mathematics and Computer Science. Volume One;* and *The Young Adult Reader's Adviser: The Best in Social Sciences and History, Science and Health. Volume Two.* New Providence, NJ: Bowker.

These volumes have been written to assist students, teachers, and librarians with the wide selection of resources available. Alphabetized by author within the subject category, each entry includes biographical information about the author including books by and about the author.*

Killen, Rosemary (project director). 1988. *The Author's Eye.* Santa Rosa, CA: American School Publishers.

Each complete program—available for authors Roald Dahl and Katherine Paterson—includes an excellent video of the author in his or her writing setting, twenty-five "Author's Notebooks," a poster, and a teacher's resource book. The terrific "Author's Notebooks," which are sold in packages of twenty-five and can be ordered separately, include letters written by the author, first drafts, notes, jottings, and favorite phrases and words. Inspiring for understanding how a writer works and for stimulating students' own writing. Very expensive.*

• Kovaks, Deborah, and James Preller. 1993. *Meet the Authors and Illustrators: 60 Creators of Favorite Children's Books Talk About Their Work. Volume Two.* New York: Scholastic Professional Books.

For each engaging two-page profile of a well-known, favorite author or illustrator, the following is included: some early memories, the creative process each goes through, a picture of the author or illustrator, selected published titles, statements by the author or illustrator, photocopies of the cover of one or two favorite books or illustrations, and a terrific activity suggested by the author or illustrator. See also Volume One, 1991. Both resources are visually appealing and filled with interest-*

ing information for students and teachers. My favorite part about these profiles is that each is written in a way that encourages young writers to write their own stories and/or create their own illustrations.

Lloyd, Pamela. 1990. *How Writers Write.* Portsmouth, NH: Heinemann.

Using a question-and-answer format, the author has put together a book that shows how writers live and work. She interviews authors such as Robert Cormier, Madeleine L'Engle, Jack Prelutsky, Seymour Simon, and Jane Yolen to find out how they write a first draft, where ideas come from, how they conduct research, and why they are writers. There are many ideas that can be shared with your students. (V.M.)

• *Meet the Author Collection.* 1993–1994. Katonah, NY: Richard C. Owen. (hardbound)

Written by the authors themselves for seven-to-ten-year-old readers and illustrated with real-life, color photographs of authors at home and at work, each of these thirty-two-page books is terrific for kids to read on their own. Even as an adult, I found these books fascinating. Readers will notice how and where authors live and write, get many of their ideas, and organize their days. The prominent children's authors in the series include Verna Aardema, James Howe, Jean Fritz, Lee Bennett Hopkins, Jane Yolen, Rafe Martin, Karla Kuskin, Paul Goble, Patricia Polacco, Margaret Mahy, Eve Bunting, Patricia McKissack, and Cynthia Rylant. Great for learning about favorite authors and for motivating reading of their books. Also terrific for motivating children's own writing. Available as individual titles.

Norby, Shirley, and Gregory Ryan. 1989. *Famous Children's Authors.* Book Two. Minneapolis, MN: T. S. Denison.

A grade-two teacher and a children's librarian have written twenty author stories for young readers to enjoy and gain information about popular authors. Each two-page entry ends with a bibliography of the authors' books. Sequel to Book One.

Quackenbush, Robert. 1985. *Once Upon a Time: A Story of the Brothers Grimm.* New York: Simon & Schuster. See annotation, p. 152b.

Rosen, Michael J. (ed.). 1993. *Speak! Children's Book Illustrators Brag About Their Dogs.* San Diego: Harcourt Brace.

Kids and adults love this book. Fortythree famous illustrators brag, in pictures and stories, about their dogs. The personalities of the dogs—and the illustrators—shine through. Editor Michael Rosen invites children to write to him and "send me a little bragging about your favorite dog." A totally entertaining and engaging book.

Rylant, Cynthia. 1993. *But I'll Be Back Again: An Autobiography by the Newbery Award-Winning Author.* New York: Beech Tree.

In this book, Rylant describes the influences on her life: her grandmother, a tiny town named Beaver, the Beatles, and Robert Kennedy. How a little girl from rural West Virginia who grew up without books became an award-winning author becomes clear after you read these words. Her books become even more meaningful as she mentions where some of her ideas and characters come from. (V.M.)

Shapiro, Miles. 1994. *Maya Angelou: Author.* New York: Chelsea House. See annotation, p. 152b.

Tunnell, Michael O., and Richard Ammon. 1993. "The Creative Process." In *The Story of Ourselves: Teaching History Through Children's Literature,* edited by Michael O. Tunnell and Richard Ammon. Portsmouth, NH: Heinemann, pp. 9–47.

Four well-known authors (Joan W. Blos, Milton Meltzer, Pam Conrad, Russell Freedman) and an illustrator (Leonard Everett Fisher) describe their own process of writing and illustrating historical fiction and nonfiction and, in so doing, make elementary through middle school students "insiders" to the process. I found the reading fascinating and saw possibilities for children's writing. For example, in writing nonfiction, Russell Freedman vividly describes his storytelling devices: creating a detailed scene that the reader can visualize, developing a character through explicit word pictures, and using telling an-

ecdotes. For the annotation of the complete text, see p. 93b.

- Turner, Robyn Montana. 1992. *Georgia O'Keeffe (Portraits of Women Artists for Children)*. New York: Little, Brown.

    This is but one in an excellent series of biographies of prominent women artists Rosa Bonheur, Mary Cassatt, Frida Kahlo, Georgia O'Keeffe, and Faith Ringgold. The books are distinctive for the informative, carefully researched text, photographs related to the artist's life, and beautiful color reproductions of the artist's work. Use as a read-aloud for the early grades. Intermediate-grade students can read them on their own. Reaffirming to young women (and young men) who are interested in art and becoming artists. Fills a need for more books on famous women.

Venezia, Mike. 1990–1994. *Getting to Know the World's Greatest Artists*. Chicago, IL: Children's Press.

    A great series for introducing young children to art and artists. Written in enlarged, clear text, the book presents the artist as a real person. Color reproductions of the artist's work plus fanciful illustrations open up the world of art to students in grades K–4. Some of the celebrated artists in the series include: Botticelli, Leonardo da Vinci, Hopper, Goya, Cassatt, Monet, Picasso, Gauguin, Rembrandt, and Van Gogh.

Winter, Jeanette, and John Winter. 1991. *Diego*. New York: Knopf. See annotation, p. 153b.

Parent Books and Resources

Baghban, Marcia. 1989. *You Can Help Your Young Child with Writing*. Newark, DE: International Reading Association.

    This pamphlet is part of a series designed to provide parents with practical ideas to use to support young learners. Beginning with anecdotes of young children writing, it describes how the child's understanding of the writing system differs from that of the adult writer. Answers to possible parent questions, such as "What about correctness?" are given, along with recommended readings for more information. A helpful guide to hand to a questioning parent! (V.M.)

Barron, Marlene. 1990. *I Learn to Read and Write the Way I Learn to Talk*. Katonah, NY: Richard C. Owen.

    Based on whole language theory and practice, this concise booklet (32 pp.) simply and clearly explains early reading and writing behaviors. Excellent to share with preschool through grade one parents.

Baskwill, Jane. 1989. *Parents and Teachers: Partners in Learning*. Richmond Hill, Ontario: Scholastic Canada. See annotation, p. 4b.

- Bialostok, Steven. 1992. *Raising Readers: Helping Your Child to Literacy*. Winnipeg, Manitoba: Peguis.

    This is a terrific book to lend or give to parents who want specific information about how children learn to read, what to look for in their children's reading, and how they can support the process. Bialostok answers the questions parents have about reading aloud, the role of phonics, skills teaching, prediction, literacy development, school, and much more. Viewing reading as a process of making meaning, he gives parents perspectives and specific strategies for helping their young children develop as readers. Every parent I have lent this book to has found it easy to read and understand and incredibly helpful.

Butler, Dorothy, and Marie Clay. 1988, 1987. *Reading Begins at Home, Writing Begins at Home*. 2nd ed. Portsmouth, NH: Heinemann.

    These companion books are very useful in helping parents to understand how young children learn to read and write, and even more important, to help them to support the process before their children enter school. Both are helpful to give to parents of first-grade children, and they are especially appreciated by parents with younger children at home. (V.M.)

Cullinan, Bernice E. 1993. *Let's Read About: Finding Books They'll Want to Read*. New York: Scholastic, Inc.

Here is a companion book to Read to Me: Raising Kids Who Love to Read. *It is filled with ideas for parents to use in creating a reading environment, for reading aloud, for finding time to read, determining appropriate books for children of different ages, and how to find needed books. The final chapters suggest specific books according to subjects of interest to children of certain ages. For example, a seven- or eight-year-old might enjoy a book of poetry, or a book about sports. Under each category, a list of annotated books is suggested. This is a useful book to give or lend to parents. (V.M.)*

Cullinan, Bernice E. 1992. *Read to Me: Raising Kids Who Love to Read.* New York: Scholastic, Inc.

Writing to help parents give a love of reading to their preschool through age twelve children and keep them reading, well-known reading educator Bernice Cullinan gives straight talk, practical ideas, and brief summaries of recommended books. Several teachers I know have ordered these in bulk and given them out to parents at the first curriculum/open house evening.

• Edwards, Sharon A., and Robert W. Maloy. 1992. *Kids Have All the Write Stuff: Inspiring Your Children to Put Pencil to Paper.* New York: Penguin Books.

This is the perfect book to hand to a parent wanting to learn more about children and the writing process. It is filled with practical ideas to support young writers, and it has many samples of what children have produced. A special "Note to Teachers" chapter answers many questions that parents raise about writing in the classroom. There is an extensive bibliography of children's books that support the writing ideas and activities in the body of the text. Although written for parents, this book also deserves a teacher audience. (V.M.)

Henderson, Anne T. October 1988. "Parents Are a School's Best Friend." *Phi Delta Kappan,* pp. 149–153.

Henderson reviews long-term research findings across diverse populations and reports that "parent involvement in almost any form appears to produce measurable gains in student achievement." While training of parents of at-risk children in home teaching proved significant, the average level of achievement for a school rose only when parents were involved in the school. Important findings for raising achievement levels in effective schools through long-term, comprehensive, well-planned parent involvement.

Hill, Mary W. 1989. *Home: Where Reading and Writing Begin.* Portsmouth, NH: Heinemann.

This book is written specifically for parents and extends the idea of parents as partners in literacy development. Many examples of the developmental nature of children's reading and writing are given. Children's literature titles fill the pages, along with many practical suggestions for parents who want to reflect and consider how they can encourage their children as readers and writers. It is a great one to hand to parents in answer to their question, "How can I help my child?" (V.M.)

International Reading Association, Newark, DE. (800 Barksdale Road, P.O. Box 8139, 19714-8139, telephone 800-336-READ)

Publishes many booklets and brochures to assist parents in helping their children develop as readers and writers. Reasonably priced and can be ordered in bulk.

Kenney, Anne, Lori Morgan, Jane Owen, Chris Sherman, and Russell Walsh (team leaders). 1992. *Teens' Favorite Books: Young Adults' Choices 1987–1992.* Newark, DE: International Reading Association. See annotation, p. 67b.

Lipson, Eden Ross. 1991. *The New York Times Parent's Guide to the Best Books for Children.* Revised and updated. New York: Random House. See annotation, p. 68b.

National Council of Teachers of English. Urbana IL (1111 Kenyon Road, 61801, telephone 800-369-NCTE). 1993. "Elementary School Practices."

This popular brochure helps parents, board members, and administrators better understand and recognize the ways in which elementary teachers are incorpo-

*rating current research on language learn-
ing in their classroom practice: single copies are free and can be copied without
permission. Multiple copies are available
for $7.00 per hundred.*

Oxley, Peggy, Jean Sperling, Lynda Mudre,
and Nancy Blume, with Moira McKenzie,
and Martha King. 1991. *Reading and
Writing: Where It All Begins: Helping
Your Children at Home.* Columbus, OH:
The Literacy Connection. (2577 Coventry
Road, 43221)

*This forty-page booklet is terrific to give
to preschool, kindergarten, and grade one
parents. Clearly illustrated and written in
a positive tone, it helps parents support
their children as they learn to read and
write. Lots of specifics are given for what
parents can and should do at home.*

Phenix, Jo, and Doreen Scott-Dunne. 1994.
Spelling for Parents. Markham, Ontario:
Pembroke Publishers, and Bothell, WA:
The Wright Group.

*This eighty-page handbook helps par-
ents understand how spelling is learned
and why we are moving away from weekly
memorization of word lists. What to teach
about spelling and how to help children
become better spellers is clearly presented.
An excellent reference for teachers too.*

Preece, Alison, and Diane Cowden. 1993. *Young
Writers in the Making: Sharing the Process with Parents.* Portsmouth, NH: Heinemann.

*This practical, 130 page book is full of
usable ideas, visuals, letters, newsletters,
and forms for communicating the writing
process of young children to parents.
From the first day of school to classroom
visits to meetings to home-school projects,
Preece and Cowden offer guidelines and
suggestions for getting parents to support
and understand an integrated, literacy-
based curriculum. The primary-grades
teacher will find this a terrific resource for
effectively communicating children's writing processes with parents.*

Stillman, Peter. 1989. *Families Writing.* Cin-
cinnati, OH: Writer's Digest Books. Distributed by Heinemann. (hardbound)

*This is a delightful book about writing
for the very best of reasons—for the family's sake—and pure enjoyment. Beginning with reasons for writing, the book is
filled with suggestions for a lifetime of
family writing activities. It's not a textbook, but a plea to tell your story—to
capture family happenings in words to be
cherished, enjoyed, and passed on to future generations. Stillman's pleasure in
writing shines through the many pieces of
his family history that are scattered
throughout the book. It's a book that I
want to share with parents, and one I
want to return to for ideas and inspira-
tions. (V.M.)*

Stoll, Donald R. (ed.). 1994. *Magazines for
Kids and Teens: A Resource for Parents,
Teachers, Librarians, and Kids!* Glassboro, NJ: Educational Press Association
of America, and Newark, DE: International Reading Association. See annotation, p. 72b.

Trelease, Jim. 1992. *Hey! Listen to This: Stories to Read Aloud.* New York: Penguin
Books. See annotation, p. 72b.

Trelease, Jim. 1990. *The New Read-Aloud
Handbook.* New York: Penguin. See annotations p. 73b.

Williams, David L., and Nancy Feyl Chavkin.
October 1989. "Essential Elements of
Strong Parent Involvement Programs."
Educational Leadership, pp. 18–20.

*Seven essential elements from successful
parent involvement programs in a five-
state area are identified and described:
written policies, administrative support,
training, partnership approach, two-way
communication, networking, and evaluation. A list of parent involvement resources is included. A useful article for
schools intent on improving parent involvement.*

Recommended Literature by Grade Level, K–12, and Supplemental Lists

Annotations for grades K–8 and supplemental lists by Susan Hepler
Annotations for grades 9–12 by Dana Noble

About These Lists

Implicit in a literature/reading program that uses real books are choice, reading for pleasure and information, and sustained daily reading time in school and at home. In addition, we need to provide time for collaborative talk about books that examines text in depth through multiple perspectives and makes connections to our lives and other texts. With high quality literature and teacher guidance, children learn to read and read to learn across the curriculum.

The following K–12, grade-level lists assume a balanced reading program that includes reading aloud, shared reading, guided reading, and independent reading as well as diverse opportunities to respond to text through listening, discussion, further reading, writing, and the visual and dramatic arts. With the exception of the kindergarten list in which books are meant to be read *to* the child, all books are meant to be read *by* and *with* the children in the guided-reading program. Books have been chosen for suitability for guided reading and literary appreciation—that is, these are books that have the power to evoke high-level discussion and personal connections to children's lives. While the grade-level placement of a book is arbitrary, that is, a title could work at

several grade levels, what is not arbitrary is the quality of the books.

Balancing the Collection

As much as possible, each grade-level collection is balanced to reflect a wide variety of literature—picture books, poetry, folktales or traditional literature, realistic fiction, historical fiction, science fiction, humor, multicultural literature, and nonfiction. Books have been carefully selected from the best of children's literature, young adult (YA) literature, and, in some cases, adult literature for both their high quality and outstanding illustrations. When a folktale has been included, a "best version" has been chosen—that is, a version that is prize-winning, easily available, and beautifully told.

In this edition, we have made a major effort to locate and include excellent multicultural literature, that is, books by and about people of color that are also books respected within the particular cultures. Recognizing that, in the near future, many more Americans will be African-American, Latino, Native American or Asian-American, we have made an effort to include the best texts and illustrations that authentically represent these ethnic groups. We believe it is important that students see themselves and their culture as connected to school literacy and that all students experience the richness and diversity of other cultures through outstanding literature. As well, we have made a deliberate effort to include more books with females as main characters. Also,

103b

picture books are included through the grades as they are not just for young children. Older students enjoy the notable illustrations, beautiful and thoughtful text, and making connections to their lives and other stories.

All titles from the 1991 edition of *Invitations* have been looked at for relevance and current publishing information. Updated comments have been added to some titles; a few titles have been deleted; many new titles have been added.

Organization

Grade-level literature lists are organized alphabetically by title. Each book annotation includes a brief summary, noteworthy characteristics about the literary and artistic quality, and possible suggestions for discussion and response. Key features of each grade-level list precede the list of books, and in the K–8 levels, this information also includes suggestions for author study.

In addition to the grade-level lists, be sure to check the supplemental lists that follow the Grade 6 list and include: "Books Which Invite Writing and Storytelling" (grades 1–6), "Wordless Books" (grades K–6), "Life Stories" (grades 2–6), and, new with this edition, "Bilingual Spanish Books—A Beginning List." Also, note the extensive listing of books and series for emergent readers in the lists between kindergarten and Grade 1: "Books Which Invite Readers into Print" and "Developing Early Reading Strategies." Some titles that previously were listed in "People in Other Lands" and "Books About Our Diverse Population" have been reabsorbed into the grade-level lists as there are now many excellent multicultural titles available, making those separate categories unnecessary.

To help you locate all recommended books easily, this edition has included recommended K–12 literature, as well as the supplemental literature lists, in the main index by title, author, and illustrator. Books on the lists in the following categories are also resorted in a "Multicultural Book List:" "African-American/Black Culture," "Asian-American/Asian Culture," "Latino," and "Native American." (see pp. 167b–169b).

A "+" next to a title means the book is also available as a Big Book. The word "series" after an annotation means that there are sequels or

at least one more book dealing with the same characters in the same setting. The paperback publisher is noted within the parentheses following the original publisher and date. In general, publishers have their own paperback imprint. If the parentheses are empty, the book was not available in paperback when *Invitations* went to press, or it may only be available through a book club. (COP) indicates that a title is currently out of print. Paperback books often go in and out of print and sometimes change publishers, so if a book is not available at a particular time, it may well be available at a later date. So that teachers and schools can afford to purchase multiple copies of books, these lists are almost completely limited to titles that are (or will be) available in paperback.

Also, keep in mind that while each of the following grade-level lists stands on its own, many titles could work well on several levels.

Easy Books

Note that within grade levels 1–12, some texts have been designated easy reading (E). That is, in comparison to the other books at this grade level, these titles should be the easiest for most students to read. This designation is to ensure that your grade-level collections include some easy-to-read titles so that all students not only discuss books (that may have been read to them aloud or through shared reading) but that all students be able to read some books with minimal assistance. One of the disturbing trends with the transition to a literature program is struggling students who never actually receive books that are easy enough for them to read. Note that books marked (E) at a grade level above you may well be appropriate at your grade level.

Building a Literature Program

These literature lists are meant to be used as a reference and starting point for dialogue in a school or district. It is recommended that six to ten copies of each selected title be purchased so books can be used for guided reading and small-group discussion. It works well if groups of teachers, librarians, and administrators sit down together, read and discuss books, and make decisions about what will work best in their own school contexts. There is no one right list or best list.

For use of literature and additional recommended titles, consult your school or public librarian, reading specialists and resource teachers, the recommended texts, journal articles and "Literacy Extension Resources" in these "blue pages" as well as chapters 3, 5, and 6 in *Invitations*. For complete, updated information on ordering trade books and literature collections from wholesalers and publishers, see *Invitations* (1994), pp. 454–459.

Literature-based or a Literature Program?

While some educators do not distinguish between a literature-based program and a literature program, we do. We see a literature program as encompassing complete texts that are each separate, bound books. Many of these books are part of the classroom library collection, housed in an attractive reading area where students are free to choose books they want to read. We see a literature-based program as part of the transition process to an integrated literacy classroom. In a literature-based program, to ease management and choice of multiple texts, a school or district purchases a program that packages authentic literature selections in one text, often with accompanying consumable activities. One of the advantages of a packaged program is that it is often well balanced with nonfiction, fiction, poetry, and multicultural selections. Among the disadvantages are that some of the original illustrations and text may be altered or missing completely, thereby changing some intended meaning. Most important, even if the text is unaltered, part of a book is not the same as reading a complete book. Since as adults we do not regularly read books in anthologies, we need to give our students the same pleasure a whole book encompasses. Especially, let's keep the magic that comes from turning each page of a favorite book in anticipation and wonder.

"Formula Fiction" Books

While we do not include popular culture series books, such as *Baby Sitters Club, Boxcar Children, Encyclopedia Brown, Goosebumps,* and *Sweet Valley High* on our lists, we take the position that these books are an acceptable genre for children. The powerful appeal of "formula fiction" series books and the excitement they generate in young readers make them worth including in children's choices for reading, if for no other reason than children read them willingly and gain confidence in themselves as readers. Because so many children get "hooked" on these series books, where the format of one book follows another and the literary merit may be questionable, they probably need these books for a while as part of a balanced literary diet, much the same way as adults read some popular fiction. It is our job to help readers broaden their reading experiences to include more mature and richer literature.

Book Clubs

Because book clubs have become a major supplier of trade books to elementary classrooms in the U.S. and because they offer a wide range of interesting books across all genres, information about the three major book clubs is included. Within each club, there are different clubs for different grade levels. Prices are discounted with average costs per book of about $1.50 to $3.00. Note that many of the books on the literature lists may first be available exclusively through book clubs but later will be available through trade publishers. Check with your local bookstore or book distributor. For information regarding the nature and use of school book clubs and how they contribute to children's literacy development, see "School Book Clubs and Literacy Development: A Descriptive Study" by Dorothy S. Strickland and Sean A. Walmsley, 1994. (Available from the National Research Center on Literature Teaching and Learning, State University of New York at Albany.)

Scholastic Book Clubs
P.O. Box 7500
Jefferson City, MO 65102–9981
800-724-2424

Scholastic has five clubs, Firefly (pre-K), See Saw (K–grade 1), Lucky (grades 2–3), Arrow (grades 4–6), and Tab (grades 7–9 and up). Monthly brochures offer forty-five to fifty titles and include award-winning books. Also offers books to teachers grouped by theme and special offers for specific curriculum areas.

Troll Book Clubs
2 Lethbridge Plaza
Mahwah, NJ 07430
800-541-1097

Troll has five clubs, Troll Pre-K/K (preschool and K), Troll 1 (grades K–1), Troll 2 (grades 2–3), Troll 3 (grades 4–6), and Troll 4 High Tops (grades 6–9). Each month about forty-five titles are offered as well as different teacher specials, such as award-winning books and theme sets that can be used in the classroom.

Trumpet Book Clubs
P.O. Box 605
Holmes, PA 19043-9865
800-826-0110

Trumpet's three clubs, Early Years (pre-K–K), Primary Years (grades 1–3) and Middle Years (grades 4–6), send monthly brochures that offer forty to forty-five titles, including books by prize-winning authors and special items such as pop-up books, theme-based text sets, books and audiotape sets, and author video visits. An In-Class catalogue for teachers allows them to order books, Big Books, and text sets—groups of quality books gathered around a central concept—at any time during the school year.

Kindergarten

This list features excellent and near-classic titles with strong story lines and themes powerful to five- and six-year-olds. While a few kindergartners may be able to read some of these books, those selected for this list are intended primarily for reading aloud, discussing, and extending in the classroom. (See the next two lists, which support new readers.) First graders and second graders already familiar with these stories will enjoy them once again as they become readers.

Some key ideas among books in this list include solving problems, being in a family, and growing or changing. Traditional literature features cumulative stories, well-known tales, Mother Goose, and patterns such as the tricky fox, threes, and folktale language. Concepts include counting one to ten, the alphabet, and days of the week. Books may also be grouped by topics such as shoes, cats, or other animals, and eating or foods.

Suggestions for kindergarten author studies include Eric Carle, Donald Crews, Lois Ehlert, Paul Galdone, Kevin Henkes, Pat Hutchins, Bill Martin, and Nancy Tafuri, among others.

1. *Annabelle Swift, Kindergartner* by Amy Schwartz. New York: Orchard, 1988. (Orchard)

   This sophisticated look at a precocious child's beginning of school has humor and a gentle treatment of fitting in at school. Annabelle has been tutored by her older sister in what she thinks is important. But it is Annabelle's own skill, being able to count money, that gives her success. Other starting school stories include Mary Serfozo's Benjamin Bigfoot *(New York: McElderry, 1993), and Dorothy Butler's* My Brown Bear Barney *(New York: Greenwillow, 1988), and Kevin Henkes's* Owen *(see p. 108b).*

2. + *Bread and Jam for Frances* by Russell Hoban, illustrated by Lillian Hoban. New York: Harper & Row, 1964. (HarperTrophy)

   Like many young children, Frances the badger has narrow food preferences but changes her mind with the help of parents and an adventurous friend. Excellent discussion starter on the advantages of and difficulties we have in trying new things. (Series)

3. + *The Carrot Seed* by Ruth Kraus, illustrated by Crockett Johnson. New York: Harper & Row, 1945. (Scholastic; HarperTrophy)

   This classic story fulfills a child's need to feel important and successful by showing how a boy plants a seed and raises a huge carrot despite his family's doubts. Works well with The Great Big Enormous Turnip *and* Titch *in a theme of "planting" (see pp. 107b & 109b).*

4. + *Chicka Chicka Boom Boom* by Bill Martin and John Archambault, illustrated by Lois Ehlert. New York: Simon & Schuster, 1989. (   )

Rhythmic narrative and alphabet both upper case and lower case tell a story of disaster when all of the lower-case letters crowd into the coconut tree. The adult capital letters come along to sort out the mess. Chantable text invites children to chime in and move with the rhythm.

5. + *Chicken Soup with Rice* by Maurice Sendak. New York: Harper & Row, 1962. (Scholastic; HarperTrophy)

    A month-by-month rhyming account of one boy's humorous uses for chicken soup that invites children to follow the pattern in making up their own verses.

6. + *Each Peach Pear Plum* by Janet and Allan Ahlberg. New York: Viking, 1979. (Puffin; Scholastic)

    Characters from Mother Goose and well-known folktales appear in an "I Spy" text pattern. As with B. G. Hennessy's The Missing Tarts *(New York: Viking Kestrel, 1989), children enjoy reviewing the familiar characters while seeing a story unfold.*

7. *Feast for 10* by Cathryn Falwell. New York: Clarion, 1993. (   )

    African-American family shops, one to ten, then counts down to supper, ten to one, as they prepare dinner. Consider how families help each other, how meals are prepared; talk about daily ways in which we use numbers, or count down to an event, such as an upcoming holiday.

8. + *Feathers for Lunch* by Lois Ehlert. San Diego: Harcourt Brace, 1990. (   )

    A humorous account of a cat's inability to catch a variety of spring birds is vibrantly illustrated with Ehlert's collage illustrations made from hand-painted paper. Various birds and flowers are rendered to scale, each discreetly labeled with its proper name. Informative in studying birds or in springtime units. Rhyming text supports new readers.

9. + *Freight Train* by Donald Crews. New York: Greenwillow, 1978. (Mulberry)

    This introduction to what a freight train is and what it does also teaches children specific car names and reinforces the naming of colors. With air-brushed illustrations that seem to move across the page, this is one in a series of Crews's books about transportation.

10. *The Gingerbread Boy* by Paul Galdone. New York: Clarion, 1975. (Clarion)

    This well-told version of a familiar cumulative tale makes a good flannel board story, mural, or story map of the action. It also reintroduces the tricky fox, a standard character of many folktales that children may already know.

11. *The Great Big Enormous Turnip* by Leo Tolstoy, illustrated by Helen Oxenbury. New York: Franklin Watts, 1968. (COP)

    In cumulative pattern, the animals, children, and the old woman line up behind the old man to try to pull the turnip out of the ground. Excellent for a classroom drama or a flannel board story.

12. + *It Begins with an A* by Stephanie Calmenson, illustrated by Marisabina Russo. New York: Hyperion, 1994. (Hyperion, Scholastic)

    This alphabetic guessing game gives four verbal and pictorial clues: "You travel in this. / It begins with an A. / It starts on the ground, / and then it flies away." Four pictures enable children to consider naturally the beginning sounds of words and to guess successfully. While some words such as camera, icing, *the soft sound of g for* giraffe, *and q for* quarter *may be difficult for children, they are eager to play the game of figuring out the mystery. Large gray letters at the end of each page invite children to read and repeat "What is it/she/he?"*

13. *Mama, Do You Love Me?* by Barbara Joosse, illustrated by Barbara Lavalee. San Francisco: Chronicle Books, 1993. (   )

    In a reassuring story set in Inuit territory, a little girl tests her mother's love by proposing all sorts of mischief and asking if she would still be loved. Useful in family units, for discussing how we know our parents love us, and for seeing mischief as a universal child behavior. Pictures accurately depict items and motifs of Inuit culture; an afterword provides background for older children. The same setting forms the backdrop for Ann Herbert Scott's On

Mother's Lap, *illustrated by Glo Coalson (New York: Clarion, 1992; Clarion).*

14. "Mother Goose"

    Kindergartners enjoy repeated hearings and chantings of these rhymes. Many collections by well-known illustrators such as Tomie dePaola, Brian Wildsmith, Arnold Lobel, and James Marshall entertain children for hours with these cornerstones of literature. See, too, Each Peach Pear Plum.

15. *The Napping House* by Audrey Wood, illustrated by Don Wood. San Diego: Harcourt Brace Jovanovich, 1984. (Harcourt)

    In cumulative pattern, this humorous story pictures a snoring granny who shares the bed with her grandson and an assortment of animals until a pesky flea climbs aboard. Children enjoy chanting the rhythmical text, noticing the flea draw closer to the sleepers in each picture, and the gradually lightening palette of colors as dawn approaches.

16. *New Shoes for Silvia* by Johanna Hurwitz, illustrated by Jerry Pinkney. New York: Morrow, 1993. (   )

    In a nonspecific Latino country in "the other America," a little girl receives the present of new shoes, but they are too big. She turns them into toys until finally one day they fit. Read the pictures for details of a rural community lovingly depicted in Pinkney's watercolor illustrations. Pair with Red Dancing Shoes *(see below) to discuss feelings about new shoes.*

17. *Owen* by Kevin Henkes. New York: Greenwillow, 1993. (   )

    Owen, a boy mouse, figures out how to take his blanket to kindergarten in spite of a busybody neighbor, Mrs. Tweezer, and her assertion that this just isn't done. (The blanket goes as handkerchiefs). The story appeals to children who are now over kindergarten anxiety as well as to older children who can look back appreciatively at Owen's resourcefulness. Henkes is a popular author whose books such as Julius, the Baby of the World *(New York: Greenwillow, 1990),* Chester's Way *(New York: Greenwillow, 1988; Puffin), and* Chrysanthemum *(New York: Greenwillow, 1991)*

all portray young children's small dilemmas of growing up.

18. *Purple, Green, and Yellow* by Robert Munsch, illustrated by Helene Desputeaux. New York: Annick Press, 1992. (Annick)

    Brigid is crazy about felt-tip markers and convinces her mother to buy 500 each of the ones that are washable, the ones that smell like foods, and finally, the indelible ones. When she can't resist coloring herself, some silly and impossible disasters occur. Children love the preposterous story and the ending joke on daddy.

19. *Read-Aloud Rhymes for the Very Young* edited by Jack Prelutsky, illustrated by Marc Brown. New York: Knopf, 1986. (   )

    Over 200 poems selected from both old and new poets to enjoy all year long. Poems about loose teeth, friendship, the seasons, animals, or holidays, are nicely balanced for humor and thoughtfulness.

20. *Red Dancing Shoes* by Denise Lewis Patrick, illustrated by James E. Ransome. New York: Tambourine, 1993. (   )

    An unnamed African-American girl receives new shoes from her grandmother and displays them by dancing around the small city neighborhood. When she nearly ruins them in the mud, her favorite great aunt helps clean her up. A soothing presentation of a childhood "tragedy" that comes out right because the community cares.

21. + *Rosie's Walk* by Pat Hutchins. New York: Macmillan, 1968. (Scholastic; Macmillan)

    One long sentence with many prepositional phrases tells of Rosie's walk before dinner. But the illustrations beg to be talked about as another tricky fox is foiled in his attempt to catch his dinner. Children can tell alternative stories, provide dialogue for the many animals pictured, or experiment with patterned shapes in their own art work.

22. *The Salamander Room* by Anne Mazer, illustrated by Steve Johnson. New York: Knopf, 1991. (Dragonfly)

    Like many kindergartners, Brian makes a pet of something he has found outside, a salamander. His mother asks various ques-

tions about how he will care for it while the illustrations show Brian in his imagination turning his room into the woods. Fanciful depiction that elicits both wishful and true stories of bug and reptile "pets."

23. + *Seven Blind Mice* by Ed Young. New York: Philomel Books, 1992. (Scholastic)

    An Indian fable, "The Elephant and the Blind Men," is given a new twist when seven blind mice each set out on a different day of the week to investigate the large Something that has come to their forest pond. Ordinal numbers, colors, and days of the week are concepts appropriate for this age level, and some children will understand the moral: you have to see the whole picture, not just a part. This Caldecott Honor Book is illustrated with Young's clean, brilliant collages.

24. + *Ten Nine Eight* by Molly Bang. New York: Greenwillow, 1983. (Scholastic; Morrow)

    An African-American girl and her father get ready for bed in a countdown counting book. Talk about bedtime rituals and solve the mystery of where the missing shoe from the "seven shoes" page has gone.

25. *The Three Bears* by Paul Galdone. New York: Clarion, 1973. (Clarion)

    A cornerstone of children's literary experiences, this story is told in a straightforward manner and illustrated with plenty of wee-little, middle-sized, and great-big items or print to encourage children to notice them. Compare treatment of the characters, the household, and humorous touches by looking at other versions of the story illustrated by David McPhail, Byron Barton, Lorinda Bryan Cauley, James Marshall, Jan Brett, and Anne Rockwell.

26. *Titch* by Pat Hutchins. New York: Macmillan, 1971. (Aladdin)

    Titch, the littlest in his family, always gets the short end of things until he plants a seed and his plant is the envy of his siblings. Good start for encouraging children to talk about aspects of being small or little or young. See also The Carrot Seed. (Series)

27. + *The Very Hungry Caterpillar* by Eric Carle. New York: Putnam, 1969. (Scholastic)

A hungry caterpillar eats his way through various foods during one week, spins a chrysalis (here called erroneously a "cocoon"), and emerges as a beautiful butterfly. Children can retell with the actual book as pictures with die-cut holes provide prediction clues.

28. *We're Going on a Bear Hunt* by Michael Rosen, illustrated by Helen Oxenbury. New York: McElderry Books, 1989. (   )

    This chantable, repetitive, predictable text invites children to chime in with hand or body motions as the teacher reads it. Good for shared reading and dramatic play as well. Note the good-natured humor and the clues that suggest this is imaginative play (a snowstorm in July?) rather than a true story.

29. *When Jeremiah Found Mrs. Ming* by Sharon Jennings, illustrated by Mireille Levert. Toronto: Annick Press, 1992. (Annick)

    In the second story in the series, Jeremiah can't think of a thing to do but Mrs. Ming lets him help, often imaginatively, with her many household tasks. Finally, with all the house in order, Mrs. Ming is ready to read a book and Jeremiah is ready to listen. While readers aren't sure whether Mrs. Ming is Jeremiah's mother, a relative, or his babysitter, she is a wonderful character. Quirky illustrations invite children to examine the pictures and talk about the humorous details. (Series)

30. *Where the Wild Things Are* by Maurice Sendak. New York: Harper & Row, 1964. (HarperTrophy)

    In this reassuring classic, Max, sent to his room for making mischief, dreams he travels to a land where he controls things. Children can notice how the pictures change, or create a wild rumpus complete with animal masks, but the most powerful aspect of the story is still parental forgiveness and love for children even when they misbehave.

31. *Yo! Yes?* by Chris Raschka. New York: Orchard, 1993. (   )

    Two boy strangers meet. One is bold, the other is shy. One is white, the other is African-American. They chat, become *friends, and go off together. This powerful story of friendship features eloquent pictures and very little text. The one or two hand-lettered words per page invite children to notice print, and while the words are not predictable, many kindergartners are so taken with the book and its message that they memorize the words and "read" it to each other.*

Books Which Invite Readers into Print

The following texts, many of which are only eight pages, are recommended for beginning emergent readers. These texts have consistent and simple structure, familiar and repetitive language patterns, very limited print, which is consistently and clearly placed on each page, and illustrations that are highly supportive of the text. These books are excellent for guiding students in developing one-to-one matching (one-to-one correspondence) of spoken to printed word, correct directionality skills, and utilization of pictures that depict most of the text. Even at this simplest level, each of these stories ends with a twist to delight the reader. Many of these stories also encourage readers to create their own versions.

For greater student success in reading a new book, introduce the new book by "talking through" the pictures and vocabulary *before* students attempt to read the book on their own. For guidelines as well as titles for selecting books for beginning readers, see especially "Selecting Books for Beginning Readers" by Barbara Peterson, pp. 119–147, in *Bridges to Literacy: Learning from Reading Recovery* by Diane Deford, Carol Lyons, and Gay Su Pinnell (Portsmouth: NH: Heinemann, 1991).

1. + *Across the Stream* by Mirra Ginsburg, illustrated by Nancy Tafuri. New York: Greenwillow, 1984. (Mulberry, Scholastic)
   Rhyming text tells of a hen's dream of escaping a fox by crossing a stream on a friendly duck's back. Notice the tiny symbols next to each page number, the many other animals in the illustrations, and discuss whether this is a dream or not. See how many other stories children can recall in which a chicken and a fox appear.

2. *All Fall Down* by Brian Wildsmith. New York: Oxford University Press, 1983. (Oxford)
   "I see" one animal standing upon another until "all fall down." Like 1 Hunter, this book can be read easily because the pictures make the text predictable. Compare with "Pardon?" Said the Giraffe and make your own falling-down story.

3. *Blue Sea* by Robert Kalan, illustrated by Donald Crews. New York: Greenwillow, 1979. (Mulberry).
   Four fish—biggest, bigger, big, and little—chase each other until finally little fish escapes them all. Although the text is very simple, with repetition, patterned language, and a different color for each fish and the words that refer to it, children will need to hear the book to put the language in their ears before reading this on their own. See also Rain *by the same pair (New York: Greenwillow, 1978; Mulberry).*

4. + *Brown Bear, Brown Bear, What Do You See?* by Bill Martin, Jr., illustrated by Eric Carle. New York: Henry Holt, 1983. ( )
   Children enjoy chanting this chain-structured story of an animal of one color who sees another animal of a different color, and so forth. Change the animals to children in the class for a new chant or make another book of differently colored bugs, other animals, or birds. See also this team's Polar Bear, Polar Bear, What Do You Hear? *(New York: Holt, 1991).*

5. + *The Bus Ride* by Anne McLean, illustrated by Justin Wager. Glenview, IL: Scott, Foresman, 1971. (Scott, Foresman)
   "A girl got on the bus. Then the bus went fast." These first two pages are repeated over and over again, but with different characters—a boy, a fox, a hippopotamus, a goat, a rhinoceros, a horse, a rabbit, and finally a bee, which forces everyone off the bus.

6. *The Cat Sat on the Mat* by Brian Wildsmith. New York: Oxford University Press, 1982. (Oxford)
   Pictures clearly show a cat on the mat but each page turn adds another animal until the annoyed cat says "Sssppstt" and everyone leaves.

7. *The Chick and the Duckling* by Mirra Ginsburg, illustrated by Jose and Ariane Aruego. New York: Macmillan, 1973. (Macmillan)

   "Me, too," says a chick as it follows an adventurous duckling's lead until disaster nearly results and the chick finally thinks for itself: "Not me!"

8. *Five Little Ducks* by Raffi, illustrated by Jose Aruego and Ariane Dewey. New York: Crown, 1989. (Crown)

   In this countdown song, five ducks disappear "over the hills and far away," one by one, until they all return to Mama Duck with ducklings and spouses of their own. Repetitive verses and refrains make this a good match for new readers.

9. *The Good Bad Cat* by Nancy Antle, illustrated by John Sanford. Grand Haven, MI: School Zone, 1993. (School Zone)

   A mischievous cat gets in the way of a chess game: "Bad cat!" But when the cat chases a mouse out of the house, it becomes a "good cat!" One sentence or phrase per page, some of which repeat at the end, supports beginning reading strategies.

10. *Have You Seen My Cat?* by Eric Carle. Saxonville, MA: Picture Book Studio, 1987. (Scholastic)

    Carle uses his brilliant collages and the repeated title plus the refrain of "that is not my cat!" to tell the story of a boy who finally finds his lost cat—and more—after a long search.

11. *Have You Seen My Duckling?* by Nancy Tafuri. New York: Greenwillow, 1984. (Viking; Morrow)

    An adventurous duckling leaves his family but is visible in each picture as a mother duck asks various pond animals, "Have you seen my duckling?" Children enjoy the visual game of hide-and-seek. Other books by Tafuri that work at this level include Who's Counting? *(New York: Greenwillow, 1986) and* Spots, Feathers, and Curly Tails *(New York: Greenwillow, 1989).*

12. *I Like Books* by Anthony Browne. New York: Knopf, 1987. (COP)

    A gorilla mentions the kinds of books he likes; among them are scary books, books about pirates, funny books, and alphabet books. Ask children to talk about "kinds of books." Create a book display on a table in the classroom based on children's categories of books they like.

13. + *I Went Walking* by Sue Williams, illustrated by Julie Vivas. Orlando, FL: Harcourt Brace Jovanovich, 1989. (   )

    In the same vein as Brown Bear, Brown Bear, What Do You See?, *a child goes walking and sees various animals who all follow her. Vivas's large illustrations can be easily seen even in large read-aloud groups. Be sure to watch for the girl tossing aside her sweater, socks, and shoes as she begins to play.*

14. *Jog Frog Jog* by Barbara Gregorich. Grand Haven, MI: School Zone, 1992. (School Zone)

    Simple story about a frog who jogs and gets chased by a dog is told in large print. Two to six words on a page and a good match between picture and story support readers. Part of a "Start to Read" series.

15. *Mary Wore Her Red Dress and Henry Wore His Green Sneakers* by Merle Peek. New York: Clarion, 1985. (Clarion)

    The verses in the song repeat what critters wore "all day long" when they attended a birthday party. The chantable or singable text is enhanced by humorous illustrations that augment the story line; the story reviews colors cleverly, as well.

16. *Monster Can't Sleep* by Virginia Mueller. New York: Puffin, 1988. (Puffin).

    It's time for bed "but Monster wasn't sleepy" repeats four times. Parents try reading a bedtime story, warm milk, and a goodnight kiss until Monster finally gets sleepy. (Series)

17. *Mouse Views: What the Class Pet Saw* by Bruce McMillan. New York: Holiday, 1993. (Holiday)

    A class's pet mouse explores the school and is seen in a variety of clear, close-up photographs as it sits on unobvious but typical classroom objects (chalk, stack of colored paper, pencil box). Readers are invited to guess what the mouse is on. The next picture confirms the child's guess with a labeled photograph of the close-up now seen in context. A school map over-

view of mouse's route invites children to map their own classroom or school, or to draw a mouse-eye view of something in their own classroom.

18. *My Book* by Ron Maris. New York: Viking Penguin, 1983. (Puffin)

    Half-pages inserted change the look of each picture as a child invites the reader to go through "my gate" and finally into "my room." The text, if not the format, invites readers to make their own book of possessions, routes to favorite spots, and so forth.

19. *Oh No, Nicky!* by Harriet Ziefert, illustrated by Richard Brown. New York: Puffin, 1992. (Puffin)

    Nicky, an adventurous little cat, is saved from trouble around the house by a bigger cat who leads him to make better choices. A sturdy lift-the-flap book that will survive many readings; large, easy-to-read text.

20. *1 Hunter* by Pat Hutchins, New York: Greenwillow, 1982. (Mulberry)

    Clues to the next page's minimal text are found on each preceding page of this counting book. Children enjoy being able to predict by finding the hidden animals.

21. *Today Is Monday* by Eric Carle. New York: Putnam, 1993. (Scholastic Book Club)

    Each day of the week is given to a particular food and the animal that eats it. Multiethnic children at the story's end are invited to a banquet: "Come and eat it up!" Carle's glorious collage and paint illustrations invite children to experiment with their own art work. The traditional song is a part of the text but the chorus, "Is everybody happy? Well, I should say," has been omitted. Teachers may want to teach the whole song, but children who experiment with word correspondence should be warned that the text will not match.

22. *What a Tale* by Brian Wildsmith. New York: Oxford University Press, 1986. (Oxford)

    Five tails, "spotted," or "bobbed," and so forth, turn out to be animals riding in a kangaroo's pouch. Silly with one small pun on the word "tail." See, too, Tail Toes Eyes Ears Nose *by Marilee Robin Burton*

(New York: Harper & Row, 1989) for more readable fun with animal parts.

23. *Where's Spot?* by Eric Hill. New York: Putnam, 1980. (Puffin)

    Finally in paperback, this classic lift-the-flap book provides children with plenty of prepositional phrases within questions: "Is he under the bed?" Whatever the hiding animal is, it answers "No" until readers find Spot. Sure to be read to pieces, so keep glue handy to mend the sturdy flaps as this is an excellent book with great child appeal.

24. *Who's Counting?* by Nancy Tafuri. New York: Greenwillow, 1986. (Mulberry)

    A puppy meets a variety of creatures that are counted out in limited, enlarged text: one squirrel, two birds, etc. Look for the puppy or some part of it in each picture plus the identifiable "main character" in the final three pictures of the puppy with his huge family.

25. *Whose Hat?* by Margaret Miller. New York: Greenwillow, 1988. (   )

    "Whose hat?", repeated six times in the text, is followed by a picture of a real-life hat (fireman, chef, nurse) with an adult wearing his or her related hat. The adjacent page pictures a child playing in the same role in the hat. Large, clear print with only one or two predictable words on a page. Compare with Ron Roy's Whose Hat Is That? *(Boston: Houghton Mifflin, 1987), which has more text but equally excellent content.*

Because it is difficult to find "literature" at this earliest emergent level and because budding readers need lots of practice on easy books, the following simple, patterned texts, all in paperback, are also recommended:

26. *Piñata: Celebrating Literacy/Celebrando la lectura* by Barbara Flores, Elena Castro, and Eddie Hernandez. Miami: DDL Books, Inc. (DDL)

    Well-done eight-page predictable story books featuring North American Latino families and real-life topics such as Mi familia (My Family), En la playa (On the Beach), La boda (The Wedding), *and* Los tamales. *The forty soft-cover books are*

*available in Spanish or English and are
perfect for bilingual classrooms.*

27. *Reading Corners 1, 1992.* San Diego: Dominie Press. (Available in Canada through Toronto: Gage Educational Publishing)

   A set of eleven books of eight pages each with titles such as I Read, I Have a Pet, I Like to Eat, *and* Baby Animals. *Fanciful illustrations support the short, predictable text.*

28. *The Story Box, Level 1.* Bothell, WA: The Wright Group, 1990.

   Some of the simplest books in this series, like In the Mirror *and* The Party, *have only several words on a page and are extremely predictable with good support from the pictures. Twenty-four titles in three sets.*

29. *This Is the Way I Go.* Allen, TX: DLM, 1976.

   A set of six books emphasizes common action words (climb, fly, run, swim, crawl, and play) in consistent, predictable language patterns. For example, in I Jump, *one page reads, "'I can jump,' said the horse." Also a good springboard for writing similar texts based on the same pattern. Works well to begin with shared writing in a small group and duplicate the new text for each student to read and illustrate.*

30. *Tiger Cub Readers* by Robert and Marlene McCracken. Winnipeg, Manitoba: Peguis, 1989.

   A set of eight books of fourteen pages each depicts basic concepts and familiar experiences. For example, in What Is This? *each animal page says, "This is a duck" or "This is a pig" with a colorful, clear illustration directly under the text. Available in little books and in* $8\frac{1}{2} \times 11$ *size.*

31. *Twig Books* by Rebel Williams. Bothell, WA: The Wright Group, 1990.

   Twig Books, Sets A, B, C, and D, each contain eight nonfiction books of eight pages each. Well done for simplicity, picture match with text, and content material. For example, Champions (Set A) *shows the symbol and a picture of the Olympics on the cover and title page. The text, spread over eight pages, reads, "People running. People jumping. People swimming. People diving. People lifting. People throwing. Champions!"*

For students who need support in learning letters of the alphabet by name and sound, *Letter Books* (compiled by Lois Markt and published by Dominie Press, San Diego, 1994) are very useful. Each ten-page booklet focuses on a letter of the alphabet by featuring a color illustration of a thing that begins with the targeted letter on one page and the word that goes with the picture on the adjacent page.

Developing Early Reading Strategies

These are highly predictable books, many with rhyme, rhythm, and repetition that make them especially predictable. Familiar sentence patterns are repeated; illustrations provide excellent support to the text; the print is very clear, sizable, and consistently placed on each page; the language structure and story line are familiar and make sense. In contrast to the highly structured "Books Which Invite Readers into Print," these texts have more words on a page, longer sentences, more descriptive language patterns, and greater narrative development. Most of these titles are also easier to read than titles on the "First Grade" list. Many of these books are songs readily available on tape or record, and chants, which further support readers.

Repeated readings of such books help young readers develop sight vocabulary, fluency, and confidence as well as strengthen early reading strategies such as one-to-one correspondence, left-to-right line sweep, use of picture, meaning, and structure cues, and use of beginning and ending consonants. (See also "Recommended Literature for Beginning Readers: Rhyme, Rhythm, and Repetition," Routman, 1988, pp. 285–290, for additional titles.)

1. *All I Am* by Eileen Row, illustrated by Helen Cogancherry. New York: Bradbury, 1990. (   )

   In short declarative sentences, such as "I am a friend. / I am a neighbor. / I am an artist. / I am a singer," a child considers all that he is and does. The book invites children to consider what adjectives and roles might describe them. *Perfect model for writing about yourself, for considering talents, roles, and qualities such as being a thinker and dreamer that are not so easy to come up with. See also* Quick as a Cricket, *page 148b, for a similar pattern using similes.*

2. + *Bright Eyes, Brown Skin* by Cheryl Willis Hudson and Bernette G. Ford, illustrated by George Ford. Orange, NJ: Just Us Books, 1990. (Sundance)

   Text in verse celebrates the physical beauty of four African-American children as they engage in typical school activities.

3. *Cookie's Week* by Cindy Ward, illustrated by Tomie dePaola. New York: Putnam, 1988. (Putnam)

   On each day of the week, a mischievous cat manages to create a new household upset. Predictable, repetitive, natural language pattern. Excellent for understanding cause and effect and for creating original stories based on the book's format and pattern.

4. + *Crocodile Beat* by Gail Jorgensen, illustrated by Patricia Mullins. Crystal Lake, IL: Rigby, 1988. (Rigby)

   This colorful animal story of a crocodile in search of his dinner naturally lends itself to drama and movement. Children love chanting the rhythmic beat of this story and seeing the surprise ending. The illustrations, comprised of collage made from tissue paper, are superb.

5. *Dear Zoo* by Rod Campbell. New York: Macmillan, 1982. (Aladdin)

   A child who writes to the zoo requesting a pet receives various animals and returns them all as unsuitable until a puppy arrives. Each animal is revealed in a lift-the-flap format that invites children to predict and see what the zoo has sent. Limited print on each page, consistent pattern, and colorful lift-up feature make this a children's favorite.

6. *Everything Grows* by Raffi, illustrated by Bruce McMillan. New York: Crown, 1987. (Crown)

   Another in the "Songs to Read" series that matches music and text with high-

quality illustrations. *See other books in this series, too.*

7. *Five Little Monkeys Jumping on the Bed* by Eileen Christelow. New York: Clarion, 1988. (Clarion)

   The traditional verse is bracketed by getting ready for bed and Mom finally getting all the little monkeys in bed only so she can gleefully jump on her bed. The verse itself is fun to chant using a countdown starting with five fingers raised.

8. *Gone Fishing* by Earlene Long, illustrated by Richard Brown. Boston: Houghton Mifflin, 1984. (Houghton Mifflin)

   A father and son spend a quiet, satisfying day fishing and being together. While there are some complex language structures, most of the text is quite simple with supportive illustrations. "A big fishing rod for my daddy" (p. 8). "A little fishing rod for me" (p. 9).

9. + *Greedy Cat* by Joy Cowley. Wellington, New Zealand: Department of Education, 1983. (Richard C. Owen)

   Children delight in Greedy Cat who continually loots "Mum's" shopping bag and who finally gets what he deserves. "Along came Greedy Cat. He looked in the shopping bag. Gobble, gobble, gobble, and that was the end of that" is spread out over four lines and repeated seven times in the story.

10. *Hush Little Baby* by Aliki. New York: Simon & Schuster, 1968. (Simon & Schuster)

    Popular folk lullaby is easily and enjoyably sung by young readers. This favorite version is illustrated in folk art style with muted colors to support the mood of the text.

11. + *In a Dark, Dark Wood* by June Melser and Joy Cowley. Auckland, New Zealand: Shortland Publications, 1980. (The Wright Group)

    Children love the suspense of finding out what's in the "dark, dark box" in the "dark, dark house." Compare with Ruth Brown's A Dark, Dark House *(New York: Dial, 1981).*

12. + *Is Your Mama a Llama?* by Deborah Guarino, illustrated by Steven Kellogg. New York: Scholastic, 1989. (Scholastic)

    A humorous story in rhyming verse fol-

lows a baby llama on visits and inquiries to various animals in a quest to determine if his mama is a llama.

13. + *It Looked Like Spilt Milk* by Charles G. Shaw. New York: Harper & Row, 1947. (Harper & Row)

"Sometimes it looked like Spilt Milk. But it wasn't Spilt Milk. / Sometimes it looked like a Rabbit. But it wasn't a Rabbit." Consistent language pattern and simple, accompanying cutouts of the objects one might "see" in cloud shapes make this easy to read and suitable for beginning patterned writing.

14. + *Joshua James Likes Trucks* by Catherine Petrie. Chicago: Children's Press, 1988. (Children's Press)

Joshua James, a young African-American boy, likes all kinds of trucks—big, little, long, short, red, green, yellow, blue, and trucks that go up and down. Very predictable text with large, clear print and matching picture cues.

15. *Just Like Daddy* by Frank Asch. New York: Simon & Schuster, 1981. (Simon & Schuster)

A gentle story of a young bear who emulates his daddy—and his mommy. Repetitive phrases and clear illustrations make this an appealing, easily readable book.

16. *Molly* by Ruth Shaw Radlauer, illustrated by Emily Arnold McCully. New York: Simon & Schuster, 1987. (Little Simon).

A disorganized but happy and independent little girl gets ready for and goes to school. Easy to read because of its limited print, the engaging story gets good support from the illustrations. (Series)

17. + *More Spaghetti I Say* by Rita Gelman. New York: Scholastic, 1987. (Scholastic)

Although the pictures are barely more than cartoons, children love this playful, rhyming book about the eating antics of two monkeys, Minnie and Freddy. (Series)

18. + *Mrs. Wishy-Washy* by Joy Cowley, illustrated by Elizabeth Fuller. Auckland, New Zealand: Shortland Publications, 1980. (The Wright Group)

"Oh, lovely mud," say the cow, the pig, and the duck before Mrs. Wishy-Washy cleans them all up. But back they go into

the puddle again. Children will sympathize with these mud-lovers. Retell the story with different animals or make a giant mural mud puddle with a variety of dirty or about-to-be dirty animals.

19. *Mud* by Wendy Cheyette Lewison, illustrated by Maryann Cocca-Leffler. New York: Random House, 1990. (Random House)

Whimsical pictures match the short, rhyming verse describing a boy and girl who are covered with mud everywhere.

20. *My Bike* by Craig Martin. Wellington, New Zealand: Department of Education, 1985. (Richard C. Owen)

Realistic photographs show a boy riding his bike each day of the week. The story is cumulative with a new episode being added for each day of the week. Good for reinforcing direction words: "over," "under," "around," "through," "up," and "down" and for writing a similar patterned story. (See pp. 142–143 for examples.) Check other titles in this Ready to Read *series.*

21. + *Noisy Nora* by Rosemary Wells. New York: Dial, 1973. (Dial)

Young readers love the rhythm and rhyme of this popular tale. Children relate to the angry frustration of young Nora who "had to wait" because her mother and father were busy with her younger siblings. Discuss other, more appropriate ways Nora could have gotten attention.

22. + *Oh, A-Hunting We Will Go* by John Langstaff. New York: Macmillan, 1974. (Aladdin)

This popular rhyming chant with music included on the final page is a favorite classic. In addition to singing the text, children enjoy adding their own original verses.

23. *Old MacDonald Had a Farm* by Glen Rounds. New York: Holiday, 1989. (Holiday)

This farmer has the usual animals plus a few surprises in the popular song. Bold, black print in four sizes clues readers into the animal's name, the sound it makes, the chorus, and connecting words. See also other versions such as Carol Jones's (New York: Houghton Mifflin, 1989), Holly Berry's (New York: North South, 1994), and Tracey Campbell Pearson's (New York: Dial, 1984), which adds additional verses, too.

24. *"Pardon?" Said the Giraffe* by Colin West. New York: Lippincott, 1986. (Harper-Trophy)

"'What's it like up there?' asked the frog . . . 'Pardon?' said the giraffe." These two language patterns alternate for most of the text as a persistent frog tries repeatedly to talk to a tall giraffe. Children enjoy the humorous ending and finding the frog on the colorful end pages. See, also by West, "Not Me," Said the Monkey *(Lippincott, 1987) and* Have You Seen the Crocodile? *(Lippincott, 1986).*

25. *Pizza Party* by Grace Maccarone, illustrated by Emily Arnold McCully. New York: Scholastic, 1994. (Scholastic)

In rhyming text of two to four words per page, children make pizza from scratch with a man who likes to cook with kids. While the text simply states "We push. / We poke. / We roll. / We joke," the illustrations reveal the process from start to finish. Children who have made pizza can dictate or write directions, making this a book that invites writing as well.

26. + *Pumpkin Pumpkin* by Jeanette Titherington. New York: Greenwillow, 1986. (Mulberry)

A boy and his grandfather plant a pumpkin seed and raise, harvest, and carve the pumpkin after carefully saving some seeds for next year's pumpkin in this life cycle book. Identify the animals that watch the pumpkin grow, and plant seeds or carve a pumpkin. (Series)

27. *Roll Over! A Counting Song* by Merle Peek. New York: Clarion, 1981. (Houghton Mifflin)

Toys in bed fall out as a boy sings the song. Finally, when the child is asleep, readers see the animals in a wall frieze. See also the lift-the-flap Roll Over! *by Mordecai Gerstein (New York: Crown, 1988).*

28. *Stop, Thief!* by Robert Kalen, illustrated by Yossi Abolafia. New York: Greenwillow, 1993. (   )

This circular story portrays the travels of an acorn as each animal snitches it from the previous one until it finally comes back to the original squirrel. Refrain of "stop, thief" invites children to chime in.

29. *Things I Like* by Anthony Browne. New York: Knopf, 1989. (COP)

A chimpanzee tells what he likes to do: painting, riding a bike, playing with toys, dressing up, and much more. Humorous illustrations strongly support the text of one to five words on each page. See also I Like Books *by the same author, p. 111b.*

30. + *What a Wonderful World* by George David Weiss and Bob Thiele, illustrated by Ashley Bryan. Littleton, MA: Sundance, 1967. (Sundance)

Inspired by the Louis Armstrong rendition, this song of praise to the marvels in the natural world is beautifully illustrated in Bryan's glowing watercolors.

31. *Wheels on the Bus.* Raffi Songs to Read, illustrated by Sylvie Kantorovitz Wickstrom. New York: Crown, 1988. (Crown)

This well-known song invites children to sing the words and follow the people on the bus as they ride to a park. Final page includes the music and additional verses. Other books in the series with pictures by different illustrators bring other well-known songs to life, allowing children to sing their way toward literacy. (Series)

32. + *Who Said Red?* by Mary Serfozo. New York: McElderry Books, 1988. (Aladdin)

Vibrant watercolor illustrations by Keiko Narahashi complement the rhyming and repetitive text. Imaginative use of language for primary color words. (Series)

33. + *Who's in the Shed?* by Brenda Parkes. Crystal Lake, IL: Rigby, 1986. (Rigby)

Increasingly enlarged cutouts give additional clues to "Who's in the shed?" Children love predicting as they go along and rereading many times. The recurring pattern is "So the sheep (and other animals) had a peep through a hole in the shed. What did she see?"

Once again, it is difficult to find "literature" children can actually read at this early level. Emerging readers needs lots of books (literally hundreds) to read and practice on daily to gain book knowledge, sight vocabulary, fluency, and confidence. Therefore, the following published series, all in paperback, are recommended for the classroom collection. Before introducing these books and sharing them with children, it is important to know children's needs and interests and be very familiar with the books. Once the child is secure with beginning reading strategies and has developed some fluency, be sure to expand your collection to include the wealth of wonderful trade books by well-known and award-winning authors and illustrators found in the grade level literature lists, literacy extension resources, your school and public libraries, children's book publishers, book clubs, and bookstores.

You have to be choosy in selecting books from the following series, but many are short, predictable texts with story language, pictures, and topics that make sense and appeal to the young reader. Some of these published series are better than others, and within a series the quality of books may vary. Some of the books in these series are by noted authors and illustrators. Many come with teacher guides of varying quality. Some focus on "skills" teaching. Our recommendation is to ignore the skills and words in isolation and focus on story enjoyment. A number of these titles are also available in Spanish. Some have accompanying Big Books and/or cassettes. Many can be ordered as individual titles, either singly or in six-packs. Others are only available as part of a package. Check with the respective publishers and/or their representatives.

For classrooms that lack sufficient numbers of needed books, try writing your own books with the students. We do this mostly in the small, guided reading group as a shared writing by scribing for and assisting the children in writing a coherent, original story that is often inspired by a book or author we have particularly enjoyed. It works well to then photocopy enough "books" so each student can illustrate and read a personal copy.

34. *Early Learning Paks.* Carmel, CA: Hampton-Brown Books, 1992–1993.

   Seven stories with rhyme and repetition are geared to second-language learners. Books are sixteen pages or twenty-four pages and vary in difficulty. See also from

Hampton-Brown, A Chorus of Cultures: Developing Literacy Through Multicultural Poetry, *an excellent anthology of over 100 poems (1993).*

35. *A First-Start Easy Reader.* Mahwah, NJ: Troll Associates, 1980–1992.

   Some recommended titles in this series of forty-four books with simple sentences and easy vocabulary include Animals at the Zoo, Betsy the Babysitter, Big Red Fire Engine, Harold's Flyaway Kite, Skating on Thin Ice, *and* Stop That Rabbit.

36. *Hello Reader! Series.* New York: Scholastic, 1992–1994.

   Some of the books in this series in levels 1 and 2 are fine for reinforcing beginning reading strategies. Several recommended, predictable books that deal with topics children can relate to are Itchy, Itchy Chicken Pox, Pizza Party *(see p. 116b),* My Messy Room, *and* Hello House! *(see p. 120b).*

37. *Literacy 2000 Satellites.* Stages 1 and 2. Crystal Lake, IL: Rigby, 1993.

   There are twenty-four books in each stage of this popular series of fiction and nonfiction books. Emergent readers enjoy reading these little eight-page books. For many more easy-to-read titles, refer to Stages 1 and 2 of the Literacy 2000 *reading collection. Some titles are more predictable than others. See also the supplemental collection of traditional tales and contemporary stories. Some favorites include* The Gingerbread Man, Who's in the Shed?, Crocodile Beat, Oh No!, Time for a Rhyme, The Enormous Watermelon, *and* Who Sank the Boat? *Teachers find that the* Literacy 2000 *Teachers' Resource has many helpful suggestions for establishing a balanced reading program.*

38. *New Way: Learning with Literature.* Austin, TX: Steck-Vaughn, 1989.

   We initially rejected this series because it is so structured, but struggling readers enjoy their "chapter book" format. Emergent readers experience much success with this series and come to know and enjoy the characters. Illustrations are clear and highly supportive in each sixteen-page text. Level

1, Red Level, books are the easiest and include nine titles. Beginning readers also have success with Level 2, Blue Level, books.

39. *Read More Books* by Dianne Frasier and Constance Compton. San Diego: Dominie Press, 1994.

    Sixteen nonfiction titles for emergent readers focus on real life and work situations such as I Am a Photographer, I Am a Dentist, I Live in an Apartment, Shopping, *and* What Do You See at the Pet Store? *Five pages of limited, clear text are supported by five pages of accompanying color photographs of related people and places. A very well-done, appealing series for emergent readers.*

40. *Read-alongs.* Stage 1. Crystal Lake, IL: Rigby, 1988.

    Six, twenty-four-page, predictable titles are available with or without cassettes for listening to and following along with the text.

41. *Reading Unlimited.* Glenview, IL: Scott, Foresman, 1976.

    Books include The Bus Ride, The Lion's Tail, Catch That Frog, Friends, Pat's New Puppy, Cats and Kittens, Victor Makes a TV, Ten Little Bears *and* Happy Faces. *An old series but great for building early reading strategies with meaningful stories.*

42. *Ready to Read Series.* Katonah, NY: Richard C. Owen, 1983.

    Developed by the Department of Education in Wellington, New Zealand, "Ready to Read" titles provide the structure and natural language upon which New Zealand's highly successful reading program is based. Some of the easiest and most notable titles for emergent readers include: T Shirts, Greedy Cat, I Can Read, Old Tuatara, *and* Sam's Mask.

43. *Rookie Readers.* Chicago: Children's Press, 1987–1993.

    Many of the titles in this series of sixty-four books are delightful as they use children's language and experiences along with rhyming verse and predictable text. Ignore the "Word List" at the end of each book. Some of the best in the series include: Bobby's Zoo; A Buzz Is Part of a Bee; Bugs!; Eat Your Peas, Louise; I Love Cats; Katie Couldn't; Katie Did It; Messy Bessey; Messy Bessey's Garden; Sometimes Things Change; Too Many Balloons; Wait, Skates!; Where is Mittens?; Bobby's Zoo; Hot Rod Harry; Hi Clouds; Collecting; Larry and the Cookie; *and* I Love Fishing.

44. *The Story Box Level 1 Read-Togethers.* Bothell, WA: The Wright Group, 1987.

    Twenty-five fiction titles, available as Big Books and little books, are predictable for emergent readers because of their rhyme, rhythm, repetition, and delightful story line. Some classic titles include Hairy Bear, Mrs. Wishy-Washy, The Big Toe, *and* In a Dark, Dark Wood. *A favorite collection for many kindergarten and grade one teachers and children.*

45. *Sunshine Books, Level 1 Fiction.* Bothell, WA: The Wright Group, 1990.

    More than one hundred titles in fourteen sets (A–J) give the emerging reader practice on eight-page stories and sixteen-page stories. Sunshine, Level 1, Teacher Guide (1992) is excellent for setting up a balanced reading-writing program.

46. *Sunshine Science, Level 1,* Sets A and B. Bothell, WA: The Wright Group, 1992.

    Topics that young children are curious about, such as skeletons, spiders, and space, are clearly presented with photo illustrations in these sixteen-page books. Eight books in each set.

47. *Tadpole Readers.* Crystal Lake, IL: Rigby, 1984.

    Twenty books written by or about young children captivate young readers with their fanciful illustrations, interesting topics, enlarged print, and easy-to-read text. Some favorites include The Trolley Ride, When Lana Was Absent, Excuses, Excuses, *and* Munching Mark. *Ideal for having children create their own versions.*

48. *Talk-About-Books* by Debbie Bailey, photos by Susan Huszar. San Diego: Dominie Press, 1994.

    Engaging color photographs of children of diverse cultural backgrounds in natural settings support the simple text of these easy-to-read books. Titles include: My Dad, My Mom, Sisters, Brothers, Toys, Shoes, Clothes, *and* Hats.

49. *Windmill Books. Set E.* Bothell, WA: The Wright Group, 1988.

   The six books in this set are ideal for emergent readers. Several of the titles are Lucy's Sore Knee, Goodnight Peter, *and* My Wonderful Chair.

Grade 1

Books on this list include many titles that first graders will be able to read on their own but not, perhaps, in the early months of school. Teachers should consider some titles as read-alouds and shared readings in the fall and as guided or shared readings as children become more proficient. New readers need the content of the previous two lists and may draw on the kindergarten list as well.

Books in this list deal with ideas of what it means to be a friend, occupations and working habits, helping others, and concepts such as egg-layers, fractions, and the nature of rivers and ponds. Traditional literature includes classic folktales in both European and African-American literature, plus the introduction of the trickster pattern.

Suggestions for first-grade author studies include Byron Barton, Tomie dePaola, Denise Fleming, Mem Fox, Arnold Lobel, James and/or Edward Marshall, Bruce McMillan, Maurice Sendak, Audrey and Don Wood, or any of the authors on the kindergarten list introduction.

1. *Alexander and the Terrible, Horrible, No Good, Very Bad Day* by Judith Viorst, illustrated by Ray Cruz. New York: Atheneum, 1972. (Aladdin)

   Alexander has numerous "terrible things" happen to him and considers moving to Australia. Good discussion or story starter about our own terrible, or even very good, days. (Series)

2. *Amos & Boris* by William Steig. New York: Farrar, Straus & Giroux, 1971. (Sunburst)

   Like Aesop's "The Lion and the Mouse," this story shows how a big and a little creature exchange help: a seagoing mouse is saved by a whale but then the beached whale is saved by a mouse. Notice the interesting language of the story, write a diary as if you were the mouse or the whale, make a tiny mouse museum of things important to Amos, and ask children to compare Steig's story with Aesop's fable. (See Teacher's Guide, Appendix B.)

3. *Anansi and the Moss-Covered Rock* by Eric A. Kimmel, illustrated by Janet Stevens. New York: Holiday, 1988. (Scholastic).

   Anansi, a lazy trickster spider from African folk tradition, gains food from all the animals through the use of a magic rock. But little Bush Deer figures out what he is doing and tricks him instead. See also Anansi Goes Fishing *(New York: Holiday, 1992), and Stevens's updated humorous illustrations present animals sitting in lawn chairs sipping sodas and listening to boom boxes. (Series)*

4. *Benjamin* by Anne Matheson. Toronto: Gage Educational Publishing, 1993. (Dancing Sun)

   In pristine photographs, special Benjamin uses his senses to appreciate the world around him. When he tells his friends about his discovery, they ridicule him until he explains how to look, listen, and smell. Good for discussing how we experience the world and, with older children, how authors notice more than simply how things look.

5. + *A Chair for My Mother* by Vera B. Williams. New York: Greenwillow, 1982. (Mulberry, Scholastic)

   A child and her waitress mother save coins to buy a comfortable armchair after their belongings are destroyed in an apartment fire. The community helps them get back on their feet, and the story provides an excellent start for a discussion of how people help each other in neighborhoods, in classrooms, and in the world. Notice Williams's selection of small pictures to highlight aspects of the larger ones. (Series)

6. + *Chickens Aren't the Only Ones* by Ruth Heller. New York: Putnam, 1981. (Putnam)

   Accurate paintings illustrate the rhyming text about all the animals that hatch from eggs: birds, reptiles, fish, insects, and even the extinct dinosaur are mentioned. An excellent discussion starter for ways scientists categorize the world and a fine introduction to a classroom study of animals.

7. + (E) *Dinosaurs, Dinosaurs* by Byron Barton. New York: Crowell, 1989. (Harper-Collins)

In three to eight words per page, Barton's deceptively simple text tells quite a bit about dinosaurs in words children can read. A triceratops family provides a story subtext that children can make into a separate story. See also the more difficult and informative sequel, Bones, Bones, Dinosaur Bones (New York: Crowell, 1990).

8. + (E) *Eating Fractions* by Bruce McMillan. Scholastic, 1991. (   )

An African-American child and a white child demonstrate fractions visually while graphics support concept of fractions by cutting of pizza, desserts, and so forth. Appetizing foods are cut into halves, thirds, or fourths. Concepts and words are reinforced with mathematical symbols and provide excellent discussion topics and impetus for dividing and depicting other food fractions.

9. *Every Time I Climb a Tree* by David McCord, illustrated by Marc Simont. Boston: Little, Brown, 1967. (Little, Brown)

The title poem invites readers to do their own dreaming from a high place, and other poems play with words, sounds, feelings, and sights. A fine introduction to a major American poet; Simont's bold illustrations seem just right for the selections.

10. (E) *Flying* by Donald Crews. New York: Greenwillow, 1986. (Mulberry)

Like other books in Crews's transportation series, this one examines aspects of flying in short phrases: "Take off. / Flying over highways. / Flying over rivers." Look for visual references to his previous titles, the meaning of the dedication, and Crews on the first page carrying a newspaper on which is written the date he completed the book. (He does this with dates, by the way, in most of his books.) Crews is an excellent author/illustrator to study in first grade because of the age-appropriate content and the fact that children can see the many patterns Crews works with in text and illustration. See two stories from the author's childhood, Bigmama's (1991) and Shortcut (1992, both New York: Greenwillow).

11. *Frog and Toad Together* by Arnold Lobel. New York: Harper & Row, 1971. (Harper-Trophy)

The steadfast Frog helps his impatient friend Toad through a series of humorous incidents in this popular series. Children enjoy laughing at Toad's impetuous acts and discussing what they would do in similar situations. Occasionally, Lobel's gentle tales provoke readers to discuss theme, or "big ideas," as well. (Series)

12. *George and Martha* by James Marshall. Boston: Houghton Mifflin, 1972. (Sandpiper)

The first collection of small stories about two large friends introduces children to this popular hippo pair. (Series)

13. (E) *Hello, House!* by Linda Hayward, illustrated by Lynn Munsinger. New York: Random House, 1988. (Random House)

Funny Brer Rabbit tale set in large type, with one to two sentences per page, introduces children to this African-American trickster.

14. *Henry and Mudge* by Cynthia Rylant, illustrated by Suçie Stevenson. New York: Macmillan, 1987. (Aladdin)

In an easy-reader format with full-color illustrations, Rylant and Stevenson tell about Henry, a boy who finally gets a pet dog. Mudge grows to 180 pounds, accompanies Henry to school, and gets lost and is found all in seven short chapters. Like Lobel, Rylant packs a lot into few words, and readers will be moved, will laugh, and will want to talk about the story. There are many books in this excellent series. (Series)

15. *I Need a Lunch Box* by Jeanette Caines, illustrated by Pat Cummings. New York: HarperCollins, 1988. (HarperTrophy)

While his first-grade sister gets many new things to start school, an unnamed African-American boy only wants a lunch box. He imagines wonderful designs for a different lunch box for each day of the week before he finally receives a present from his father. Children can design their own perfect and outrageous lunch boxes *or decide on the ideal contents to fill them after reading this story. Pair with the easy-to-read* Harry Gets Ready for School *by Harriet Ziefert, illustrated by Mavis Smith (New York: Puffin, 1991) for a discussion of how we get ready for the start of a school year. See* Jamal's Busy Day *by Wade Hudson, illustrated by George Ford (Orange, NJ: Just Us Books, 1991) for a comparison of an African-American child's school "work day" with that of his parents.*

16. (E) *In a Small, Small Pond* by Denise Fleming. New York: Henry Holt, 1993.
   (   )
   In this Caldecott Honor Book, the life cycle of a pond is illustrated by bright illustrations made of dyed paper pulp poured through stencils. Minimal text imaginatively placed on the page notes what animals come to life in a pond in the spring and ends with the pond dormant as deep winter sets in. See also Fleming's other concept books such as Barnyard Banter *(1994),* Count! *(1992), and* In the Tall, Tall Grass *(1991).*

17. *Ira Sleeps Over* by Bernard Waber. Boston: Houghton Mifflin, 1972. (Sandpiper)
   The universal problem of how to save face even though you want your teddy bear with you on a sleepover is explored in this family story. Ask why Ira decides to take his bear after all. Most children have bedtime rituals and special toys or blankets that they enjoy comparing. In a sequel, Ira Says Goodbye *(Boston: Houghton Mifflin, 1988), Ira's best friend moves away but not so far that the boys can't visit each other. (Series)*

18. *Jamaica's Find* by Juanita Havill, illustrated by Anne Sibley O'Brien. Boston: Houghton Mifflin, 1986. (Sandpiper)
   An African-American girl finds a stuffed dog and contemplates keeping it. But when she takes it to the park office, she makes a new friend. (Series)

19. *Little Bear* by Else Holmelund Minarik, illustrated by Maurice Sendak. New York: Harper & Row, 1957. (HarperTrophy)
   One of the very first early-reader books, as well as one of the finest, presents Little Bear and his friends to children. Elegantly

told but with a controlled vocabulary, the stories have endured for over thirty years. Ask children how Little Bear is like and unlike human children. Jean Van Leeuwen's series beginning with Tales of Oliver Pig, *illustrated by Arnold Lobel (New York: Dial, 1979), provides some of the same reader satisfactions with its humanized pig family growing up. Check other books in the "I-Can-Read" format published by HarperCollins, Macmillan, Dial, Scholastic, Puffin, and others to introduce readers who are ready for more text to beginning "chapter books." (Series)*

20. *The Little Red Hen* by Paul Galdone. New York: Clarion, 1974. (Clarion)
   If you don't do any of the work, then you don't get any of the hen's bread. Notice the words "Not I" are cleverly illustrated. Encourage retelling with pictured seeds, wheat, flour, bread, and the four folktale characters. For another humorous take on working, see Martin Waddell's funny Farmer Duck *(Cambridge, MA: Candlewick, 1991) with beautiful springtime settings painted by Helen Oxenbury and* A Job for Wittilda *by Caralyn and Mark Buechner (New York: Dial, 1993).*

21. *Little Red Riding Hood* by Trina Schart Hyman. New York: Holiday, 1983. (Holiday)
   This classic folktale features the hungry wolf and the helpful huntsman as well as wonderfully illustrated borders and small vignettes. Watch the cat. See Self-Portrait: Trina Schart Hyman *(Addison-Wesley, 1981, p. 153b) and tell children about the importance of this story to the author. Compare Lisbeth Zwerger's illustrations for the same story.*

22. (E) *My Best Friend* by Pat Hutchins. New York: Greenwillow, 1993. (   )
   Two black friends and one is better at everything than the other one. However, when they sleep over, the second friend can keep her friend from being scared by the blowing curtains. Good story to discuss friendships, differences in competencies, self-esteem, and self-confidence.

23. (E) *My River* by Shari Halpern. New York: Scholastic, 1992. (Scholastic)
   One short sentence per page, such as

"It's my river," shows a turtle on a log. Successive pages of one short sentence and an illustration of a different animal show the diversity of a river ecosystem: "It's everyone's river." Good for discussion of interdependence of species and what one finds in and along a river.

24. + *One of Three* by Angela Johnson, illustrated by David Soman. New York: Orchard, 1991. (Sundance)

    The youngest of three African-American sisters tells how happy she is to be part of this urban family, even if the two older girls leave her behind sometimes.

25. *A Painter* by Douglas Florian. New York: Greenwillow, 1993. (   )

    Part of the "How We Work" series, this book has about one large-print sentence per page illustrated in bold watercolors. Each title features a man or woman at work. Text varies in difficulty from the more detailed but still simple A Chef to the very easy An Auto Mechanic. (Series)

26. *Pierre* by Maurice Sendak. New York: Harper, 1962. (HarperTrophy)

    Originally a part of the four-book Nutshell Library, this is also published separately. Pierre doesn't care about anything until a lion eats him. After the lion coughs him up, Pierre cares! Rhyming text, repetitive phrases, and the saucy Pierre captivate readers, and the five short chapters support the idea that children are reading longer books. A classic.

27. *The Random House Book of Poetry for Children*, edited by Jack Prelutsky. New York: Random House, 1983. (   )

    Over 500 poems are divided into sections on nature, seasons, children, humor, people, and food ("I'm Hungry!"); other poems invite children to enjoy poetry. An excellent selection from which to choose all year long.

28. *Shoes from Grandpa* by Mem Fox, illustrated by Patricia Mullins. New York: Orchard, 1989. (Orchard)

    Jessie, an active girl, is given new clothes by various members of her family. As the cumulative tale builds and she is encumbered by layers of clothes, she asks if someone could just buy her some jeans?

Torn-paper collage illustrations, lines of text with some internal rhythmic verse, the cumulative pattern of the story, plus a modern girl who has a common complaint make this compelling and easy to read.

29. *Three by the Sea* by Edward Marshall, illustrated by James Marshall. New York: Dial, 1981. (Dial Easy-to-Read)

    Three short stories present a girl and two boys who are entertaining each other before they go for a swim. Humor is found in unexpected plot twists and, as usual, in Marshall's droll illustrations. Teachers will appreciate, too, the hilarious contrast between a bland story Lolly reads from her school basal text and the lively story her friend Sam tells instead. (Series)

30. + *Time for a Rhyme* illustrated by Marjorie Gardner, Heather Philpott, and Jane Tanner. Crystal Lake, IL: Rigby, 1982. (Rigby)

    Nursery rhymes, some well known and others not, are presented with lively illustrations for children who may not be familiar with Mother Goose. (See also annotation for "Mother Goose" on the kindergarten list, p. 108b.)

31. *Tom* by Tomie dePaola. New York: Putnam, 1993. (   )

    An autobiographical picture book. Grandfather shows Tommy interesting things about the butcher business and the grocery store he owns. When Tommy takes to school two chicken feet decorated with nail polish, he gets into trouble, but his grandfather just winks and says "We'll just have to think of something else to do." Wonderful relationship and a good introduction to dePaola's many types of books. See his autobiographical The Art Lesson (New York: Putnam, 1989, see p. 97b); an example of his nonfiction such as Charlie Needs a Cloak (New York: Simon & Schuster, 1990); a story that draws on his Italian heritage such as + Strega Nona (New York: Simon & Schuster, 1979; Scholastic); or one of his many traditional stories or picture books. A great author to study at this grade or the next.

32. *Too Many Tamales* by Gary Soto, illustrated by Ed Martinez. New York: Putnam, 1993. (   )

*When Maria helps her mother make ta-
males for the family Christmas Eve celebration, she thinks she has worked her
mother's ring into the filling. So she convinces her cousins to help her eat the
whole plate of food in order to find the
ring. Rich paintings depict this extended
Latino family as all begin once again to
make the replacement holiday tamales.*

33. *Wiley and the Hairy Man* by Molly Bang.
New York: Macmillan, 1976. (Aladdin)
*In this traditional African-American
folktale, the Hairy Man threatens Wiley
and his mother until they trick him three
times. Trickery, magic, wise mothers, and
the number three are common motifs in
folktales, and children might think of other
stories with these patterns.*

34. *City Kids* by Lorraine Wilson. Crystal
Lake, IL: Rigby, 1987.
*This series of sixty little books about the
everyday experiences of children—from the
teacher getting mad, to cooking spaghetti,
or getting new sneakers or a haircut—are
terrific for enjoying reading and encouraging writing. Humorous illustrations and
natural language make them kid favorites.
Struggling older readers enjoy them, too.*

Grade 2

The books on this list reflect a second grader's
desire for increasing knowledge of the world,
its geography, its people, and its ecology. In
addition, a variety of easy-reader formatted
books and chapter books encourage readers to
take on more text.

Some unifying ideas of books here include
living in a family, diversity in relationships,
friendship, caring for the earth, valuing cultural diversity, considering nonfiction formats,
occupations and work, animal behavior, and
periods in American history. Traditional literature includes the comparison of Anansi versions and the introduction of other tricksters;
the cross-cultural variants of the "good person
rewarded/greedy person punished"; and an
echo from the first grade list, a variant of "Red
Riding Hood."

New readers at this grade may need to return to the previous three lists to build fluency
and confidence. Consider, too, revisiting books
on the previous lists that are thematically related to this one as a way of helping children
see patterns in idea, genre, or structure.

Suggestions for second-grade author studies
include Verna Aardema, Marc Brown, Gail
Gibbons, Steven Kellogg, Bill Peet, Brian
Pinkney, James Stevenson, Vera B. Williams,
plus others on previous lists.

1. (E) *Abuela* by Arthur Dorros, illustrated by
Elisa Kleven. New York: Dutton, 1991.
(   )
*Latino child and her grandmother af-
fectionately spend time together, which
the child Rosalba recalls as a flying journey over New York City. Vibrant illustrations, incidental Spanish words translated
into English in context support speakers of
both languages in this joyous intergenerational adventure.*

2. *The Adventures of Spider* by Joyce Cooper
Arkhurst, illustrated by Jerry Pinkney.
Boston: Little, Brown, 1964. (Scholastic)
*Told with the rhythm, sounds, and ca-
dences of African oral tradition, these
tales reveal the trickster nature of Anansi,
the spider. Look for the interesting fea-
tures of African folktales. Compare the
character of Anansi and the language of
the story in Gail Haley's* A Story, a Story
*(New York: Atheneum, 1970) or Gerald
McDermott's* Anansi the Spider *(New
York: Holt, Rinehart and Winston, 1972).
See also* Anansi and the Moss-Covered
Rock, *p. 119b. Invite children to write
their own tales. (Series)*

3. *Amazing Grace* by Mary Hoffman, illustrated by Caroline Binch. New York: Dial,
1991. (   )
*A black child who loves to read is glow-
ingly depicted in illustration and text.
When Grace is told by her classmates that
she can't play Peter Pan because she is
black and a girl, her grandmother takes
her to see a famous black ballerina from
Trinidad. Excellence convinces Grace that
she can be Peter Pan and her tryout performance convinces everyone that if you
put your mind to it, you can do anything
you want.*

4. *Amelia's Road* by Linda Jacobs Altman, illustrated by Enrique O. Sanchez. New York: Lee & Low, 1993. (Lee & Low)

   As a child of migrant workers, Amelia is tired of moving and wishes for a place of her own. She finally appropriates a giant tree and buries a box of memories as a way of creating her own spot. Also available in Spanish edition.

5. *Animal Fact/Animal Fable* by Seymour Simon, illustrated by Diane deGroat. New York: Crown, 1979. (Crown)

   In a clever guessing-game format, Simon presents simple statements about animals that may be true or false. When the reader turns the page, his prediction is confirmed or not by a paragraph of facts and two factual illustrations, one usually a close-up. In addition to provoking children to reconsider "common knowledge," this book also provides a lively format children may use in their own report writing. See numerous other books by Simon, one of the foremost writers of nonfiction for children.

6. *Borreguita and the Coyote* by Verna Aardema, illustrated by Petra Mathers. New York: Knopf, 1991. (   )

   In this Mexican trickster tale, a sheep outwits a coyote three times in familiar folktale patterns. Coyote is usually the traditional trickster in Southwest Native American tales and the pattern of the tricky one being "outfoxed" can be found in other trickster tales such as those of Brer Rabbit and the Anansi stories on this and previous lists.

7. *Charlotte's Web* by E. B. White, illustrated by Garth Williams. New York: Harper & Row, 1952. (Harper)

   This beloved animal fantasy has become a classic because of its timelessness. A spider's efforts to save a young pig are chronicled in graceful prose. The gentle humor, development of the animal characters, Fern's growth from young child to young girl, the themes of friendship, growing up, and the cycle of life and death make this a powerful book for young readers.

8. (E) *A Country Far Away* by Nigel Gray, illustrated by Philippe Dupasquier. New York: Orchard, 1988. (Orchard)

   A single text is illustrated as it pertains to two different settings. The top half of the page presents a rural African savannah culture; the bottom half, a suburban western culture. Besides demonstrating a good visual format for comparison, this is an excellent discussion book for similarities and differences. Pair with Galimoto (below) and look at a map of Africa to see what you can discover.

9. *The Courage of Sarah Noble* by Alice Dalgliesh, illustrated by Leonard Weisgard. New York: Scribner, 1954. (Aladdin)

   Eight-year-old Sarah's courage is proved in many ways when she accompanies her father into the wilderness to cook for him while he builds a cabin for their family. A realistic picture of part of life in "olden days" and a fine discussion of what bravery and courage are. Teachers may want to note the unconscious racist attitudes conveyed when Sarah is annoyed because the Indians don't speak English and her father renames a Native American man John because he can't pronounce his name— reflections of another era's attitudes toward nonwhite populations. It is still, however, an excellent discussion book and a favorite at this grade.

10. *The Day of Ahmed's Secret* by Florence Parry Heide, illustrated by Ted Lewin. New York: Lothrop, Lee and Shepard, 1990. (   )

    Ahmed, an Egyptian boy of about eight, delivers bottled gas to his customers in Cairo. When he finally learns to write his name, it is a big day in the family. Children who look at the mix of ancient and modern aspects of Egyptian life depicted in the illustrations and consider the message of the story gain valuable experience in seeing "like an anthropologist" or reading between the lines. For other books that deal with the theme of valuing literacy, see Patricia Polacco's The Bee Tree (New York: Putnam, 1993) set in Amish country, the African-American Papa's Stories by Dolores Johnson (New York: Macmillan, 1994), and the South Africa–set Over the Green Hills by Rachel Isadora (New York: Greenwillow, 1992). Children can draw inspiration from these books to talk about when they learned to read and write.

11. *Do Not Open* by Brinton Turkle. New York: Dutton, 1981. (Puffin)

When Miss Moody opens a blue glass bottle she finds at the seashore, an evil genie is let loose. But it proves no match for the tricks of Miss Moody and her cat. Recall the trick and ask children to think of other stories, such as "Puss in Boots" or "The Brave Little Tailor," in which trickery is important.

12. *Dr. De Soto* by William Steig. New York: Farrar, Straus & Giroux, 1982. (Sunburst)

A clever mouse dentist tricks a fox patient. Notice the many contrivances that help the dentist in his office, elicit children's knowledge of the fox character from other folktales, and introduce children to other modern tales by this popular author. See also Dr. De Soto Goes to Africa (*New York: Farrar, Straus & Giroux, 1992). (Series*)

13. (E) *Friday Night Is Papa Night* by Ruth A. Sonneborn, illustrated by Emily A. McCully. New York: Viking, 1970. (Puffin)

Pedro and his Hispanic family wait for Papa, who is working at two jobs, to come home on Friday. When Papa finally arrives, it is after midnight but the family gathers for a joyous celebration because Friday is "the nicest night." Children might talk of their own family celebrations or special times after hearing this story.

14. *Galimoto* by Karen Lynn Williams, illustrated by Catherine Stock. New York: Lothrop, Lee and Shepard, 1990. (Mulberry)

Kondi lives in Malawi and spends a day constructing a galimoto, a vehicle made from bits of wire. This story of resourcefulness, determination, and enterprise is glowingly depicted in watercolors and reveals much about contemporary village life on the shores of Lake Malawi.

15. *The Great Kapok Tree* by Lynne Cherry. San Diego: Harcourt Brace, 1990. (   )

A Brazilian woodcutter is persuaded not to cut down a kapok tree, the primary source of life for so many animals, when each one comes to him in a dream. Like My River (*see p. 121b*), this book encourages children to talk about interdependence of species and the importance of rain forests to our world. See also Un Paseo por el bosque lluvioso, *page 154b.*

16. *Honey I Love: And Other Poems* by Eloise Greenfield, illustrated by Leo and Diane Dillon. New York: Harper & Row, 1978. (HarperTrophy)

Greenfield presents a jump-rope rhyme, chants, observations on people and the neighborhood, and thoughts in the voice of a young African-American child. Illustrations in warm browns and sepias are as sensitive as these poems that celebrate a child's world.

17. + *How Much Is a Millon?* by David M. Schwartz, illustrated by Steven Kellogg. New York: Lothrop, Lee and Shepard, 1985. (Mulberry)

Help for the reader in conceptualizing large numbers. Follow up with estimating, finding funny illustrations, inventing rules for the game suggested in Kellogg's humorous illustrations, and read the sequel by the same team, If You Made a Million (*New York: Lothrop, Lee and Shepard, 1989). (Series*)

18. *How My Parents Learned to Eat* by Ina R. Friedman, illustrated by Allen Say. Boston: Houghton Mifflin, 1984. (Sandpiper)

A girl recounts how her American father and her Japanese mother each learned to eat with an unfamiliar utensil, which explains why in their house they sometimes eat with knives and forks and sometimes with chopsticks.

19. *I Want a Dog* by Dayal Kaur Khalsa. New York: Crown, 1987. (Dragonfly)

May badgers her parents for a pet dog but they are firm in their refusal. So May puts a leash on her white rollerskate and treats it like the longed-for pet. Dog lovers will admire the many dogs crowding the pictures, but children will respond to May's persistent "Try, try, try again," which eventually wins her parents over. The "Henry and Mudge" series by Cynthia Rylant (see Grade 1 list) fits well with stories about children who want pets.

20. (E) *Lionel in the Fall* by Stephen Krensky, illustrated by Susanna Natti. New York: Dial, 1987. (Puffin)

    In four short chapters, Lionel goes back to school and deals with new-teacher anxieties, friendships, and Halloween. Like Cynthia Rylant's *Henry and Mudge Under the Yellow Moon (New York: Macmillan, 1987), which is also set in the fall and is presented in easy-reader format, these short chapters enable children to see their daily lives reflected in books. Good for beginning the school year because of the fall setting and the reading level.*

21. *The Little Painter of Sabana Grande* by Patricia Maloney Markun, illustrated by Robert Casilla. New York: Bradbury, 1993. (   )

    Based on an actual incident, this story tells of a Panamanian boy artist who, lacking paper, painted his work on the sides of his house. Neighbors asked him to paint theirs, too, and the resultant beauty moved everyone. Good discussion book, like Galimoto *(see p. 125b) for using what you have to make something beautiful.*

22. *Lon Po Po: A Red-Riding Hood Story from China* by Ed Young. New York: Philomel, 1989. (   )

    Unlike the story most familiar to children, this one presents three daughters who, in disobeying their mother, let an old wolf into the house. But the eldest outwits the wolf in this Chinese story. Locate China on the map, discuss how this older version and Hyman's (see list for Grade 1) compare, and wonder over the mysterious dedication. Young has also illustrated a Chinese "Cinderella" variant, Yeh Shen *(see p. 138b).*

23. *Mary Marony and the Snake* illustrated by Blanche Sims. New York: Putnam, 1992. (   )

    Nervous about starting second grade in a new school, Mary is afraid that the children will make fun of her stuttering. An understanding mother, a matter-of-fact teacher, and the speech therapist help Mary gain the respect of her classmates. Six chapters, black and white drawings, and a length of sixty-four pages make this a good choice when readers are ready for chapter books. (Series)

24. *Me & Neesie* by Eloise Greenfield, illustrated by Moneta Barnett. New York: Harper & Row, 1975. (HarperTrophy)

    Janell's imaginary friend, Neesie, causes trouble as Janell deals with anxiety over starting school. But new friends at school solve some of the problem in this African-American girl's small moment of growing up.

25. *Monarch Butterfly* by Gail Gibbons. New York: Holiday, 1989. (Holiday)

    Gibbons introduces the life cycle of the monarch in numerous close-ups, with labels, a migration map, and some monarch lore. Directions for raising a pupa are given. Gibbons is a wonderful author to know for her lively, useful presentation of so many child-popular informational topics.

26. *An Octopus Is Amazing* by Patricia Lauber, illustrated by Holly Keller. New York: Crowell, 1990. (   )

    An excellent informational book in the "Let's-Read-and-Find-Out" series, this uses illustrations, labels, diagrams, and examples to present this fascinating animal. Good for discussion about how nonfiction conveys information. Lauber is an excellent nonfiction author to know. (Series)

27. + *Ox-Cart Man* by Donald Hall, illustrated by Barbara Cooney. New York: Viking, 1979. (Scholastic)

    This lyrical journey from fall to spring in the life of one early nineteenth-century family in New England is a paean to a self-sufficient life. Compare a child's life in this book with that portrayed in The Courage of Sarah Noble, *or with modern children's lives.*

28. *Owl Moon* by Jane Yolen, illustrated by John Schoenherr. New York: Philomel, 1987. (   )

    A girl's owling trek with her father late one winter night is beautifully evoked in stunning watercolors and poetic prose. Children might enjoy writing or telling of their own memorable experiences with the natural or nocturnal world.

29. *Pass It On: African-American Poetry for Children* selected by Wade Hudson, illustrated by Floyd Cooper. New York: Scholastic, 1993. (   )

    A varied selection of well-known contemporary and traditional poets such as Clifton, Hughes, Giovanni, Greenfield, Cullen, and Grimes is accompanied by Floyd Cooper's rich oil paintings. Subjects of poems include family life and play, pain and enduring, history, strength, and hope. Poems were selected for their power to pass on values to children.

30. *The Patchwork Quilt* by Valerie Flournoy, illustrated by Jerry Pinkney. New York: Dial, 1985. (   )

    Tanya, an African-American child, has a new understanding of the importance of family when she and her mother finish a patchwork quilt her ailing grandmother had started. Discuss how families help each other and the special "gifts" people in families share with each other.

31. *Rabbit's Judgment* by Suzanne Crowder Han, illustrated by Yumi Heo. New York: Henry Holt, 1994. (   )

    A bilingual story told in both Korean and English concerns a treacherous tiger who promises not to hurt the man who helps him out of a deep pit. A clever rabbit tricks the tiger and saves the man in this authentic tale whose striking, impressionistic illustrations enlarge a child's artistic eye.

32. (E) *The Smallest Cow in the World* by Katherine Paterson, illustrated by Jane Clark Brown. New York: HarperCollins, 1991. (HarperTrophy)

    When Marvin's family moves to take care of another Vermont farm, he misses an ornery cow that has been sold and becomes a bit ornery himself. When he creates an imaginary and comforting miniature cow and keeps it in a small bottle, he is ridiculed at school until his family and his sister's new friend show their appreciation for his creative solution in adapting to the move. The sixty-four-page easy-reader with eloquent illustrations is a good book for discussing how people help

each other adjust to changes as well as what farm life is like in a rural area.

33. *The Stories Julian Tells* by Ann Cameron, illustrated by Ann Strugnell. New York: Knopf, 1981. (Knopf)

    Six chapters introduce the imaginative Julian, his younger brother Hugh, and their friend Gloria. Strugnell's pictures of this loving African-American family and their often funny encounters are an added plus. First book in a popular series. (Series)

34. *The Talking Eggs* by Robert D. San Souci, illustrated by Jerry Pinkney. New York: Dial, 1989. (   )

    A poor widow favors her lazy daughter over the industrious one, but the good girl is rewarded by a strange old lady while the lazy one gets nothing but snakes, bugs, and scorpions in this Creole variation on a common folktale theme. Let children compare this cross-cultural theme variant in Jose Aruego and Ariane Dewey's Philippine Rockabye Crocodile (New York: Greenwillow, 1988; Mulberry); Momoko Ishii's Japanese The Tongue-Cut Sparrow, translated by Katherine Paterson, illustrated by Suekichi Akaba (New York: Dutton, 1983); Samuel Marshak's Russian The Month-Brothers, illustrated by Diane Stanley (New York: Morrow, 1983), and Mufaro's Beautiful Daughters, see page 132b.

35. (E) *Three Wishes* by Lucille Clifton, illustrated by Michael Hays. New York: Doubleday, 1992. (Dell)

    Nobie, in African-American dialect, tells of the lucky penny she has found on New Year's Day and the falling out with her best friend as a result. See the Grade 1 list for other books about friendship plus books such as Russell Hoban's A Bargain for Frances (New York: Harper, 1970; Scholastic; Harper) and Kevin Henke's Chester's Way (New York: Greenwillow, 1988).

36. *A Toad for Tuesday* by Russell E. Erickson. New York: Lothrop, Lee and Shepard, 1974. (Beech Tree)

    The unlikely friendship that develops between a cranky, messy owl and a good-tempered, orderly toad works well as a

springboard for other books about friendship. Readers ready for short chapter
books will enjoy the first of four adventure
stories featuring the toad brothers Morton
and Warton. (Series)

37. (E) + *Tommy at the Grocery Store* by Bill
Grossman, illustrated by Victoria Chess.
New York: HarperCollins, 1989. (Harper-
Trophy)
   *A piggy mother loses her son at the
grocery store and successive others purchase the boy thinking he is food of various sorts. Silly rhyming fun based on puns
on body parts: human ears vs. ears of
corn, or bottle necks, or potato eyes, for
instance. Easy-reading format assisted by
rhyme is great for shared reading.*

38. (E) *Wagon Wheels* by Barbara Brenner,
illustrated by Don Bolognese. New York:
Harper & Row, 1978. (HarperTrophy)
   *In easy-reader format, the beginning
settlement of Nicodemus, Kansas, is seen
through the eyes of two African-American
boys as they walk toward their new prairie home.*

39. (E) + *Where the Forest Meets the Sea* by
Jeannie Baker. New York: Greenwillow,
1987. (Scholastic)
   *Through striking collage illustrations,
readers explore with a modern boy a tropi-
cal rain forest in Australia. Throughout,
the pictures of ghostly images of past life
in the forest as well as ghostly images of
possible futures for this forest raise questions about how humans value rain forests
and wild land in general. A thought-provoking and beautiful book. See also* The
Great Kapok Tree *(p. 125b), and* Rain Forest *by Helen Cowcher (New York: Farrar
Straus & Giroux, 1988; Sunburst) to develop an ecological theme.*

40. *Wump World* by Bill Peet. Boston: Houghton
Mifflin, 1970. (Houghton Mifflin)
   *This delightfully illustrated tale of grass-
eating Wumps, peaceful creatures whose
world is ruined by pollution and the misuse of natural resources, is both a clever
tale and a catalyst for discussion of the
pollution of our world. Be sure to check*

for other Bill Peet titles (over twenty in
paperback).

41. "Adam Joshua" Series by Janice Lee Smith,
illustrated by Dick Gackenbach. New York:
HarperCollins. (HarperTrophy)
   *This novel series presents in five to
seven illustrated chapters a school setting
in which second and third graders deal
with the fun, dilemmas, and daily occurrences of being in school. Adam's dog gets
into school; the science fair is likely to be
won by a boy whose father helped him;
show-and-tell gets out of hand, and so
forth. Once children have read one book,
the rest seem easy. Good starts are* The
Monster in the Third Dresser Drawer
(1981), It's Not Easy Being George *(1991),
or* The Turkey's Side of It: Adam Joshua's
Thanksgiving *(1990, all New York: HarperCollins; HarperTrophy). Length varies
from 76 to 176 pages.*

Grade 3

Books on this list include chapter books (novels) that present children with diverse fantasy
and realism. In addition, nonfiction presented
in straightforward fashion, or embedded in a
story, is included to show children how information can be conveyed by narrative, charts,
graphs, maps, labels, small features enlarged
in closeups to show details, and so forth. Children in their own nonfiction writing can be
invited to use techniques they discover in guided
reading of these books.

Beautifully illustrated picture books for older
children introduce important discussion topics
such as being of two cultures, the value of
taking risks, and the importance of individual
principled action. One person may make a
difference. Children at this age may need to
be reminded that just because a book has illustrations doesn't mean that it is for little kids.

Relationships between generations in a family are a prominent theme of books on this list,
as well as on previous lists. In addition, books
set in other countries continue to broaden a
child's conception of the world. Books from
various genres may also be grouped under the
very broad topics of animals, humor, or as by

or about Latinos (see the "Multicultural Book List," page 168b, and the Bilingual Spanish Books list, page 153b, for books about Latino experiences).

Traditional literature includes selections from the folktales of the United States: Native American, African-American, and tall tales plus a series to introduce folktales by country, an excellent way to help children organize their reading.

Suggestions for third grade author studies include Beverly Cleary, Barbara Cooney, Johanna Hurwitz, Trina Schart Hyman, Dick King-Smith, Giulio and Betty Maestro, Margaret Mahy, Jerry Pinkney, Patricia Polacco, and William Steig plus any authors on the previous grade list introduction.

1. (E) *Abuela's Weave* by Omar S. Castaneda, illustrated by Enrique O. Sanchez. New York: Lee & Low, 1993. (Lee & Low)

In picture-book format, Esperanza is asked by her Abuela to sell their woven goods in the Guatemalan marketplace because Abuela thinks customers will be scared off by her facial birthmark. But the beautiful weavings speak for themselves and sell quickly in the market to people used to machine-made goods.

2. *Amazing Spiders* by Alexandra Parsons, photographs by Jerry Young. New York: Knopf, 1990. (Knopf)

With beautiful full-color photographs that reveal multiple details, this informational book series is organized around a dozen topics listed in the contents. Other books in the series invite readers to talk about birds, mammals, and snakes. The parent volumes are "Eyewitness Books," a more densely packed series for older readers. (Series)

3. *Annie and the Old One* by Miska Miles, illustrated by Peter Parnall. New York: Little, Brown, 1971. (Little, Brown)

Parnall's sensitive illustrations match this story of a Navajo girl, Annie, and her denial and gradual acceptance of her weaving grandmother's eventual death when she completes her work.

4. *Arthur, for the Very First Time* by Patricia MacLachlan, illustrated by Lloyd Bloom. New York: HarperCollins, 1980. (Harper-Trophy)

Sent to visit his relatives on a farm, Arthur retreats passively into being an observer until his friendship with the exuberant Moira, her veterinarian father, and his eccentric relatives pulls him out of his shell. Arthur's transformation from "Mouse" to himself is believable and entertaining. Discuss the meaning of the title. 128 pages, illustrations.

5. *Chicken Sunday* by Patricia Polacco. New York: Philomel, 1992. (   )

Despite differences in religion, sex, and race, young Patricia is best friend of Winston and Stewart Washington and she considers their grandmother, Miss Eula, her own. The three children earn Miss Eula an Easter hat from a Russian Jewish shopkeeper when they sell Ukrainian decorated eggs in his shop in order to convince him that they have not pelted his shop with eggs. Themes of understanding and friendship across generations and glorious art work make this picture book sing. Polacco is an excellent author/illustrator to study as children can discover how her books draw on her own childhood. Begin with her Meteor! *(New York: Putnam, 1987), the funny* Some Birthday! *(New York: Simon & Schuster, 1991), and* The Keeping Quilt *(New York: Simon & Schuster, 1988) plus her illustrated autobiography,* Firetalking *(New York: Richard C. Owen, 1994).*

6. *Class Clown* by Johanna Hurwitz, illustrated by Sheila Hamanaka. New York: William Morrow, 1987. (Scholastic)

First novel in a readable, realistic fiction series dealing with the same class of children. In eight large-print illustrated chapters, Lucas changes during the school year from being the class goof-off to a responsible leader of the class minicircus. In each successive novel in the series the class gets older, but the reading levels remain fairly stable so that some readers may wish to tackle the four books. (Series)

7. *The Comeback Dog* by Jane Resh Thomas, illustrated by Troy Howell. Boston:

Houghton Mifflin, 1981. (Bantam Sky-lark)

Daniel rescues a near-dead dog from a ditch, revives it, and tries to make it love him. Subtly the author gives the reader clues as to Daniel's feelings in this graceful and poignant novel of what loving is all about. (Series)

8. *Crow Boy* by Taro Yashima. New York: Viking, 1955. (Puffin)

Chibi is too shy to participate in school in this Japanese village until a sympathetic teacher helps him to blossom and metamorphose—beautifully symbolized as flower and butterfly by the book's endpapers.

9. *Danny the Champion of the World* by Roald Dahl. New York: Knopf, 1975. (Bantam)

Danny's father's secret poaching in Victor Hazel's wood provides the opportunity for discussion on the morality of poaching. Children enjoy this adventure of a loving, fun-filled relationship between a father and son as told by a master storyteller. See The Author's Eye, *p. 98b, for information about how Dahl works as a writer.*

10. *The Discovery of the Americas* by Betsy Maestro, illustrated by Giulio Maestro. New York: Lothrop, Lee and Shepard, 1991. (Mulberry)

An in-depth look at how North America became populated starting with the Bering Land Bridge. Evidence is clearly presented in picture book format so that children review possible visits of Phoenicians, Irish monks, Japanese fishermen, Vikings, and so forth. Appendices, tables of dates, large detailed illustrations, and maps are excellent examples of how informational books "work" and provide children with format examples for their own writing. The Maestros write top-rate nonfiction books.

11. + *Earthworms* by Keith Pigdon and Marilyn Woolley, illustrated by Sadie and Suzanne Pascoe. Cleveland: Modern Curriculum Press, 1989. (Modern Curriculum Press)

Clear illustrations in a variety of formats with labels, cross-sections, examples, cutaways, and graphs help readers understand earthworms. By discussing how information is conveyed in nonfiction texts, teachers can help children be better users of reference material. Directions for making a wormery are included.

12. *Favorite Fairy Tales Told in England* retold by Virginia Haviland, illustrated by Maxie Chambliss. New York: Beech Tree, 1994. (1959) (Beech Tree)

Before the era of the single, gloriously illustrated folktale, these collections were and still are the best source for knowing the major folktales from a particular country. The excellent series encompasses sixteen countries. Look to the well-illustrated single-tale editions for authentic, lively pictures, but read these collections for authentic text that reads aloud well.

13. *The Fortune-Teller* by Lloyd Alexander, illustrated by Trina Schart Hyman. Boston: Dutton, 1992. (   )

This humorous trickster story is set in the African country of Cameroon. Rich illustrations provide much local detail, and the clever story shows a smart man quick to take advantage of a profitable situation. Look for accurate depiction of a Cameroon marketplace plus the two little lizards hidden in each double-page spread. For more books set in Africa, see Galimoto *(page 125b) and* A Country Far Away *(page 124b).*

14. (E) *The Great White Man-Eating Shark* by Margaret Mahy, illustrated by Jonathan Allan. Boston: Dial, 1990. (   )

A hilarious story of justice delivered is told about a selfish boy who disguises himself as a shark to scare the other swimmers out of his favorite Australian swimming hole. It works until a lady shark falls in love with his disguise. The deadpan telling and the humor of the pictures are fine emphasis to the moral. A good introduction to the humor of this well-known New Zealand author who writes both picture books and novels.

15. *Halmoni and the Picnic* by Sook Nyul Choi, illustrated by Karen M. Dugan. Boston: Houghton Mifflin, 1993. (   )

A Korean grandmother feels embarrassed and out of place in this country until the third graders in her granddaughter's school welcome her and the Korean food she brings to a class picnic. *Intergenerational relationship between grandparent and child is part of many books on these lists. See on this list* Abuela's Weave, Knots on a Counting Rope, Annie and the Old One, *and* Uncle Jed's Barbershop *for a beginning. Be sure to see previous lists for the topic of grandparents, also.*

16. *I Hate English* by Ellen Levine, illustrated by Steve Bjorkman. New York: Scholastic, 1989. (Scholastic)

    Mei-Mei, a recent immigrant from Hong Kong, refuses to speak English until an astute new teacher helps her by reading to her and taking her places. How does it feel to be in a new place? How do people learn to speak a new language? Other books that help children talk about the difficulties in learning a new language include Muriel Stanek's story of a Latino girl, I Speak English for My Mom, *illustrated by Judith Friedman (Niles, IL: Whitman, 1989) and Bud Howlett's story of a girl from El Salvador,* I'm New Here *(Boston: Houghton Mifflin, 1993.)*

17. *I'll Meet You at the Cucumbers* by Lilian Moore, illustrated by Sharon Woodring. New York: Atheneum, 1988. (Skylark)

    Adam Mouse considers his own country world the ultimate setting until his pen pal Amanda invites him to the city. There, Adam discovers that he is a poet. This simple animal fantasy novel asks children to consider what poetry is and does. Pair with poetry or with a version of the fable "The Country Mouse and the City Mouse." Discuss what poets do. Debate the merits of a city or country life.

18. (E) + *Knots on a Counting Rope* by Bill Martin, Jr., and John Archambault, illustrated by Ted Rand. New York: Holt, 1987. (Holt)

    Stunningly illustrated, this picture book tells of a blind Navajo boy who loves to hear his grandfather recite his birth story and other stories of the boy's life. For each telling, the old man ties one knot on a rope; when the rope is completely knotted, the boy will be able to tell the stories from his own memory. *A perfect catalyst for telling our own birth stories but a fine discussion book, too, for its many layers of meaning.*

19. *Koko's Kitten* by Francine Patterson, photographs by Ronald H. Cohn. New York: Scholastic, 1985. (Scholastic)

    In this nonfiction photo-essay, Dr. Patterson tells how she began to teach Koko the gorilla to speak in American Sign Language (ASL). Talk about how gorillas communicate in the wild and what Patterson has taught here. Discuss what the pictures show us, or perhaps give them captions. How might understanding animals be important to humans? (Series)

20. *Mirette on the High Wire* by Emily Arnold McCully. New York: Putnam, 1992. ( )

    In this 1993 Caldecott Award–winning picture book, a Parisian girl in the last century makes friends with a failed high-wire artist. As he teaches her to walk the wire, he regains his strength and courage as well. Good for discussing the ways we gather courage, and how older and younger may help each other. The ending invites reader speculation on what happens next.

21. *Miss Rumphius* by Barbara Cooney. New York: Viking, 1982. (Puffin)

    As a child, Miss Rumphius wishes to see faraway places, live by the sea, and make the world more beautiful. As a grown-up, she accomplishes all three in this picture book set in the previous century. Consider how each of us could make the world more beautiful; talk about dreams we have. Read about others who made some part of the world beautiful, such as Johnny Appleseed, George Washington Carver, or The Man Who Planted Trees *by Michael McCurdy (New York: Chelsea Green, 1986).*

22. *Molly's Pilgrim* by Barbara Cohen, illustrated by Michael J. Deraney. New York: Lothrop, Lee and Shepard, 1983. (Skylark)

    The girls in her turn-of-the-century class make fun of her imperfect English, and Molly thinks she will never belong. When she brings her Pilgrim doll dressed like a Russian immigrant to school for the Thanks-

giving project, her teacher saves the day. Touching story, based on a true incident, and a good discussion book.

23. *More Stories Julian Tells* by Ann Cameron, illustrated by Ann Strugnell. New York: Knopf, 1986. (Knopf)

    Julian, who is about eight or nine, his younger brother Huey, and his friend Gloria think of interesting ways to overcome summer boredom with a little help from the boy's dad. Warm, African-American family with typical family exchanges; the second book about Julian. (Series)

24. + *Mufaro's Beautiful Daughters* by John Steptoe. New York: Lothrop, Lee and Shepard, 1987. (Mulberry)

    The king is choosing a wife, and two beautiful sisters journey to his village. But the mean-spirited sister does not pass the three tests while the kind and gentle Nyasha naturally succeeds. Notice the lush flora and fauna of Zimbabwe. Ask children to compare the good sister/bad sister pattern found in The Talking Eggs, *p. 127b.*

25. *Nathaniel Talking* by Eloise Greenfield, illustrated by Jan Spivey Gilchrest. New York: Writers and Readers Publishing, 1988. (Black Butterfly)

    In a variety of free-verse poetry, some of which borrows from rap and the twelve-bar blues, nine-year-old Nathaniel shares thoughts on growing up, his proud and loving family, tolerance for variety in people and in music, and memories. Each poem is a gem that evokes response and dialogue about what is important. Try choral reading. Greenfield includes directions for writing your own twelve-bar blues.

26. (E) *Nettie's Trip South* by Ann Turner, illustrated by Ronald Himler. New York: Macmillan, 1987. (Scholastic)

    This simple but eloquent, illustrated story is presented as a letter from a white ten-year-old girl to her friend about what she has felt and discovered about slavery in the pre–Civil War South.

27. *Paul Bunyan* by Steven Kellogg. New York: Morrow, 1984. (Mulberry)

    Children need to know about the only folktale tradition indigenous to the United States—the tall tale. Kellogg's series does a fine job of introducing America's tall-tale heroes of Bunyan, Mike Fink, Johnny Appleseed, and Pecos Bill. See, too, another series by Ariane Dewey, in easy-reader format, and recent collections such as Amy L. Cohn's From Sea to Shining Sea *(New York: Scholastic, 1993) and Mary Pope Osborne's* American Tall Tales *(New York: Knopf, 1991.)*

28. *Poem Stew*, edited by William Cole, illustrated by Karen Ann Weinhaus. New York: Lippincott, 1981. (HarperTrophy)

    Over fifty poems celebrate food, funny eaters both real and weird, and our fascination with what we eat. Finger-snapping rhythm, catchy rhymes, and a variety of topics make this an excellent collection for chants, choral reading, before-lunch laughing, and pure enjoyment.

29. *Ralph S. Mouse* by Beverly Cleary, illustrated by Paul O. Zelinsky. New York: Morrow, 1982. (Dell; Avon)

    While earlier Ralph novels introduced the mouse and his boy companions, this fantasy novel is set in a school classroom and, like Mouse Views *(see page 111b), it seems perfectly believable. A prize-winning film was made of this book, combining live action and puppetry (Los Angeles: Churchill Films, 1991). In Elaine Scott's excellent informational* Look Alive *(New York: Morrow, 1992), text and photos explain how this movie was made. (Series)*

30. *Ramona Quimby, Age 8* by Beverly Cleary, illustrated by Alan Tiegreen. New York: Morrow, 1981. (Dell Yearling)

    Ramona deals with changes in her life and grows up a little. Children identify with Ramona's trying to be a third grader, a younger sister, and a decent person all at once. (Series)

31. *Raven: A Trickster Tale from the Pacific Northwest* by Gerald McDermott. San Diego: Harcourt Brace, 1993. (   )

    Simple, rhythmic language and bold, stylish illustrations reflect the oral and artistic traditions of the Pacific Northwest Native Americans in this story of the trickster Raven and how he brought light from the sky world to the people. Seek out other Native American tales that explain natural phenomena, such as those found in the myth collection by Natalia M. Belting, Moon Was Tired of Walking on Air, illustrated by Will Hillenbrand (Boston: Houghton Mifflin, 1992), or other tales of Native American tricksters such as coyote, Mouse Woman, or Paul Goble's "Iktomi" stories.

32. (E) *The Skirt* by Gary Soto, illustrated by Eric Velasquez. New York: Delacorte, 1992. (Dell)

    A short novel of eight chapters tells how Miata Ramirez left her tiered folklorico dancing skirt on the school bus and how she retrieved it. Strong Latino family in a situation many third graders can identify with—that of losing something and what to tell your parents. No glossary but most of the incidental Spanish words are translatable. 74 pages.

33. *Stone Fox* by John R. Gardiner, illustrated by Marcia Sewell. New York: Crowell, 1980. (HarperTrophy)

    Ten-year-old Willy enters a sled dog race against the legendary Indian Stone Fox in order to pay off the back taxes on his grandfather's Wyoming farm. Readers will never forget this masterfully told and moving story set in the 1800s.

34. *The Tales of Uncle Remus: The Adventures of Brer Rabbit* by Julius Lester, illustrated by Jerry Pinkney. Boston: Dial, 1988.
    (   )

    No child should miss these classic stories of the African-American trickster, Brer Rabbit, because they are a part of our cultural history, extremely funny, and so freshly told here that listeners can almost see the storyteller in front of them. The four-book series features collections of familiar and not-so-well-known stories. Be sure you read Lester's introductions so that you know what he is doing and from what historical tradition his retellings spring. Children will enjoy comparing this to the series by Van Dyke Parks, illustrated by Barry Moser, which begins with Jump! The Adventures of Brer Rabbit *(San Diego: Harcourt Brace Jovanovich, 1986.) (Series)*

35. *Uncle Jed's Barbershop* by Margaree King Mitchell, illustrated by James Ransome. New York: Simon & Schuster, 1993.
    (   )

    An African-American barber realizes his dream of opening his own barbershop after years of using his savings to help others in crisis. The neighborhood rejoices in his success and the hard work it took to get there. Good picture book catalyst for a discussing tenacity, entrepreneurship, special family members, and how the community supports its members.

36. + (E) *Vejigante Masquerader* by Lulu Delacre. New York: Scholastic, 1993. (Scholastic)

    A Puerto Rican boy makes his own costume with adult help so that he can join the older boys in Carnival mischief. When a goat eats part of his costume, it seems like disaster until his mother helps make it right. See also Delacre's song collections Arroz con leche *(1989) and* Las navidades *(1990, both Scholastic) from Latin America.*

37. *What's the Big Idea, Ben Franklin?* by Jean Fritz, illustrated by Margot Tomes. New York: Coward, McCann & Geoghegan, 1976. (Coward)

    Jean Fritz has the knack of making facts lively, interesting, and even funny in her series of well-illustrated authentic biographies of famous people. Create a time line of Franklin's life, marvel over his achievements, or compare information in this book with a fiction account, such as Robert Lawson's Ben and Me *told by Ben's mouse companion (Boston: Little, Brown, 1939). (Series)*

38. (E) *Wild Weather: Tornadoes* by Lorraine Jean Hopping, illustrated by Jody Wheeler. New York: Scholastic, 1993. (Scholastic)

    This "Hello Reading" book presents information in six short chapters about tornadoes across the United States. Notice tables, diagrams, and the "blow-up" of a map segment to help children see how information is conveyed. Other nonfiction books in this series include books about manatees, ants, and the Titanic.

39. (E) *The Year of the Panda* by Miriam Schlein, illustrated by Kam Mak. New York: Crowell, 1990. (HarperTrophy)

   This eighty-page novel addresses the dilemma of mainland Chinese who need arable land but are being raided by the giant pandas who need bamboo as their range is reduced by farming. A boy raises a baby giant panda before turning it over to a rehabilitation and reintroduction center. Pair with Judy Allen's Panda, *illustrated by Tudor Humphries (Cambridge, MA: Candlewick Press, 1993).*

Grade 4

Books in this list include settings other than the United States and books about people of two cultures. As would be expected, these titles often present some of the dilemmas and responsibilities being human entails—our role in preserving endangered species, the comparison of life in third-world countries with aspects of American life, relationships among family members, and our developing values. Be sure to check previous lists for related titles.

Novels include several kinds of fantasy (animal, science fiction, and high fantasy) and realism both thoughtful and humorous. We have also included titles that invite readers to laugh, depend on some maturity to see what's funny, and appeal to a nine-year-old's sense of humor.

Poetry, short stories, picture books for older children, and informational books extend readers' experiences with text. "Cinderella" variants and folktale parodies draw attention to the many ways authors and illustrators help children reflect on and modify their understanding of this genre.

Suggestions for fourth grade author studies include Paul Fleischman, Sid Fleischman, Paul Goble, Eloise Greenfield, Patricia McKissack, Jack Prelutsky, Cynthia Rylant, Jon Sciezska, Chris Van Allsburg, and Jane Yolen, plus any authors on the previous grade list introductions.

1. *Anastasia Krupnik* by Lois Lowry. Boston: Houghton Mifflin, 1979. (Bantam)

   Anastasia, a budding poet and a thoughtful fourth grader, is initially annoyed at her parents for having a new baby. But the death of her grandmother, the arrival of baby Sam, and her increasing sense of the importance of family help her change her mind. Anastasia's lists at the end of each chapter suggest by inference her gradual changes of heart in this first Anastasia story. (Series)

2. (E) *Appalachia: Voices of Sleeping Birds* by Cynthia Rylant, illustrated by Barry Moser. San Diego: Harcourt Brace, 1991. (   )

   In evocative prose, Rylant presents the mountains and hollers of Appalachia so that readers can feel and sense the place. Pair with Shiloh *(see p. 137b) and let children see how different authors create and evoke a sense of setting beyond appearances.*

3. *Beauty and the Beast* by Michael Hague. New York: Holt, 1989. (Holt)

   This classic story of a beast transformed by love invites children to talk about how and why people change both in stories and in real life. Encourage critical thinking by comparing this version with others such as Beauty and the Beast *by Mordicai Gerstein (New York: Dutton, 1989); by Marianna Mayer, illustrated by Mercer Mayer (New York: Macmillan, 1978); or by Jan Brett (Boston: Houghton Mifflin, 1989).*

4. (E) *Best Wishes* by Cynthia Rylant, photographs by Carlo Ontal. Katonah, NY: Richard C. Owen, 1992. (   )

   Excellent photographs illuminate the author's discussion of her life as a writer in Ohio and West Virginia. Readers will notice echoes and origins of many of Rylant's ideas, settings, and characters here. See other titles in this "Meet the Author Collection" (p. 99b). See also Rylant's autobiographical But I'll Be Back Again, *Orchard, 1989 (Beech Tree).*

5. *Bunnicula* by Deborah and James Howe. New York: Atheneum, 1971. (Camelot)

   What if a pet rabbit really is a vampire? Chester the cat believes he has discovered one and sets out to prove to the human family that he is right. Told by the laconic family dog Harold with doglike observations and concerns for food, this first story in the series is humorous and fast-moving. Chil-

dren enjoy comparing the vampire lore in this book with traditional lore. (Series)

6. *Dynamite Dinah* by Claudia Mills. New York: Macmillan, 1990. (Macmillan)

Ten-year-old Dinah craves attention and thinks of a million creative things to attract others to her. When her baby brother comes along, family relationships become more complex before Dinah can accept responsibility. Good book for discussing relationships with family and friends and the joys and dilemmas of being a person with dramatic flair. (Series)

7. *Every Living Thing* by Cynthia Rylant, illustrated by S. D. Schindler. New York: Bradbury, 1985. (Aladdin)

Twelve challenging but never sentimental short stories invite readers to consider little moments of growth in children and adults. The first story, "Slower Than the Rest," reminds readers of the wonder of human diversity as it aligns a child with special needs and a turtle against a hurried world. The last, "Shell," uses a common metaphor in a symbolic way that young readers can understand.

8. *The Frog Prince Continued* by Jon Scieszka, illustrated by Steve Johnson. New York: Viking, 1991. (Puffin)

What happens after the princess marries the frog prince? This silly sequel helps children see how folktales may be turned around and played with. It may be their first experience with the literary device of allusion, as well. Scieszka's collection of The Stinky Cheese Man and Other Fairly Stupid Tales (New York: Viking, 1992) parodies at least ten well-known folktales. Donna Jo Napoli's novel treatment of The Prince of the Pond (New York: Dutton, 1992) is a full-fledged narrative that begins with a frog sitting in the middle of a pile of clothes. (See Cinder Edna, page 145b, for more fooling-with-folktale inspiration before asking children to write their own spoofs).

9. (E) *Go Fish* by Mary Stolz, illustrated by Pat Cummings. New York: HarperCollins, 1991. (HarperTrophy)

Six illustrated chapters reveal eight-year-old Thomas's learning about his African-American heritage from his grandfather.

Florida Gulf Coast setting, fishing, and storytelling are all part of this quiet story. 73 pages. (Series)

10. (E) *The Gold Coin* by Alma Flor Ada. New York: Macmillan, 1991. (Aladdin)

A young thief follows an old healer woman around in an effort to steal her gold coin. Set in Central America, this picturebook tale invites children to consider how much money is enough, and the value of work, friendship, and community.

11. (E) *Grandfather's Journey* by Allan Say. Boston: Houghton Mifflin, 1993. (   )

In the manner of reminiscence, this 1994 Caldecott Award–winner presents Say's grandfather, who came to America from Japan at the turn of the century. This picture book for older readers speaks on many levels. From a mention of the destruction of World War II, to knowing and understanding our grandparents, to the feelings one has on being a part of two cultures, there is much to discuss. See also a sequel written earlier, Tree of Cranes (Houghton Mifflin, 1991). Themes in this book echo titles found in previous lists, as well.

12. *The Green Book* by Jill Paton Walsh, illustrated by Lloyd Bloom. New York: Farrar, Straus & Giroux, 1982. (Sunburst)

Vivid writing tells the story of a family from the future who must leave Earth to colonize a new planet. How do they survive? What is the importance of stories in a new land? This thought-provoking short novel begins and ends with the same sentence, a magical discovery for fourth graders. Paperback edition often omits the illustrations, so be sure to secure at least one hardbound edition for the classroom.

13. *The Hundred Penny Box* by Sharon Bell Mathis, illustrated by Leon and Diane Dillon. New York: Viking Penguin, 1975. (Puffin)

Michael's great great aunt Dewbet is 100 years old and keeps an old box full of pennies to help her remember each of her birthdays. When Michael's mother wants to throw out the box, Michael tries to save all the stories of her life. This moving story of emotions in an extended African-American family is a catalyst for talking about our own family histories. What would children tell for each year or penny in their lives so far?

14. (E) *Knights of the Kitchen Table* by Jon Scieszka, illustrated by Lane Smith. New York: Viking, 1991. (Viking)

This funny, time-slip fantasy series introduces three boys, "the Time Warp Trio," who visit times past. Uncommitted readers find these stories compelling, hip, and humorous. While there isn't much to discuss, there is plenty to laugh about, and Lane Smith's line drawings and snappy dialogue move the story along quickly. (Series)

15. *The Lion, the Witch and the Wardrobe* by C. S. Lewis. New York: Macmillan, 1950. (Collier)

Four children free Narnia from the spell of the White Witch in this first of a seven-book series. A modern classic. (Series)

16. (E) *The Most Beautiful Place in the World* by Ann Cameron, illustrated by Thomas B. Allen. New York: Knopf, 1988. (Random House)

Seven-year-old Juan struggles with poverty and parental abandonment but is supported by his own intelligence, determination, and the love of his grandmother. Set in Guatemala, this is a universal story of growing into your own skin and up to your own potential.

17. *The Real Thief* by William Steig. New York: Farrar, Straus & Giroux, 1973. (Sunburst)

While stretching the vocabulary of readers, Steig tells the story of Gawain the goose, guard of the Royal Treasury, who is wrongly accused of stealing, until a repentant mouse confesses. Discuss the consequences of accusing without evidence. A good introduction to a popular author and illustrator. Be sure to have Steig's Dominic (*New York: Farrar, Straus & Giroux, 1984*) and Abel's Island (*New York: Farrar, Straus & Giroux, 1985*) on hand as well.

18. *The Rough-Face Girl* by Rafe Martin, illustrated by David Shannon. New York: Putnam, 1992. (Scholastic)

A traditional Algonquin story also known as "Little Burnt Face," this "Cinderella" variant supports the Native American belief that only those who walk humbly can truly see. When the Rough-Face Girl is able to do what her two haughty sisters cannot, which is to see the supreme being in all of his glory, she is made beautiful in his eyes and becomes his bride. Some children may recognize the theme, the transforming power of love, as similar to "Beauty and the Beast."

19. (E) *Sachiko Means Happiness* by Kimiko Sakai, illustrated by Tomie Arai. San Francisco: Children's Book Press, 1990.
(   )

Sachiko, a child of Asian descent, is angry because her senile grandmother does not know her, but her sympathy overcomes her anger and sadness, at least for a moment. Pair this picture book with The Hundred Penny Box (*see above*). Loop the Loop by Barbara Dugan, illustrated by James Stevenson (*New York: Greenwillow, 1992*) also deals with an elderly person's senility and memory loss, but readers get to know the magnificently sassy Mrs. Simpson before she goes into a nursing home. Children born to older parents are increasingly likely to know a senile relative or visit a nursing home, and books such as these help foster open discussion.

20. *Sarah, Plain and Tall* by Patricia MacLachlan. New York: Harper & Row, 1985. (HarperTrophy)

In spare prose, Anna tells how Sarah came from Maine after her father places an ad for a wife in an eastern newspaper. Colors and music form a continuous thread through this touching story of family life on the pioneer prairie. See also a sequel, Skylark (*New York: HarperCollins, 1994*), in which the drought-ridden family returns to Sarah's beloved Maine. See also Brett Harvey's stories of her grandmother's prairie days in My Prairie Year (*New York: Holiday, 1986*) and My Prairie Christmas (*New York: Holiday, 1990*), both illustrated by Deborah Kogan Ray.

21. (E) *Scooter* by Vera B. Williams. New York: Greenwillow, 1993. (Mulberry)

In short, profusely illustrated chapters,

the personalities and relationships of the neighbors in Elana Rose Rosen's apartment building and neighborhood are explored. The exuberant spirit of Elana, the witty drawings, and the theme of making new friends when you've moved give this book child appeal. Good for discussing how the community supports its members, too.

22. *Shiloh* by Phyllis Reynolds Naylor. New York: Atheneum, 1991. (Dell)

    Eleven-year-old Marty shelters a dog from an abusive owner without the knowledge of his parents. The book elicits all sorts of discussion with fourth graders: What is honorable behavior? What are the consequences of lying? Is the "villain" bad? Told in first person in West Virginian regional dialect, this book is an excellent example of how an author creates well-rounded characters and a sense of place.

23. (E) *Skinnybones* by Barbara Park. New York: Knopf, 1982. (Knopf)

    Like Knights of the Kitchen Table *(see p. 136b), this lead title in a series keeps children, especially boys, interested in reading. Wisecracking Alex, the smallest boy on his baseball team, tells his own story about entering a commercial-writing contest and his encounters with the school bully. The first chapter is a side-splitting, laugh-inducing read-aloud. (Series)*

24. (E) *Song of the Trees* by Mildred Taylor, illustrated by Jerry Pinkney. New York: Dial, 1975. (Bantam)

    A short chapter book that depicts an African-American family in the Depression who protect the family's stand of giant old trees from the dishonest white loggers. This introduces the Logans, whose larger story is told in Roll of Thunder, Hear My Cry. *(See Grade 6 list.) (Series)*

25. *Sunken Treasure* by Gail Gibbons. New York: Crowell, 1988. (HarperTrophy)

    In this nonfiction book, Gibbons tells of the sinking in 1622 of the ship Atocha, its discovery and the raising of the treasure, its preserving, cataloguing, and distribution, and other famous treasure-laden shipwrecks. Text is succinct, and information-bearing illustrations invite study and discussion. *See, too, other works of nonfiction by this prolific author on such topics as lighthouses, the building of skyscrapers, the post office, and a host of other subjects.*

26. *A Taste of Blackberries* by Doris Buchanan Smith, illustrated by Charles Robinson. New York: Crowell, 1973. (HarperTrophy)

    A young boy describes his friendship with Jamie and his feelings about Jamie's sudden death from a bee sting. Pair this with Mavis Jukes's sensitive and subtle Blackberries in the Dark *(New York: Knopf, 1985; Dell) for another boy who carries on after the death of someone special, in this case, his grandfather.*

27. (E) *Tiger* by Judy Allen, illustrated by Tudor Humphries. Cambridge, MA: Candlewick, 1992. (Candlewick)

    A village in South China hires a man to shoot a potentially dangerous tiger. The man shoots it, but with a camera, not a gun. Elegant and accurate pictures depict the tiger with reverence and sympathy. A "tiger fact sheet" ends this picture-book blend of information contained within a story. Humphries and Allen have also created informative stories about a whale, a panda, and an elephant in this same format. The series provides excellent inspiration to children who have gathered information about an animal and don't want to write a report. (Series)

28. *The Whipping Boy* by Sid Fleischman, illustrated by Peter Sis. New York: Greenwillow, 1986. (Troll)

    The theme is like "The Prince and the Pauper" with a light, humorous touch as Jemmy, whipping boy to Prince Brat, leads his prince through a series of adventures. Fun to read aloud and a good introduction to an author whose quasi-historical settings pique our interest while his humor and apt similies makes us laugh.

29. *Yang the Youngest and His Terrible Ear* by Lensey Namioka. Boston: Little, Brown, 1992. (Little)

    Two boys, one who is Chinese-American, the other white, must balance their passions for baseball and violin playing with their fathers' conflicting expectations for them. Humorously told, this novel al-

lows children to discuss the theme of balancing your own needs and desires with those of your parents as you grow up. It also reveals the cultural contrasts new immigrants to this country encounter.

30. *Yeh Shen: A Cinderella Story from China* by Ai-Ling Louie, illustrated by Ed Young. New York: Philomel, 1982. (Putnam)

    This version predates the European versions and raises the question of where folktales come from and how they travel. Notice the author's prefatory note, the illustrator's use of the fish motif, and of course the comparisons to the German or French "Cinderella." See also Shirley Climo's The Egyptian Cinderella, *illustrated by Ruth Heller (New York: Crowell, 1989) and* The Korean Cinderella, *by the same pair (Crowell, 1993). See also the parodies listed with* Cinder Edna, *page 145b.*

31. The books of Chris Van Allsburg.

    While Van Allsburg's books are unlikely to be available in paperback, he is an author/illustrator all children should know. Check out his books from the library and let children read them in chronological order to see how the artist's themes change, how his endings feature twists, where "Fritz" the dog is hidden, and how the artist's uses of color, frames, and point of view change and develop.

Grade 5

More of the world, its people, and human dilemmas are included in the novels on this list. Books set in China form a basis for possible study of one country. Several books have historical settings: the Revolutionary War, often introduced in this grade, World War II, plus one book that is an outcome of the Vietnam War. In addition, the theme of survival—in history, in realistic fiction, and in fantasy—is introduced here at the age at which many children believe themselves prepared to "go it alone." Realistic fiction includes more complex relationships among families and friends than have been presented in previous lists.

Dragons, both from the East and from the West, and one fantasy novel featuring a dragon,

are introduced to present a continuing character in traditional literature. Parodies of folktales introduced in the previous list work equally well here as a chance for children to play with form and content of folktales with which they are familiar. The *pourquoi* pattern of folktales is included both as an organizer for tales children already know and as a model for writing.

Suggestions for fifth-grade author studies include Mitsumasa Anno, Natalie Babbitt, Betsy Byars, Jean Craighead George, Virginia Hamilton, Lois Lowry, Eve Merriam, Phyllis Reynolds Naylor, Yoshiko Uchida, plus any authors on the previous grade list introductions.

1. *A Blue-Eyed Daisy* by Cynthia Rylant. New York: Bradbury, 1985. (Dell Yearling)

   Like short glimpses into someone else's life, these chapters present a picture of Ellie's eleventh year. Understated prose, the telling phrase, and a way of letting readers see and understand people truly characterize Rylant's writing.

2. *The Borrowers* by Mary Norton, illustrated by Beth and Joe Krush. San Diego: Harcourt Brace Jovanovich, 1953. (Odyssey)

   This classic asks readers to take another point of view, that of people merely inches tall. A believable story with well-drawn characters and aptly described miniature settings. (Series)

3. *Bridge to Terabithia* by Katherine Paterson, illustrated by Donna Diamond. New York: Crowell, 1977. (HarperTrophy)

   A friendship between an impoverished boy and a girl whose parents have come to rural Virginia to reexamine their values grows, then ends abruptly when one dies in a flash flood. A catalyst for discussion of friendship, the story also examines many sorts of bridges: across cultures, across ages, between sexes.

4. *The Cat's Purr* by Ashley Bryan. New York: Atheneum, 1985. (   )

   In the oral language of the storyteller, Bryan explains why the cat and rat are enemies and how the cat got its purr. The explanatory or pourquoi story pattern is found throughout the world. Use many examples to introduce the genre before asking children to write their own folktales about some natural phenomena. Pos-

sible choices include Shonto Begay's Navajo story, *Ma'ii and Cousin Horned Toad (New York: Scholastic, 1992),* Flora's Brazilian story of *Feathers Like a Rainbow (New York: Harper, 1989),* and Verna Aardema's tale from Kenya, *Why Mosquitoes Buzz in People's Ears (New York: Dial, 1975).*

5. *Chi-Hoon: A Korean Girl* by Patricia McMahon, photographs by Michael F. O'Brien. Honesdale, PA: Boyds Mill, 1993. (   )

    Color photographs, a narrative, and excerpts from the life of an eight-year-old Korean girl give children insight into modern-day Korean life. See, too, Peggy Thomson's City Kids in China, *photographs by Paul Conklin (New York: HarperCollins, 1993) for excellent nonfiction about children's Asian contemporaries halfway around the world.*

6. (E) *Class President* by Johanna Hurwitz, illustrated by Sheila Hamanaka. New York: Morrow, 1990. (Morrow)

    The fifth-grade class officer election attracts Cricket, a confident but self-centered girl, and a Latino boy, Julio, who doesn't think he has the talent for the job but proves it to his classmates and, finally, to himself. The fourth in the series, School Spirit *(New York: Morrow, 1994) continues Julio's quiet development as an activist. (Series)*

7. *Dealing with Dragons* by Patricia Wrede. New York: Harcourt Brace, 1990. (Scholastic)

    Princess Cimorene, tired of her passive castle life, apprentices herself to a dragon and helps rid the dragon world of evil wizards. Humorous references to the conventions and content of folktales let children read as insiders who know the references. Introduce it by asking children to round up what they know about princesses and dragons. (Series)

8. *Dear Mr. Henshaw* by Beverly Cleary, illustrated by Paul O. Zelinsky. New York: Morrow, 1983. (Dell Yearling)

    Readers must draw inferences from this story told completely in letters written by sixth grader Leigh Botts to the author of his favorite books. This honest portrayal of a child in a single-parent family also

suggests that readers might discuss the making of a writer and a problem solver. *(Series)*

9. *The Dragon's Pearl* by Julie Lawson, illustrated by Paul Morin. New York: Clarion, 1993. (   )

    The traditional eastern dragon offers an interesting comparison with the usually better-known western dragon. In an effort to save a valuable dragon's pearl from robbers, a boy swallows it, only to transform himself into a dragon. Collage and highly textured illustrations are burnished with gold, the symbol of Chinese royalty. For other presentations of Chinese dragons, see Darcy Pattison's The River Dragon, *illustrated by Jean and Mou-sien Tseng (New York: Lothrop, 1993) or Deborah Nourse Lattimore's* The Dragon's Robe *(New York: HarperCollins, 1990).*

10. *The Dream Keeper* by Langston Hughes, illustrated by Brian Pinkney. New York: Knopf, 1994. (   )

    "Mother to Son," "Dreams," and "My People" are among the many well-known poems in this collection of this revered African-American poet's work. First published in 1932, this new edition is elegantly illustrated with Pinkney's scratchboard illustrations.

11. (E) *Germy Blew It—Again* by Rebecca Jones. Holt, 1988. (Knopf)

    The second in a popular and funny series about Jeremy Bluett, a budding entrepreneur whose plans to profit from raising and selling gerbils almost work. Jeremy's frequently imagined encounters with newspaper reporters, which appear as italicized text, let readers laugh over the disparity between how Jeremy sees himself and what is really about to happen. A book to keep readers reading. (Series)

12. *In the Year of the Boar and Jackie Robinson* by Bette Bao Lord, illustrated by Marc Simont. New York: Harper & Row, 1984. (HarperTrophy)

    Twelve chapters chronicle the year (1947) that Shirley Temple Wong, newly arrived in Brooklyn from China, becomes an American. Baseball's great Jackie Robinson is an important catalyst in Shirley's Americani-

zation. Teammates *by Peter Golenbock and illustrated by Paul Bacon (San Diego: Harcourt Brace Jovanovich, 1990) presents the significance of Robinson to the integration of major league baseball in picture-book format.*

13. *Journey to Topaz* by Yoshiko Uchida, illustrated by Donald Carrick. New York: Scribner, 1971. (Creative Arts Book Company)

    Based on the WWII incarceration in American camps of 110,000 Japanese-Americans, this story is told through the eyes of Yuki. See Behind Barbed Wire *by Daniel S. Davis (New York: Dutton, 1982), for more information on the emotional and political aspects of this moving story. See also the picture book,* Baseball Saved Us *by Ken Mochizuki, illustrated by Dom Lee (New York: Lee & Low, 1993) for another view of internment-camp life, this one in Idaho. (Series)*

14. *Jump Ship to Freedom* by Christopher and James Lincoln Collier. New York: Delacorte, 1981. (Dell)

    Continental Congress's problems with redeeming the scrip paid to soldiers to fight in the Revolutionary War form the backdrop for this story of an African-American boy who struggles to gain self-esteem. Historically accurate in period detail, language, and fact, this is one of the few books for elementary children that presents African-American views of the Revolutionary period. Contains the controversial word "nigger," which is explained in an afterword discussing the historical accuracy of the book. Pair with Avi's The Fighting Ground *(New York: Lippincott, 1984). (Series)*

15. *The Land I Lost: Adventures of a Boy in Vietnam* by Huyn Quang Nhuong, illustrated by Vo-Dinh Mai. New York: Harper & Row, 1982. (HarperTrophy)

    The author tells of his boyhood in a Vietnamese hamlet with his college-educated father, his work with a water buffalo named Tank, and the daily life where crocodiles might threaten, monkeys could cause mischief, and the threat of war was imminent.

16. *Me, Mop, and the Moondance Kid* by Walter Dean Myers. New York: Delacorte, 1988. (Dell)

    A lighthearted, fast paced novel concerns an African-American boy's urban experiences on a baseball team with his brother and a girl they met at an orphanage from which the two boys were recently adopted. Introduces a popular author who has written extensively for adolescents. See, also, a sequel called Me, Moondance, and the Nagasaki Knights *(New York: Delacorte, 1992). (Series)*

17. *Morning Girl* by Michael Dorris. New York: Hyperion, 1992. (Hyperion)

    A Caribbean Taino Native American girl's life is made believable and engages reader sympathies. The book ends as Columbus and his men are coming to the island for the first time. Young readers, who have some inkling of what will happen to the Tainos next, are irate at Columbus's diary excerpt, which reports that the Tainos are ignorant but friendly and would make good slaves. Pair this with many of the excellent, partial or fictionalized biographies of Columbus; see also The Discovery of the Americas, *page 130b.*

18. *My Side of the Mountain* by Jean Craighead George. New York: Dutton, 1975. (Puffin)

    A stirring story about one boy's survival in the Catskills. Authentic details, nature closely observed, and a character who is very much like a fifth grader make this a powerful discussion story and a natural for follow-up with activities. Be sure to have on hand the sequel, On the Far Side of the Mountain *(New York: Dutton, 1989), for interested readers. (Series)*

19. *Number the Stars* by Lois Lowry. Boston: Houghton Mifflin, 1989. (Dell Yearling)

    During World War II, one Danish girl's small, brave act saves Jews from the Nazis. Children identify with the main character, and the story serves as an introduction to the historical period as well. Marie McSwigan's popular Snow Treasure *(New York: Dutton, 1942; Scholastic) set in this time period is a story of a brave group of children who smuggled gold out of Nor-*

way under the Nazis' noses. See also Journey to Topaz *(p. 140b)*.

20. *On My Honor* by Marion Dane Bauer. Boston: Houghton Mifflin, 1986. (Dell Yearling)

What is honor? When Joel's best friend Tony goads him into swimming in a dangerous river and Tony drowns, Joel is left to ponder that question. Honor, a sympathetic and honest father, and a responsible boy who makes one mistake he'll have to live with make this a powerful catalyst for discussion.

21. (E) *Onion Tears* by Diana Kidd, illustrated by Lucy Montgomery. New York: Orchard, 1989. (Beech Tree)

Deceptively simple in appearance, this novel is told in short bits, small vignettes, letters, and poems by a Vietnamese boat person who has made her way to Australia. Good for teaching readers how to read between the lines, how to notice small clues to large ideas, it also presents another view of two cultures coming together.

22. *The People Could Fly* by Virginia Hamilton, illustrated by Leo and Diane Dillon. New York: Knopf, 1985. (Knopf)

African-American folktales, divided into four sections of animal, fanciful, supernatural, and slave tales of freedom, are richly told and powerfully illustrated. Part of everyone's multicultural American heritage.

23. *The Pinballs* by Betsy Byars. New York: Harper & Row, 1977. (HarperTrophy)

Three foster children learn to care for each other in this humorous but also moving account of one summer in the Masons' home. Note the way characters remember events, the use of figurative language, and how and why Carlie especially changes her attitude.

24. *Redwall* by Brian Jacques. New York: Philomel, 1986. (Putnam)

The first book in the series about a crusader mouse and his protection of the Redwall Abbey from Cluny the Scourge, a rat, is a fast-paced, good-guys-versus-bad fantasy. While the book is long, it is not difficult or complex and provides real reader satisfaction. *(Series)*

25. (E) *Saint George and the Dragon* by Margaret Hodges, illustrated by Trina Schart Hyman. Boston: Little, Brown, 1984. (Little, Brown)

In addition to telling a story popular in the Middle Ages, this version is painstakingly illustrated to reflect the rich symbolism of medieval art. Look for fairies vying with angels and for the significant flowers. Look, too, for the author delivering the manuscript to the illustrator on the back cover.

26. *Spin a Soft Black Song* by Nikki Giovanni, illustrated by George Martins. New York: Farrar, Straus & Giroux, 1985. (Sunburst)

Poems about African-American children in families, living and playing in the city, and loving life, are explored. No punctuation or upper-case letters make readers work a little harder for the ample rewards.

27. *The Story of Money* by Betsy Maestro, illustrated by Giulio Maestro. New York: Clarion, 1993. (   )

The history of our money system, from trade and barter to coins and dollars, is traced. Useful end matter presents money of other countries, unusual money, and other interesting facts. Since making and having money is a preoccupation of this age group, you may want to pair this with books about entrepreneurs, or start a school store or other money-making project.

28. *A Stranger Came Ashore* by Mollie Hunter. New York: Harper & Row, 1975. (HarperTrophy)

Finn Learson says he is a survivor of a shipwreck, but Robbie and his grandfather don't trust him. Rightly so, because Finn Learson is a Selkie, a man upon the land but a Selkie in the sea, and he is out to steal Robbie's sister in this well-written, mysterious fantasy. Foreshadowing provides many clues. Find out more about Selkies. Keep a class-compiled glossary of Shetland Island terms and clues to help readers stay located in the story.

29. *Tentacles: The Amazing World of Octopus, Squid, and Their Relatives* by James Martin. New York: Crown, 1993. (   )

Lucid and beautifully illustrated intro-duction to general characteristics of cepha-lopods. Separate chapters by animal, dia-grams, photographs, a glossary, and an index do much to teach children about information format while interesting them in a biological class of animals. Compare the density and treatment of information on the octopus with a book on the Grade 2 list, An Octopus Is Amazing, *page 126b.*

30. (E) *Toughboy and Sister* by Kirkpatrick Hill. New York: Macmillan, 1990. (Puffin)

    A Canadian Athabascan boy and his sister survive the summer at the family fish camp when their father dies from his alcoholism. Short, cliff-hanger chapters make this an easier read than Hatchet, *see page 143b.* (Series)

31. *Tuck Everlasting* by Natalie Babbitt. New York: Farrar, Straus & Giroux, 1975. (Sunburst)

    Overprotected Winnie Foster makes a decision to help the Tucks, and her life is changed forever in this fantasy, which considers what it might be like to live forever. With a preface and an afterword that introduce readers to the layers of mean-ing and symbolism a well-written story may have, this story is a modern classic.

Grade 6

Survival in many settings is a theme of this list: Who survives? How? What do they learn? What do they need beyond satisfying food and shelter needs? (See books on the previous list, too.) Books on this level also include diverse historical periods, settings, genres, themes, and types of characters. Fables are presented as a part of traditional literature and as a model for writing.

Since children mature at differing rates, be sure to consider titles on the previous list if readers have missed them. In addition, call attention to other books by these well-known, worthwhile authors to encourage children to keep reading and talking about books.

Suggestions for sixth-grade author studies include Betsy Byars, James Cross Giblin, Mary Downing Hahn, Walter Dean Myers, Scott O'Dell, Katherine Paterson, Gary Paulsen,

Mildred Taylor, Cynthia Voigt, plus any authors on the previous grade list introductions.

1. *Aesop's Fables* illustrated by Heidi Holder. New York: Viking, 1981. (Puffin)

    Nine fables of human foibles follow the pattern: animal characters, spare and pre-cise telling, and an ending moral. It is often easier for children to compose their own fables if they first generate a list of morals or lessons, since the sole purpose of a fable is to teach. See also Fables, *page 146b.*

2. *All the Small Poems* by Valerie Worth, illus-trated by Natalie Babbitt. New York: Far-rar, Straus & Giroux, 1987. (Sunburst)

    Four of the poet's books in one volume. Valerie Worth has the knack of condensing the essence of things and making the amazingly right comparisons between the animate and inanimate. A magnet trades "secrets with the North Pole"; a jack-o'-lantern has a "vegetable skull." This disci-plined free verse might encourage students to look closely, make connections, elimi-nate excess words, and create their own small poems.

3. *Child of the Owl* by Lawrence Yep. New York: Harper & Row, 1988. (Dell)

    When the very American Casey is sent to live with her Chinese grandmother in San Francisco's Chinatown, she begins to realize and finally to accept her family heritage as well as her own unique strengths.

4. *Cousins* by Virginia Hamilton. New York: Philomel, 1990. (Scholastic)

    An African-American Ohio family, di-verse in its members, supports Cammy as she tries to cope with the death of a cousin whom she has hated. This powerful book elicits lengthy discussions about family re-lationships. One of this excellent writer's most readable books. See also The Gold Cadillac *for another story of African-Ameri-can extended families.*

5. *Cracker Jackson* by Betsy Byars. New York: Viking Penguin, 1985. (Puffin)

    What should eleven-year-old Cracker do when he discovers that his favorite for-mer babysitter is being abused by her hus-band? Byars is an author every fifth and sixth grader should know for her under-

standing of what it is like to be a kid becoming a young adult, her excellent writing, her humor, and her way of dealing with difficult topics sympathetically and fairly.

6. *The Dark is Rising* by Susan Cooper, illustrated by Alan Cober. New York: Atheneum, 1973. (Aladdin)

On his twelfth birthday, Will discovers he is the last of the old ones and must join the battle outside time against the dark. With many echoes of Welsh myth and legend to ground it, this fantasy draws on many familiar patterns children know from television or movies as well as from other books: the old mentor, the young and unready hero, magical talismans, the struggle between good and evil, and the power of ancient magic. The second in a five-book series. (Series)

7. *Dicey's Song* by Cynthia Voigt. New York: Atheneum, 1983. (Fawcett)

In Homecoming (*New York: Atheneum, 1981*), a near-orphaned Dicey and her three siblings walked from Connecticut to the Maryland shore to live with their grandmother. This sequel deals with the prickly peace they all must make and with Dicey's growing maturity, independence, and understanding about family. There are many other books in the Tillerman family saga. (Series)

8. *From Hand to Mouth: Or How We Invented Knives, Forks, Spoons, and Chopsticks & the Table Manners to Go with Them* by James Cross Giblin. New York: Crowell, 1987. (Harper)

This premier author of nonfiction has made a career of taking unusual subjects (milk, chairs, chimney sweeps) or more predictable ones (the Rosetta stone, unicorns) and making them fascinating. Moving through prehistory to present day and across the globe, Giblin shows how utensils evolved out of necessity, style, economics, and social customs. A good way to view world history plus a good example of how asking interesting questions can lead you around the world in search of answers.

9. (E) *The Gold Cadillac* by Mildred Taylor, illustrated by Michael Hays. New York: Dial, 1987. (Bantam)

This short, powerful novel set in the 1950s reveals the differences between the North and South when segregation was still overt. A family attempts to drive their newly purchased Cadillac from Cleveland to Mississippi only to see the father imprisoned briefly because the local police believe that a black man could not possibly own this car but must have stolen it.

10. *The Great Gilly Hopkins* by Katherine Paterson. New York: Crowell, 1978. (HarperTrophy)

Smart-aleck Gilly finally meets her match in Maime Trotter, the last of a series of foster parents Gilly is placed with. Gilly's gradual change of heart and the hilarity of some scenes impel readers to the story's conclusion. Readers may need some help in discussing the ending as Gilly gets exactly what she has wanted . . . but it is not to stay with Trotter. Is this happy or not?

11. *Hatchet* by Gary Paulsen. New York: Bradbury, 1987. (Puffin)

After a plane crash, thirteen-year-old Brian spends fifty-four days in the wilderness learning to survive with only the aid of a hatchet given him by his mother. He also reconciles his parents' divorce. Group with other survival stories across genres to compare which qualities make a survivor; how a survivor changes; what beyond food, shelter, and safety (e.g., companions, art, music) helps a survivor; and so forth. (Series)

12. *Homesick: My Own Story* by Jean Fritz, illustrated by Margot Tomes. New York: Putnam, 1982. (Dell Yearling)

A famous author writes of her childhood in China before the Boxer Rebellion and her longed-for trip back to the United States in a hum'orous and authentic voice. Be sure to discuss why the book is titled "homesick."

13. *Island of the Blue Dolphins* by Scott O'Dell, illustrated by Ted Lewin. Boston: Houghton Mifflin, 1960. (Dell Yearling)

A California Indian girl, Karana, survives on an island for eighteen years. Based on fact, this popular story raises many questions about whether "rescue" by Spanish priests was necessarily a good thing. (Series)

14. *Journey to Jo'burg: A South African Story* by Beverley Naidoo, illustrated by Eric Velasquez. New York: Lippincott, 1985. (HarperTrophy)

When the baby suddenly becomes ill, thirteen-year-old Naledi journeys from their village to find her Mma working in far-off Johannesburg. Readers may gain some understanding of the painful struggles South Africans endured in the time of Apartheid. The sequel, Chain of Fire *(New York: Lippincott, 1990), follows Naledi in her fifteenth year. (Series)*

15. *Letters from a Slave Girl: The Story of Harriet Jacobs* by Mary E. Lyons. New York: Macmillan, 1992. (   )

This fictionalized account of Harriet Jacobs, born a slave in North Carolina in 1813, presents a character who ran away from her three-year-old mistress to hide in her grandmother's attic for seven years. Her observations, written in dialect based on Jacobs's own writing and on other slave narratives, give readers a remarkable picture of this tragic historical period. See also Many Thousand Gone, page 152b.

16. *Lincoln: A Photobiography* by Russell Freedman. New York: Clarion, 1987. (Clarion)

Quoting often from Lincoln and using a variety of primary sources, Freedman makes the man come alive. Readers learn "the facts" about this president and come to understand the ideas for which he stood, his background, the tenor of the times, and the legacy he has left. Biography at its finest.

17. (E) *Missing May* by Cynthia Rylant. New York: Orchard, 1992. (Orchard)

When Summer's beloved May, who has cared for her for the last six years, dies, Summer has to keep May's husband Ob from despair and willing himself to die. This family, eccentric, quirky, and wonderful, makes itself into a new one that includes the memory and the power of May's love in this short but powerful novel by one of our greatest writers of children's fiction. See also Best Wishes, page 134b.

18. *Mrs. Frisby and the Rats of NIMH* by Robert C. O'Brien, illustrated by Zena Bernstein. New York: Atheneum, 1971. (Aladdin)

Where can rats with human intelligence find a place that does not rely on theft and that won't be discovered and destroyed by humans? This complex and fast-moving story deals with the themes of courage and self-determination. Sequels written by O'Brien's daughter, Jane Conly, continue the story. (Series)

19. *Roll of Thunder, Hear My Cry* by Mildred Taylor, illustrated by Jerry Pinkney. New York: Dial, 1976. (Puffin)

Being an African-American family in rural Mississippi in the 1930s has rewarding moments as well as grim ones for the Logan family. Nine-year-old Cassie observes racial tension, her mother's struggle to maintain her teaching job, and her own father's dramatic rescue of an African-American teenager from a lynch mob. This story invites children to make links between Lincoln's time, the Depression era, and the present in the lives of African-Americans. See also Song of the Trees, p. 137b. (Series)

20. (E) *Sadako and the Thousand Paper Cranes* by Eleanor Coerr, illustrated by Ronald Himler. New York: Putnam, 1977. (Dell Yearling)

Based on the true story of Sadako Sasaki, who died of radiation poisoning when she was twelve. The heroine to the children of Japan is commemorated by a memorial in Hiroshima Peace Park where children leave paper cranes made in her honor. A short but thoroughly moving story. Coerr has also retold a shorter picture-book version, Sadako, *illustrated by Ed Young (New York: Putnam, 1993).*

21. *The Sign of the Beaver* by Elizabeth Speare. Boston: Houghton Mifflin, 1983. (Dell Yearling)

Left to attend his family's wilderness cabin in Maine, Matt cannot cope without the help of Attean, a woodland Indian. Consider what gifts each boy leaves with the other, who is freer, what qualities help Matt survive, and whether this story portrays Indians fairly. Compare the survival skills and the character of Matt with that of Brian *in* Hatchet.

22. *Something Upstairs: A Tale of Ghosts* by Avi. New York: Orchard, 1988. (Avon)

Time-slip fantasy in which a boy in Rhode Island discovers that the stain on the floor of his room is really very old blood. He is able to slip back in time and help a young slave boy who is trying to prevent bloodshed of his people. Historically accurate, this story makes the reader wonder what might have happened if one state had abolished slavery years before 1863, as this one nearly did.

23. *Time for Andrew: A Ghost Story* by Mary Downing Hahn. New York: Clarion, 1994. (   )

    The author, best known for her very popular Wait Till Helen Comes *(New York: Clarion, 1986; Avon), tells a riveting ghost story set at the turn of the century when there is no cure for diphtheria. Andrew from the present day trades places with his namesake in the past so that he may recover from this dread disease, only to discover that the cured boy refuses to return to the past. Both boys become stronger in their resolves and change as a result of their experiences. Hahn's satisfying ending is not typical of most time-slip fantasies. Use this story to discuss conventions of this kind of fantasy as well as an introduction to Hahn's work.*

24. *Where the Red Fern Grows* by Wilson Rawls. New York: Doubleday, 1961. (Bantam)

    Billy trains his dogs to be a fine hunting team in the Ozarks in this heartwarming and sentimental tale of the devotion between animals and humans. A long-time favorite with both adults and young readers.

Books Which Invite Writing and Storytelling (Grades 1–6)

The books on this list value storytelling or are natural models for encouraging children to write, either because of strong story models, definitive formats, patterned organization, or some other device. Many of these books appeal to primary children as stories but may be reread and extended on a different level by older children. Check the titles, too, in the Wordless Books list, page 149b, for writing extension possibilities.

1. *Aesop's Fables,* see page 142b.
2. *All I Am,* see page 113b.
3. *All the Small Poems,* see page 142b.
4. Alphabet Books

   Numerous alphabet books suggest ways for children to organize writing. Illuminations by Jonathan Hunt (New York: Bradbury, 1989) provides medieval information from "alchemist" to "zither," suggesting that children could organize information from a thematic unit study in this manner. Aster Aardvark's Alphabet Adventures by Steven Kellogg (New York: Morrow Junior Books, 1987) is told strictly by the letters: "After Aster applied herself and achieved an A. . . ." Chris Van Allsburg's sinister The Z Was Zapped (Boston: Houghton Mifflin, 1987) or Mary Azarian's woodcut A Farmer's Alphabet (Boston: David Godine, 1981) are other provocative compendiums. Maurice Sendak's Alligators All Around (New York: HarperCollins, 1962) suggests two-word phrases a child could attribute to another animal. Assemble a number of alphabet books, look at how they are organized, and invite children to try their hands at the ones that are appropriate to this grade level. See also the kindergarten list, pp. 106b–110b.

5. *Animal Fact/Animal Fable,* see page 124b.
6. *The Book of Pigericks* by Arnold Lobel. New York: Harper & Row, 1982. (HarperTrophy)

   Zany pigs in all sizes parade through these imaginative limericks. Children can laugh at Lobel's efforts and create their own using this familiar pattern. Be sure to share a few limericks by the masters, Edward Lear and Ogden Nash.

7. *The Cat's Purr,* see page 138b.
8. *Chicken Sunday,* see page 129b.
9. *Cinder Edna* by Ellen Jackson, illustrated by Kevin O'Malley. New York: Lothrop, Lee and Shepard, 1994. (   )

   In a second story, running parallel to the "Cinderella" story, Edna earns her dress, takes the bus that quits running at midnight, wears loafers as better for dancing, and marries the prince's younger brother who runs the palace recycling plant. See also Sidney Rella and the Glass

Sneaker *by Bernice Myers (New York: Macmillan, 1986). Several other updates of traditional folktales with strong feminine heroines include* Princess Smartypants *(New York: Putnam, 1986), Michael Emberley's urban "Red Riding Hood" story,* Ruby *(Boston: Little, Brown, 1990) and Tony Johnston's* The Cowboy and the Black-Eyed Pea *(New York: Putnam, 1992). Collect parodies and show children how authors vary the setting, change the sex, age, or specie of the main character, and play with traditional tales before you turn them loose on their own updates or parodies. See also* The Frog Prince Continued, *page 135b.*

10. *The Day of Ahmed's Secret, see page 124b.*

11. *Dear Annie* by Judith Caseley. New York: Greenwillow, 1991. (Mulberry)

    Grandfather writes to Annie as she grows towards school age until finally she is able to write back to him. Her show-and-tell item is a shoe box of all of Grandpa's letters to her, inspiring the whole class to make a bulletin board of letters from everyone. The book draws attention to diverse written correspondence and invites children to write to someone they care about.

12. *Don't Forget to Write* by Martina Selway. Nashville, TN: Ideals, 1992. (Ideals)

    One long letter written to her mother over a few weeks' time shows how "old Ginger Nut," as her grandfather calls her, changes her mind about visiting her grandparents. Children can write about their own visits, imaginary visits, or simply see an ongoing letter, which is really a form of journal writing.

13. *Everybody Needs a Rock* by Byrd Baylor, illustrated by Peter Parnall. New York: Scribner, 1974. (Aladdin)

    Ten "rules for finding a rock" guide this poetic text. Parnall's black-line illustrations evoke the landscape of special places, as well. Suggest to children that they find a special rock, seashell, flower, or tree and write new rules. Try illustrating in shades of one color and black line as Parnall does. Other titles by this team, such as Your Own Best Secret Place *(1979),* I'm in Charge of Celebrations *(1986), or* The Way to Start a Day *(1978) (all New York: Scribner) also provide models.*

14. *Fables* by Arnold Lobel. New York: Harper & Row, 1980. (HarperTrophy)

    Following the models of Aesop and La Fontaine, Lobel has created twenty original fables with morals such as "Even the taking of small risks will add excitement to life." It is often easier to start with the moral and work backwards to create the story. Using Aesop, for instance, borrow morals and ask children to create another version that suits this moral. Children who have read such excellent fable collections as Tom Paxton's Aesop's Fables *(New York: Morrow Junior Books, 1988), Harold Jones's* Tales from Aesop *(New York: Watts/Julia MacRae, 1982), or Eve Rice's* Once in a Wood: Ten Tales from Aesop *(New York: Greenwillow, 1979) will have more to bring to this.*

15. *Faint Frogs Feeling Feverish* by Lilian Obligado. New York: Viking Penguin, 1983. (Puffin)

    Alliterative phrases tickle the tongue in this collection of tongue twisters. Susan Purviance's and Marcia O'Shell's Alphabet Annie Announces an All-American Album *(Boston: Houghton Mifflin, 1988) is loaded with alliterative sentences. Nicola Bayley's counting rhyme,* One Old Oxford Ox *(New York: Atheneum, 1977), presents a dozen animals actively engaged.* A Snake Is Totally Tail *by Judi Barrett (New York: Atheneum, 1983) includes clever alliterative and figurative descriptions of animals. Introducing children to literary devices helps sharpen their sensitivity to language use and provides them with ways of enlivening their writing. Expect some overuse first!*

16. *Family Pictures/Cuadros de familia* by Carmen Lomas Garza. As told to Harriet Rohmer. Spanish version by Rosalma Zubizarreta. San Francisco: Children's Book Press, 1990. (Children's Book Press)

    Paintings depict the Chicana artist's childhood in Texas with such details as shopping in the open market, killing a chicken for dinner, and parties. Presented in Eng-

lish and Spanish, the text encourages children to draw, talk, or write about their own "family pictures."

17. *Fortunately* by Remy Charlip. New York: Macmillan, 1964. (Aladdin)

    Fortunately, Ned got a party invitation; unfortunately, the party was in Florida and Ned lives in New York. In this strongly patterned story, Ned meets each setback with improbable innovation. Using this model, children can create their own preposterous adventures with dinosaurs, at the circus, under the earth, and so on.

18. *Go Fish,* see page 135b.

19. *Hailstones and Halibut Bones: Adventures in Color* by Mary O'Neill, with new illustrations by John Walner. New York: Doubleday, 1989. (COP)

    O'Neill describes not only things that are red or blue or gray; she also evokes the smell or taste or sounds of a color. While children try their hands at their own color poems, return to the book frequently to help writers see how the poet works. An earlier edition illustrated by Leonard Weisgard (Doubleday, 1969), provides more subtle pictures for the same text. See, too, Eve Merriam's "A Yell for Yellow" in Jamboree: Rhymes for All Times (New York: Dell Yearling, 1984).

20. + *A House Is a House for Me* by Mary Ann Hoberman, illustrated by Betty Fraser. New York: Harper & Row, 1978. (Puffin)

    What constitutes a house? There are obvious ones in this rollicking, rhyming text, but there are also unique ones; a carton is a house for a cracker, or peaches are houses for peach pits. Children's illustrated examples of other literal or metaphorical houses make a good class book and help introduce figurative language.

21. *I Am Wings,* see page 158b.

22. *I Need a Lunch Box,* see page 120b.

23. *The Important Book* by Margaret Wise Brown. New York: Harper & Row, 1949. (HarperTrophy)

    What is important about a flower? This book asks readers to look at essences. Children can generate their own important

attributes for a favorite article, something in nature, or a special time.

24. *In a Pickle and Other Funny Idioms* by Marvin Terban, illustrated by Giulio Maestro. New York: Clarion, 1983. (Clarion)

    "In a pickle" and thirty other common American idioms are presented and explained. Other titles in the series introduce a variety of literary devices. Ask children to glean idioms from everyday use, such as expressions using body parts ("have a heart") or using "line" ("bee-line," "lining track," "line of vision"). Activities such as this make children much more sensitive to figurative language in their own as well as others' writings. (Series)

25. *The Jolly Postman, or Other People's Letters* by Janet and Allan Ahlberg. Boston: Little, Brown, 1986. (   )

    A postman delivers letters to fairy tale and folktale characters. Actual letters in a variety of formats (e.g., advertising circular, invitation, postcard, announcement, lawyer's letterhead, etc.) may be removed from real envelopes. After a study of folktales, brainstorm who might write what sorts of letters. Provide various sizes of envelopes, card stock, different sizes of stationery, and plenty of time for drafts.

26. *Mouse Letters* by Michelle Cartlidge. New York: Dutton, 1993.

    This miniature book, about 2" × 2", includes actual small envelopes that hold letters from mice inviting a non-visible child to a garden party. Children can create miniature letters from fairies, from book characters, or from animals, and display them in the classroom. To make your own tiny envelopes, take apart a regular envelope and reduce the size by cutting an equal amount from the original margin. Refold and glue. (Series)

27. *The Mysteries of Harris Burdick* by Chris Van Allsburg. Boston: Houghton Mifflin, 1984. (   )

    Fourteen mysterious stories are each suggested with a title, picture, and a single line of text. "Archie Smith, Boy Wonder" shows a sleeping boy observed by five shining lights while the text states, "A tiny voice asked, 'Is he the one?'" Van Allsburg's provocative phrase invites children to provide the beginning and end as they make their own whole stories. On another plane, ask children to think of their own provocative sentences, titles, and illustrations.

28. *Nathaniel Talking*, see page 132b.

29. *One Sun* by Bruce McMillan. New York: Holiday, 1990. (   )

    In what he calls "terse verse," McMillan presents two-word rhyming phrases dealing with the beach: sand hand / lone stone / snail trail, and so forth. Children can generate their own terse verses while older children can sustain the idea within a topic such as a trip to the small mall or the new zoo. See also his Play Day *(New York: Holiday, 1991).*

30. *The Popcorn Book* by Tomie dePaola. New York: Holiday, 1978. (Holiday)

    Information about popcorn is conveyed in a variety of formats suggesting that children might frame their reports in something other than straight narrative: "My report is about. . . ." Labels under pictures, cartoons, conversational balloons, and a recipe are some of the features. See, too, Animal Fact/Animal Fable, *p. 124b, and Joanna Cole's "Magic Schoolbus" series for other challenging informational formats.*

31. *Quick as a Cricket* by Audrey Wood, illustrated by Don Wood. Clarkston, MI: Child's Play, 1982. (Child's Play)

    A child likens aspects of himself to those of animals: "I'm as slow as a snail" or "I'm as loud as a lion." Young children can make their own books of comparisons. Older ones could decide which of these expressions are trite or predictable and write their own fresh similes.

32. *Sister*, see page 156b.

33. *Someday* by Charlotte Zolotow, illustrated by Arnold Lobel. New York: Harper & Row, 1965. (HarperTrophy)

    While many children write their own "someday" stories as wishes for the future, others are able to catch the irony of "Someday . . . my brother will introduce me to his friends and say 'This is my sister,' instead of 'Here's the family creep.'"

34. *Stringbean's Trip to the Shining Sea* by Vera B. Williams and Jennifer Williams. New York: Greenwillow, 1988. (Scholastic)

    This story of Stringbean's trip with his brother in a camper looks like a book of bound postcards. Readers construct Stringbean's trip, his adventures, and his feelings from what the two boys write on the backs of the postcards. Clever stamps, funny pictures on the cards, and the whole novelty of having to infer the story make this a winner with children. Simply retelling the story is a challenge. To recast the format, ask what if some other character who went on a physical or psychological journey wrote back periodically to her family.

35. *Tell Me a Story, Mama* by Angela Johnson, illustrated by David Soman. New York: Orchard, 1989. (Orchard)

    A girl asks her mother to tell stories of when Mama was little, but the girl ends up retelling them all herself. Italic typeface indicates the mother's talk. The way this family has shown its love for its members throughout the generations comes strongly through in the stories the mother has told. Children can write about their own family stories, interview grandparents, or tell favorite family stories.

36. *Tiger*, see page 137b.

37. *The True Story of the 3 Little Pigs* by A. Wolf as told to Jon Scieszka, illustrated by Lane Smith. New York: Viking Kestrel, 1989. (Scholastic)

    For introducing point of view, there is no better book. The wolf tells of how his bad cold and the pigs' rudeness forced him to act. This hilarious story suggests other folktale characters who might tell their true stories if children would be their voices: Jack's giant, Gretel's witch, or Wiley's hairy man. Build on this experience by asking children to consider another character's point of view in a novel.

38. *When I Was Little* by Toyomi Igus, illustrated by Higgins Bond. Orange, NJ: Just Us Books, 1992. (Just Us)

    Noel, a young African-American boy, hangs out at the old fishing hole with Grandpa. The fishing spot is surrounded by condos and houses now, but Grandpa can recreate life as it used to be when he tells Noel stories of "when I was little." The reminiscences about iceboxes, outhouses, phonographs, and first autos are depicted in black-and-white illustrations interspersed among the full-color of the present day. Ask older relatives for their stories of the olden days.

39. *When I Was Little: A Four-Year-Old's Memoir of Her Youth* by Jamie Lee Curtis, illustrated by Laura Cornell. New York: HarperCollins, 1993. (   )

    A backward look told from the advanced viewpoint of a four-year-old with action-packed, detailed contrasting illustrations. Encourage children to tell their own "little" stories. Pair with a forward look, When I'm Big *by Debi Gliori (Cambridge, MA: Candlewick Press, 1992; Candlewick), in which a boy imagines the bizarre and wonderful things he will have, wear, and do when he is older.*

Wordless Books (Grades K–6)

Wordless books must rely on the illustrations to do the work. All of these titles provide excellent discussion possibilities, and some present children with the opportunity to create narratives. They suggest that children become adept at "reading the pictures" and noticing how the illustrator engages us.

1. *The Angel and the Soldier* by Peter Collington. New York: Knopf, 1987. (COP)

    While a young girl sleeps, her toy angel rescues her toy soldier from the clutches of pirates who live in a ship on top of the piano. Richly evoked by the soft, coloredpencil drawings and seen from the perspective of tiny beings, this story suggests how we might see the world through someone else's eyes.

2. *Anno's USA* by Mitsumaso Anno. New York: Philomel Books, 1983. (Philomel)

    Anno's lone traveler makes his way from Hawaii to California and across the country moving freely in time. Each doublepage spread may show bits from a region's history, famous people and landmarks, fine arts allusions, and well-known characters from children's literature or from "Sesame

Street," as well as Anno's trademark optical illusions. Older children, with their greater knowledge of the world, spend hours pondering, naming, and laughing over their discoveries. (Series)

3. *Changes, Changes* by Pat Hutchins. New York: Macmillan, 1971. (Aladdin)

    Entirely with block shapes, Hutchins shows a man and woman who build a block house and dismantle it to produce a fire engine, a boat, and various other things.

4. *Deep in the Forest* by Brinton Turkle. New York: Dutton, 1976. (Puffin)

    This is a mirror of "The Three Bears" but it is a little bear cub who crawls into a Colonial log cabin to wreak havoc. Notice the bear crawling into and out of the pictures that neatly frame this clever story. Pair with versions of The Three Bears, p. 109b.

5. *First Snow* by Emily Arnold McCully. New York: Harper & Row, 1985. (HarperTrophy)

    The mouse family goes sledding but the littlest mouse is afraid to go down the hill. When she finally gets up her courage, the family can't get her off the slopes. Other books in the series chronicle the arrival of a new baby, a family picnic, a Christmas celebration, and the beginning of school. All have strong narrative possibilities. (Series)

6. *Follow Me!* by Nancy Tafuri. New York: Greenwillow, 1990. (   )

    A baby sea lion explores his rocky island while curiously following a red crab. But his mother is always watching. Retell the story in a pattern of conversation between the baby and its mother, or make a story in which a language pattern is repeated: "The baby seal did —————. Mother watched from the rocks." See also Tafuri's Jungle Walk *(New York: Greenwillow, 1988).*

7. *Free Fall* by David Wiesner. New York: Clarion, 1988. (Mulberry)

    While studying an atlas, a boy falls asleep and has an adventure in a surreal landscape that curiously reflects aspects of his room furnishings. The dreamlike quality of the story becomes richer the more one studies the pictures. Obtain several copies *of the book and lay the pictures out in a frieze-like sequence to see how one page exactly blends into the next. Children might write their own dream sequences or imagine that several items in their bedrooms come to life in a story.*

8. *Frog Goes to Dinner* by Mercer Mayer. New York: Dial, 1967. (Dial)

    Chaos results when a boy discovers his pet frog has ridden in his pocket to a fancy restaurant. Jealousy is the theme of One Frog Too Many *(New York: Dial, 1975).* (Series)

9. *Is It Red? Is It Yellow? Is It Blue?* by Tana Hoban. New York: Greenwillow, 1978. (Mulberry)

    Hoban's colorful photographs of common city scenes, children doing things, and articles invite talk, not only about colors but about what is going on, about shapes, or about associations. Good for introducing children to this prolific creator of photographed concept books.

10. *Mouse Around* by Pat Schories. New York: Farrar, Straus & Giroux, 1991. (Sunburst)

    A mouse leaves his nest undiscovered in the pocket of a plumber and has a series of imaginative adventures as it goes from pocket to rolled newspaper to shopping bag to paper cup and so on in the everyday world of people. Numerous pictures of various sizes show close-ups and details, making this a good book for small groups of children to work with in a collaborative retelling.

11. + *Niki's Walk* by Jane Tanner. Cleveland: Modern Curriculum Press, 1987. (MCP)

    Niki and his mother go for a walk in this urban setting; celebrate someone's birthday in a park; and see a variety of sights such as a construction site, boats on the river, a tow truck removing a wrecked car, and so forth. Much to talk about with early elementary children. Take a walk and discuss what you see. Write a group story.

12. *Peter Spier's Rain* by Peter Spier. New York: Doubleday, 1982. (Doubleday)

    A brother and sister explore their wet neighborhood and engage in hundreds of activities before returning home for a hot bath and cocoa. Writing possibilities include telling about the day from the point of view of one of the children or writing about what you would like to do on a rainy day.

13. *The Silver Pony* by Lynd Ward. New York: Houghton Mifflin, 1973. (Houghton Mifflin)

    This long story depicts a lonely farm boy who fantasizes about the trips he takes on his beautiful winged pony. When his family finds him lying ill outside, their present of a real pony helps the boy bring his fantasy and his real world together. Older children can better sustain the narrative possibilities of this story.

14. *The Snowman* by Raymond Briggs. New York: Random House, 1978. (Random)

    A small boy has a wonderful nighttime adventure with his snowman who can fly. In the morning, though, his friend has melted. Observant children may notice that the story takes place in Britain when they see landmarks and other clues.

15. *Sunshine* by Jan Ormerod. New York: Lothrop, Lee and Shepard, 1981. (Mulberry)

    A small girl's morning routine as she prepares for school is speeded up when she shows her parents what time it is. The same warm family feeling is created in the sequel Moonlight *(New York: Lothrop, Lee and Shepard, 1982; Mulberry).*

16. *Tuesday* by David Wiesner. New York: Clarion, 1991. (   )

    As the moon rises, so do frogs on their lily pads. They glide over a sleeping village, through laundry, into an open window to discover late-night TV, and over a surprised dog. The magic stops when the sun begins to rise. A perplexed news crew tries to figure out what has happened. Funny pictures encourage children to make up dialogue for the many frogs and animals who witness the improbable situation. See, too, Wiesner's also nearly wordless June 26, 1999 *(Clarion, 1992).*

Life Stories (Grades 2–6)

With the many fine picture book and novel-sized autobiographies and biographies available, children are no longer confined to the often dry series books of individual lives. This list introduces authors of biographies and involves children in the lives of some people who made the world a different place because of their actions. Many kinds of biographies as well as a partial autobiography are included here.

1. *Alvin Ailey* by Andrea Davis Pinkney, illustrated by Brian Pinkney. New York: Hyperion, 1993. (   )

    From his early beginnings in Texas to his teen years in Los Angeles through his founding of his famous dance theater in New York, the life of this well-known black dancer is chronicled. Pinkney's swirling scratchboard illustrations capture motion and energy of the man during his triumphant years.

2. *Diego,* see page 153b.

3. *The Double Life of Pocahontas* by Jean Fritz. New York: Putnam, 1983. (Puffin)

    This complete biography covers the short twenty-one years of Pocahontas' life lived in the early 1600s. Fritz writes elegantly about the encounters of the Native Americans with Captain John Smith and the early Virginia settlers. See, too, other titles about Stonewall Jackson, James Madison, and Benedict Arnold by our foremost writer of biographies for children.

4. *El Chino* by Allen Say. Boston: Houghton Mifflin, 1990. (   )

    Bong Way "Billy" Wong, a Chinese American raised in Nogales, Arizona, always dreamed of being a great athlete. But it wasn't until he discovered bullfighting that he found his true calling. Say's radiant watercolors illuminate this true story of a man who pursued his unconventional dream.

5. *Flight: The Journey of Charles Lindbergh* by Robert Burleigh, illustrated by Mike Wimmer. New York: Philomel, 1991. (   )

    In poetic text and compelling illustration this book evokes the feelings and emotions of Lindbergh during his famous flight in 1927. Inspiring partial biography also speaks to having a dream and realizing it. See also the more biographical but less

beautiful Lindbergh *by Chris Demarest (Crown, 1993).*

6. *The Glorious Flight: Across the Channel with Louis Bleriot* by Alice and Martin Provensen. New York: Viking, 1983. (Puffin)

    With many historical and background details that invite readers to speculate about life in 1909, the authors involve children in this famous flight.

7. *The Great Alexander the Great* by Joe Lasker. New York: Viking, 1983. (Puffin)

    The vividly illustrated life of Alexander, who ruled the land from Greece to India, is highlighted with particular emphasis on his bravado, imagination, and his friendship with his horse, "Bucephalus." See, too, Lasker's The Boy Who Loved Music *(New York: Penguin, 1979) for an imaginative rendering of how Haydn came to compose the "Farewell" Symphony.*

8. *Homesick,* see page 143b.

9. *Indian Chiefs* by Russell Freedman. New York: Holiday, 1982. (Holiday)

    Aspects of the lives of six Indian leaders who led their people in moments of crisis in the middle 1800s. This collection of partial biographies, illustrated with photographs from the period, enables older readers to see the settling of the West from multiple perspectives. See Freedman's many other excellent biographies, including Lincoln: A Photobiography, *p. 144b.*

10. *James Weldon Johnson: "Lift Every Voice and Sing"* by Patricia and Fredrick McKissack. Chicago: Children's Press, 1990. (Children's Press).

    The life of this civil rights leader and author of the famous song of the title is presented in large print with black-and-white photographs from the period. A chronology of events in the person's life ends each book in this useful biography series. (Series)

11. *Johnny Appleseed* by Steven Kellogg. New York: Morrow, 1988. (Morrow)

    The life of John Chapman is based on fact, but many legends surround this famous planter, as well. In this exuberantly illustrated picture book, children might separate the fact from the fiction and compare Kellogg's version with Aliki's The Story of Johnny Appleseed *(Englewood Cliffs, NJ: Prentice Hall, 1963)* or with Reeve Lindbergh's poetic Johnny Appleseed, *illustrated by Kathy Jakobsen (New York: Joy Street/Little, Brown, 1990).*

12. *Keep the Lights Burning, Abbie* by Peter and Connie Roop, illustrated by Peter E. Hanson. Minneapolis, MN: Carolrhoda Books, 1985. (Carolrhoda)

 In easy-reader format, this fictionalized biographical sketch tells of one month in Abbie Burgess's life when a storm left her father on the mainland and Abbie took care of her sick mother and her siblings while keeping a Maine lighthouse working in 1856. A note tells readers more about Abbie's life.

13. *The Land I Lost,* see page 140b.

14. *The Last Princess: The Story of Princess Ka'iulani of Hawai'i* by Fay Stanley, illustrated by Diane Stanley. New York: Macmillan, 1991. (   )

 This sad story of the annexation of the sovereign nation of Hawai'i to the United States is offset by the proud dignity of the young princess, the last of royalty to rule the island, as she tried to convince Grover Cleveland of her people's right to sovereignty. Part of Stanley's biographical series, beautifully illustrated. See also Stanley's Charles Dickens: The Man Who Had Great Expectations *(Morrow, 1993). (Series)*

15. *Laura Ingalls Wilder* by Gwenda Blair, illustrated by Thomas B. Allen. New York: Putnam, 1981. (Putnam)

 In more demanding vocabulary than the type size would suggest, Blair rounds up details that cover but expand upon this well-known author's life as portrayed in her "Little House" books.

16. *Many Thousand Gone* by Virginia Hamilton, illustrated by Leo and Diane Dillon. New York: Knopf, 1993. (   )

 Short biographical vignettes of famous resistors to slavery, African-Americans and others, trace the history of slavery in the United States. Well-known figures such as Harriet Tubman, Frederick Douglass, Sojourner Truth, and Dred Scott as well as those less well-known give readers

background in the history of slavery and those who protested.

17. *Maya Angelou: Author* by Miles Shapiro. New York: Chelsea House, 1994. (Chelsea House)

 One of the "Black Americans of Achievement" series, this powerful biography does not spare middle schoolers the details of life for an African-American person in the United States from the 1930s when Angelou was growing up to the present day. Photographs present political, social, and economic aspects of the author's time but do not show her until the 1970s when she became well known for her writing. The publisher also features a series of biographies for younger readers, "Junior World Biographies." (Series)

18. *Once upon a Time: A Story of the Brothers Grimm* by Robert Quackenbush. New York: Simon & Schuster, 1985. (   )

 This lighthearted, simplified biography introduces readers to the two brothers who collected folklore and enabled many now-familiar tales to be rendered into print in the early 1800s. Quackenbush has written and illustrated many simplified biographies of such people as Thomas Edison and Peter Stuyvesant. (Series)

19. *The One Bad Thing About Father* by F. N. Monjo, illustrated by Richard Cuffari. New York: Holt, 1974. (HarperTrophy)

 In easy-reader format, readers see Theodore Roosevelt through the eyes of his son Quentin, who maintained that the only bad thing about his father was that he was president, and so his whole family, including the irrepressible Alice Roosevelt, had to live at the White House. See other simplified biographies by this author about such people as Thomas Jefferson and Benjamin Franklin.

20. *A Picture Book of Simon Bolivar* by David A. Adler, illustrated by Robert Casillo. New York: Holiday, 1992. (Holiday)

 The famous South American liberator's life story is chronicled. David Adler's picture-book biographies fill a real need. They present accurate information, attractively illustrated, in an easy-to-read format of one or two paragraphs per page. Subjects currently feature several U.S. presidents, Harriet Tubman, Frederick Douglass, Helen Keller, Florence Nightingale, and others. "Notes from the author" and a helpful chronology of the subject's life end most volumes. Highly useful for reluctant older readers as well. (Series)

21. *Self-Portrait: Trina Schart Hyman* by Trina Schart Hyman. New York: Harper & Row, 1989. (   )

    In her familiar bold black line and color, Hyman reveals her personal connection with the folktales she has illustrated and discusses her training as an illustrator, her marriage, and her country household. Bound to send children back to her books for another look, and an inspiration to budding artists, as well. (Series)

22. *Shaka, King of the Zulus* by Diane Stanley and Peter Vennema, illustrated by Diane Stanley. New York: Morrow, 1988. (Mulberry)

    The famous leader of one of the largest African armies ever assembled at a period when European explorers were "discovering" the continent is seen in dramatic, detailed illustration and text. This picturebook biography does not ignore Shaka's cruelty but sets it in the context of tribal beliefs of the time. See, too, this team's other titles, such as Good Queen Bess *(New York: Four Winds, 1990) and* Peter the Great *(New York: Four Winds, 1986) by this team.*

23. So Far from the Bamboo Grove, see page 159b.

24. *Traitor: The Case of Benedict Arnold*, see page 159b.

25. *A Weed Is a Flower: The Life of George Washington Carver* by Aliki. New York: Simon & Schuster, 1988.

    In brief, easy-reader format, Aliki captures simply the story of a man born a slave who became a great research scientist. See also her simplified biographies of Benjamin Franklin and Johnny Appleseed.

26. *Where Do You Think You're Going, Christopher Columbus?* by Jean Fritz, illustrated by Margot Tomes. New York: Putnam, 1980. (Putnam)

    In lively but entirely factual detail, Fritz

captures the man's courage and pride, as well as the attitudes of his times. Information-bearing illustrations, end notes, and a helpful index introduce children to the use of these valuable tools. (Series)

Bilingual Spanish Books: A Beginning List

To address the needs of the growing number of Latino students in our schools to read both in their first language and in English, we have included books that are bilingual. That is, the text is in English and Spanish on each page. In order to become literate in their first language and maintain this literacy while acquiring English, children may read texts with both languages. Such texts are also helpful for English-speaking students to learn Spanish.

Be sure to check with mainstream publishers such as HarperCollins, Morrow, Scholastic, and others such as Lee & Low Books who are now providing their own lines of bilingual books. Look, too, for those such as Farrar, Straus & Giroux, who are republishing Spanish translations of their own books, in this case under the "Mirasol" imprint. Children's Book Press publishes many bilingual titles, some of uneven literary or illustrative quality, so be selective.

For strategies and support for the teaching of second-language learners using a whole language approach, see "Whole Language Learning and Teaching for Second Language Learners" by Yvonne Freeman and David Freeman in *Reading Process and Practice: From Socio-Psycholinguistics to Whole Language* by Constance Weaver (Portsmouth, NH: Heinemann, 1994, pp. 558–629).

1. *Carlos and the Squash Plant / Carlos y la planta de calabaza* by Jan Romero Stevens, illustrated by Jeanne Arnold. Flagstaff, AZ: Northland, 1993. (   )

    A humorous, inventive tall tale concerns Carlos who doesn't take a bath when his mother tells him to. A squash plant grows from his ear until finally he scrubs himself. A recipe for a squash dish called Calabacitas *is included.*

2. *Diego* by Jeanette Winter and John Winter. New York: Knopf, 1991. (   )

    Over half of the text of this short biog-

raphy of Diego Rivera depicts his child-hood. The rest encapsulates his contributions to art, both in his native Mexico and in the world. Small, bordered, square illustrations depicting his life open up to one contrasting double-page illustration to suggest the scale in which the muralist worked.

3. *Family Pictures,* see page 146b.

4. *Margaret and Margarita / Margarita y Margaret* by Lynn Reiser. New York: Morrow, 1993. (   )

    Two parallel stories of little girls who go to the park with their mothers. English language is rendered on one page in pink letters, Spanish on another in blue. As the two girls play together and begin to use each other's languages, the intermingled blue and pink words reflect this blending. The theme of friendship fits well with other titles on the kindergarten, first, and second grade lists.

5. *The Piñata Maker / El piñatero* by George Ancona. San Diego: Harcourt Brace, 1994. (Harcourt Brace)

    The process by which a Oaxacan craftsman makes piñatas and paper puppet heads is shown in color photographs, pictures, and full paragraphs. While no specific directions are given, children can easily make their own modified piñatas following this process.

6. *Un paseo por el bosque lluvioso / A Walk in the Rainforest* by Kristin Joy Pratt. Nevada City, CA: Dawn, 1993. (Dawn)

    In alphabet-book format, aspects and inhabitants of the South and Central American rain forests are presented. Elegant paintings and informative short paragraphs provide background and information in child-alluring ways.

7. *Uncle Nacho's Hat / El sombrero del tio Nacho,* adapted by Harriet Rohmer, illustrated by Mira Reisberg. San Francisco: Children's Book Press, 1989. (CBP)

    In this story based on a Nicaraguan folktale, Uncle Nacho can't seem to get rid of his old hat when he is given a new one by his niece. Finally he is able to discard it when it returns to him in shreds. It is his niece who encourages him to forget it

and get on with life. An afterword note gives further background.

8. *Vejigante Masquerader,* see page 133b.

9. + *The Woman Who Outshone the Sun: La mujer que billaba aun mas que el sol* from a poem by Alejandro Cruz Martinez, translated by Rosalma Zubizarreta, illustrated by Fernando Olivera. San Francisco: Children's Book Press, 1991. (CPB, Scholastic)

    Based on a legend, this story shows what happens when people do not honor each other, and when a river dries up. An ecological tale as well as a story of human values.

Grade 7

Books at this level continue to deal with friendships, growing up, becoming independent, and considering consequences of actions. They also continue to present wider world views. The short story genre is introduced in two volumes.

As on the previous two grade lists, many of the authors here have written extensively for the middle school age group, and once readers are familiar with an author, they tend to want to read more of that person's books. Teachers should introduce many authors and their works to readers as encouragement and advice. This is the age at which children, because of school and extracurricular demands, often stop most of their recreational reading and do not return until after adolescence—or perhaps ever.

Suggestions for seventh grade author studies include Patricia Beatty, Pam Conrad, Paula Fox, Virginia Hamilton, Gary Soto, Lawrence Yep, plus many others on the previous three grade list introductions.

1. (E) *Baseball in April* by Gary Soto. San Diego: Harcourt Brace Jovanovich, 1990. (Odyssey)

    Small day-to-day events in a California (Mexican-American) Latino community much like the author's Fresno are presented in this short story collection of eleven selections. For and about middle schoolers, these stories present themes of friendship, independence, love, success, and family relationships. See other Soto collections, too, such as Local News *(San Diego: Harcourt Brace, 1993) or his novel,* Taking Sides *(San Diego: Harcourt Brace, 1991).*

2. *Bull Run* by Paul Fleischman, illustrated by David Frampton. New York: HarperCollins, 1993. (Harper)

 Fleischman, an innovative writer, introduces aspects of this famous opening Civil War battle as seen in sixteen short first-person vignettes. People include a horse-lover, a black man, a sketch artist, a slave woman, a local landowner, and others whose stories often fold into each other. One event from different perspectives raises the discussion of how our expectations and our experiences color what we see and understand. Also an excellent introduction to the War Between the States. See, too, his historical novels, Saturnalia (1990) and Path of the Pale Horse (1983, both Harper).

3. (E) *The Burning Questions of Bingo Brown* by Betsy Byars. New York: Viking Penguin, 1988. (Puffin)

 Bingo wonders about girlfriends, his use of mousse, his teacher's sanity, and his family. Byars combines humorous dialogue and adolescent concerns deftly and believably. (Series)

4. *Children of the Dust Bowl: The True Story of the School at Weedpatch Camp* by Jerry Stanley, illustrated with photographs. New York: Crown, 1992. (Crown)

 Against the backdrop of the Dust Bowl Era, Stanley tells of the Oklahoman migration to an unwelcoming California. Ostracized by Californians as "dumb Okies," the children went without education until one group pulled together in this true story to create their own school. From two derelict buildings it grew into classrooms, a shop, a science lab, and a full curriculum. Children helped build it by selling produce from school gardens and hammering nails. The school still exists today and is a tribute not only to how industry can overcome hardship but to how prejudice can be transformed. Excellent nonfiction and compelling photographs introduce children to a historical period they may know only through the movie "The Wizard of Oz."

5. *A Day No Pigs Would Die* by Robert Newton Peck. New York: Knopf, 1972. (Dell Yearling)

 In the Depression, thirteen-year-old Rob comes to understand his Vermont father's quiet dignity, his willingness to admit to errors, and his ability to do what must be done for the family to survive.

6. *Dragon's Gate* by Lawrence Yep. New York: HarperCollins, 1993. (   )

 Newbery runner-up. A boy called Otter flees China to work on building the railroads on the Golden Mountain, the Sierra Nevadas of California, only to find that he has been misinformed about life for him here. Disillusioned, he becomes involved in the first strike of Chinese railworkers in a little-written-about period in American history. The title has a literal as well as symbolic meaning for Otter.

7. *A Girl Called Boy* by Belinda Hurmence. New York: Clarion, 1982. (Clarion)

 While fingering a family soapstone carving, a sarcastic African-American girl is transported back to the past where her short hair and blue jeans cause her to be mistaken for a runaway slave. This time-slip fantasy is historically accurate but framed within a contemporary viewpoint.

8. *The Giver* by Lois Lowry. Boston: Houghton Mifflin, 1993. (Houghton Mifflin)

 1994 Newbery winner and great discussion book about choices. In a future utopian society, children are given their occupational training beginning at age twelve. Jonas's occupation will be to receive the memories of this society—pleasurable but annoying ones concerning snow as well as painful and horrible ones such as war. It is only when he discovers that euthanasia will kill his adopted baby brother that Jonas rebels. An enigmatic ending, powerful themes, the plan and nature of dystopias, and a believable protagonist make this book eminently discussable. See also Z for Zachariah (p. 157b).

9. *Grab Hands and Run* by Frances Temple. New York: Orchard, 1993. (   )

 Felipe, his mother, and his five-year-old sister flee from a city in El Salvador after his father disappears. His memories of his father (who he learns is dead), his grandparents, and his dog pull back at him *as they sustain the fleeing family. The book hints at the massacres and atrocities that propelled so many Central Americans northward, and presents background for why people immigrate.*

10. *The House of Dies Drear* by Virginia Hamilton, illustrated by Eros Keith. New York: Macmillan, 1968. (Macmillan)

    Weird and terrifying but ultimately explainable happenings threaten an African-American professor and his family, who are staying in a house that was a former Underground Railroad stop. Thomas Small and his family finally solve the mystery in this fast-paced story. (Series)

11. *Jacob Have I Loved* by Katherine Paterson. New York: Crowell, 1980. (HarperCollins)

    Louise develops from a jealous and bitter twin sister to an emotionally healthy adult on an island in the Chesapeake Bay in the 1940s. Rich with well-developed characters, allusions, and multiple themes.

12. *Jayhawker* by Patricia Beatty. New York: Morrow, 1991. (   )

    Stealing slaves from neighboring Missouri to freedom in Kansas, a Kansas boy, Lije, is part of events stemming from Lincoln's Emancipation Proclamation. Readers also meet other historical figures, such as Jesse James, Jim Hickok, and John Brown. Accurate Civil War background plus a suspenseful introduction to Beatty's many other novels set in the Civil War period and during the settling of the West.

13. *Julie of the Wolves* by Jean Craighead George. New York: Harper & Row, 1972. (HarperTrophy)

    Miyax, a thirteen-year-old Eskimo girl, runs away on the tundra and survives with a pack of wolves. Themes of coming of age and ecology, and details of the true behavior of wolves. (Series)

14. *The Middle of Somewhere: A Story of South Africa* by Sheila Gordon. New York: Orchard, 1989. (Bantam)

    The struggle of an African family to continue to live in their home village, which white South Africans want for a suburb. A story with strong values of brotherhood and persistence ending with the release of

Nelson Mandela. See, too, Journey to Jo'burg *on p. 144b.*

15. (E) *The Monument* by Gary Paulsen. New York: Delacorte, 1991. (   )

    One of Paulsen's shorter, nonsurvival stories asks the reader to consider what constitutes a monument to the war dead? Rocky, a mixed-race thirteen-year-old with a bad leg, sees the adult world more clearly and considers what art can do. Good discussion novel and a quick read.

16. *My Brother Sam Is Dead* by James Lincoln Collier and Christopher Collier. New York: Four Winds, 1974. (Scholastic)

    Conflicting loyalties and the injuries inflicted on the innocent during the Revolutionary War are seen through the eyes of Sam's younger brother Tim. See also the Colliers' trilogy about African-Americans during this war, which begins with Jump Ship to Freedom, *p. 140b.*

17. *Prairie Songs* by Pam Conrad. New York: Harper & Row, 1985. (HarperTrophy)

    Louise's simple pioneer existence is changed forever by the arrival of a doctor and his elegant, though mentally unbalanced, wife. Figurative and descriptive language, as well as an accurate picture of pioneer living, bring this time closer. See, too, Conrad's My Daniel *(New York: Harper & Row, 1989), told in two settings, present and pioneer days.*

18. (E) *The Shooting of Dan McGrew* by Robert W. Service, illustrated by Ted Harrison. Boston: David R. Godine, 1988. (   )

    Life at the Malamute Saloon, as told by Dawson City's resident poet, is boldly brought to life by Harrison's vivid paintings. See, too, Harrison's treatment of Service's The Cremation of Sam McGee *(New York: Greenwillow, 1987).*

19. (E) *Sister* by Eloise Greenfield, drawings by Monetta Barrett. New York: Harper, 1974. (HarperTrophy)

    Thirteen-year-old African-American Doretha struggles with her identity in the family until she rereads her book of memories that she started when she was nine. Chapter headings reveal the age at which

Doretha wrote the diary entries—a record of hard times, good times, the times that make her strong now. Students might reflect, journal-style, upon their own strong memories that make them who they are now.

20. *Summer of My German Soldier* by Bette Greene. New York: Dial, 1973. (Bantam)
    Told from the viewpoint of a twelve-year-old Jewish girl in a small Arkansas town who befriends a Nazi POW. Amid prejudice and anger, he leaves her to grow up with knowledge that she is a "person of worth." (Series)

21. *True Confessions of Charlotte Doyle* by Avi. New York: Orchard, 1990. (Orchard)
    A girl, through an accident of fate, becomes the only female aboard a ship bound for America from England in 1832. In first-person narrative, Charlotte tells how she became involved in mutiny, a raging storm, and treachery among the sailors before coming ashore a changed person with a new perspective on what it means to be female.

22. *Village by the Sea* by Paula Fox. New York: Orchard, 1988. (Dell Yearling)
    With her father facing surgery, Emma goes to visit her quixotic aunt at the seashore and learns something about love, envy, rage, and finally forgiveness in this powerful psychological novel.

23. *Where the Lilies Bloom* by Vera and Bill Cleaver, illustrated by James Spanfeller. New York: Lippincott, 1969. (HarperCollins)
    A fourteen-year-old Appalachian girl keeps her family together after her parents' death by trying to teach them "wildcrafting" and the art of being close-mouthed in this survival story. (Series)

24. (E) *Within Reach*, edited by Don Gallo. New York: HarperCollins, 1993.
    (   )
    Ten short stories by popular authors, such as Robert Lipsyte, Judie Angell, Constance Greene, and Pam Conrad, join less well-known ones to tell diverse stories for middle-grade readers. Author biographies

included. *Good for introducing theme, genre, discussion, and authors quickly.*

25. *The Wright Brothers: How They Invented the Airplane* by Russell Freedman, with original photographs by Wilbur and Orville Wright. New York: Holiday, 1991. (Holiday)
    Working from primary source material, Freedman captures interest by making readers feel as if they were eyewitnesses to history. Pair with Lawrence Yep's fictionalized account of a Chinese-American's work with airplanes at the turn of the century, Dragonwings (New York: HarperCollins, 1975).

26. *Z for Zachariah* by Robert C. O'Brien. New York: Atheneum, 1965. (Macmillan)
    Ann Burden, the sole survivor of her valley after a nuclear explosion, contemplates a solitary existence. Her discovery of a sick man brings her initial hope, but her diary in which she tells the story chronicles her disillusionment and her final departure with hope of finding other survivors. See also a very different future imagined in The Lake at the End of the World *by Christine MacDonald (New York: Dial, 1988), and* The Giver, *p. 155b.*

Grade 8

Patterns in this list include many titles that help readers consider how a family in any setting can help or impede the growth of its members. Two compelling fantasies deal with individual responsibility and possibilities in a future setting or in an imagined world. As in the previous list, complex themes, characters, and literary presentations put new but not unmanageable demands on young adult readers.

Suggestions for author studies include Avi, Sue Ellen Bridgers, Peter Dickinson, Russell Freedman, Diana Wynne Jones, William Sleator, Cynthia Voigt, plus many others on the previous three grade lists.

1. *All Together Now* by Sue Ellen Bridgers. New York: Knopf, 1979. (Bantam)
    While spending the summer with her grandparents, twelve-year-old Casey makes friends with a retarded man and begins to

consider responsibility, friendship, and the nature of families in this richly characterized, often humorously told, novel.

2. (E) *The Borning Room* by Paul Fleischman. New York: HarperCollins, 1991. (Harper)

A short, powerful novel of the memories of an Ohio farm girl, told solely through scenes centering on the room in the family's house where people die and are born. Besides being a remarkable picture of frontier life from the mid-1800s through into the new century, this story shows how an author incorporates effortlessly the historical research that makes the period come alive. Runaway slaves, seances, electricity, the endless cycles of farm life, chloroform as a wonder drug, and rural entertainment come to life in Fleischman's powerful story of one life cycle. Help readers see the many allusions, metaphors, and similes Fleischman uses so seamlessly. See also the four-generation story Jericho by Janet Hickman (New York: Greenwillow, 1994).

3. *Borrowed Children* by George Ella Lyon. New York: Orchard, 1988. (COP)

Mandy knows her ticket out of her Kentucky hill house is education and is brokenhearted to have to stay home to care for the latest addition to her siblings in the 1920s. But a well-earned trip to Memphis relatives becomes a journey of self-discovery and gives her a new perspective, both on her family and on her dreams.

4. *Crazy Lady* by Jane Conly. New York: HarperCollins, 1993. (   )

Vernon, an academic failure, hangs out in the Baltimore streets desperate to resolve his problems. He is befriended by Maxine and Roland, an alcoholic and her retarded son, both of whom Vernon used to taunt. A retired teacher Maxine finds to tutor Vernon asks as payment that he help the boy and his mother, which tests but eventually reveals Vernon's true strengths. Poignant, contemporary, true, and many readers will identify with the pain of exclusion and the problems and rewards of compassion.

5. *Eva* by Peter Dickinson. New York: Delacorte, 1989. (Dell)

In a future time, a girl's brain is trans-

planted into a chimpanzee's body, partly to save her life but partly to further research. This passionate and eloquent story raises questions about ecology, responsible science, and the nature of humankind.

6. (E) *The Highwayman* by Alfred Noyes, illustrated by Charles Keeping. New York: Oxford University Press, 1981. (COP)

This tragic narrative poem of love and loyalty is dramatically illustrated. Keeping reverses his striking pictures from black on white to a ghostly white on black after the highwayman's death.

7. (E) *I Am Wings: Poems About Love* by Ralph Fletcher. New York: Bradbury, 1994. (   )

Taken singly, each poem is about some aspect of adolescent love. But, read as a narrative, the collection could chronicle a relationship from first glance to final breaking up from the standpoint of a boy. Good reading and free-verse approach encourages writers to try their own hands at unrhymed poems that convey strong feelings. See also Paul Janeczko's anthology Preposterous: Poems of Youth (New York: Orchard, 1991).

8. *I Will Call It Georgie's Blues* by Suzanne Newton. New York: Viking, 1983. (Dell Yearling)

Controlled by the conservative views of his minister family and expectations of his small southern town, fifteen-year-old Neal secretly studies to be a jazz pianist. A coming-of-age story compellingly told.

9. *The Moves Make the Man* by Bruce Brooks. New York: Harper & Row, 1984. (Harper)

A white boy and African-American boy form a tenuous friendship based on their admiration for each other's sports prowess, one in baseball, the other in basketball. Themes of overcoming prejudice, dealing with mental illness, and growing up, as well as near-poetic descriptions of playing "hoop."

10. *Nothing But the Truth* by Avi. New York: Orchard, 1991. (Avon)

A ninth grader failing English can't participate in sports. His plan to be transferred from both his English teacher and a failing grade is to hum the national anthem when it is played over the loud-speaker. The ensuing events become issues of First Amendment rights and of national attention. Thoughtfully presented ideas in a variety of formats, from letters and memos to newspaper articles, speech transcripts, and diary entries by one of children's literature's most challenging writers.

11. *The Outsiders* by S. E. Hinton. New York: Viking, 1967. (Dell Yearling)

    In this classic gang novel, "Greasers" face death and struggle with peer relationships, poverty, and a search for self. Realistically written and fast paced.

12. *Scorpions* by Walter Dean Myers. New York: Harper & Row, 1988. (Harper Keypoint)

    When Jamal inherits gang leadership and a gun from his imprisoned brother, he can't seem to find a way out. Gritty portrayal of the consequences of impetuous action set in Harlem.

13. *Shabanu: Daughter of the Wind* by Suzanne Fisher Staples. New York: Knopf, 1989. (Random)

    At twelve, the youngest daughter of a modern-day Pakistani camel herder knows her culture demands that she must be married but chafes against her fate. A vivid portrayal of life and death in the desert world and a dramatic coming-of-age story of a brave young girl. (Series)

14. *So Far From the Bamboo Grove* by Yoko Kawashima Watkins. New York: Lothrop, Lee and Shepard, 1986. (Beech Tree)

    This fictionalized autobiography tells of eleven-year-old Yoko's escape from Korea to Japan in 1945, when Korea was ridding itself of anyone with hated Japanese ancestry. A harrowing story of courage with a unique perspective on World War II. See also Year of Impossible Goodbyes *by Sook Nyul Choi (Boston: Houghton Mifflin, 1991), which takes place within the same setting and time period. (Series)*

15. *A Solitary Blue* by Cynthia Voigt. New York: Atheneum, 1984. (Scholastic)

    The gradual development of a loving relationship between Jeff and his divorced father takes place only after Jeff, too, has been psychologically wounded by his irre-sponsible mother. Dicey Tillerman, from Voigt's other novels, figures in Jeff's healing as well. (Series)

16. (E) *Toning the Sweep* by Angela Johnson. New York: Orchard, 1993. (Scholastic)

    Moving among different perspectives, the author skillfully tells parts of the story of three generations. Fourteen-year-old Emily has come with her mother to move her cancer-ridden grandmother Ola from the desert back to Cleveland. Past events from Ola's Alabama upbringing, Emmie's mother's inability to face the fact of her father's brutal murder as an "uppity nigger," and Emmie's newfound courage blend into an emotional story about facing life squarely.

17. *Traitor: The Case of Benedict Arnold* by Jean Fritz. New York: Viking, 1981. (Puffin)

    Arnold's enthusiastic, impetuous, and reckless personality leads him finally to disappointment and treason. A gripping biography of a complex personality seen against the Revolutionary War period.

18. *A Wizard of Earthsea* by Ursula LeGuin, illustrated by Ruth Robbins. New York: Parnassus Press, 1968. (Bantam)

    Pride and arrogance cause Ged, a young wizard, to call up a shadow that threatens all of Earthsea until Ged can face what he has done. Powerful themes of maintaining balance and harmony, personal responsibility, and self-knowledge, as well as an elegant telling, make this classic high fantasy a standard against which others are measured. (Series)

Grades 9 and 10

The concerns, conflicts, pain, and discoveries of adolescents dominate the literature on this list. Characters struggle with pressure from their peers and parents and with the harsh realities of twentieth-century society. Traditional classics and very current fiction are both represented for students to discover great literature and models for their own writing. A special effort has been made to add literature that explores human differences—racial, cultural, physical, and psychological.

1. *Betsey Brown* by Ntozake Shange. New York: St. Martin's Press, 1985. (St. Martin's)

    Thirteen-year-old Betsey is part of a large, boisterous black family living in St. Louis in 1959, the year of forced school integration. Besides the normal problems and wonders of adolescence, sexual awakenings, fitting in with the group, and self-identity crises, Betsey must quickly learn about racial hatred and how to deal with it. The novel raises questions about how cultural heritage affects identity and what social activism costs in human terms.

2. *Bless the Beasts and the Children* by Glendon Swarthout. New York: Doubleday, 1970. (Pocketbooks)

    A group of emotionally handicapped adolescents grow in maturity and self-esteem through their sensitivity to the plight of the buffaloes near their Arizona camp. Readers are challenged by the storytelling through dream sequences and flashbacks in this coming-of-age novel and drawn to its conservationist theme.

3. *The Catcher in the Rye* by J. D. Salinger. Boston: Little, Brown, 1951. (Bantam)

    This classic young adult novel presents the conflicts of innocence and experience and adolescent angst in an irreverent, touching way. Students identify with Holden Caulfield through his run-ins with authority, parents, and insensitive people everywhere. Invites discussion of issues of sexuality, individuality, ethics, and moral values.

4. (E) *The Chocolate War* by Robert Cormier. New York: Pantheon, 1974. (Dell)

    A powerful story of a high school boy who refuses to sell chocolates for his Catholic high school. Jerry stands up against the cold and calculating Brother Leon and the school's secret society. Encourages students to question the uses of power and authority and the responsibilities of the individual to "dare to disturb the universe."

5. (E) *Eight Plus One* by Robert Cormier. New York: Pantheon, 1980. (Dell)

    Cormier's nine short stories are glimpses into the daily lives and concerns of young people: the mystical world of fathers, the shifting of adolescent friendships, discov-eries about love, and the mistakes of youth. Cormier's brief stories are mirrors for students to look into and see themselves.

6. *Fahrenheit 451* by Ray Bradbury. New York: Ballantine, 1953. (Ballantine)

    Told with poetic power, a classic science fiction tale filled with technological wonders and a chilling warning of the dangers of censorship. Montag is a fireman in the cold and ominous future where fires are not extinguished but used to destroy books, the enemy of people in a world where thinking is dangerous. Connects with current issue of language censorship.

7. *Forbidden City* by William Bell. New York: Bantam Starfire, 1990. (Bantam Starfire)

    At age seventeen Alex has the rare opportunity to witness history when his photo-journalist father is assigned to cover Beijing during the 1989 student democratic uprising in Tiananmen Square. Along with Alex the reader acquires a quick education in Chinese politics and customs, but when friends and acquaintances become targets of political reprisal and eventually all foreigners' lives are endangered, the reporter's fascination turns to horror and despair. Students will be exposed to the personal loss and destruction that war as presented in history books seldom teaches. See also Emily Neville's The China Year *(New York: HarperCollins, 1991), which takes place in the same time frame.*

8. (E) *The Girl in the Box* by Ouida Sebestyen. Boston: Little, Brown, 1988. (Bantam)

    A sixteen-year-old girl writes notes to the world from a small cellar room where she is being held after a kidnapping. Her only solace is a typewriter; with it she attempts to make sense of the crime, her fear, and, in the process, her life as a teen-ager. Unusual style and "audience" make for interesting writing model. Issues of mortality and the enduring human spirit may prompt discussion.

9. *A Hero Ain't Nothin' But a Sandwich* by Alice Childress. New York: Coward, McCann & Geoghegan, 1973. (Putnam)

    Benjie is a young African-American boy struggling for identity in the ghetto and rapidly becoming addicted to heroin. Told by a variety of narrators and viewpoints, this short novel offers insights into the roles of friends, teachers, and family in their efforts to help Benjie and the complex forces that propel the boy toward his escape from the bleak world around him.

10. *The Hitchhiker's Guide to the Galaxy* by Douglas Adams. New York: Crown, 1979. (Pocket Books) *(Series)*

   A comic science fiction story of the end of the world and one human's consequent outer space adventures. Adams' characters are as likely to say something significant as absurd in this satire of our bureaucratic systems and materialistic values. Readers enjoy the word play and wit of this hip, well-written story, the first of a series by Adams.

11. (E) *Home before Dark* by Sue Ellen Bridgers. New York: Knopf, 1976. (Bantam)

   Vivid characterization pulls readers into the world of a family of migrant workers searching for roots. Excellent writing models for teenage writers in this story of a girl's strength and love. It may prompt reactions to issues of sexual desire and family loyalties.

12. (E) *The Island* by Gary Paulsen. New York: Franklin Watts, 1988. (Dell)

   Very unusual style and structure make this novel of self-discovery an interesting study for young readers. At fifteen, Wil Neuton finds an island one summer that wakens him to nature, meditation, art, and writing as a way to his own growth. Each chapter opens with an entry from Wil's journal, and interspersed with the traditional narration are Wil's own pieces of writing. Students may be led to ask questions about the meanings of their own existence through their reading.

13. (E) *Jack* by A. M. Homes. New York: Macmillan, 1989. (Vintage)

   Fifteen-year-old Jack has juggled loyalties to his divorced mother and father for three years after an acrimonious divorce, and is devastated when he learns that his father is gay. Through the help of his friends and the efforts of his parents, Jack begins to accept the circumstances and how they affect him. The need for self-acceptance

and tolerance for differences is particularly important for young people; this novel offers an opportunity to explore this sensitively.

14. *Kaffir Boy* by Mark Mathabane. New York: Macmillan, 1986. (NAL)

   Autobiography of an African-American boy growing up with the horrors of poverty and racial persecution in modern South Africa. The experiences of Johannes and his family give students a real glimpse into the struggles that beset blacks in South Africa.

15. (E) *Linger* by M. E. Kerr. New York: HarperCollins, 1993. (   )

   When his brother leaves with the other enlisted men to fight in the Gulf War and the town beauty becomes his brother's pen pal, Gary feels nothing but envy for his brother. By the novel's end Gary is wiser about the realities of war, about relationships, and about hypocrisy among the rich and respectable in his small town. Students will find the theme of appearance vs. reality on several levels worth discussion in this story concerning recent history.

16. (E) *Lizard* by Dennis Covington. New York: Delacorte, 1991. (Dell)

   Lizard is a remarkable character, a fourteen-year-old boy deformed from birth with eyes that look different directions and a nose flattened to one side. Committed to the state school for the retarded by an uncaring parent, Lizard learns that his future is up to him. When a group of itinerant actors free him to play Caliban in their production of Shakespeare's "The Tempest," Lizard learns about human nature and discovers his own humanity. This finely written novel will prompt discussion about our feelings about people with disabilities and makes an excellent companion to the study of "The Tempest."

17. (E) *The Man from the Other Side* by Uri Orlev. Boston: Houghton Mifflin, 1991. (   )

   True story of a fourteen-year-old boy's experience in Warsaw during World War II. Marek discovers for himself how the Nazis are persecuting the Jews as he and his Catholic father sell food and supplies to Jews in hiding. An exciting story of risky intrigues and narrow escapes, this story also provides young readers an insight about the period of the Holocaust from a new perspective.

18. *The Miracle Worker* by William Gibson. New York: Atheneum, 1960. (Bantam)

    Inspiring dramatization of the story of Helen Keller and her remarkable teacher Anne Sullivan. Students are fascinated by the violent struggle between Anne and Helen. Gibson's focus allows students to see the handicaps of each member of the family, and readers gain insight into how we all handicap ourselves. It also invites the study of stagecraft.

19. *Night* by Elie Wiesel. New York: Hill & Wang, 1960. (Bantam)

    A personal account of a teenage boy's terrifying experiences in the Nazi death camps of World War II. Students identify with Elie through the first-person narrative. The stark reality of the events of the Holocaust promotes study of survival behavior and provokes student interest in this important historical event.

20. *Night Kites* by M. E. Kerr. New York: Harper & Row, 1986. (HarperCollins)

    Seventeen-year-old Erick is an average teenager facing the adolescent concerns of dating, friendships, and school, but must come to terms with a much more devastating problem when he learns that his older brother has AIDS. Readers are presented with realistic conflict for discussion of family reaction to homosexuality and disease.

21. *Of Mice and Men* by John Steinbeck. New York: Viking, 1938. (Viking Penguin)

    Classic American novel of the Depression era in our history and a very readable book. Students are drawn into the friendship between the mentally retarded Lennie and his companion George. Offers readers both an important view of America and an opportunity to examine their own needs for attention, love, and friendship.

22. *Reflections on a Gift of Watermelon Pickle*, edited by Stephen Dunning et al. New York: Lothrop, Lee and Shepard 1966. ( )

    A now-classic collection of modern verse by a wide variety of well- and little-known poets arranged in short thematic sections or grouped by subject matter. A wealth of poetic forms and ideas for student writing or talking.

23. (E) *Running Loose* by Chris Crutcher. New York: Morrow, 1983. (Dell)

    The humorous, gently sarcastic tone of the narration pulls readers into this book about adolescent pressures to succeed and be popular. Struggles of conscience of the main character provide excellent entries into discussion and self-questioning for teenage readers.

24. *Somehow Tenderness Survives* selected by Hazel Rochman. New York: Harper & Row, 1988. (HarperCollins)

    These ten stories of the pain and sadness of racial separation in southern Africa are powerful and very moving records of loss felt by both white and black people. Told by such fine writers as Nadine Gordimer and Doris Lessing, each story focuses on relationships strained or torn by the attitudes of apartheid. An excellent personal history, and also an opportunity for students to experience the personal effects of society's unjust laws.

25. (E) *Somewhere in the Darkness* by Walter Dean Myers. New York: Scholastic, 1992. (Scholastic)

    Jimmy Little is a fourteen-year-old boy who lives in New York with Mama Jean, his only known "mother," when suddenly his father who has been in prison shows up at his door. Myers's depiction of a boy discovering what it means to have a father and a man trying to learn to be a father as they travel across the U.S. is sensitive and engaging. The novel offers students a chance to question the responsibilities of children to their parents, and vice versa, and perhaps to reevaluate the power of parental love.

26. *A Summer Life* by Gary Soto. Hanover, NH: University Press of New England, 1990. (Dell)

    These brief stories and essays by and about a Chicano boy growing up in southern California wonderfully present the imagination and energy of youth. Writing with rich imagery and vivid language, Soto conveys the innocence, humor, joy, and pain of children spending their summer days amid rust and garbage on the hot, weed-covered asphalt of Los Angeles. These pieces are excellent models for student personal writing.

27. (E) *Visions*, edited by Donald R. Gallo. New York: Dell, 1987. (Dell)

    Nineteen short stories by authors familiar to and loved by young adults explore issues of acceptance by peers, asserting independence, desire and longing—a full range of adolescent and human concerns. Variety in tone runs from tragic to comic, in subject from fantasy to gritty reality. Valuable source to engage teens in literature and the genre of the short story.

28. *A Yellow Raft on Blue Water* by Michael Dorris. New York: Holt, 1987. (Warner)

    This stylistically interesting story, told through three narrators, a daughter, mother, and grandmother, presents the struggles of an American Indian family to accept the bleak remains of their heritage on the reservation. Rayona is fifteen, the daughter of a black man and Indian woman and trying to understand a mother who seems not to care for her, but when the same events are revealed through other points of view, the novel takes on tragic power. The book may prompt exploration of diverse points of view and acceptance of differences.

Grades 11 and 12

War and survival, mental illness, social injustice, and personal versus societal responsibility are some of the many themes explored in the literature from this list. Students nearing adulthood may satisfy their needs to answer questions about the world through their reading of serious, thought-provoking literature. Again, new books have been selected to reflect racial and cultural diversity for students to explore.

1. *After the First Death* by Robert Cormier. New York: Pantheon, 1979. (Dell)

   Political thriller about terrorists who hijack a busload of children. Readers view the situation through the eyes of Miro, a

young, well-trained killer; Katie, the teenage bus driver; and Ben, the son of a patriotic general. These young views bring into a public drama the issue of what matters more, human life and emotion or political systems and loyalties.

2. *Black Ice* by Lorene Cary. New York: Knopf, 1991. (Vintage)

   True account of the life of a teenage African-American girl from a poor family dealing with the challenges and pressures of attending an Ivy League prep school in New Hampshire. The author, who eventually became a teacher herself, confronts social and racial stereotypes with respect to education. An inspiring story of success in overcoming barriers, this account will help young people understand the social pressures black teenagers face today.

3. *Black Voices*, edited by Abraham Chapman. New York: New American Library, 1968. (NAL)

   A lengthy anthology of poetry, short stories, fiction, and nonfiction by African-American writers, with biographical sketches. Provides serious readers with a survey of African-American literature. Also offers humor, engaging narratives, and thought-provoking short pieces for important discussion of racial conditions in this country.

4. *Children of a Lesser God* by Mark Medoff. Salt Lake City: Gibbs M. Smith, 1987. (Gibbs M. Smith)

   An award-winning play about a teacher who falls in love with one of his students, a young deaf woman, and tries to bridge the gap between the hearing and deaf worlds. In the process, he learns about the strength and dignity of deaf people. This very readable and engaging drama will enable students to gain an understanding of deaf attitudes and culture.

5. (E) *Fallen Angels* by Walter Dean Myers. New York: Scholastic, 1988. (Scholastic)

   Told by a young African-American man from the streets of New York, this story of a tour of duty in Vietnam evokes the boredom and terror of soldiers thrown into a war they do not understand or know how to fight. Racial conflict mixes with the conflicts of conscience and courage that characterize war novels. Provides valuable context for understanding contemporary American history.

6. *The House on Mango Street* by Sandra Cisneros. New York: Vintage, 1989. (Vintage)

A *personal account of a girl and her Mexican family growing up in Chicago. Told with poetic language and sensitive detail, this series of brief vignettes documents the pain and joy of adolescent longings amidst the poverty and prejudice experienced by the Latino community. The creativity and power of these stories will serve as writing models for young writers and offer experiences for discussion about the point of view of a minority group.*

7. *I Know Why the Caged Bird Sings* by Maya Angelou. New York: Random House, 1969. (Bantam)

An *African-American woman tells her moving story of childhood and adolescence. Angelou's writing is fresh, engaging, and poetic. She offers insights about African-American values and culture as well as the pain and joy of being young. Invites personal response from students.*

8. (E) *I Had Seen Castles* by Cynthia Rylant. New York: Harcourt Brace, 1993. (   )

As *an old man, John Dante recalls his life at seventeen as he experienced America's reaction to Pearl Harbor and the emotional build-up to his enlisting to fight in World War II. This sad, poignant story brings out the cruelty and terrible injustice of war as it affects two young people in love. Very simple and moving, the novel may prompt students to think of war in real and personal terms.*

9. (E) *If Rock and Roll Were a Machine* by Terry Davis. New York: Delacorte, 1992. (Bantam)

Bert *Bowden is a seventeen-year-old boy who has suffered a year of humiliation from a grade-school teacher who was trying to cure his impulsive behavior, but who has destroyed his spirit and self-confidence. Through the love and parenting of a high school teacher and a middle-aged biker, he begins to value himself. The novel's interesting style may inspire some*

student experimentation with narration; the concept of gaining self-respect through integrity will appeal to teenage readers.

10. *In Country* by Bobbie Ann Mason. New York: Harper & Row, 1985. (HarperCollins)

Coming *to terms with the scars from the Vietnam War in small-town Kentucky during the 1980s, this book shows the pain and confusion of vets and their families. Well-drawn characters and an interesting narrative style. Provides students with insights about conflicting attitudes toward this war and may prompt comparisons to current global events.*

11. (E) *Join In,* edited by Donald R. Gallo. New York: Delacorte, 1993. (   )

Seventeen *short stories of characters from a variety of ethnic backgrounds, this collection examines the lives of American Indians, Puerto Ricans, Vietnamese, and others as they deal with life in America. Told by well-known and respected young adult writers and others, these stories offer insights to student readers about a variety of cultures and ways of looking at the world as well as prompt self-examination of attitudes Americans have about people of other cultural backgrounds.*

12. *A Lesson Before Dying* by Ernest J. Gaines. New York: Knopf, 1993. (   )

Set *in Louisiana in the 1940s, this novel about a young black man seeking dignity amid racial intolerance demonstrates the power of helping our fellow man. A young black teacher visits a condemned teenager in prison to teach him how to die and gains his own reward, an understanding of his own sense of humanity. An excellent historical document and, more importantly, a fine work of fiction that offers students an opportunity to explore the question of what it means to be human.*

13. *Lord of the Flies* by William Golding. New York: Putnam, 1954. (Perigee)

Classic *British novel of the ancient struggle between civilization and chaos. Rich details of setting offer students opportunities for seeing craftsmanship while physical and moral conflicts provide for discussion topics.*

14. (E) *Memory* by Margaret Mahy. New York: Macmillan, 1987. (Dell)

   Students may empathize with the plight of the elderly in this story of a teenager's reluctant involvement with an Alzheimer's disease victim. From the New Zealand setting readers also get a glimpse into political unrest there. Especially well-drawn characterization will engage students and spur inquiry into their social responsibility to the elderly.

15. (E) *Midnight Hour Encores* by Bruce Brooks. New York: Harper & Row, 1986. (HarperCollins)

   Offers readers a glimpse into the life of a young musical prodigy through authentic details. Ideals of the hippie movement of the 1960s contrast with present-day realities of divorce and materialist values and raise worthwhile questions for young readers.

16. *The Nick Adams Stories* by Ernest Hemingway. New York: Scribner, 1972. (Scribner)

   Hemingway's stories of the young Nick in Michigan bring up issues important to young people: friendship, loyalty, love and sex, and peer pressure. Very readable. Hemingway's powerful narratives are filled with the ambiguity and mystery of adolescence. An excellent source for discussion and writing ideas.

17. *One Flew over the Cuckoo's Nest* by Ken Kesey. New York: Viking, 1962. (NAL)

   Kesey's antihero, R. P. McMurphy, is both a scoundrel and a saint as he helps a group of beaten men overcome the system that has destroyed their manhood. The uses and misuses of power and the belief in oneself are important questions for students to consider in this classic contemporary novel.

18. *Ordinary People* by Judith Guest. New York: Viking, 1976. (Viking Penguin)

   Story of a teenager's struggle to accept his brother's death and find his own identity. Conrad learns to face the demons of guilt and rejection that torture him and face up to his family, which is falling apart. Catalyst for study of family dynamics and pressures on young people today.

19. *A Raisin in the Sun* by Lorraine Hansberry. New York: Random House, 1959. (NAL)

   The voices of an African-American family struggling against poverty and with one another's needs pull readers into this drama. Family loyalty, the need for a strong black identity, and the frustration of the American dream just beyond the grasp of the Younger family are relevant for discussion.

20. (E) *Remembering the Good Times* by Richard Peck. New York: Delacorte, 1985. (Dell)

   First-person narrative of a young man recalling his bittersweet memories of junior high and high school, the powerful bonds of friendship forged with two friends, and the horror of dealing with the suicide of one. Very engaging prose style will pull readers into the story. May inspire study of psychological pressures of family life and society.

21. *A Separate Peace* by John Knowles. New York: Macmillan, 1959. (Bantam)

   The global conflict of World War II is the backdrop of this story of prep school students discovering their own sources of conflict. Shifting friendships and loyalties, peer pressure, and confusion about identity complicate the last days of youth before the war. High school students faced with pressures of the real world connect with these lives powerfully.

22. *Slaughterhouse-Five* by Kurt Vonnegut, Jr. New York: Delacorte, 1969. (Dell)

   The story of Billy Pilgrim's life, affected as it is by the devastation he witnessed in the bombing of Dresden, Germany, in World War II. The horrors of war and issues of government hypocrisy, individuality, and family intrigue students, and Vonnegut's humorous, offbeat style is engaging to young sensibilities.

23. *Soul Catcher* by Frank Herbert. New York: Putnam, 1972. (Berkley)

   An American Indian takes revenge against the white man for the oppression of his people by kidnapping the son of a state official. Authentic details of Indian culture and philosophy invite comparison to popular American thought and values.

Narrative techniques of multiple first person, letters, and news reports may offer students models for their own experimentation.

24. (E) *Staying Fat for Sarah Byrnes* by Chris Crutcher. New York: Greenwillow, 1993. (   )

    A novel about young people dealing courageously with the difficulties of child abuse and alienation. "Moby," a high school senior who has struggled with obesity since early childhood, fights to save his friend Sarah, whose scars from a terrible childhood burn have made her a social outcast. Young readers will find the novel engaging, and the themes of loyalty in friendship and dealing with the evil of child abuse worthy of discussion.

25. *The Tao of Pooh* by Benjamin Hoff. New York: Dutton, 1982. (Viking)

    This funny and thought-provoking explanation of ancient Chinese philosophy through the stories of Pooh, Piglet, Eeyore, Rabbit, and Christopher Robin are lessons about how to live our lives from a refreshingly offbeat point of view. Students will gain a rudimentary understanding of Daoism, enjoy the wit and humor of Hoff, and find in these parables rather esoteric concepts to be explored.

26. *Wide Sargasso Sea* by Jean Rhys. New York: Norton, 1966. (Norton)

    A prequel to Brontë's Jane Eyre, *this novel tells the story of a young native Caribbean girl's life as a mixed child of British and Jamaican heritage from childhood through marriage and immigration to England. A finely written account of the attitudes and prejudices of traditional views toward "natives" told in stream-of-consciousness style, the novel will provoke discussion about various types of prejudice in a male-dominated world.*

Multicultural Book List

For full publishing information and annotations for the following titles, please refer to the page numbers given below.

African-American/Black Culture

Adventures of Spider, The. See page 123b.

Alvin Ailey. See page 151b.

Amazing Grace. See page 123b.

Anansi and the Moss-Covered Rock. See page 119b.

Betsey Brown. See page 160b.

Black Ice. See page 163b.

Black Voices. See page 163b.

Bright Eyes, Brown Skin. See page 114b.

Cat's Purr, The. See page 138b.

Chicken Sunday. See page 129b.

Country Far Away, A. See page 124b.

Cousins. See page 142b.

Dream Keeper, The. See page 139b.

Eating Fractions. See page 120b.

Fallen Angels. See page 163b.

Feast for 10. See page 107b.

Flying. See page 120b.

Fortune-Teller, The. See page 130b.

Freight Train. See page 107b.

Galimoto. See page 125b.

Girl Called Boy, A. See page 155b.

Go Fish. See page 135b.

Gold Cadillac, The. See page 143b.

Hero Ain't Nothin' But a Sandwich, A. See page 160b.

Honey I Love: And Other Poems. See page 125b.

House of Dies Drear, The. See page 156b.

Hundred Penny Box, The. See page 135b.

I Know Why the Caged Bird Sings. See page 164b.

I Need a Lunch Box. See page 120b.

Jamaica's Find. See page 121b.

James Weldon Johnson. See page 151b.

Jayhawker. See page 156b.

Join In. See page 164b.

Joshua James Likes Trucks. See page 115b.

Journey to Jo'burg. See page 144b.

Jump Ship to Freedom. See page 140b.

Kaffir Boy. See page 161b.

Lesson Before Dying, A. See page 164b.

Letters from a Slave Girl. See page 144b.

Maya Angelou. See page 152b.

Me & Neesie. See page 126b.

Me, Mop, and the Moondance Kid. See page 140b.

Middle of Somewhere, The. See page 156b.

More Stories Julian Tells. See page 132b.

Moves Make the Man, The. See page 158b.

Mufaro's Beautiful Daughters. See page 132b.

My Best Friend. See page 121b.

Nathaniel Talking. See page 132b.

Nettie's Trip South. See page 132b.

Niki's Walk. See page 150b.

One of Three. See page 122b.

Pass It On. See page 127b.

Patchwork Quilt, The. See page 127b.

People Could Fly, The. See page 141b.

Raisin in the Sun, A. See page 165b.

Red Dancing Shoes. See page 108b.

Roll of Thunder, Hear My Cry. See page 144b.

Scorpions. See page 159b.

Shaka, King of the Zulus. See page 153b.

Sister. See page 156b.

Somehow Tenderness Survives. See page 162b.

Something Upstairs. See page 144b.

Song of the Trees. See page 137b.

Somewhere in the Darkness. See page 162b.

Spin a Soft Black Song. See page 141b.

Stories Julian Tells, The. See page 127b.

Tales of Uncle Remus, The. See page 133b.

Talking Eggs, The. See page 127b.

Tell Me a Story, Mama. See page 148b.

Ten Nine Eight. See page 109b.

Three Wishes. See page 127b.

Toning the Sweep. See page 159b.

Uncle Jed's Barbershop. See page 133b.

Wagon Wheels. See page 128b.

Weed is a Flower, A. See page 153b.

What a Wonderful World. See page 116b.

When I Was Little. See page 148b.

Wide Sargasso Sea. See page 166b.

Wiley and the Hairy Man. See page 123b.

Yo! Yes? See page 109b.

Asian-American/Asian Culture

Chi-Hoon. See page 139b.

Child of the Owl. See page 142b.

Dragon's Gate. See page 155b.

Dragon's Pearl, The. See page 139b.

El Chino. See page 151b.

Forbidden City. See page 160b.

Grandfather's Journey. See page 135b.

Halmoni and the Picnic. See page 130b.

How My Parents Learned to Eat. See page 125b.

I Hate English. See page 131b.

In the Year of the Boar and Jackie Robinson. See page 139b.

Join In. See page 164b.

Journey to Topaz. See page 140b.

Lon Po Po. See page 126b.

Onion Tears. See page 141b.

Rabbit's Judgment. See page 127b.

Sachiko Means Happiness. See page 136b.

Sadako and the Thousand Paper Cranes. See page 144b.

Seven Blind Mice. See page 109b.

So Far from the Bamboo Grove. See page 159b.

Tiger. See page 137b.

Yang the Youngest and His Terrible Ear. See page 137b.

Year of the Panda, The. See page 134b.

Yeh Shen. See page 138b.

Latino

Abuela. See page 123b.

Abuela's Weave. See page 129b.

Amelia's Road. See page 124b.

Baseball in April. See page 154b.

Borreguita and the Coyote. See page 124b.

Carlos and the Squash Plant. See page 153b.

Chair for My Mother, A. See page 119b.

Class President. See page 139b.

Diego. See page 153b.

El Chino. See page 151b.

Family Pictures. See page 146b.

Friday Night is Papa Night. See page 125b.

Gold Coin, The. See page 135b.

Grab Hands and Run. See page 155b.

Great Kapok Tree, The. See page 125b.

House on Mango Street, The. See page 164b.

I Speak English for My Mom. See page 131b.

I'm New Here. See page 131b.

Join In. See page 164b.

Little Painter of Sabana Grande, The. See page 126b.

Margaret and Margarita. See page 154b.

Most Beautiful Place in the World, The. See page 136b.

New Shoes for Sylvia. See page 108b.

Picture Book of Simon Bolivar, A. See page 152b.

Piñata. See page 112b.

Piñata Maker, The. See page 154b.

Skirt, The. See page 133b.

Summer Life, A. See page 162b.

Too Many Tamales. See page 122b.

Uncle Nacho's Hat. See page 154b.

Vejigante Masquerader. See page 133b.

Walk in the Rainforest, A. See page 154b.

Woman Who Outshone the Sun, The. See page
    154b.

Native American

Annie and the Old One. See page 129b.
Courage of Sarah Noble, The. See page 124b.
Discovery of the Americas, The. See page 130b.
Double Life of Pocahontas, The. See page 151b.
Indian Chiefs. See page 151b.
Island of the Blue Dolphins. See page 143b.
Join In. See page 164b.
Julie of the Wolves. See page 156b.
Knots on a Counting Rope. See page 131b.
Last Princess, The. See page 152b.
Mama, Do You Love Me? See page 107b.
Morning Girl. See page 140b.
Raven. See page 132b.
Rough-Face Girl, The. See page 136b.
Sign of the Beaver, The. See page 144b.
Soul Catcher. See page 165b.
Stone Fox. See page 133b.
Toughboy and Sister. See page 142b.
Yellow Raft on Blue Water, A. See page 163b.

Appendix A:
A Folk/Fairy
Tale Unit for
Grades 3–6

Folk/fairy tales are stories that have been handed down through the years in oral or written form.

Older students may enjoy and appreciate a unit focusing on comparative analysis of variants of popular folk and fairy tales. Tales such as *Cinderella, Rumpelstiltskin, Sleeping Beauty, Beauty and the Beast, Hansel and Gretel,* and *Little Red Riding Hood* have popular versions from different countries. Check with your librarian for titles.

Younger students also enjoy listening to and comparing different versions of favorite fairy tales such as *The Three Bears, Little Red Riding Hood,* and *Stone Soup.*

Rationale for Doing a Unit on Folk and Fairy Tales

1. Folk/fairy tales are a literary genre that is part of children's cultural heritage.
2. Folk/fairy tales deal with important themes: good triumphs over evil, perseverance and hard work pay off; lucid thinking solves problems; unselfishness is rewarded; justice will be done.
3. While some fairy tales are very violent, they provide an acceptable way for children to deal with violence.
4. Children feel connected with parents and grandparents by reading the same tales that past generations have read.
5. Folk/fairy tales have a wonderful, rich vocabulary.
6. Folk/fairy tales are appealing to all children.
7. Folk/fairy tales stimulate children's imagination.
8. Children of varying abilities are exposed to different levels of meaning.
9. Folktales are important for understanding various customs and cultures.
10. A large selection of fairy tales is readily available from the school and/or public libraries, making it easy for the teacher to gather a classroom collection. (You do not need special funds to do a folk/fairy tale unit.)
11. If your school mandates the basal text, you can still supplement it—or set it aside for a month—with an authentic literature unit.

Larger Understandings/Major Concepts

1. Folk/fairy tales can be interpreted many different ways depending on point of view, country of origin, and culture.
2. A clearly defined differentiation between good and evil—as presented in folk/fairy tales—can heighten awareness of consequences of behavior and help students make connections to problems in our society that are not so clearly defined.

3. Some things in life, like folk/fairy tales, have remained consistent through the ages for parents and grandparents and can be a vehicle for connectedness between generations.

Planning

Plan on four to six weeks for an in-depth study. Divide the class heterogeneously into three groups for literature discussion, and be sure each student has a literature response log for recording reactions to the folktales. (See "Literature Response Logs" and "Literature Discussion Groups" in chapter 6 for procedures.) While some books will be read aloud by the teacher, most will be read silently by the students. Students keep a record of all folk/fairy tales read in their literature response log or in a separate folder (see Figure A-1).

Gather a collection of folk/fairy tales for the classroom, allowing at least four books per student. A class of twenty-five students should have about one hundred books. Some of these should be duplicate copies to allow for paired reading and small-group discussion. Try also to get as many different-quality versions of the tales as you can to allow for comparative analysis. See the bibliography at the end of this appendix for a sampling of folktales from our libraries that have worked well. You may also want to consult the following resources for specific titles, ideas, and other recommended resources. The unit presented here acknowledges the following valuable resources for some of the ideas and activities.

Figure A-1   Record of Folk/Fairy Tales Read by A Student

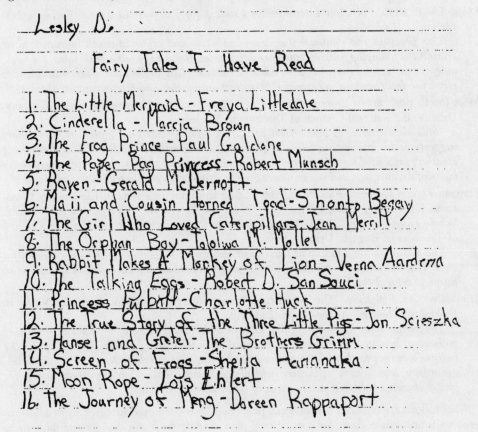

Lesley D.

Fairy Tales I Have Read

1. The Little Mermaid - Freya Littledale
2. Cinderella - Marcia Brown
3. The Frog Prince - Paul Galdone
4. The Paper Bag Princess - Robert Munsch
5. Raven - Gerald McDermott
6. Maii and Cousin Horned Toad - Shonto Begay
7. The Girl Who Loved Caterpillars - Jean Merrill
8. The Orphan Boy - Tololwa M. Mollel
9. Rabbit Makes A Monkey of Lion - Verna Aardema
10. The Talking Eggs - Robert D. San Souci
11. Princess Furball - Charlotte Huck
12. The True Story of the Three Little Pigs - Jon Scieszka
13. Hansel and Gretel - The Brothers Grimm
14. Screen of Frogs - Sheila Hamanaka
15. Moon Rope - Lois Ehlert
16. The Journey of Meng - Doreen Rappaport

Resources

Blatt, Gloria T. (ed.). 1993. *Once Upon a Folk Tale: Capturing the Folklore Process with Children.* New York: Teachers College Press. See annotation, p. 61b.

Bosma, Bette. 1992. *Fairy Tales, Fables, Legends, and Myths: Using Folk Literature in Your Classroom.* 2nd ed. New York: Teachers College Press. See annotation, p. 61b.

Goforth, Frances S., and Carolyn V. Spillman. 1994. *Using Folk Literature in the Classroom: Encouraging Children to Read and Write.* Phoenix, AZ: Oryx Press. See annotation, p. 65b.

Huck, Charlotte S., Susan Hepler, and Janet Hickman. 1993. "Traditional Literature." In *Children's Literature in the Elementary School.* 5th ed. (pp. 251–307). Fort Worth, TX: Harcourt Brace.

> *Various types of folktales are discussed, such as cumulative tales and beast tales. Characteristics of folktales, including plot structures, characterization, style, themes, and motifs, are elaborated. Variations of popular folk and fairy tales from around the world are shared.*

Hurst, Carol Otis. November–December 1985. "The World of Once upon a Time." *Early Years/K–8,* pp. 26–31.

> Carol Hurst presents thirty-five wonderful activities to go along with fairy tales. Pick and choose what will work for you and your students.

Moss, Joy F. 1994. "Modern Fairy Tales and Traditional Literature: Revisions and Retellings." In *Using Literature in the Middle Grades: A Thematic Approach* (pp. 43–62). Norwood, MA: Christopher-Gordon. See annotation, p. 69b.

Moss, Joy F. 1990. *Focus on Literature: A Context for Literacy Learning.* Katonah, NY: Richard C. Owen.

> *This practical text connects theory and practice and offers in-depth literature units around the following focuses: transformation tales, Baba Yaga tales, devil tales, cat tales, magic object tales, bird tales, wish tales, horse tales, Cinderella tales. Each unit includes plans for daily sessions, meaningful literature extensions, and bibliographies of tales.*

Moss Joy F. 1984. *Focus Units in Literature. A Handbook for Elementary School Teachers.* Urbana, IL: National Council of Teachers of English.

> *"Folktale Patterns: A Focus Unit for Grades Three and Four," pp. 107–124, offers suggestions for connecting folktales from different countries. References and teaching ideas are presented for three patterns: the theft of magical objects, the use of superpowers by helpful characters, and stories where greedy characters wind up with little ("circle tales").*

Spritzer, Daune Rebecca. Fall 1988. "Integrating the Language Arts in Elementary Classroom Using Fairy Tales, Fables, and Traditional Literature." *Oregon English.* Theme: *Whole Language,* pp. 23–26. (Journal available for purchase through National Council of Teachers of English, Urbana, Illinois)

> *The author shares a workable four- to six-week unit on folktales with lots of thoughtful ideas and activities for the classroom teacher. Included are examples of questions to promote critical thinking.*

Trousdale, Ann. Fall 1989. "The True Bride: Perceptions of Beauty and Feminine Virtue in Folktales." *The New Advocate,* pp. 239–248.

> *The author notes variants of fairy tales in which the virtues of the female characters go beyond beauty. For example, in* Mufaro's Beautiful Daughters *by John Steptoe, the heroine emerges for her character, not her beauty. Other tales cited have truthfulness, generosity, and loyalty as virtues held above beauty. This is an important article for giving students balanced perspectives of heroines in fairy tales.*

What follows are eighteen instructional plans that have been used successfully in a heterogeneous fourth-grade class. An instructional plan may be used one day, several days, or as long as several weeks. You will find that certain plans will need to be repeated to allow enough time for a concept or activity to be understood and fully discussed.

Allowing about one hour and thirty minutes each day for the folk/fairy tale unit has worked well. This time includes following through on the instructional plan as well as sharing problems and successes. For example, students and teacher may take the time to respond to a written draft of an original fairy tale or share completed storymaps or fairy tales. Note that samples of students' work that have been included come from average students.

The following plans are meant to be used only as a guide. You will want to change the sequence to suit your class needs, to delete some activities, and to add others.

Instructional Plan One: Characteristics of Fairy Tales (whole class)

Brainstorm with the class the characteristics of familiar fairy tales. Have a student act as scribe and list them on chart paper. Post the chart where it is easily visible and accessible. The chart is revised throughout the unit as new insights appear.

Characteristics usually mentioned include:

1. Happens in the past—time period not defined
2. Usually has a happy ending
3. May involve the supernatural
4. Often has a clear conflict between good and evil
5. Often begins with "Once upon a time"
6. Often includes a task, which if completed, brings a reward
7. All have plots and problems
8. Often includes a magic object/person to protect or help the main character
9. Often have brave heroes who rescue a helpless maiden
10. Main character sometimes gets fooled
11. Usually has to do with royalty
12. May have a fairy godmother, fairies, elves, or a witch

Instructional Plan Two: Characteristics of Fairy Tales (independently)

From the classroom collection of fairy tales you gathered, have the students select a fairy tale to read independently. Instructions to students: "Read your fairy tale silently. As you are reading, take notes in your literature response log on the characteristics you find that make this a fairy tale. Use the characteristics we listed on our chart, as well as any we may have missed."

After students have individually read the books or worked in pairs—jotting down the characteristics they found in their literature response logs—meet in literature discussion groups. Students share their discoveries.

Instructional Plan Three: Characteristics of Fairy Tales

As a whole-class activity, revise the list of characteristics on the chart. Students then select a new book and follow procedures for Instructional Plan 2. Sharing can be whole class, in pairs, or in discussion groups.

Instructional Plan Four: Comparative Analysis of Fairy Tale Variants (ongoing activity, can be combined with other plans)

Over a period of several weeks, read to the students, or have available for them to read silently, as many versions of one fairy tale as you can locate. Students note some of the points of difference in their logs. *Cinderella,* which has many variants, is one tale that works well. Students' favorites have included:

Cinderella by Charles Perrault; Amy Ehrlick, reteller; illustrated by Susan Jeffers (Dial, 1985).

Cinder Edna by Ellen Jackson, illustrated by Kevin O'Malley (Lothrop, Lee and Shepard, 1994). See annotation, p. 145b.

Mufaro's Beautiful Daughters by John Steptoe (Lothrop, Lee and Shepard, 1987). See annotation, p. 132b.

Princess Furball by Charlotte Huck, illustrated by Anita Lobel (Greenwillow, 1989).

The Rough Face Girl by Rafe Martin, illustrated by David Shannon (Putnam, 1992). See annotation, p. 136b.

The Talking Eggs by Robert D. San Souci, illustrated by Jerry Pinkney (Dial, 1989). See Annotation, p. 127b.

Yeh Shen: A Cinderella Story from China by Ai-Ling Louie, illustrated by Ed Young (Putnam, 1982). See annotation, p. 138b.

A comprehensive listing of *Cinderella* variants is included in *Focus on Literature* by Joy Moss, pp. 183–185. Check with your librarian for other well-known tales with multiple variants.

Instructional Plan Five: Settings in Fairy Tales

As a whole class, discuss what a setting is. Note the settings in tales read so far, and ask the children to be prepared to describe the setting in the tale they read today. In their logs, students write a paragraph describing the setting of their tale. After the tales have been read silently and paragraphs written, students meet in literature discussion group(s) and focus on the settings in their tales.

Instructional Plan Six: Use of Storymapping Format (demonstration)

Read aloud a favorite fairy tale and demonstrate, with input from the students, how to construct a storymap. This can be done on the chalkboard, on the overhead projector, or on large chart paper. This activity is done whole class with teacher guidance that invites student participation. Each student fills in his own copy of the storymap, which is kept and used as a reference model for constructing other storymaps (see Figure A-2).

Storymapping Format

Title of Story
Author
Setting (where and when)
Characters (who)
Problem
Action: 1, 2, 3. . .(as many as needed)
Resolution (use key words from the story)

Instructional Plan Seven: Storymapping (practice phase; repeat this activity two or three times)

Pair the children within a literature discussion group. Assign them the task of reading a self-selected fairy tale with their partner and mapping it according to the format (see Figure A-3). This activity can also be done individually or as a small group.

Instructional Plan Eight: Comparing/Contrasting Fairy Tales (optional; depends on availability; check with your librarian)

Show a film or filmstrip of a folk or fairy tale. Then read the book to the class and compare main character, setting, illustrations, and outcomes.

Which was more exciting? Which let you sense what was going to happen next more clearly? Which used more descriptive language? What elements of the fairy tale were different?

Instructional Plan Nine: Focusing on Magic

As a whole class, the element of magic is discussed as it has occurred in fairy tales read up to this point. Every student then selects and reads a new fairy tale independently. The students take notes in their literature response logs on:

- What if the magic didn't work?
- Find the magic moment in the fairy tale and speculate on what would happen if the magic failed.

Students share their speculations in literature discussion groups.

Figure A-2   A Storymap Done Whole Class With Teacher Guidance

Lindsay Kathleen
Campbell

STORY MAPPING FORMAT

Title of Story Hansel and Greatal By The Brothers Grimm

Setting (where and when) Large Forest, witches house, long ago

Characters (who) Hansel and Gretal and Woodcutter and witch

Problem Getting away and back home

Action

  1. stepmother kicking them out

  2. Lost in woods (2 times)   6. Getting home

  3. Captured by the witch

  4. Deal with the witch

  5. money / jewels

Resolution (use key words from the story)

      Jewels/stepmother gone/Kill Witch/
      Get home

Note: Resolution will tell how the problem was solved.

       Actions will be main happenings in the story.

Instructional Plan Ten: Dramatizing Fairy Tales

Since several fairy tales have been read by now, ask the children to name some that would be good for dramatization. List the tales on the board. Divide the children into small groups of four or five. Let each group select a tale from the list and prepare to act it out for the rest of the class. The groups should be instructed to keep the tales fairly simple. No costumes or scenery are necessary. Items on hand in the classroom can be used as props. After about thirty minutes, the students give their presentations. Students could use *Tales for Telling from Around the World* (Medlicott, 1992), which contains many tales to retell or dramatize.

Instructional Plan Eleven: Math Activity

Read aloud a version of *Little Red Riding Hood.* Then give the following homework assignment:

"How many miles is it to your grandmother's (or grandparents') house?"

The next day, have students push pins on a world map to show where grandmothers (or grandparents) live. Make a graph showing how many miles away most grandmothers live. This makes an interesting bulletin board.

Instructional Plan Twelve: Comparative Analysis of Fairy Tale Variants (may take several days)

Based on the many fairy tales students have now heard and read, brainstorm, whole class, the main categories that could be compared in the fairy tale variants. List the categories on the chalkboard. Some categories that fourth graders came up with for variants of *Cinderella*

Figure A-3   A Student's Storymap of Screen of Frogs

STORY MAPPING FORMAT

Title of Story Screen of Frogs

Setting (where and when) Long ago Japan

Characters (who) Koji Frog

Problem Koji does not want to work

Action

1. He begins selling the fields, lakes and mountains for money.
2. He only has one house, a lake and a mountain left.
3. The begs him not to sell his land.

(as many as needed)
4. He sells all his posesions and keeps the land.

Resolution (use key words from the story)

He learned the value of work.

Note: Resolution will tell how the problem was solved.

Actions will be main happenings in the story.

included: personalities of main character; qualities of Cinderella, stepmothers, or trouble-makers; why Cinderella was chosen as bride; helpers; ending.

In small groups of four or five have the students work together to make comparison charts. Students list the variants across the top of the chart. Each group chooses the categories it thinks are important to compare and lists them down the left side of the chart. See Figure A-4 for charts that resulted from two different groups. Each group then presents its findings to the entire class. Discussion with agreement and disagreement will result. Acting out favorite variants, for peers and other classes, can also follow this activity.

Instructional Plan Thirteen: Recognizing Different Points of View

This lesson will focus on recognizing a different point of view in fairy tales. Features of satire and parody can be included for older students. The teacher reads aloud *The True Story of the 3 Little Pigs* by A. Wolf as told to John Scieszka. This humorous tale convincingly presents a wolf's reasons for the misfortunes of the three pigs. Differences between this tale and the traditional tale elicit a lively discussion. Among other things, students note that point of view can make a difference in how a character is perceived.

Then ask the children to tell you the characteristics of a traditional prince and princess fairy tale. List them on the chalkboard. Next, read the nontraditional tale *The Paper Bag Princess* by Robert N. Munsch to the class. This is a facetious story of a modern-day princess who saves the prince and then decides he's not to her liking. (If you have multiple copies, students can read in pairs.) Following the reading, have the students answer the following question in their literature response logs: "What different points of view does the author present?"

Meet in response groups, or whole class, and share the contrasts between the traditional prince and princess tale and *The Paper Bag Princess*. See Figure A-5 for a chart that resulted from a whole-class discussion.

Use the book *The Girl Who Loved Caterpillars* (Merill, 1992), a telling of a young Japanese woman in twelfth-century Japan who resists social and family pressures as she befriends caterpillars and other socially unacceptable creatures. Have students discuss issues of inde-pendence and what the tale might have been like if the protagonist were male.

Instructional Plan Fourteen: Becoming Aware of the Role of Illustrations in Folk and Fairy Tales

Most notable fairy tales, such as *Moon Rope* (Ehlert, 1992) and *Raven: A Trickster Tale from the Pacific Northwest* (McDermott, 1993), have outstanding, vibrant illustrations. Discuss the role and impact of illustration in folk and fairy tales, the importance of art in different cultures, and compare illustration styles and techniques of different books. Also, use the "Author/Illustrator Books and Resources" on page 97b to share information about notable illustrators. Students can work in small groups to note characteristics and comparisons of illustrations in fairy tales. In preparation for writing their own fairy tales, they can begin to think about the role that illustration will play in their own tales.

Instructional Plan Fifteen: Developing a Good Lead for an Original Fairy Tale (may take several days)

Today students will concentrate on the way storytellers begin their stories. The teacher, or students working individually or in pairs, rereads just the first paragraph of several familiar fairy tales. Ask the students: "Which beginning makes you curious about what is going to happen? Why? Which beginning tells you the most about the story? What information does the author give in the first paragraph?"

Brainstorm a topic for the beginning of a fairy tale that the class could write about. Create

Figure A-4   Comparison Charts for "Cinderella" variants: Two Different Group Interpretatons

	Grimm's Cinderella	Perrault's Cinderella	Mufaro's Beautiful Daughters	Princess Furball	Vasilisa The Beautiful
Personalities of Main Character	Clever Sometimes depressed -Kind	nice/Kind smart sensitive mostly happy	Kind willing helpful giving generous	smart, Kind clever, tricky,	beautiful Kind loving Sweet giving willing
Why Prince or King chooses her	She's beautiful Kind -She's got nice clothes	She's pretty, has beautiful clothes, Kind, considerate	helpful past test Kind gentle willing beautiful	makes good soup beautiful giving	beautiful good weaver good helper cooperative
Helpers	Animals	fairy God mother	Nyoka and father	nurse	magic doll
~~Stepmother~~ ~~Trouble-~~ ~~matore~~ Family History	Mother dies replaced by step mother step mother brings two step sisters	Mother dies God mother helps Cinderella Cinderella has two stepsisters	no mother loveable father mean, picky, greedy sister	mother died	mother dies father remarries leaves town mother gives Vas. a magic doll
Ending	Gorry happily	There's a wedding happily ever after	prove sister wrong Marriage Happy Ending	marriage happy	wedding happy ending

"unedited"

	Grimm's Cinderella	Princess Furball	Mufaro's Beautiful Daughters	Tattercoats	Vasilisa The Beautiful
Personalities of Mischief-Makers	Stepsisters- greedy, spoild, jealous Stepmother- jealous, evil	father- promises hand in marrage to an Oger.	Manyana- selfish imiture selfcentered impolite, rude consided	Maids- inconsiderate grandfather- stubborn	Babayaga- 1/2 + 1/2 stepsisters-jealous rude, cruel, inconsiderate, selfish stepmother-self centered, self concieted
Qualities of Cinderella	Kind and pretty extremly Good	smart, Kind, beautiful genours	Kind, genours, caring, beautiful	beautiful, sad, getting happer every day	beautiful, Kind genours, Tough
Why choose Cinderella as bride	Because the shoe fit and beauty and the blood was running from the stepsisters feet	Food, Trickery + beauty.	Beautiful + kind to everyone.	He loved- Tattercoats for her beauty	Because she was beautifu and her very beautiful clothing
ending	doves-pecked out eyes of stepsisters. happily ever after for Cinderella	Happy ending for Furball	Happy ending for Nyasha	sadly ends for grandfather happily ends for Tattercoats	Vasalisa kept doll in pocket all the time stepsisters burnt to ashes
helpers	Birds	Nurse	Snake	goose Header geese	Doll

"unedited"

several beginnings as a shared writing. Analyze each one. Which one would make you want to read on? Why? (Use the overhead projector or large chart paper so students can refer back to the shared writing.)

Have the children work in partners and write the beginning of a fairy tale or rewrite a new beginning for a favorite tale. Share these beginnings in a response-group format, having students and the teacher note what is well done and offering suggestions for improvements.

Instructional Plan Sixteen: Revising a Good Lead (whole class)

Using a student's fairy tale beginning (with the student's permission) on the overhead projector, revise for content and clarity as a whole class. Then have students work in pairs revising their fairy tale beginnings. Share in response groups.

Instructional Plan Seventeen: Storymapping an Original Fairy Tale

Have students storymap the fairy tales they have started writing. This will cause them to plan the characters, the problem, the action, and the resolution. To clarify their storymap, students can also draw a picture of the characters in the setting. This enables the students to be descriptive in their writing. Have a sharing time at the end of the period. This activity will take more than one period.

Instructional Plan Eighteen: Writing an Original Fairy Tale

When students have mapped out their fairy tales and conferenced with the teacher or peer group, they may begin writing their fairy tale. The tale will go through the writing process:

Figure A-5   Comparison Chart from Whole-Class Discussion

**Comparing Traditional Tales with Princes and Princesses to
The Paperbag Princess by Robert Munsch**

Traditional Tale	The Paperbag Princess
Usual point of view	Different point of view
beautiful princess, beautifully dressed	beautiful, not well dressed (in paper bag)
helpless princess	independent princess, not helpless
kind prince	conceited prince
prince saves princess	princess saves prince
prince and princess get married	princess refuses to marry prince
not much humor	very humorous
evil person fought	evil force outwitted
ball, helping person	no ball, no helping person
happy ending	not happy about break-up, but happy to be
illustrations—clear, beautiful	separated from prince
begins "Once upon a time..."	illustrations—modern, humorous
ends "...happily ever after."	not usual beginning or ending words

Figures A-6 and A-7   Two Students' Mock Classified Ads

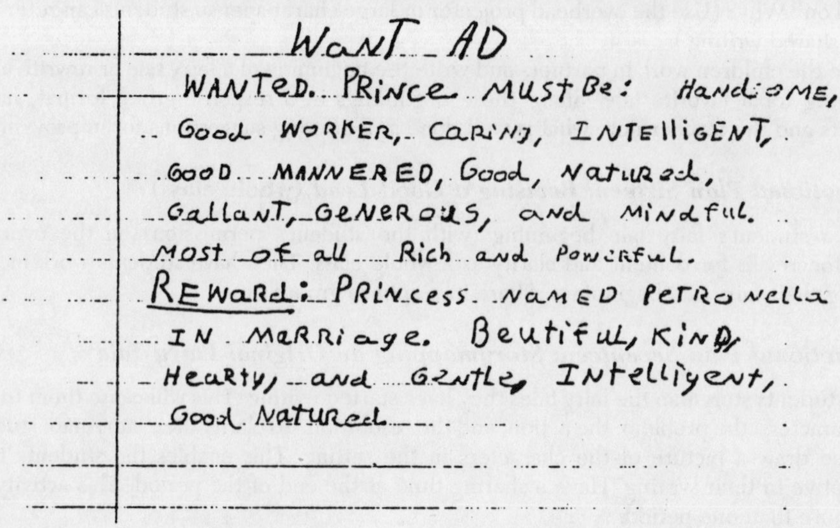

WanT AD

WANTeD. PRince MUSt Be: Handime,
Good WORKER, CaRinJ, INTElligeNT,
Good MANNERED, Good, Natured,
Gallant, GeNeROuS, and Mindful.
Most of all Rich and PowerfuL.
REWaRd: PRincess NAMED PeTRoNella
IN MaRRiage. Beutiful, KiNd,
Hearty, and Gentle, Intelliyent,
Good Natured

rough draft, conference, revision, editing, final copy. This will take several weeks to bring to completion. Completed tales are shared and displayed in the classroom.

Optional Activities (allow student choice)

(For students who have completed fairy tales and/or for end of unit projects)

- *Math activity*   Write down the fairy tales read in class. Have children select their favorites. (Pass out a survey or interview classmates.) Graph the results on a large chart.
- *Diary*   Write a diary entry as if you were the fairy tale character after a major event has occurred, for example, the Beast after Beauty fails to return, Cinderella after the ball, Little Red Riding Hood after she meets the wolf in the woods.
- *Filmstrip*   Using a kit for filmstrips that contains blank film and markers, have students make a filmstrip of a fairy tale. Students also prepare an accompanying script, which they read when presenting the filmstrip to the class.
- *New fairy tale*   Create a new version of a well-known tale. Have students storymap the tale first, and note how this version will be different. Also encourage tales from different points of view. For example, students could choose to write *Little Red Riding Hood* from the wolf's point of view, *Beauty and the Beast* from the vantage point of the Beast, or *The Three Billy Goats Gruff* from the troll's point of view.
- *Newspaper*   Use a newspaper format to write headlines, articles, classified ads, and editorials about fairy tale characters. For example, an ad might be written looking for Cinderella's lost slipper; a headline might read: "Children Foil Witch and Reap Bounty"; an editorial might call for the arrest of the wolf after he has demolished two pigs' houses. Captions and illustrations could be included (see Figures A-6 through A-8).
- *Riddle Book*   Write riddles about characters from fairy tales and share them with other classes. Each page would have an illustration and a riddle, for example, a picture of a cat in hat and boots. The riddle might say, "He was a very clever cat. Who was he?" The back page would list the answers to the riddles. (The answer to the above riddle is Puss

Figure A-7

LOST

A slipper, a pure glass slipper. A very, small, pure glass slipper. With high heels and very narrow. It was lost at the ball on May 7, 1800. The prince at the castle is looking for it. <u>REWARD</u>: dance one dance, your choice with the prince. You should return the slipper to the castle immediately.

by Lindsay

from *Puss in Boots*.) These riddle books can be made clear and easy enough for first- or second-graders to enjoy.

- *Crossword puzzle*   Design a fairy tale crossword puzzle using words frequently used in fairy tales, such as: prince, princess, witch, Hansel, wolf, pigs, forest, stepmother, spell, magic (see Figure A-9).
- *Dramatization of point of view*   A small group of students plans a dramatization of *The Three Little Pigs* from the wolf's point of view, using and adapting the dialogue from the book *The True Story of the 3 Little Pigs* by John Scieszka. Before presenting the drama, the group reminds the audience of the traditional tale by recalling specific events in the familiar version. This dramatization could be presented to other classrooms.
- *Dialogue*   Two students write a conversation between two fairy characters. It can be taped, written in dramatic form, or read orally as Readers Theatre.
- *Game*   Keeping the theme of a familiar fairy tale, students enjoy designing original games with cards and directions. Students use tagboard and make colorful drawings of events and motifs from the fairy tale. This is an excellent activity for a pair of students. When the game is completed, the students put it to the test by having other students play it.
- *Crafts/arts*   Make a gift for a fairy tale character. The gift could be something the fairy tale character could use to get out of a difficult situation.
- *Fairy tale party*   Under the supervision of the teacher, plan a fairy tale party for another class to attend. The students design and send out invitations. Refreshments are planned, and volunteers bring them in. Students are asked to give presentations such as: the filmstrip, dramatization of the fairy tale books written by the students, and art projects completed. This party is held near the end of the unit (see Figure A-10).

Fairy Tales/Folktales

The tales listed here are just a sampling of the wonderful folk and fairy tales that exist. For additional titles and ways to use them, look for the many annotations of recommended folktales and fairy tales included in the grade-level literature lists in these "blue pages." Also, check with a librarian, and use the "Resources" on page 172b to locate other quality titles.

Figure A-8   A Student's Mock Newspaper Article

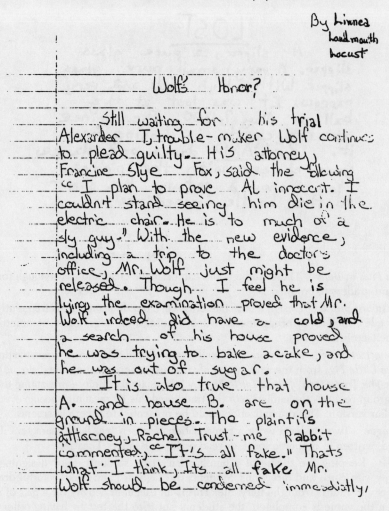

By Linnea Loudmouth Locust

Wolf's Honor?

Still waiting for his trial Alexander T. trouble-maker Wolf continues to plead guilty. His attorney, Francine Slye Fox, said the following "I plan to prove Al innocent. I couldn't stand seeing him die in the electric chair. He is to much of a sly guy." With the new evidence, including a trip to the doctors office, Mr. Wolf just might be released. Though I feel he is lying, the examination proved that Mr. Wolf indeed did have a cold, and a search of his house proved he was trying to bake a cake, and he was out of sugar.

It is also true that house A. and house B. are on the ground in pieces. The plaintifs attlorney, Rachel Trust-me Rabbit commented, "It's all fake." Thats what I think, Its all fake Mr. Wolf should be condemed immediatly,

Anderson, Hans Christian. 1987. *The Snow Queen*. Illustrated by Bernadette Watts. New York: North-South Books.

Anderson, Hans Christian. 1981. *The Wild Swans*. Pictures by Susan Jeffers. Retold by Amy Ehrlich. New York: Dial.

Brown, Marcia. 1954. *Cinderella*. New York: Macmillan.

Cauley, Lorinda Bryan. 1986. *Puss in Boots*. New York: Harcourt Brace Jovanovich.

Demi. *The Magic Boat*. 1990. New York: Henry Holt.

Ehlert, Lois. 1992. *Moon Rope*. New York: Harcourt Brace Jovanovich.

Gipson, Morrell. 1984. *Rip Van Winkle*. New York: Doubleday.

Goble, Paul. 1993. *The Lost Children*. New York: Bradbury Press.

Grimm, The Brothers. 1986. *Grimm's Fairy Tales*. Illustrated by Richard Walz. Racine, WI: Western Publishing.

Figure A-8 (Continued)

before he kills any other
innocent pig, person, or peacock.
All pigs will live in terror untill
Mr. Wolf is condemmed and put to
death.
After talking to the last little
pig, Mr. Patric Spared Pig, I am
toatlly convinced the story from
the wolf's point of view is a
complete lie.
He knocked down the houses
trying to get at the pigs, buried his
sugar, and rigged it to make it look
like he was baking a cake.
The only thing that is
real is the cold. Tough luck Mr.
Alexander T. Wolf.

By Marie Frisof

Grimm, The Brothers. 1981. *Hansel and Gretel.* Illustrated by Anthony Browne. New York: Knopf.

Grimm, The Brothers. 1980. *Hansel and Gretel.* Pictures by Susan Jeffers. New York: Dial.

Grimm, The Brothers. 1983. *Little Red Riding Hood.* Retold and illustrated by Trina Schart Hyman. New York: Holiday.

Grimm, The Brothers. 1982. *Rapunzel.* Retold by Barbara Rogasky. Illustrated by Trina Schart Hyman. New York: Holiday.

Grimm, The Brothers. 1983. *Rumpelstiltskin.* Illustrated by Donna Diamond. New York: Holiday.

Grimm, The Brothers. n. d. *Snow White and Rose Red.* Retold and illustrated by Bernadette Watts. New York: North-South Books.

Hamanaka, Sheila. 1993. *Screen of Frogs: An Old Tale.* New York: Orchard Books.

Haley, Gail. 1986. *Jack and the Bean Tree.* New York: Crown.

Haviland, Virginia. 1994. *Favorite Fairy Tales Told in England.* Illustrated by Maxie Chambliss. New York: Beech Tree. See annotation, p. 130b.

Hodges, Margaret. 1984. *Saint George and the Dragon.* Illustrated by Trina Schart Hyman. Boston: Little, Brown. See annotation, p. 141b.

Huck, Charlotte. 1989. *Princess Furball.* Illustrated by Anita Lobel. New York: Greenwillow.

Hyman, Trina Schart. 1977. *The Sleeping Beauty.* Boston: Little, Brown.

Littledale, Freya. 1986. *The Little Mermaid.* Illustrated by Daniel San Souci. New York: Scholastic.

Magnus, Erica. 1986. *The Boy and the Devil.* Minneapolis, MN: Carolrhoda Books.

Figure A-9   Fairy Tale Crossword Puzzle

Alam G:
Dina L.   Fairy Tale Crossword Puzzle

Down

1. One of the seven Dwarfs
3. A poison food that Snow White Ate
5. Cinderella lost her glass _____.
7. Jack sold his cow for some magic _____.
9. Rumple Stilkkin _____ straw into gold.

Across

2. A reptile, that was turned to a prince.
4. It ate Little Red Riding Hood.
6. The opposite of Beauty
7. Goldilocks went into this animals house
8. Mirror, Mirror, on the _____
10. Little Red Riding Hood Picked _____, for her Grandmother.

Mayer, Mercer. 1980. *East of the Sun and West of the Moon.* New York: Four Winds Press.

McDermott, Gerald. 1993. *Raven: A Trickster Tale from the Pacific Northwest.* New York: Harcourt Brace. See annotation, p. 132b.

Medlicott, Mary (ed.). 1992. *Tales for Telling from Around the World.* Illustrated by Sue Williams. New York: Kingfisher Books.

Merrill, Jean. 1992. *The Girl Who Loved Caterpillars: A Twelfth-Century Tale from Japan.* Illustrated by Floyd Cooper. New York: Philomel Books.

Mollel, Tololwa M. 1991. *An Orphan Boy: A Maasai Story.* Illustrated by Paul Morin. New York: Clarion.

Figure A-10 A Student's Welcome Note to a Fairy Tale Party

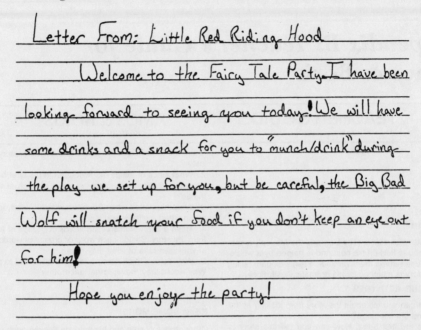

Letter From: Little Red Riding Hood

Welcome to the Fairy Tale Party. I have been looking forward to seeing you today! We will have some drinks and a snack for you to "munch/drink" during the play we set up for you, but be careful, the Big Bad Wolf will snatch your food if you don't keep an eye out for him!

Hope you enjoy the party!

Munsch, Robert. 1980. *The Paper Bag Princess*. Toronto: Annick Press.

Ransome, Arthur. 1968. *The Fool of the World and the Flying Ship*. New York: Farrar, Straus, & Giroux.

Rappaport, Doreen. 1991. *The Journey of Meng: A Chinese Legend*. Illustrated by Yan Ming-Yi. New York: Dial Books for Young Readers.

Scieszka, Jon. 1989. *The True Story of the 3 Little Pigs*. Illustrated by Lane Smith. New York: Viking Kestrel.

Steel, Flora Annie. 1976. *Tattercoats*. Illustrated by Diane Goode. New York: Bradbury.

Steptoe, John. 1987. *Mufaro's Beautiful Daughters*. New York: Lothrop, Lee, and Shepard. See annotation, p. 132b.

Whitney, Thomas. 1970. *Vasilisa the Beautiful*. Illustrated by Nonny Hogrogian. New York: Macmillan.

Yolen, Jane. 1987. *The Girl Who Loved the Wind*. Illustrated by Ed Young. New York: Crowell.

Appendix B: Teacher's Guide for Amos & Boris

TEACHER'S GUIDE
by Susan Hepler

AMOS & BORIS
by William Steig

SUMMARY

In this story, similar to "The Lion and the Mouse", a sea-going mouse falls off his boat and is helped by a whale. The mouse returns the favor later. Steig's elegant telling of the story is matched by his dramatic illustrations.

INITIATING ACTIVITIES

1. What can you tell about the story from looking at the cover and the title page?
2. Read the first page. How can you tell this story is going to be unusual? What do you notice about the words?

THINKING CRITICALLY

1. How did Boris the whale help Amos? How did Amos return the favor? Does this sound like any other story you know?
2. What kinds of things did Amos put in his boat before he set out? What use might he make of each of these things?
3. What happened when Boris "sounded"? What does it mean when a whale "sounds"?
4. Make a chart of interesting words or groups of words from the story. Beside each word or groups of words, put in your own idea of what they mean.
5. Why do you think Amos and Boris were sad to part? Why would they "never forget each other"?

READ SOME MORE!

Other stories of little and big animals helping each other are The Lion and The Rat, illustrated by Brian Wildsmith, and The Lion and The Mouse, illustrated by Ed Young. Other modern-day fables include Marcia Brown's Once a Mouse, Leo Lionni's Frederick, Arnold Lobel's Fables, and John Ciardi's John J. Plenty and Fiddler Dan.

H.P. Kopplemann Inc., P.O. Box 145, 140 Van Block Ave., Hartford, CT 06141-0145   203-549-6210   1-800-243-7724   IN CT 1-800-842-2165

DO IT YOURSELF

1 Make a display of the things Amos took along in the Rodent. Label each one and make a title for your display.

2 Make a mouse-sized model of the Rodent. Write a description of how you made the model or tell something about it.

3 Pretend that you are Amos telling your grandchildren about your wonderful adventure. Tell or write this story for them.

4 Write a newspaper article telling how "Whale Is Saved During Hurricane Yetta".

5 Paint a picture of your favorite part of the story. Write or tell about your picture.

6 Make a picture of another meeting Amos and Boris might have. Write or tell about your picture.

7 Keep a diary as Amos or Boris would have kept it and report each day's adventures.

by William Steig

Reprinted with permission of H.P. Kopplemann Inc., Hartford, CT.

Appendix C: Teacher's Guide for Journey to Topaz

TEACHER'S GUIDE
by Susan Hepler,

JOURNEY TO TOPAZ
by Yoshiko Uchida

About the Story

Eleven-year-old Yuki Sakane and her family are evacuated to a Japanese internment camp at the beginning of the United States' war against Japan. This restrained story is based on the author's experiences during World War II and reflects the quiet dignity, courage, and loyalty with which Japanese-Americans dealt with this unjust treatment.

Initiating Activities

1. What can you predict about this story by looking at the front cover and the Contents? What feelings does the cover try to show?

2. Read the first paragraph of the Prologue aloud. What do you know about World War II? (Read aloud the whole Prologue before reading the story, or after finishing, depending on the level of students.)

3. Do you know any people now, or in times past, who have been forced to leave their homes and live in guarded camps? What feelings might these people have had?

Thinking Critically

Chapter 1: "Strangers at the Door" (Pages 1–9)

1. Who is in Yuki's family? What can you tell about them? How are they like families you know? How are they different?

2. Why does the FBI come to Yuki's house? What do they do there?

Chapters 2–3: "The Long Wait" and "A Lonely Christmas" (Pages 11–29)

3. Why does Mother serve tea to the FBI men? How do you think the FBI men feel about the Sakane family? Why do you think that?

4. Besides serving tea, what other Japanese customs does Mother keep?

5. What are Issei? Nissei?

6. What has happened to Father? Why do you think this has happened? Is Father guilty of any crime?

7. What is the "evacuation"? Who ordered it? Why? How does the Sakane family feel about this? How does Mr. Jamieson feel about this?

Chapter 4: "Ten Days to Pack" (Pages 31–39)

8. What things do Japanese-Americans have to give up or stop doing before they are to be evacuated?

9. What preparations do the Sakane family make before going to the evacuation camp? What do you think is hardest for each person to give up?

10. Do all Caucasian people feel that the Japanese-Americans are being treated fairly?

Chapters 5–6: "Inside the Barbed Wire" and "Home is a Horse Stall" (Pages 41–58)

11. How does the Sakane "apartment" compare with their former home?

12. What small things give the Sakane family comfort at Tanforan?

Chapters 7–8: "A New Friend" and "Ken Spoils a Party" (Pages 59–74)

13. If the Sakane family had made a list of their complaints about the situation at Tanforan, what things would be on that list?

14. Why is Chapter 8's title a good one? What does Ken's decision mean for Yuki and her mother?

Chapters 9–10: "A New Rumor" and "Goodbye, Tanforan" (Pages 75–91)

15. Why do you think Yuki is glad to be back in school? Have you ever felt that way?

16. Yuki and Emi play "Jan Ken Po." What game does this sound like? What do you call "zoris"?

17. What is Yuki trying to tell Ken when she gives him not a half but a whole candy bar?

18. Mr. Kurihara says America is making prisoners of its own citizens. But Mother has an answer for him (page 90) beginning, "Fear has made this country do something . . ." What do you think Mother means?

Chapters 11–12: "A Home in the Desert" and "Dust Storm" (Pages 93–109)

19. On a map of the western United States, locate and label: where Father is; the Sakanes' former home town; Tanforan; and the route to Topaz. The last two may take some detective work.

20. Is Topaz a better place than Tanforan? Why or why not?

21. What is a *trilobite*, the gift Yuki gave to Emi?

Chapters 13–15: "A Last Visit," "Tragedy at Dusk," and "Good News" (Pages 111–129)

22. How have Yuki's feelings changed toward Mr. Kurihara? How does he die? Why? How does the camp show their grief? What does Yuki do? Why?

23. What happy occurrences make Yuki feel a little more hopeful?

24. Why do you think Ken feels so distant from his family?

Chapters 16–17: "Another Goodbye" and "Hello, World" (Pages 131–149)

25. What are the arguments for Ken's joining the all-Nisei army unit? What are the arguments against it? What is Father's advice? What would you have done? Why?

26. Why does Mr. Toda feel so bad?

27. Why can the Sakane family go free in Utah but not in any West Coast state?

28. The Sakane family has many friends both in and out of camp. Which ones help them through the hard times? How? Who do you think helps the most? Why?

29. Do you think this experience may change Yuki? How?

187b

DO IT YOURSELF

1 Pretend you are a friend to Yuki, like Mimi or Mrs. Jamieson, and fix a box of things you'd send to her in Topaz to cheer her up. Make a table display and label your gifts.

2 Mimi gave Yuki a red-covered diary in which to keep her thoughts. Write four or five entries Yuki might have made during some of the difficult or happy times in the story. Don't forget details to make it interesting.

3 Look up "Japanese Internment Camps" in magazines from 1942. What else can you find out from these articles?

4 Write the letters Yuki would write to Mr. Toda or to Emi after she and her family settled in Salt Lake City. What do you imagine might happen next?

5 Invite a Japanese-American person into your classroom to talk about Japanese customs they still keep. Or locate someone who may know about internment camps and ask them to talk about them to the class.

6 Make a book of Japanese customs that were followed by the Sakane family, such as Dolls Festival Day, paperfolding, using certain words, serving tea, and so forth. Do some research on other Japanese customs and report your findings to the class using your informational book.

READ SOME MORE!
Journey Home is a sequel to this story, and The Eternal Spring of Mr. Ito by Sheila Garrigue tells of a Japanese-Canadian family's difficulty during this time. Yoshiko Uchida has also written many other books about the experiences of Japanese-Americans. An excellent informational book about the internment camps with many illustrations is Behind Barbed Wire by Daniel S. Davis.

Reprinted with permission of H. P. Kopplemann Inc., Hartford, CT.

Appendix D:
Using the
Goldilocks
Strategy to
Choose Books*

Easy Books

Ask myself these questions. If I am answering yes, this book is probably an EASY book for me. I'll have fun reading it.

1. Have I read it lots of times before?
2. Do I understand the story?
3. Do I know (can I understand) almost every word?
4. Can I read it smoothly?

Just Right Books

Ask myself these questions. If I am answering yes, this book is probably a JUST RIGHT book for me. I'll give it a try.

1. Is this book new to me?
2. Do I understand what I've read so far?
3. Are there just a few words per page I don't know?
4. When I read are some places smooth and some choppy?
5. Can someone help me with this book? Who?

Hard Books

Ask myself these questions. If I am answering yes, this book is probably a HARD book for me. I'll spend a little time with it now. I'll give it another try later (perhaps in a couple of months).

1. Are there more than a few words on each page I don't know?
2. Am I confused about what is happening in this book? Do I feel bored?
3. When I read, does it sound pretty choppy?
4. Is everyone else busy and unable to help me?
5. Is there a way to get this book closer to a Just Right?

From "Lessons from Goldilocks: 'Somebody's Been Choosing My Books But I Can Make My Own Choices Now!'" by Marilyn M. Ohlhausen and Mary Jepsen. *The New Advocate*, Vol. 5, No. 1, Winter 1992, p. 36. Norwood, MA: Christopher-Gordon. Reprinted with permission of the authors.

---

* Students can also generate their own version of the Goldilocks Strategy. With teacher guidance, students brainstorm how good readers successfully choose books. The teacher transcribes students' thoughts onto a chart that is displayed in the classroom.

Appendix E: A Sliding Mask and a "Flag"

A Sliding Mask

I keep two sizes on hand, one to use with Big Books and the other for regular-size text on the overhead projector or in the small-group or one-to-one reading situation. The slide fits into the slot and is moved to mask, gradually expose, and highlight features of text. Below

(actual size)
4"

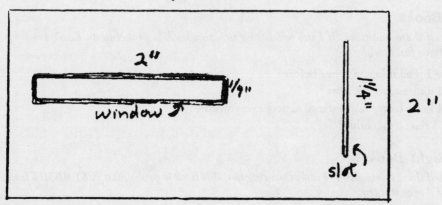

Big book size: 6 1/2" x 2 1/2" (shown reduced)

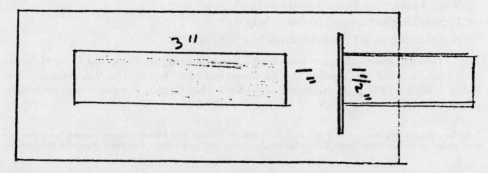

are two sizes that I use. I outline the windows with black magic marker to make the print stand out. Check the text size of your books to determine what sizes will work well for you. Construct with tagboard or file cards.

A *"Flag"*

I use tongue depressors and tagboard to construct flags of different sizes. I usually keep three sizes on hand. I tape or glue the rectangular size tagboard onto the tongue depressor. Experiment to get the sizes that work for you. The size of the flag determines how long a word you can highlight.

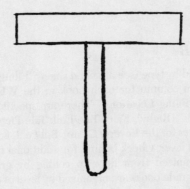

Use

With the overhead projector and screen, you can use a "flag" to call attention to a word. Place the flag on the screen behind you (not on the transparency on the overhead projector) directly over the particular word you want to highlight. Slowly and steadily move the flag away from the screen. The flag lifts the word off the screen and moves it onto the flag. The word is taken out of context so it can be studied or highlighted. Then the word goes back into context by moving the flag back onto the word on the screen. This is a dramatic visual technique that is easy and effective to use with students of all ages.

Appendix F:
Notes on Use of
the WEB
1993–1994

Organization of WEB

Books are organized and filed by type (see attached sheet, "Filing Locations"). The literature sign-out book has a location column for each book in the WEB that corresponds to the abbreviations listed under "Filing Locations." There are specific Animal, other Nonfiction, Biography, Poetry, "City Kids" (Rigby), Fairy Tale/Folk Tale Picture Books, and Audiotapes. There are also separate shelves for the Beverly Cleary, Bill Peet, and William Steig collections. All books are shelved in one layer. Check behind for additional copies of a title.

All fiction books are organized from floor to ceiling by grade level. Books are filed alphabetically by title. First-grade books are organized by level of difficulty. Each level is then filed alphabetically by title. For your reference there is a listing of these books by level in a separate reference book ("WEB Collection: Sorted by Location") in the WEB room. Big Books are also filed alphabetically by title, in large boxes next to the WEB. All second, third, and fourth grade core books are located in a cabinet in the hall outside the WEB room.

Notices of upcoming whole language workshops are posted on one wall.

Periodically, you may want to check in the file folders for each of the core books. The folders are continually being updated with additional information/activities about these books. They are housed on a top shelf in the WEB.

Our WEB room coordinator is Donna Jackson. She will be glad to have a meeting with all Mercer parent volunteers to train them on book repair or WEB organization.

Book Sign-Out and Return

All WEB books are listed alphabetically by title in the sign-out book and include notations for the recommended grade level, the number of books in the collection, and the shelving location of book. Note that the sign-out book also includes a separate reference listing of all books in these categories: Big Books, Biography, Bill Peet, Poetry, William Steig, Beverly Cleary, Animals, Nonfiction, City Kids, Fairy Tale/Folk Tale Picture Books, Science core Books, Audiotapes, and second, third, and fourth grade core books. There are also listings of books by difficulty level in the first-grade fiction area. The sign-out book also has a listing of new titles added during the year.

It is necessary that all books be signed out and signed in with your initials, number of copies taken, and the dates so teachers know where books are and so we can maintain an accurate record-keeping system. If you are signing out many titles at one time and need assistance recording the titles in our WEB sign-out book, please arrange for a parent volunteer from your room to help you. You may want to choose one parent volunteer to assist you all year with signing out, signing in, shelving, and repairing books. Please return books to their proper location and grade level. The books are marked for easy return. All first-grade fiction books are filed within the color-coded shelves. All the other books have the type of book marked in red ink on the inside upper right corner. Fiction books for grades two, three, and four will have that number on this corner. Please return them repaired and bound with rubber bands for easier storage. Be sure you return books in alphabetical order by the title. This includes all Big Books.

Also, note the list of core books per grade level is posted on one wall. Those titles may be used only at the designated grade level or higher grade level.

Each teacher is supposed to have a personal copy of each core book to use as a teacher's guide. See Dr. Stokes if you need any titles.

Classroom Procedures

Each book has a number and school stamp on the inside front cover. To ensure that students take responsibility for core books and WEB books, be sure to note the number of the book each student receives. Work out your own accountability system. Please take the time to talk with your students about taking responsibility for our books. For example, books should not be placed open on a desk face down, because it weakens the spine. Have your students use book marks.

Book Repairs

The care and handling of our books is a high priority and needs to be discussed with all students. You may want to invite an older student in to talk about this with younger students.

Your room representative will be responsible for recruiting a parent from your room to repair books monthly.

As best as we were able, most books were repaired in June and are in good shape. Core books that were cancelled have been replaced. In some cases, you will need to have students or parent volunteers repair the books before you use them. It is necessary that we all assume responsibility for book repair to ensure long life for our books. Please be sure books are repaired before you return them.

Book mending tape is available in the WEB room. Fourth graders, previously trained in book repair, can be used to demonstrate book repair to students in grades two and three. Some teachers have found that it works well to assign specific students to this ongoing task. Kindergarten and first-grade teachers may want to get some parent volunteers or upper-grade students to keep up with book repair. There are two book repair machines for your use and students can easily be taught to use them. These machines can be signed out through Regie.

Lost and Damaged Books

If a book is lost, encourage the student to purchase a replacement copy (it is tedious work to order and replace single copies). Otherwise, the student should be charged a $3.00 replacement fee for the lost book. There is a form to be used for this. A copy is attached. More are available in the WEB room.

Monies collected for lost books should be turned into the office along with the title of the lost book. Please keep a record of all books that have been lost and paid for (and give that list to Regie in June) so we know what books to replace.

Fines should be assessed for damaged books. Repair charges can range from $.25 to $1.00. The money will be used for book replacement and WEB supplies.

See Regie or Donna Jackson for any assistance/concerns/suggestions. We are better organized this year, due to everyone's input and cooperation.

WEB BOOKS

Date _____

Dear Parent,

Your child _____ has lost/damaged the following book(s):

Title   Author

_____

_____

_____

_____

Please send in _____ for damage/replacement cost.

Comments:

_____

Classroom teacher

Appendix G: General Guidelines to Students for Submitting Stories, Poems, or Manuscripts to Publishers

- The writing should belong to you, the student. While adults may respond to the writing, ownership and authorship must remain with the student.
- Conference with your teacher and peers as you go through the authoring cycle. Allow plenty of time for thinking, creating, sharing, revising, and editing.
- Check to see that your material fits the format of the publication to which you are submitting. If unsure, write to the publisher with specific questions.
- Make as many of your changes as possible in the revising and editing stages prior to submitting your finished manuscript. In that way, the voice of the author can be completely respected.
- If you are interested in including illustrations, check with the publisher to see if illustrations are accepted. Be sure to acknowledge the illustrator if you are collaborating with another person in the process.
- Send only your best stories or manuscript.
- Submit to only one publisher at a time. Keep a copy of your submission with the name of the publisher and date sent.
- Acknowledgment of those who have helped you is recommended.
- Submissions should be typed, word processed, or in your very best handwriting.
- All manuscripts submitted should be copyrighted by the use of the "c" with a circle around it, the date, and the name of the author. It's also a good idea to seal the original in an envelope, mail it to the author's home address by registered mail, and keep it sealed, as proof of authorship.
- Enclose a self-addressed, stamped envelope for future correspondence.
- The publisher will notify you if the manuscript is accepted. While royalties are not usual, the publisher will discuss any business aspects with the author.
- The publishing time period varies with each book. Usually publication occurs within six months to eighteen months after a submission is received by the publisher. Just as the authoring cycle takes time, so does the publishing cycle. If a submission is accepted, any necessary conferencing will usually occur by telephone or letter.
- Don't be discouraged if you are rejected. Most writers receive multiple rejections before getting an acceptance.

Regie Routman gratefully acknowledges the input of children's publisher Billie White Price of Quality Publishing in Conway, South Carolina.

Appendix H:
Spelling
Interview

NAME: _____ Grade _____ Date _____

1. Are you a good speller? _____

   Why do you think so? _____

   _____

   _____

2. What makes someone a good speller? _____

   _____

   _____

3. What do you do when you don't know how to spell a word? _____

   _____

   _____

4. If someone is having trouble spelling a word how could you help that person? _____

   _____

   _____

5. Is it important to be a good speller? Why or why not? _____

   _____

   _____

Appendix I

HAVE-A-GO

Copy Word	1st Attempt	2nd Attempt	Standard Spelling

Appendix J:
Communicating
with Parents

J1: Getting Parents Involved

GETTING PARENTS INVOLVED

Children who take pride in expressing their ideas in writing may become discouraged if parents criticize their approximations, particularly the use of temporary spellings. The more knowledgeable parents are about the writing process, the more supportive and enthusiastic they are likely to be about their children's work. The following letter may be copied or paraphrased to help parents better understand the writing process.

Dear Parents,

Some parents have been wondering why children in early primary grades are bringing home papers with temporary spellings that haven't been corrected.

Do you remember when your child learned to talk? She probably made many "mistakes" or approximations, in speech, and they didn't bother you much. You may have corrected a few, now and then, but mostly you included the child in the events of everyday life, encouraged the child to talk, and enjoyed the conversations. You probably knew, as parents do, that children learn to talk the way they learn to sit up and crawl and walk—they learn to talk by talking.

Learning to write works the same way. For example, early in the year, one child wrote:

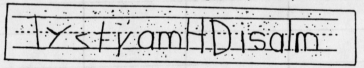

Now this doesn't look like your writing any more than a child's early words sound like your speech. But it's a tremendous piece of work! First of all, and most important, this child knows that written language is supposed to mean something, and he knows exactly what it means:

I was watching TV at my house. Then I saw a little mouse.

Just about every letter stands for one word in the story.

I y s   tv a m H   D i s a l   m
I was (watching)   TV at my house.   Then I saw a little mouse.

Some developmental stages in writing come before this one, and others come after. From this sample we see that the child knows the following:

- print proceeds in a straight line from left to right across a page
- print is made up of letters

- letters come in upper and lower case
- letters stand for sounds in the words he wants to write.

Later on the child wrote the following response to a story about two friends playing together:

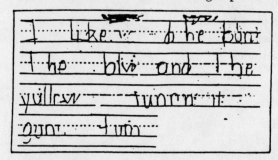

I like the part (where) the blue
and the yellow turn into green
from (author's name)

The writing still doesn't look like yours, but it's closer.

Since writing the earlier sample, this child has learned that:
- written language is made up of words separated by spaces
- each word between spaces stands for one word in speech
- written words are made up of a number of different letters
- there are a number of letter/sound combinations in each word (both beginning and ending sounds are included here)
- when you "know" a word (The), you spell it the same way every time
- if you don't "know" a word, you can use what you do know about letters and sounds to say what you mean until you learn the dictionary spelling
- you self-correct your own writing when it doesn't look right to you, just as children self-correct their own speech
- punctuation is part of written language.

That's a lot to have learned, and the child has doubtless learned more that cannot be documented by looking at this one sample alone.

Teachers help children learn to write the way parents and families help them learn to talk. If we put all our energy into correcting temporary spellings, children get discouraged and lose a natural desire to write. They learn from heavy correction that meaning is less important than spelling the words right.

If we invite them to use their oral language in their writing, even though they can't spell all the words correctly, we free them to say what they mean. And, in fact, as the examples show, they learn a lot about writing in general, and spelling in particular, from the risks they take along the way. Children learn to write by writing, and we are most helpful to them when we appreciate and encourage their "best attempts."

Is there a time for teaching particular points of spelling, grammar, punctuation, and handwriting? Yes. Full group and individual conferences address such points as the need is noted in the children's own writing.

Is there a time when children correct their work and turn out finished copy? Yes—when publishing or 'going public.' In very early grades the children do the hard work—writing the stories—and we make the corrections. As children become more experienced, they begin to take responsibility for this work, too.

I hope this letter helps you to share some of your child's joy in writing, much as you share his/her pleasure in speaking.

Sincerely,

Fall 1988 Newsletter, Whole Language Teachers Association, 16 Concord Road, Sudbury, MA 01776. Reproduced with permission.

J2: Ways to Help Your Child with Reading at Home

Setting the Atmosphere

Help your child find a quiet, comfortable place to read.

Have your child see you as a reading model.

Read aloud to your child. Reread favorite stories.

Read with your child.

Discuss the stories you read together.

Recognize the value of silent reading.

Keep reading time enjoyable and relaxed.

Responding to Errors in Reading

Based on the way most of us were taught to read, we have told the child to "sound it out" when he comes to an unknown word. While phonics is an important part of reading, reading for meaning is the primary goal. To produce independent readers who monitor and correct themselves as they read, the following prompts are recommended *before* saying "sound it out."

- Give your child wait time of 5 to 10 seconds. See what he attempts to do to help himself.
- "What would make sense there?"
- "What do you think that word could be?"
- "Use the picture to help you figure out what it could be."
- "Go back to the beginning and try that again."
- "Skip over it and read to the end of the sentence (or paragraph). Now what do you think it is?"
- "Put in a word that would make sense there."
- "You read that word before on another page. See if you can find it."
- "Look at how that word begins. Start it out and keep reading."
- Tell your child the word.

Most important, focus on what your child is doing well and attempting to do. Remain loving and supportive. When your child is having difficulty and trying to work out the trouble spots, comments such as the following are suggested:

- "Good for you. I like the way you tried to work that out."
- "That was a good try. Yes, that word would make sense there."
- "I like the way you looked at the picture to help yourself."
- "I like the way you went back to the beginning of the sentence and tried that again. That's what good readers do."
- "You are becoming a good reader. I'm proud of you."

Regie Routman, language arts resource teacher

J3: Letter to Parents Explaining Independent Reading Program

September 1994

Dear Parents,

W.E.B. (Wonderfully Exciting Books) is an important component of our reading program. The student self-selects books from our classroom, school, public, or home library for independent reading.

Your child and I will have frequent opportunities to discuss what has been read independently. The W. E. B. book will be used for reading at home and may also be used for independent reading during language arts time or during S. S. R. (Sustained Silent Reading). A record of your child's daily reading and a list of completed books will be kept in the classroom.

Your child's responsibility is to read for about thirty minutes each evening and to carry the book back and forth to school each day in a waterproof bag. Your child is also expected to take good care of this book. There will be a fine for damaged books or a replacement fee for lost or severely damaged books.

Over the school year, consistent daily reading will expose your child to various author's styles and will improve your child's fluency, vocabulary, comprehension, and writing. Our main goal is that your child will enjoy reading and choose to read for pleasure.

Please join with me in helping to create an environment where our children can enjoy books for a lifetime. Together we can build a community of readers.

Thank you for your help, support, and cooperation with our W. E. B. program.

Sincerely yours,

Please indicate that you have read this letter.

_____

(signature of parent or guardian)

$J4_1$ & $J4_2$: *Explanation of Integrated Spelling Program*

September 1994

Dear Parents,

The purpose of this letter is to introduce our spelling program to you. We support the philosophy that views spelling as an integral part of the total language arts program. We believe children develop spelling strategies through purposeful daily reading and writing. Therefore, your child will be creating personal spelling lists from daily writing, high-frequency words, and content-area words in the curriculum. Through research and our own teaching experiences, we have found that children are most interested in learning to spell words they need to use to communicate. We have also found that the more children read and write, the better they read, write, and spell.

We will emphasize three strategies in helping your child become a better speller:

- discovering and applying the rules and patterns
- proofreading
- using the dictionary and other resources

These are the same strategies adults use when trying to spell a word.

When your child asks you how to spell a word, here are some questions you can ask that may help him/her figure out the correct spelling:

Does it look right?

Can you try writing it another way?

How does the word start? How does it end?

Have you seen that word somewhere else? Can you find it for me?

What sounds do you hear?

After your child's attempts, verify the spelling by confirming the correct spelling or supplying it. Encourage your child to write the word as a whole, from memory, rather than copying it one letter at a time. Also use the attached sheet "Am I Becoming a Good Speller?", which your child has in his spelling folder, as a guide.

Keep in mind that the goal is not perfect spelling, which we as adults are still developing. The goal is to have children become more aware of spelling strategies and to be able to express themselves legibly, competently, and confidently when writing. Remember, there is no reason to learn to spell if you don't write; writing must come first.

Here are some suggested writing activities to promote writing at home:

notes to each other

greeting cards and invitations

lists for shopping, trips, gifts, parties

letters to grandparents, relatives, and friends

signs

posters

bumper stickers

recipes

songs

phone messages

post cards

puzzles
imaginative stories
jokes and riddles
cartoons
menus
map for a planned trip
diary of a trip
captions for photo pictures

We welcome your cooperation, participation, and questions concerning the spelling program. Please feel free to contact us.

Sincerely,
Elaine Weiner, second grade teacher
Linda Cooper, third grade teacher
Regie Routman, language arts resource teacher
Dr. Bernice Stokes, principal

J4₂

September 1993

Dear Families,

Your child will not be using a spelling book this year, but I will be teaching spelling! My goal is to move your child from invented spelling to conventional spelling through daily reading and writing activities and using many of the rules and patterns found in traditional spelling programs.

Each week your child will bring home 5 to 10 new words that she/he has chosen (sometimes with my help) to learn. Your child's weekly personal list is a combination of words chosen from journal entries, class themes, and high frequency words used in reading and writing. A few minutes each night will ensure success.

Please have your child bring in a name and address of a friend or relative that she would like to correspond with during the school year. This person will become your child's pen-pal.

Sincerely,

Loretta Martin

Loretta Martin

By Loretta Martin, grade 2 teacher

Parents as Allies in Children's Education

"How can I help my children learn to read and write?"

Parents who ask this question can become valuable allies—all we need do is encourage them to take active roles in helping with their children's education. In particular, parents can be especially helpful in conveying to children the idea that there are good reasons for learning to read and write.

The following are some of the ideas my colleagues and I have suggested to parents in our community, ideas that they say have worked well for them and that they have enjoyed using:

1. Be a role model for reading

- Let your children see you reading different materials for different reasons and encourage them to do the same.
- Join a book club.
- Give you children books or magazine subscriptions as gifts.
- Visit the library on a regular basis.

2. Read to your children every day

- Find a quiet spot.
- Choose interesting material.
- Encourage your children to read to you, to each other and to other members of the family.

3. Provide opportunities for listening to audio tapes and for watching selected TV programs

- Encourage your children to listen to recordings by authors or storytellers.
- Make your own recordings of your children's favourite selections.
- Allow your children to select from the program guide appropriate TV programs for viewing. Their viewing time may constitute one full evening a week, or one or two programs each night. Ask for a written schedule showing times, channels and selected programs. (Make it a rule that they have to vary the times and/or channels.)

4. Provide opportunities for reading

- Collect simple recipes and allow your children time to do some cooking.
- Always leave lots of notes for your children. Place them on the fridge door or in their lunch boxes. Sometimes it's fun to leave notes about tasks and include promised rewards for tasks that are completed. An example might be: "Please clean your rooms when you get home from school. When you're finished we'll all go out to eat at the shopping centre this evening."
- Play board games that encourage reading or word play.

5. Be a Role model for writing

- Allow your children to see you writing every day for different reasons, business and pleasure.
- Be positive. Don't overemphasize errors in your children's grammar, punctuation or spelling.

6. Provide opportunities for writing

- Set up a writing corner. Have a good selection of materials available. Vary the paper (lined and unlined) by size, colour, texture and shape.
- Purchase blank books or make your own by sewing pages together. Wallpaper scraps make good covers.
- Encourage your children to share what they've written.
- Encourage your children to proofread what they've written.
- Provide an incentive for your children to write by typing out some of their writings. If possible, allow them to use a typewriter or word processor themselves.
- Encourage your children to keep a special diary for private writing where they can freely express feelings and opinions. Promise them you will respect their privacy.
- Keep a communal journal when travelling as a family so all the members can write about what they see and discover.
- Have your children assist you in writing out grocery lists. If your children come with you when you go shopping, have them check off items as you pick them out.

7. Encourage the writing of letters

- Encourage your children to write thank you notes for presents received.
- Encourage your children to write to grandparents and other relatives and friends.

8. Encourage Creativity

- Encourage your children to rewrite TV commercials—or make up new ones.
- Encourage your children to perform commercials or plays that they've written.
- Encourage your children to illustrate their writing—start a file of pictures, photos, illustrations and cartoons for your children to use in illustrating their writing. (Such a file can be a great tool in helping to motivate the reluctant writer.)

Above all, let your children know that reading and writing are meaningful activities. It's true that we learn to read and write for practical reasons, but it's also true that reading and writing are tremendous sources of enjoyment.

By Shary Rea, B. Ed. (elementary school teacher, Alberta, Canada). Reprinted by permission.

J6: Letter to Parents to Help Make Book Covers

SHAKER HEIGHTS CITY SCHOOL DISTRICT

MERCER SCHOOL
23325 Wimbledon Road
Shaker Heights, Ohio 44122
(216) 921-1400

BERNICE STOKES, Ph.D.   April 13
Principal

Dear Parents:

I am writing to you to request your help with an urgent need for the publishing program for the first and second grades. We have run out of book covers! A wonderful emergency! Our estimation is that the children in the school have used over 1500 covers since the beginning of school and most of those have been in the first and second grades. (Most book covers for the upper grades are made as part of a classroom project.)

I would like to ask for volunteers to help us with the covers. I will package for you the supplies and directions necessary to make 10 covers. All you will need to do is to provide glue and about one hour of your time. The covers can be returned in the manila envelope we send home with your supplies.

If you are interested in helping us please fill out the tear sheet below and return it to your classroom teacher.

Thank you for your help in making this important program a success.

Susan Long
Parent Volunteer Coordinator
Mercer School

NAME _____

Classroom teacher _____

I will do _____ packet(s) of book covers.

Thank you.

Year of the Young Reader

J7: Request to Parents to Make Book Covers

BOOK-MAKING WORKSHOP

Wednesday, May 31
District Library Media Center
Woodbury School
9:30 A.M.—3:00 P.M.

This is a "drop in" workshop for kindergarten and first grade parents on making wallpaper book covers for the district's first grade publishing program.

Come when you can, for as long as you can, and learn the easy craft of book-cover making. We need to make hundreds of book covers to replenish our stock so that the Boulevard, Fernway, Lomond, Mercer, and Onaway Publishing Companies are ready to go next fall.

We plan to have as much fun as quilters at a quilting bee so please join us if you can.

—Marianne Sopko

J8: Communicating with Parents about the Reading-Writing Program

PARENTS NEWSLETTER

ONAWAY ELEMENTARY SCHOOL—GRADE 3

October 1993

My goals for this school year:

- to continue to promote a positive self image in each student;
- to foster a learning environment which focuses on cooperation and respect for others;
- to individualize educational approaches in order to meet your child's needs;
- to become a community of learners who communicate compassionately.

My thoughts on education:

- All learners must be respected.
- All students can learn.
- Focusing on the strengths must come first when looking at learners.
- The goal of education is independence.
- The learning process is highly valued and lifelong.
- The teacher is a facilitator and co-learner.
- Learners need to make choices and decisions about the curriculum.
- Collaboration builds communities of learners who support and learn from each other.

The Curriculum

I. COMPONENTS OF THE READING PROGRAM

A. Intensive Reading

1. Whole Class Reading
   Everyone is reading and discussing the same book. The students read in pairs, read silently, and I read to them.
2. Literature Response Groups
   Students engage in conversations about the core book in small groups. They keep a response log to respond to the book.
3. Specific Needs Groups
   Students are grouped according to specific needs, such as a strategy for reading or an enrichment book.
4. Read Aloud Daily to the Children.

B. Extensive Reading

1. WEB Program
   WEB stands for Wonderful Exciting Books. The goal of the program is to help the children become lifelong readers by providing them with quality literature and encouraging them to read. The students are required to read for at least 20 minutes each night.

They keep a record of the books they read in their WEB log. At the completion of a book, I interview the student about the book.

2. RAP

RAP stands for Reading Any Place. Each day the students and I read for 20 to 30 minutes silently. The goal of RAP is to educate their imaginations and grow as readers.

3. Reading with Younger Children

We read with a kindergarten class every Friday.

4. Literature Extension Activities

The students often do activities that extend the literature they read in reading group or that is read aloud to them daily. Some examples are:

- Readers Theatre
- Wanted Posters
- Book Sales
- Murals/Dioramas

II. COMPONENTS OF THE WRITING PROGRAM

A. Writing Workshop

The goal is to create a community in which writing matters because it's done for real reasons by real writers who ache with caring about their topic. The students write stories, research reports, letters, and class newspapers. The writing process is emphasized, including:

1. prewriting;
2. drafting;
3. revising;
4. editing;
5. publishing.

Conferencing is an important component of Writing Workshop. Each student is expected to publish at least one book per semester.

B. Poetry Workshop

The goal is to open up a world of feelings and give a voice to an experience of life. During this time we read, share and discuss poetry. We write poems using different styles of poetry in our writer's notebook. We also enjoy our "poet of the week" who reads a poem each morning to start our day.

III. SPELLING

Spelling is an integral part of the total language arts program. I believe children develop spelling strategies through purposeful daily reading and writing. Therefore, your child will be creating personal spelling lists from daily writing, high frequency words and content areas words from the curriculum.

I will emphasize three strategies in helping your child become a better speller:

1. Through discovery and application, we will identify rules and patterns.
2. We will use the skill of proofreading.
3. We will use the dictionary and other resources.

By Julie Beers, grade 3 teacher

J9: Communicating with Parents Through a Student Newspaper

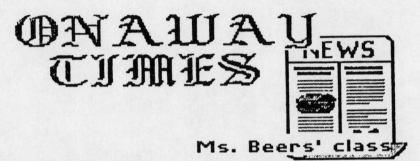

Reading

In Miss Beers class we read <u>Stone Fox</u>. Stone Fox is an Indian. He won all of his races. Little Willy just ran one race. He won $5,000. Grandfather got better. We read the book in reading groups. Miss Beers put questions on the board, and we answered the questions in our reading log.

**Article by
Joseph Simon
Jr. Editor**

Hi. My name is Sarah VanAken, your Onaway Times reporter. In reading group we read <u>Stone Fox.</u> <u>Stone Fox</u> was about a boy named Little Willy and his grandfather and how Willy fought to win the race for the money to pay back the taxes to keep the farm. After we read the book, Mrs. Douglass' class came and watched the movie with us. After the movie we got into groups and made a small Venn diagram to show how the book and the movie were the same and different. We talked about things only in the movie, things only in the book, and things that were in both. Then we put it all together and made a big Venn diagram and that's what we did for Stone Fox.

I.W.T. Stands for independent work time. The teacher gave us a folder and gave us some sheets of paper for a homonym book shaped like pears. Then we write sentences. She gave us a sheet of activities to work on too. She gave us a poster to make. We are drawing pictures and writing sentences about <u>Stone Fox.</u>

**Article by
Siquia Whitley**

Cover page, grade 3, Julie Beers's class.

J10: Letter to Parents Guiding Book Club Selection

Dear Parents,

Attached is the current Lucky Book Club order form. Lucky Book Club provides you with the opportunity to purchase good literature for your child at very reasonable prices. You are not obligated, however, to purchase anything.

If you do choose to take advantage of this opportunity, I would recommend the following books from this month's selections:

Please return the order form and your payment to school by _____. Make checks payable to Lucky Book Club.

Thanks.

Adapted from an idea developed by Nellie Edge.
For information on Book Clubs, see page 105b.

J11: Involving Parents in Evaluating Journal Writing

Dear Families,

Yes, it IS report card time again! Please read carefully the attached writing criteria which the class has developed. We discussed the characteristics of good first grade writing. The most important criteria, those that have to do with meaning, are listed first. The criteria which have to do with readability are of secondary importance and, therefore, are listed second.

Your child has brought his/her writing journal home this weekend. Please look through the journal and notice the progress he/she has made. Point out how his/her writing has improved since the beginning of first grade. Emphasize the positive. Please resist the urge to criticize.

On Monday, please return the student/adult comment sheet. Refer to the writing criteria to specifically note those elements of good first grade writing which your child is using.

Your input is very important. I appreciate this opportunity for you to celebrate your child's growth. Also, please be sure to remind your child to bring the journal back on Monday. Thank you.

Sincerely,

Peg Rimedio

What is good first grade writing? (Spring)

Developed by Room 5 students, 4/2/92

°°It makes sense.

°°The story is all about the same thing.

°°The writer is brave enough to write words the way they are said and spell them the way they sound.

°°The story tells a LOT about the subject.

°°The writer uses ALL the ideas in his/her head.

°°The writer changes the story to make it better.

°°The writing is original.

°°Ideas are written in the right order.

°° = About Meaning
     Most important

°There are spaces between words.

°The writer uses words for free.

°He/she uses some conventional spelling.

°He/she uses periods (.) at the end of sentences.

°He/she uses commas (,) to stop a little.

°He/she uses capital letters at the beginning of sentences, for names, days, and months, "I," names of states and countries, teams, etc.

°He/she skips spaces between lines.

° = About Readability
    Important

by Peg Rimedio

April 26, 1994

Dear Families,

Your child has been very busy with reading, writing, and spelling this year. As a result of the numerous and varied reading and writing activities (along with instruction and study), your child's spelling has improved. As your child continues to read and write, to use spelling rules as well as the dictionary, his/her spelling will continue to improve.

Many of the students have reached a stage in their spelling development which has allowed them to learn and to apply spelling rules and strategies. The rules and strategies taught this year are beginning to make sense, although reminders and review are always in progress.

Attached is the core spelling list for the second grade and your child's latest spelling check. Those words missed have become the primary focus for your child's individual list for the remainder of the year. If all or only a few words are misspelled, your child will continue to pull words for his/her journal and theme words. If your child is an excellent speller, he/she will continue to receive instruction revolving around spelling rules and strategies and dictionary skills based on the child's needs.

Please use the list to reinforce your child's spelling progress. A few minutes each night will aid classroom instruction.

Thank you,

Loretta Martin

Loretta Martin

Appendix K: Do Nothing to Destroy the Joy

Do Nothing to Destroy the Joy

How often have you heard someone say, "Yes, I use literature in my classroom. I DO Whole Language"? But, the reality is that Whole Language is not just having a classroom full of books and it is not something we "do." Whole Language is not a method or a set collection of ideas and activities. It is a mindset . . . a philosophy of teaching; a belief system about how children learn. It is, among other things, a belief that learning is easiest when it is from whole to part, when it is in authentic contexts, and when it is purposeful for the learner . . . Whole Language is not static; it is a definition in process. It is a label for mutually supportive ideologies and conventions. Whole Language "thrives on the principle that literacy tasks should never be ends unto themselves; instead they should be means to other ends, such as learning, enjoyment, persuasion, and communication" (Pearson, 1989). And so, when teachers employ literature in their classrooms and believe themselves to be "Whole Language teachers," they give consideration to these tenets.

Upon entering a classroom, what is it that allows one to distinguish a Whole Language classroom from a more traditional environment? At first glance it may seem that the activity being carried out in both rooms is very similar . . . there are several books; children are reading to themselves or the teacher is reading to them. But, in reality, it is only on this very superficial level, like leaving the lid on the cookie jar or the envelope on the letter, that the resemblance exists. When one ventures further to remove the lid or the envelope and take a closer look within the children's environments, there are certain common characteristics to the activities that one sees in a Whole Language classroom which are often lacking in more traditional settings. Activities relating to literature in Whole Language classrooms are authentic learning experiences which focus on exploring, problem solving and questioning . . . they are not isolated skills taught out of context. Activities are meaningful to the learner as the child finds himself/herself engaged in purposeful learning; learning in which the child takes an active part and builds upon his/her prior experiences to make sense of the world. In a Whole Language classroom, children are allowed to make choices and encouraged to become risk takers.

If a teacher is reading to his children just to fill in time at the end of the day and leaves no time for reflection or discussion . . . that's not Whole Language. Or if there is time for discussion and the only questions the teacher asks are efferent whereby the teacher is simply pulling information from the text . . . the who, the what, the where . . . forgetting to include the aesthetic aspect . . . how did you feel? how did you think? why? that's not Whole Language. If the teacher plans a worksheet on critical thinking as a follow-up activity to a story that the children have read or listened to . . . that's not Whole Language. (Indeed, it is instead a contradiction to the words "critical thinking" themselves.) If a teacher has a list of words taken from the story that he expects the children to recite and memorize before he introduces them to the story . . . that's not Whole Language either. Yes, this teacher is using literature in his classroom but the activities designed around the literature have been contrived and elude an air of basalization.

I have heard Yvonne Siu-Runyan say, "How sad it would be if our students groaned when we presented literature to them because we didn't know how to use it effectively." A prime example of stabbing literature though the heart to let it die a quick death occurred in our own family.

My daughter, in grade 8, was presented with a new novel to read over the weekend. Her assignment was not to read the novel and reflect upon its power and beauty, nor was it to relate to a particular character or to question and wonder about some of the events which took place but instead it was as follows: "Read the entire 146 pages. While you are reading make a list of 100 words that you don't know the meaning of. Find the meanings in your dictionary." Needless to say, she hated the novel before she even began to read it . . . the enchantment that good literature brings was lost before it was even given a chance. Instead of sighing because the words before her elicited a deeply felt pleasure, she sighed in disgust and despair. Yes, my daughter, being the studious and conscientious young lady that she is, listed 100 words (she said that she knew what most of them meant anyway but she NEEDED 100 words) and returned to class on Monday mumbling under her breath about "the stupid book" she had to read. As the assignment was so arduous, many of her classmates had not completed it, and so the teacher decided to give them class time to work at it. My daughter's reward for having completed this bastardization of literature was to find 25 more words! I ask you, what would have been so sinful about reading the book for reading's sake! What would have been so wrong with happiness or laughter or fright or sadness as an outcome of reading this novel? This was NOT Whole Language!

But, on the other hand, if you enter a classroom and the teacher is reading a book to the children and you can sense by the tone of the teacher's voice and by the way he/she engages himself/herself in the print and helps the children interact with the text, that the literature yields a satisfaction that is true and lasting . . . this IS Whole Language. If before or during the reading the teacher gives the children opportunities to take risks by asking predictions, if he/she stops to ask, "How did that make you feel?", if the teacher helps children make sense of their world by helping see similarities to their own lives . . . this IS Whole Language. If after reading several of Mem Fox's books and expressing interest about the animals of Australia, these children engage in research and map reading . . . this IS Whole Language.

Dorothy Menosky in her wisdom says, "Do nothing that will destroy the joy!" How many teachers feel that as long as they are using literature vs. basal readers, they are "doing" Whole Language and profess to be "Whole Language teachers"? But nothing can be further from the truth. We must always be asking ourselves whether the activities our children engage in, in relation to literature, are purposeful and authentic. Are they functional? Do they encourage risk-taking? Do we, through our use of literature in the classroom invite children inside the cover of another book and another and another? We, as Whole Language teachers, must remember to tread softly so as not to "destroy the joy."

by Peterette M. Dolyniuk
Language Development Teacher
River East School Division #9
Winnipeg, Manitoba
Canada
Reprinted with permission of the author.

Pearson, P. David. 1989. "Commentary . . . Reading the Whole Language Movement." *Elementary School Journal* 90(2).

Appendix L: Questions to Think About in Choosing a Writing Topic

What do I keep thinking about?

What do I know a lot about?

What do I know how to do really well?

What is important to me?

What do I want to find out more about?

Who or what do I care a lot about?

Who is someone important to me that I want to write about?

What do I like to do?

What was an important time in my life?

If I think back to an earlier time, what do I remember?

What am I worried about?

What am I happy about?

What am I angry about?

Inspired by *Shoptalk* by Donald Murray, pages 79–80. Heinemann, 1990.

Appendix M: Teachers' Self Evaluation: Observations About the Student as a Reader/Writer

M1: Observations About the Student as a Reader

- Chooses to read;
- Selects appropriate reading materials;
- Reads a variety of genres;
- Uses a variety of strategies to make sense of print:
    prediction
    semantics (sentence sense, pictures)
    syntax (grammar, punctuation, paragraphing)
    phonics
    self-correction
    prior knowledge
- Reads with fluency;
- Understands text;
- Actively participates in literature discussion groups:
    makes thoughtful comments
    listens attentively
    responds to peers
- Responds to literature:
    shares reading
    writes effective responses to literature
    completes literature-related activities
    keeps record of reading
- Requests appropriate help as needed;
- Utilizes resources;
- Puts forth best effort

M2: Observations About the Student as a Writer

- Chooses to write;
- Selects own writing topics;
- Writes in a variety of genres;
- Uses a variety of strategies to create meaningful writing:
    adherence to topic
    appropriate and interesting vocabulary
    logical development
    description and detail
    sentence and paragraph sense
    punctuation and capitalization
    standard spelling of high frequency words
    appropriate invented spelling
    awareness of audience
- Actively participates in writing conferences:
    listens attentively
    makes meaningful comments to peers
    considers suggestions for own writing
- Willing and able to revise writing;
- Proofreads and edits for meaning, mechanics, and spelling;
- Requests appropriate help as needed;
- Utilizes resources;
- Shares writing;
- Puts forth best effort

Appendix N: Self-Evaluation Forms

N1: Self-Evaluation: Reading

Name _____ Grade _____ Date _____

What is your favorite book that you've read?

Why is it your favorite?

How have you changed as a reader?

What do you want to do better as a reader?

N2: Self-Evaluation: Journal Writing

Name _____ Grade _____ Date _____

What is your best journal entry?

Why is it your best?

What are you doing now as a writer that you weren't doing before?

What do you want to do better as a writer?

Self-Evaluation

_____ Discussion Group

Name _____   Date _____

Book/Topic _____

1. What did I do well today (and/or improve on) during group discussion?

2. What do I still need to improve on during group discussion?

N4: Self-Evaluation Form for Any Grade or Area

Name _____

Date _____

Subject _____

What I can do well	What I find hard

What I am doing better	What I am going to work on next

N5: Ways to Involve Students in Self-Evaluation

- Interviews/Attitude surveys
- Conferences
- Audiotapes
- Reflection logs
- Editing earlier writing samples
- Noting difficult words and questions when reading
- Rating books
- Self-evaluation forms
  literature discussion
  behavior
  group work
  academic areas
  strengths, weaknesses, goal setting
- Making choices
  books
  writing topics
  projects
- Rubrics
- Report cards
- Selecting work for portfolios

N6: Weekly Self-Evaluation

Weekly Evaluation

Name _____ Date _____

This week I learned

What was most important to me this week was

I did very well

I am confused about

I want to work on

Student signature _____
Teacher signature _____
Parent signature _____

N7: A Self-Evaluation Checklist for Teachers

Am I reading literature aloud to students every day?

Am I providing time and choice daily for students to read and write on self-selected books and topics?

Am I noticing and commenting on what students are doing well and are able to do?

Are students in my class excited about learning?

Am I a happy and effective reading and writing model for my students?

Am I taking the time to demonstrate and not just assigning?

Are my questions allowing for varied responses and interpretations?

Am I equally respectful of all students regardless of culture and background?

Are my expectations high for all students?

Do students know and understand how they will be evaluated or graded?

Are my responses to students, both orally and in writing, specific and helpful?

Am I using the "red pencil" sparingly, or not at all?

Are children in my classroom feeling successful, regardless of their abilities?

Do I provide regular opportunities for students to share and collaborate?

Is the work students are doing meaningful and purposeful?

Am I encouraging students to solve their own problems and take ownership of their learning?

Am I providing opportunities for students to reflect on their progress?

Are my evaluation procedures consistent with my philosophy and my teaching?

Am I communicating effectively with parents and administrators?

Appendix O: Approaches to Teaching Reading

Meaning-Centered Approach

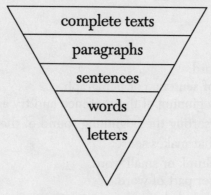

complete texts
paragraphs
sentences
words
letters

Skills Approach

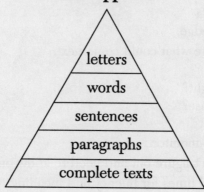

letters
words
sentences
paragraphs
complete texts

Appendix P:
Reading
Strategies for
Unknown Words

- Skip the difficult word.
    Read on to end of sentence or paragraph.
    Go back to the beginning of the sentence and try again.
- Read on. Reread inserting the beginning sound of the unknown word.
- Substitute a word that makes sense.
- Look for a known chunk or small word.
    Use finger to cover part of word.
- Read the word using only beginning and ending sounds.
    Read the word without the vowels.
- Look for picture cues.
- Link to prior knowledge.
- Predict and anticipate what could come next.
- Cross check.
    "Does it sound right?"
    "Does it make sense?"
    "Does it look right?"
- Self-correct and self-monitor.
- Write words you can't figure out and need to know on Post-Its.
- Read passage several times for fluency and meaning.

Use errors as an opportunity to problem solve.

by Regie Routman

Appendix Q:
Authentic
Assessment:
Some Examples

- interviews/surveys
- anecdotal records
- reading records
- literature response logs
- journals
- learning logs
- self-evaluations
- writing samples
- audiotapes
- videotapes
- projects
- running records
- retellings

Index